The Right to Self-Determination in International Law

ELEMENTS OF INTERNATIONAL LAW

Elements of International Law represents a fresh approach in the literature of international law. It is a long series of short books. *Elements* adopts an objective, non-argumentative approach to its subject matter, focusing on narrowly defined core topics in international law. Eventually, the series will offer a comprehensive treatment of the whole of the field. At the same time, each individual title will be a reliable go-to source for practicing international lawyers, judges and arbitrators, government and military officers, scholars, teachers, and students engaged in the discipline of international law.

PREVIOUSLY PUBLISHED TITLES IN THIS SERIES

Business and Human Rights
Robert McCorquodale

Treaties
Richard Gardiner

The Law of International Financial Institutions
Daniel D. Bradlow

Occupation in International Law
Eliav Lieblich and Eyal Benvenisti

Arms Control and Disarmament Law
Stuart Casey-Maslen

International Law of Taxation
Peter Hongler

Jus Cogens
Dinah Shelton

The International Tribunal for the Law of the Sea
Kriangsak Kittichaisaree

International Law in the Russian Legal System
William E. Butler

The Right to Self-Determination in International Law

Thomas Weatherall

OXFORD
UNIVERSITY PRESS

Oxford University Press is a department of the University of Oxford. It furthers the University's objective of excellence in research, scholarship, and education by publishing worldwide. Oxford is a registered trade mark of Oxford University Press in the UK and in certain other countries.

Published in the United States of America by Oxford University Press
198 Madison Avenue, New York, NY 10016, United States of America.

Library of Congress Cataloging-in-Publication Data
Names: Weatherall, Thomas author
Title: The right to self-determination in international law / Thomas Weatherall.
Description: New York : Oxford University Press, 2025. |
Series: Elements of international law series | Includes bibliographical references and index.
Identifiers: LCCN 2025037452 (print) | LCCN 2025037453 (ebook) |
ISBN 9780197798089 paperback | ISBN 9780197798072 hardback |
ISBN 9780197798102 updf | ISBN 9780197798096 epub | ISBN 9780197798119 online
Subjects: LCSH: International Covenant on Civil and Political Rights (1966 December 16) |
International Covenant on Economic, Social, and Cultural Rights (1966 December 16) |
Self-determination, National | Sovereignty | International law | LCGFT: Law materials
Classification: LCC KZ1269 .W43 2026 (print) |
LCC KZ1269 (ebook) | DDC 320.1/5—dc23/eng/20250812
LC record available at https://lccn.loc.gov/2025037452
LC ebook record available at https://lccn.loc.gov/2025037453

DOI: 10.1093/9780197798119.001.0001

Paperback printed by Integrated Books International, United States of America
Hardback printed by Bridgeport National Bindery, Inc., United States of America

The manufacturer's authorized representative in the EU for product safety is
Oxford University Press España S.A. of Parque Empresarial San Fernando de Henares,
Avenida de Castilla, 2–28830 Madrid (www.oup.es/en or product.safety@oup.com).
OUP España S.A. also acts as importer into Spain of products made by the manufacturer.

Note to Readers

This publication is designed to provide accurate and authoritative information in regard to the subject matter covered. It is based upon sources believed to be accurate and reliable and is intended to be current as of the time it was written. It is sold with the understanding that the publisher is not engaged in rendering legal, accounting, or other professional services. If legal advice or other expert assistance is required, the services of a competent professional person should be sought. Also, to confirm that the information has not been affected or changed by recent developments, traditional legal research techniques should be used, including checking primary sources where appropriate.

(Based on the Declaration of Principles jointly adopted by a Committee of the American Bar Association and a Committee of Publishers and Associations.)

For Charlie and Pippa

Series Editors' Preface

Elements of International Law represents a fresh approach to the literature of international law. It is a long series of short books. Following the traditional path of an international law textbook, *Elements*, rather than treating the whole of the field in one heavy volume, focuses on more narrowly defined subject matters.

There is nothing like *Elements*. It treats particular topics of international law much more extensively and in significantly more depth than traditional international law texts or encyclopaedias. As each book in the *Elements* series has a relatively narrow focus, it provides a comprehensive treatment of a specialized subject matter, in comparison to the more limited treatment of the same subject matter in other general works.

Like a classic textbook, *Elements* aims to provide objective statements of the law. The series does not concern itself with the academic niches filled ably by doctoral theses, nor include works which take an argumentative point of view, already well done by the OUP *Monograph* series. Except in length and integration, *Elements* is for substantive topics comparable to OUP's *Commentary* series on individual treaties. Each book is exhaustively footnoted in respect of international legal practice and scholarship, including treaties, diplomatic practice, decisions by international and municipal courts and arbitral tribunals, resolutions and acts of international organizations, and commentary by the most authoritative jurists.

Elements adopts an objective, non-argumentative approach to its many subject matters and constitutes a reliable go-to source for practicing international lawyers, judges and arbitrators, government and military lawyers, and scholars, teachers, and students engaged in the discipline of international law.

Mark Janis
Douglas Guilfoyle
Stephan Schill
Bruno Simma
Kimberley Trapp

Preface

Readers may notice that among the scholars cited throughout this book, two in particular stand out. The influences of Marc Weller and James Crawford, leading authorities on self-determination, are self-evident. It is their personal kindness that I wish to recognize at the outset.

Marc Weller was my doctoral supervisor at Cambridge and, since even before I arrived to begin my studies, he emphatically supported my pursuit of answers to difficult questions in international law. Without the opportunity to study *jus cogens* that he made possible, I am quite certain this book would never have been written. My good fortune has continued through a friendship with Professor Weller. This includes, among other things, his finding time to review a draft of my manuscript while working towards solutions to the world's most pressing challenges. His reactions to the manuscript helped to sharpen the final work.

At Cambridge, I was also fortunate to know James Crawford as Whewell Professor of International Law. Professor Crawford kindly agreed to serve as one of my thesis examiners. True to form as a harsh but fair examiner, Professor Crawford helped me successfully land my dissertation. I last saw Judge Crawford years later at a reception in Washington, as a newly minted attorney at the State Department. After asking about my work, which at the time involved World's Fairs of all things, he responded with a wry smile: 'Well, we can't always be thinking about *jus cogens*.'

Indeed, competing interests in theory and practice often lead down divergent paths. But, from time to time, the two for me have happily converged. My assignment as the department's self-determination lawyer was one of those moments. The extraordinary opportunity to practice the law of self-determination is what ultimately led me to embark on this book. While I have written this book in my personal capacity, it is informed by my experience across a diversity of fora and contexts in which self-determination arises. Shaped by the perspective of practice, and in the spirit of the *Elements* series, the goal of this book is to provide 'an objective, non-argumentative approach' to the right to self-determination of utility to scholars and practitioners of international law alike. Consequently, this book accepts as given that the international law of self-determination is an imperfect regime and seeks only to capture the law as it is (*lex lata*) without probing or prejudicing what it perhaps ought to be (*lex ferenda*).

In the course of writing this book, I have enjoyed the benefit of further help that deserves recognition. I sincerely appreciate the support of Oxford University Press, including in particular Robert Cavooris and Rebecca Lewis. The anonymous reviewers and Delegates of Oxford University Press provided invaluable guidance at the outset of this project, and the editors of the *Elements* series offered helpful reactions, especially Mark Janis. This book is much better for them. Professor S. James Anaya provided thoughtful reactions that informed how this book approaches Indigenous Peoples and their right to self-determination. I also extend my thanks to Sarah Hunter, Cliff Johnson, and Peter Tzeng for their reviews, which improved the book. Finally, as ever, I am grateful to my family—my wife Emily and daughter Charlie, the light of my life, and our newest addition Pippa, as well as my parents and sister, Claire—for everything.

Thomas Weatherall
Washington, DC

Contents

Table of Cases

INTERNATIONAL COURT OF JUSTICE

PERMANENT COURT OF INTERNATIONAL JUSTICE

ARBITRATION AWARDS, DECISIONS, AND OPINIONS

INTERNATIONAL CRIMINAL COURT

INTERNATIONAL CRIMINAL TRIBUNAL FOR THE FORMER YUGOSLAVIA

AFRICAN COMMISSION ON HUMAN AND PEOPLES' RIGHTS

AFRICAN COURT ON HUMAN AND PEOPLES' RIGHTS

COURT OF JUSTICE OF THE EUROPEAN UNION

EUROPEAN COURT OF HUMAN RIGHTS

INTER-AMERICAN COMMISSION ON HUMAN RIGHTS

INTER-AMERICAN COURT OF HUMAN RIGHTS

HUMAN RIGHTS COMMITTEE

AUSTRALIA

CANADA

RUSSIA

SOUTH AFRICA

SRI LANKA

UNITED KINGDOM

UNITED STATES

Abbreviations

ACHPR	African Charter on Human and Peoples' Rights
ACHR	American Convention on Human Rights
ACommHPR	African Commission on Human and Peoples' Rights
ACtHPR	African Court on Human and Peoples' Rights
ADRIP	American Declaration on the Rights of Indigenous Peoples
CESCR	Committee on Economic, Social and Cultural Rights
CIL	customary international law
CJEU	Court of Justice of the European Union
FRD	Friendly Relations Declaration
GAOR	General Assembly Official Records
HRC	Human Rights Committee
IACHR	Inter-American Commission on Human Rights
IACtHR	Inter-American Court of Human Rights
ICC	International Criminal Court
ICCPR	International Covenant on Civil and Political Rights
ICESCR	International Covenant on Economic, Social and Cultural Rights
ICJ	International Court of Justice
ILC	International Law Commission
ILO	International Labour Organisation
ITLOS	International Tribunal for the Law of the Sea
LNTS	League of Nations Treaty Series
NSGT	Non-Self-Governing Territory
OPT	Occupied Palestinian Territory
PCIJ	Permanent Court of International Justice
UN	United Nations
UNCLOS	United Nations Convention on the Law of the Sea
UNDRIP	United Nations Declaration on the Rights of Indigenous Peoples
UNGA	United Nations General Assembly
UNSC	United Nations Security Council
UNTS	United Nations Treaty Series
VCLT	Vienna Convention on the Law of Treaties
AJIL	*American Journal of International Law*
CUP	Cambridge University Press

EJIL	*European Journal of International Law*
ICLQ	*International and Comparative Law Quarterly*
ILM	International Legal Materials
ILR	International Law Reports
OUP	Oxford University Press
RIAA	Reports of International Arbitral Awards
YbILC	*Yearbook of the International Law Commission*

Introduction

Self-Determination in Theory and Practice

The right to self-determination is the right of peoples to freely determine their political status and freely pursue their economic, social, and cultural development.[1] The brevity of this definition disguises deep legal and political complexity. During the interwar period, self-determination was aptly described as 'a principle of justice and of liberty, expressed by a vague and general formula which has given rise to the most varied interpretations and differences of opinion'.[2]

In the aftermath of the First World War, self-determination had been conceived 'as an ordering principle for international society',[3] though its early expression in the League of Nations system was modest in its limited application to the disposition of colonies and other territories of the defeated belligerents following the war. The status of self-determination in international law during this period remained contested, and no entitlement to self-determination was codified as a rule of positive international law.[4] The

[1] International Covenant on Civil and Political Rights art 1, 999 United Nations Treaty Series (UNTS) 171 (16 Dec 1966, entered into force 23 Mar 1976); International Covenant on Economic, Social and Cultural Rights art 1, 993 UNTS 3 (16 Dec 1966, entered into force 3 Jan 1976).

[2] *Report submitted to the Council of the League of Nations by the Commission of Rapporteurs*, League of Nations Council Doc B7.21/68/106 (16 Apr 1921) (hereinafter 1921 Aaland Islands Report) 27.

[3] Erez Manela, *The Wilsonian Moment: Self-Determination and the International Origins of Anticolonial Nationalism* (OUP 2007) 11 (quoting James Mayall, *Nationalism and International Society* (CUP 1990) 44–45).

[4] 1921 Aaland Islands Report 27; *Report of the International Committee of Jurists entrusted by the Council of the League of Nations with the task of giving an advisory opinion upon the legal aspects of the Aaland Islands Question* (Oct 1920) *League of Nations Official Journal*, Special Supplement No 3, 5. As noted in these reports, the principle found expression only in 'a certain number' of treaties. For discussion of postwar application of the principle, see Ian Brownlie, 'An Essay in the History of the Principle of Self-Determination' in C. H. Alexandrowicz (ed), *Grotian Society Papers 1968* (Martinus Nijhoff 1970) 94–95.

The Right to Self-Determination in International Law. Thomas Weatherall, Oxford University Press.
 DOI: 10.1093/9780197798119.003.0001

UN Charter is the first multilateral instrument to enshrine the principle of self-determination. Under the UN Charter, the focus of the application of the principle of self-determination and associated institutional mechanisms would be decolonization, and it is in this context that the right to self-determination was brought into relief. Although self-determination focused initially on decolonization, 'that was only because the peoples of Trust and Non-Self-Governing Territories had not yet attained independence. The right would be proclaimed' in international law 'as a universal right and for all time'.[5] Challenges to the application of the right to self-determination outside the context of decolonization were presented at the end of the twentieth century, by the dissolution of States and emergence of new ones, leading to refinement of the right. Most recently, the right to self-determination has seen a period of contestation that has offered opportunities for further clarification, particularly through the caselaw of the International Court of Justice (ICJ).

During its development, the law of self-determination evolved markedly: as a principle of friendly relations articulated in Article 1 of the UN Charter, a right codified in Article 1 common to the International Covenant on Civil and Political Rights (ICCPR) and International Covenant on Economic, Social and Cultural Rights (ICESCR), and a rule of customary international law (CIL) giving rise to obligations in which the international community shares a common legal interest. Today, the right to self-determination is recognized as an 'inalienable right',[6] one expressed domestically as a 'fundamental human right',[7] and exercised internationally as a 'right to independence'.[8] '[I]t is one of the essential principles of contemporary international law.'[9]

Self-determination serves as an organizing principle for the international community of States. States are often defined in international law as

[5] *Report of the Third Committee*, A/3077 (8 Dec 1955) (Draft International Covenants on Human Rights) (hereinafter A/3077) para 39.

[6] See e.g. *Legal Consequences arising from the Policies and Practices of Israel in the Occupied Palestinian Territory, including East Jerusalem*, Advisory Opinion, ICJ Rep 2024 (hereinafter *Palestine* (2024)) paras 233, 257.

[7] *Legal Consequences of the Separation of the Chagos Archipelago from Mauritius in 1965*, Advisory Opinion, ICJ Rep 2019, 95 (hereinafter *Chagos* (2019)) para 144.

[8] *Accordance with International Law of the Unilateral Declaration of Independence in Respect of Kosovo*, Advisory Opinion, ICJ Rep 2010, 403 (hereinafter *Kosovo* (2010)) para 79.

[9] *East Timor (Portugal v Australia)*, Judgment, ICJ Rep 1995, 90 para 29.

legal persons possessing four attributes: a permanent population, a defined territory, government, and the capacity to enter into relations with other States.[10] The right to self-determination and its associated obligations may be understood in terms of these elements and, in effect, set out a relationship amongst them. In practice, self-determination is guided by a territorial approach, according to which the contours of the right are identified in relation to defined territorial units. The subjects and beneficiaries of the right to self-determination are, in turn, the populations of such territorial units, predominantly States but also certain other territories, which constitute peoples for purposes of the right to self-determination. The right of such peoples to self-determination is understood to possess a dual nature. The internal or domestic aspect of the right to self-determination is concerned with the relationship between a people and its government. The external or international aspect of the right to self-determination addresses the freedom of peoples from outside interference to exercise self-government and pursue their development. These aspects of self-determination are complementary.[11] And, in this way, the right to self-determination sets out expectations (with legal force) as to the relationship among the constitutive elements of the State. It is little wonder, then, that Article 1 of the UN Charter defines the purposes of the United Nations (UN) to include the development of friendly relations based on respect for the principle of equal rights and self-determination of peoples.

To this end, self-determination has been a driver of the postwar, UN - based international order as one increasingly free of relationships of colonial subordination. The UN Charter imposed specific, affirmative obligations upon States responsible for the administration of non-independent territories designed to unwind such relationships of subordination and bring about an end to colonialism and realization of self-determination for all peoples. During the drafting of the two human rights covenants, it was observed that '[t]he United Nations could not promote the principle of self-determination of peoples . . . without promoting the right of the peoples of non-self-governing and trust territories to self-government or independence . . . or

[10] Convention on Rights and Duties of States adopted by the Seventh International Conference of American States art 1, 165 League of Nations Treaty Series (LNTS) 19 (26 Dec 1933, entered into force 26 Dec 1934).

[11] See similarly James Crawford, *The Creation of States in International Law* (2nd edn, OUP 2006) 150.

vice versa'.[12] Notably, the provisions of the UN Charter addressing Non-Self-Governing Territories and Trust Territories contain the only obligations of States related to self-determination in the UN Charter. Looking forward, international law imposed negative obligations upon States that prohibit new subordinate relationships through alien subjugation, domination, and exploitation comparable to colonial relationships, thereby safeguarding the right of all peoples to self-determination. Recognition of self-determination as a right belonging to all peoples is part and parcel of its success as an organizing principle for the international community. It is in this sense that the right to self-determination constitutes a 'right to independence'.[13]

The right to self-determination also gives rise to obligations owed by the State towards its people closely related to their enjoyment of human rights and fundamental freedoms. The inclusion of provisions on self-determination as Article 1 of the two human rights covenants is understood to reflect the importance of the right as an 'essential condition' to the enjoyment of the human rights enumerated in the covenants.[14] The corollary was noted by the Third Committee of the United Nations General Assembly (UNGA) during the drafting of the covenants: 'To be deprived of the right of self-determination entailed the loss of individual human rights.'[15] Self-determination, a collective right belonging to peoples, and the enjoyment and exercise of individual rights are interdependent, thereby accounting for the prominent inclusion of the right to self-determination in the two human rights covenants, a linkage also reflected in other international instruments. Obligations of the State towards its own people arising from the right to self-determination are interrelated with its human rights obligations. It is in this regard that the right to self-determination is viewed as a 'fundamental human right'.[16] The right to self-determination is, in this way, 'fulfilled' in the normal course by a people through its collective exercise of human rights 'within the framework of an existing state'.[17]

[12] Draft International Covenants on Human Rights: Annotation, Prepared by the Secretary-General, A/2929 (1 July 1955) ch IV para 7.

[13] *Kosovo* (2010) para 79.

[14] HRC, *CCPR General Comment No. 12: The Right to Self-Determination of Peoples (Art 1)* (1984) para 1.

[15] A/3077 para 40.

[16] *Palestine* (2024) para 233 (citing *Chagos* (2019) para 144).

[17] *Reference re Secession of Quebec* [1998] 2 SCR 217 para 126.

There is, however, no accepted definition of 'peoples' for purposes of the right to self-determination. This presents an obvious challenge, as Sir Ivor Jennings observed in the early years of the United Nations:

> Nearly forty years ago a Professor of Political Science who was also President of the United States, President Wilson, enunciated a doctrine which was ridiculous, but which was widely accepted as a sensible proposition, the doctrine of self-determination. On the surface it seemed reasonable: let the people decide. It was in fact ridiculous because the people cannot decide until somebody decides who are the people.[18]

The development of a right to self-determination in international law despite the absence of a definition of 'peoples' can be explained by the close practical relationship between the right to self-determination and territorial sovereignty. The right to self-determination has developed within the framework of, and in reference to, principles of sovereignty and territorial integrity. As the African Court of Human and Peoples' Rights put it, 'the right to self-determination is essentially related to peoples' right to ownership over a particular territory and their political status over that territory'.[19] This approach can be traced to the principal international instruments—the UN Charter and the two human rights covenants—that respectively codified self-determination as a principle and as a right in international law. Understanding 'peoples' to be the populations of territorial units, as separately defined in international law and entitled to independence and sovereignty, obviates the more contested exercise of defining and distinguishing peoples for purposes the right to self-determination.

By virtue of this territorial orientation, self-determination in international law operates comfortably within a State-centric international order. This result is ironic yet unsurprising. Historically, self-determination has been viewed with circumspection, as a potentially destabilizing principle posing great risk to existing structures of political power. Robert Lansing, Woodrow Wilson's Secretary of State, wrote that '[t]he phrase is simply loaded with dynamite. It will raise hopes which can never be realized. . . . In the end it

[18] Ivor Jennings, *The Approach to Self-Government* ([1956] CUP 2011) 55–56.

[19] *Bernard Anbataayela Mornah v Benin et al*, ACtHPR, No 028/2018, Judgment, para 301 (22 Sept 2022).

is bound to be discredited, to be called the dream of an idealist who failed to realize the danger until too late to check those who attempted to put the principle in force'.[20] In a similar vein, negotiations over provisions on self-determination in the UN Charter and the Friendly Relations Declaration (FRD) reflected deep concern among States that self-determination could be construed as an entitlement to secession or even as a license to use force to such end.[21] The recognition of a right to self-determination in international law is undoubtedly revolutionary, but its codification and crystallization has been calibrated within a legal framework of obligations of States, consequences for their breach, and remedies under international law. Even if the right to self-determination fundamentally redefined relations within the international community, and in so doing dramatically grew its membership, the right did not fundamentally alter the territorial units of its members.[22]

Notwithstanding the limitations of the right as one operating within the parameters of State sovereignty and territorial integrity, self-determination remains 'a principle of justice and of liberty' at the heart of the contemporary rules-based international order. The right to self-determination promises a world of free States by conferring upon all peoples the freedom to determine their political status and to pursue their economic, social, and cultural development. The right to self-determination further entitles the peoples of those free States to governments representing the whole of their populations, the realization of which is contingent upon respect for the exercise of human rights and fundamental freedoms.

The work of self-determination remains both incomplete and ongoing. The *Chagos Archipelago* (2019) ICJ advisory opinion regarding the decolonization of Mauritius, and the nearly two dozen resolutions on decolonization adopted annually by the UNGA through its Fourth Committee, are illustrative in this regard. Beyond decolonization, the right to self-determination faces challenges on many fronts. For instance, the entitlement of the people

[20] Robert Lansing, *The Peace Negotiations: A Personal Narrative* (Houghton Mifflin Company 1921) 97. For contemporary commentary of a similar tenor, see Charles Noble Gregory, 'The Neutralization of the Aaland Islands' (1923) 17(1) *AJIL* 63, 76.

[21] See e.g. Summary Report of Sixth Meeting of Committee I/1, Doc 343, I/1/16, in (1945) 6 *UN Conference on International Organization* 296; *Report of the Special Committee on Principles of International Law concerning Friendly Relations and Co-operation among States*, A/7326 (1968) paras 164, 190; *Report of the Special Committee on Principles of International Law Concerning Friendly Relations and Co-Operation Among States*, A/7619 (1969) para 279.

[22] Christian Tomuschat, 'Secession and Self-Determination' in Marcelo G. Kohen (ed), *Secession: International Perspectives* (CUP 2006) 25.

of Palestine to self-determination continues to be a focal point of international relations—recently addressed by the Human Rights Committee (HRC), UNGA, and even the International Criminal Court (ICC)[23]—and was the subject of a second ICJ advisory opinion in 2024. States continue to grapple with assertions of the rights of Indigenous Peoples, now often under the right to self-determination. Across the world, democracy is said to be in decline and authoritarianism is on the rise; military coups supplant democratically elected governments and in so doing upend the exercise by peoples of their right to self-determination.[24] And aggression against Ukraine represents a profound threat to the right to self-determination, which is both under attack and erroneously wielded as a cynical justification for the purported annexation of territory by the Russian Federation.[25]

Despite the challenges it faces today, the weight of international law is on the side of the right to self-determination. The right to self-determination is not merely honoured in the breach. Its sources evince the breadth and depth with which the right to self-determination is recognized by States. This widespread recognition is matched by a diverse institutional architecture with the capacity to promote the implementation and enforcement of obligations arising under the right to self-determination. The United Nations, the ICJ, and a host of international and regional treaty bodies remain seized with the right to self-determination and have advanced the right through an expansive jurisprudence and practice. This jurisprudence and practice play a central role in efforts to promote the universal realization of the right to self-determination.

[23] See e.g. A/HRC/Res/55/30 (12 Apr 2024); A/Res/78/192 (22 Dec 2023); *Decision on the 'Prosecution request pursuant to article 19(3) for a ruling on the Court's territorial jurisdiction in Palestine'*, PTC I, ICC-01/18-143 (5 Feb 2021) paras 119–23.

[24] See Tom Ginsburg, *Democracies and International Law* (CUP 2021) 9.

[25] *Signing of treaties on accession of Donetsk and Lugansk people's republics and Zaporozhye and Kherson regions to Russia*, http://en.kremlin.ru/events/president/news/69465 (30 Sept 2022) ('It is undoubtedly their right, an inherent right sealed in Article 1 of the UN Charter, which directly states the principle of equal rights and self-determination of peoples'). A similar abuse of the doctrine of self-determination is seen in Russia's treatment of Abkhazia and South Ossetia: see Marc Weller, *Escaping the Self-Determination Trap* (Martinus Nijhoff 2008) 67–69. This approach is borrowed from Bolshevik/Soviet practice: see Lauri Mälksoo, 'The Soviet Approach to the Right of Peoples to Self-determination: Russia's Farewell to *jus publicum europaeum*' (2017) 19 *Journal of the History of International Law* 200, 200–18. It also bears resemblance to invocation of the principle to justify annexations by Germany and Italy during the Second World War. See Report of Rapporteur, Subcommittee I/1/A, to Committee I/1, June 1, 1945, Doc 723, I/1/A/19, in (1945) 6 *UN Conference on International Organization* 696, 703–04; Report of Rapporteur of Committee 1 to Commission I, Doc 944, I/1/34(l), in (1945) 6 *UN Conference on International Organization* 446, 455.

PART I
SOURCES

Part I examines sources of the right to self-determination in international law, with chapters on historical foundations, binding international instruments, non-binding resolutions and declarations, ICJ judgments and opinions, and the normative status of self-determination. This Part provides a comprehensive reference on sources of the right to self-determination, with commentary on the contributions of these sources to the international law of self-determination.

1 Historical Antecedents

a. Overview

The historical context underlying the emergence of the right to self-determination in international law informs how and why the right has developed into its current form in positive international law. This chapter begins by identifying expressions of the idea of self-determination and its corollaries prior to the formation of the League of Nations, beginning with the American Revolution through the First World War. This chapter then discusses the influence of self-determination in the League of Nations system, namely in the Mandate System established by the Covenant of the League of Nations for the administration of former colonies and territories of defeated belligerents of the First World War, and in the Aaland Islands arbitration. The final part of this chapter evaluates the 1941 Atlantic Charter, an early expression of aspects of a universal entitlement to self-determination, which was endorsed by most of the States that would comprise the initial membership of the United Nations. This historical context provides the foundation for the subsequent incorporation of self-determination as a principle and as a right of peoples in formal sources of international law after the Second World War.

b. Revolution and Independence

Long before the contemporary nomenclature of self-determination, aspects of self-determination were reflected in declarations of independence.[1] Early theories of resistance are found in the works of jurists including Grotius, whose influential support for a right to resistance in extreme circumstances

[1] *Accordance with International Law of the Unilateral Declaration of Independence in Respect of Kosovo*, Advisory Opinion, ICJ Rep 2010, 403 (hereinafter *Kosovo* (2010)) para 79.

The Right to Self-Determination in International Law. Thomas Weatherall, Oxford University Press.
 DOI: 10.1093/9780197798119.003.0002

was rooted in popular sovereignty and a natural right of punishment.[2] The American Revolution was based in a claim to independence notable for its articulation of the principal elements of contemporary self-determination and, accordingly, has been regarded as the historical and conceptual origin of the principle.[3] Interrelated assertions of independence from colonial rule and representative government were set out in the Declaration of Independence of 4 July 1776. The Declaration, which presented the grievances of the American colonists against King George III of England, articulated an entitlement of the American people to independence from British subjugation and to representative government.[4]

In this way, the Declaration presented a concept of self-government operating both internally and externally, a duality characteristic of the contemporary right to self-determination. The Declaration asserted an entitlement to representative government whose authority is interrelated with human rights. The appeal of the Declaration to natural law as the source of such rights ('that all men are created equal, that they are endowed by their Creator with certain unalienable Rights') provided the basis for an entitlement to representative government.[5] The Declaration also asserted an entitlement to 'separate and equal station' among sovereign States ('powers of the earth'), 'to which the Laws of Nature and of Nature's God entitle them', as 'Free and Independent States'. Not only does such a claim bespeak a 'Right' to independence from foreign subordination, but also a duty on the part of other States to respect that right.[6] This claim, too, is rooted in natural law. Natural law, as applied to inter-State relations, was understood during the period as the law of nations.[7] The Declaration's reference to 'a decent Respect to the Opinions

[2] Marco Barducci, *Hugo Grotius and the Century of Revolution, 1613–1718: Transnational Reception in English Political Thought* (OUP 2017) 46 ff.

[3] James Crawford, 'Opinion: Third Party Obligations with respect to Israeli Settlements in the Occupied Palestinian Territories' para 106 (24 Jan 2012). See also Ian Brownlie, 'The Rights of Peoples in Modern International Law' (1985) 33 *Bulletin of the Australian Society of Legal Philosophy* 104, 107.

[4] *Declaration of Independence* (4 July 1776).

[5] Thomas G. West, *The Political Theory of the American Founding: Natural Rights, Public Policy, and the Moral Conditions of Freedom* (CUP 2017) 21. See e.g. John Locke, 'The Second Treatise of Government' chs II–IV, VII, in *Two Treatises of Government* ([1689] Mark Goldie ed, Everyman 2003).

[6] West (n 5) 35. The claim to independence by the American people was asserted in particular against Great Britain.

[7] William Blackstone, *Commentaries on the Laws of England*, bk IV, ch V, 66 (4th edn, Clarendon Press 1770) ('The law of nations is a system of rules, deducible by natural reason, and established by universal consent among the civilized inhabitants of the world [] in order

of Mankind' is itself a recognition of the law of nations.[8] In sum, the assertions of internal and external self-government in the Declaration were based in legal principles which, consistent with the jurisprudence of the period, were oriented in natural law and its expression as the law of nations.[9]

The American Revolution provides a compelling, if *sui generis*, illustration of the mutually reinforcing elements of freedom from foreign subordination and representative government that constitute the contemporary right to self-determination.[10] The way the Declaration utilized the law of nations to present these elements as legal rights was without precedent.[11] Thomas Paine enthusiastically wrote, in reaction to the American Revolution, that '[w]e have it in our power to begin the world over again. . . . The birth-day of a new world is at hand'.[12] Indeed, Enlightenment ideals that influenced the American Revolution also animated the French Revolution,[13] which espoused the human rights and popular sovereignty of the French people.[14] The French Revolution is often also considered to be a historical point of reference in the narrative of self-determination.[15]

to decide all disputes, to regulate all ceremonies and civilities, and to insure the observance of justice and good faith, in that intercourse which must frequently occur between two or more independent states, and the individuals belonging to each'). See Hugo Grotius, *De Jure Belli ac Pacis Libri Tres* ([1646] Francis W. Kelsey et al tr, James Brown Scott ed, Clarendon Press 1925); Samuel Pufendorf, *De Jure Naturae et Gentium Libri Octo* ([1688] C. H. Oldfather & W. A. Oldfather tr, James Brown Scott ed, Clarendon Press 1934); Emer de Vattel, *The Law of Nations* ([1797] Béla Kapossy & Richard Whatmore eds, Liberty Fund 2008).

---

[8] Edward Dumbauld, 'Independence under International Law' (1976) 70(3) *AJIL* 425. See *Ware v Hylton*, 3 US (Dall.) 199, 281 (1796).

[9] Mark W. Janis, *America and the Law of Nations 1776–1939* (OUP 2010) 25; Edwin D. Dickinson, 'The Law of Nations as part of the National Law of the United States' (1952) 101 *University of Pennsylvania Law Review* 26, 34–36. See also Ian Brownlie, 'An Essay in the History of the Principle of Self-Determination' in C. H. Alexandrowicz (ed), *Grotian Society Papers 1968* (Martinus Nijhoff 1970) 90–92 (discussing the 'ideological roots of self-determination').

[10] Umozurike Oji Umozurike, *Self-Determination in International Law* (Archon Books 1972) 8.

[11] Janis (n 9) 26.

[12] Thomas Paine, *Common Sense* ([1776] Isaac Kramnick ed, Penguin 1986) 120.

[13] See e.g. Jean-Jacque Rousseau, 'The Social Contract' bk 1 ch 6, in *The Social Contract and Discourses* ([1762] G. D. H. Cole tr, Everyman 2003). See David Armitage, *The Declaration of Independence: A Global History* (Harvard University Press 2007) 67, 89–90.

[14] *Declaration of the Rights of Man and of the Citizen Adopted by the National Assembly during its Sessions on August 20, 21, 25 and 26, 1789, and Approved by the King.*

[15] Brownlie (n 3) 107; Antonio Cassese, *Self-Determination of Peoples: A Legal Reappraisal* (CUP 1995) 11–13; A. Rigo Sureda, *The Evolution of the Right of Self-Determination: A study of United Nations Practice* (A. W. Sijthoff 1973) 17–18. See Edward James Kolla, *Sovereignty,*

Coinciding with the period of the American and French revolutions, legal positivism emerged as what would become the prevailing philosophy of jurisprudence, which eschewed natural law as a source of legal rights and duties.[16] The law of nations was rejected by legal positivism,[17] and was largely succeeded conceptually by what Jeremy Bentham would refer to as 'international law'.[18] Whatever support the law of nations provided to claims to self-government, its natural law foundations would not substantiate an entitlement to self-determination in positive international law.[19]

Legal positivism is predicated upon on a formal source of law—a sovereign—from which law derives its authority.[20] Positive international law accordingly consists of rules created by sovereign States, the principal legal subjects of international law, to advance their interests.[21] Through the lens of a positivist legal system, one initially admitting States as its exclusive legal subjects, independence was regarded not as an entitlement of peoples cognizable through the law of nations, but rather, as an incident of the sovereignty of the State. Independence may therefore be viewed as a criterion of statehood.[22] The relationship between independence and the sovereignty of the

International Law, and the French Revolution (CUP 2017) 86–87 (distinguishing separation of Avignon from papal authority and integration by France following a plebiscite in 1791).

---

16 John Austin, *Lectures on Jurisprudence, or, The Philosophy of Positive Law* (3rd edn, Robert Campbell ed, John Murray 1869); Hans Kelsen, *General Theory of Law and State* (Harvard University Press 1949); H. L. A. Hart, *The Concept of Law* (3rd edn, OUP 2012). See Hans J. Morgenthau, 'Positivism, Functionalism, and International Law' (1940) 34(2) *AJIL* 260.

17 Hart (n 16) 231.

18 Jeremy Bentham, *An Introduction to the Principles of Morals and Legislation* ([1780] Clarendon Press 1876) x. See Mark W. Janis, 'Jeremy Bentham and the Fashioning of "International Law"' (1984) 78(2) *AJIL* 405.

19 Bentham contributed to the British response to the US Declaration of Independence and is understood to have authored the critical 'Short Review of the Declaration', which rejected the natural law foundations of the Declaration. See [Jeremy Bentham,] 'Short Review of the Declaration' in [John Lind and Jeremy Bentham,] *An Answer to the Declaration of the American Congress* (4th edn 1776) 119. In his critique of the French Declaration on the Rights and Duties of Man and the Citizen, Bentham famously referred to its invocation of natural rights founded on natural law as 'nonsense upon stilts': Jeremy Bentham, 'Nonsense upon Stilts' [1792] in Philip Schofield, Catherine Pease-Watkin & Cyprian Blamires (eds), *Rights, Representation, and Reform: Nonsense upon Stilts and other Writings on the French Revolution* (Clarendon Press 2002) 330. See Armitage (n 13) 78–80 (describing Bentham as 'a link between the American and French Revolutions' in this regard).

20 Austin (n 16) 81, 87–88.

21 *The Case of the S.S. 'Lotus'*, PCIJ Series A No 10, Judgment No 9 (7 Sept 1927) 18.

22 Convention on Rights and Duties of States adopted by the Seventh International Conference of American States art 1(d), 165 LNTS 19 (26 Dec 1933, entered into force 26 Dec

State was described by Vattel as a hallmark of an international community of States.[23]

> Every nation which governs itself, under what form soever, without dependence on any foreign power, is a *sovereign state*. Its rights are naturally the same as those of any other state. Such are the moral persons who live together in a natural society, subject to the law of nations. To give a nation a right to make an immediate figure in this grand society, it is sufficient that it be really sovereign and independent, that is, that it governs itself by its own authority and laws.[24]

The independence of the sovereign State exhibits internal and external elements, but inures to the benefit of the State qua State.

> [S]overeignty is *independence*. It is *external* independence with regard to the liberty of action outside its borders in the intercourse with other States which a State enjoys. It is *internal* independence with regard to the liberty of action of a State inside its borders[.][25]

As an emanation of the sovereignty of the State, independence in this sense retrenches certain features of the inter-State system necessary for the realization of self-determination. However, this conceptualization of the sovereignty of the State is quite different from the popular sovereignty of the American and French revolutions. Until the middle of the twentieth century, international law generally paid no regard to the peoples residing within States (or territories under their control), whose treatment remained the exclusive domain of the State.[26] International law of the period provided

1934) ('The State as a person of international law should possess the . . . capacity to enter into relations with the other States').

---

[23] Vattel is 'generally seen as the harbinger of unrestrained positivism': Marc Weller, 'Foreword' in Thomas Weatherall, *Jus Cogens: International Law and Social Contract* (CUP 2015) xii.

[24] Vattel (n 7) I.I.4 (emphasis in original).

[25] Lassa Oppenheim, I *International Law* s 123 (Ronald F. Roxburgh ed, 3rd edn, Longmans, Green & Co 1920) (emphasis in original).

[26] The notable exception being the system of protections for minorities under the League of Nations, centred on 'Minority Treaties' concluded between the League of Nations and newly established States (as well as States defeated during the First World War) to safeguard certain

nothing by way of an actionable entitlement to self-government. Formally, international law was agnostic towards claims to independence.[27]

Only during the second half of the twentieth century would international law recognize a right of peoples to self-government through independence. In this way, self-determination in international law bridged conceptualizations of State sovereignty and popular sovereignty. The First World War and its aftermath saw early indications of a shift in international law in this direction, away from an exclusionary focus on States, one which would come to fruition after the Second World War. During this period, self-determination became a prominent subject of political discourse, a development often attributed to the ardent support for the principle by US President Woodrow Wilson.[28] Wilson frequently proposed elements of the principle of self-determination as necessary for achieving peace during the First World War.[29]

rights of members of minority groups. See Helmer Rosting, 'Protection of Minorities by the League of Nations' (1923) 17(4) *AJIL* 641.

---

[27] *Kosovo* (2010) para 79.

[28] Theodore S. Woolsey, 'Self-Determination' (1919) 13(2) *AJIL* 302, 303; David Raič, *Statehood and the Law of Self-Determination* (Kluwer Law International 2002) 177–84; Brownlie (n 9) 94; Cassese (n 15) 19–23. Vladimir Lenin is also sometimes mentioned alongside Wilson in this regard. See e.g. ibid 14–19. But see Lauri Mälksoo, 'The Soviet Approach to the Right of Peoples to Self-determination: Russia's Farewell to *jus publicum europaeum*' (2017) 19 *Journal of the History of International Law* 200, 203 ('[I]t is a misunderstanding to mention in one breath Lenin's (the Bolsheviks') and Wilson's concepts of self-determination as 'precursors' in international law. The Soviet concept of the right of peoples to self-determination was adopted for tactical and propaganda purposes and had little in common with the liberal democratic concept of this right, which saw in it an end in itself'). See also Raič (supra) 184–88. See V. I. Lenin, 'The Right of Nations to Self-Determination' in *Imperialism and the National Question* ([1914] Verso 2024) (describing self-determination as an entitlement to secession in service of liberation of the proletariat).

[29] See e.g. 'An Address to the Senate of the United States' (22 Jan 1917) in Arthur S. Link (ed), 40 *The Papers of Woodrow Wilson* (Princeton University Press 1982) 533, 536–37 ('No peace can last, or ought to last, which does not recognize and accept the principle that governments derive all their just powers from the consent of the governed, and that no right anywhere exists to hand peoples about from sovereignty to sovereignty as if they were property'); 'An Address to a Joint Session of Congress'(8 Jan 1918) in Arthur S. Link (ed), 45 *The Papers of Woodrow Wilson* (Princeton University Press 1984) 534, 537–38 (setting out fourteen points to achieve peace, including the 'political independence and territorial integrity [of] great and small states alike' and opportunities 'of autonomous development' to minority nationalities in Central Europe). The UK was explicit in this regard: see 'Address of the British Prime Minister (Lloyd George) before the Trade Union Conference at London, January 5, 1918' in Joseph V. Fuller (ed), I *Papers Relating to the Foreign Relations of the United States, 1918, Supplement 1, The World War* (US Government Printing Office 1933) 4, 11–12 ('We are fighting for a just and a lasting peace, and we believe that before permanent peace can be hoped for three conditions must be fulfilled . . . a territorial settlement must be secured, based on the right of self-determination or the consent of the governed').

A provision expressly referring to self-determination had been proposed by Wilson for inclusion in the League of Nations Covenant, though reference to self-determination was not adopted in the final text.[30] Although the Treaty of Versailles (1919), which brought an end to the First World War and contained the Covenant of the League of Nations, included no express reference to self-determination, the concept found expression through the disposition of colonies and other territories of the defeated belligerents.[31] The Covenant of the League of Nations thereby contains the first, albeit narrow, multilateral application of the principle of self-determination in positive international law.[32]

c. League of Nations

Despite the prominence of the principle of self-determination in the political discourse of the First World War, an entitlement to self-determination was not codified as a rule of positive international law in the League of Nations system.[33] Even so, self-determination remained influential during the interwar period, as illustrated by two expressions of the principle. First, the Mandate System implemented the principle of self-determination in relation to colonies and other territories of the defeated belligerents of the First

[30] 'Wilson's Third Draft or Second Paris Draft, January 20, 1919' art III, reprinted in David Hunter Miller, II *The Drafting of the Covenant* (G. P. Putnam's Sons 1928) 98, 99. See also 'Wilson's Second Draft or First Paris Draft, January 10, 1919 with Comments and Suggestions by D. H. M.' art III, reprinted in Miller (supra) 65, 70; 'Wilson's First Draft' art III, reprinted in Miller (supra) 12, 12–13.

[31] The Treaty of Peace Between the Allied and Associated Powers and Germany (June 28, 1919), in Joseph V. Fuller (ed), XIII *Papers Relating to the Foreign Relations of the United States, The Paris Peace Conference, 1919*, Annex I (US Government Printing Office 1947) (hereinafter Treaty of Versailles).

[32] See H. Duncan Hall, *Mandates, Dependencies and Trusteeship* (Stevens & Sons Ltd 1948) 93–97. See also Brownlie (n 9) 94–97.

[33] *Report of the International Committee of Jurists entrusted by the Council of the League of Nations with the task of giving an advisory opinion upon the legal aspects of the Aaland Islands Question*, (Oct 1920) *League of Nations Official Journal*, Special Supplement No 3 (hereinafter 1920 Aaland Islands Report) 5; *Report submitted to the Council of the League of Nations by the Commission of Rapporteurs*, League of Nations Council Doc B7.21/68/106 (16 Apr 1921) (hereinafter 1921 Aaland Islands Report) 27. As noted in these reports, the principle found expression only in 'a certain number' of treaties. For discussion of postwar bilateral agreements applying the principle to settle territorial disputes, see Brownlie (n 9) 94–95.

World War.[34] Second, arbitration of the Aaland Islands dispute under the auspices of the League of Nations provided authoritative recognition of the principle of self-determination. These expressions of self-determination in the League of Nations system are considered in turn.

i. Mandate System

The Mandate System was established by the Covenant of the League of Nations to address the political status of German colonies and territories of the Ottoman Empire inhabited by non-Turkish populations after the First World War.[35] Under the Treaty of Versailles (1919), Germany renounced its claims to overseas territories to the Principal Allied and Associated Powers.[36] Turkey similarly renounced its claims to dependent territories under the Treaty of Lausanne (1923).[37] Territories emerging from German and Turkish rule were regarded as unprepared, to varying degrees, to exercise sovereignty as independent States.[38] Under the peace treaties, the Principal Allied and Associated Powers selected States ('Mandatory Powers') to administer these former German and Turkish territories ('Mandates').[39] The Covenant of the League of Nations established a system for Mandates, based on principles of non-annexation and that the well-being and development of such peoples form a 'sacred trust of civilization', to facilitate their achievement of self-government through self-determination.[40]

[34] See 'The Smuts Plan', reprinted in Miller (n 30) 23, 24 ff ('The Position and Powers of the League'). See *Legal Consequences for States of the Continued Presence of South Africa in Namibia (South West Africa) notwithstanding Security Council Resolution 276 (1970)*, Advisory Opinion, ICJ Rep 1971, 16 (hereinafter *Namibia* (1971)) para 52.

[35] For general background, see Hall (n 32) 29–35; *The Mandates System: Origin—Principles—Application*, League of Nations Doc 1945.VI.A.1 (1945) (hereinafter *Mandates System*).

[36] Treaty of Versailles art 119.

[37] Treaty of Peace, 28 LNTS 11 (*signed at* Lausanne, 24 July 1923). Article 132 of the Treaty of Sèvres contained a similar provision but never entered into force, and was superseded by the Treaty of Lausanne: *Mandates System* 18–19.

[38] *Mandates System* 14. See also Umozurike (n 10) 34.

[39] *Mandates System* 19. See Hall (n 32) 30–31.

[40] *International Status of South-West Africa*, Advisory Opinion, ICJ Rep 1950, 128 (hereinafter *South-West Africa* (1950)) 131; *Namibia* (1971) paras 45, 52–53. See Hall (n 32) 80; *Mandates System* 13–18. See also Chapter 7.b.i.1. For critique of the Mandate System, and subsequent Trusteeship System, as 'perpetuating Western domination', see Evan J. Criddle, 'A Sacred Trust of Civilization' in Andrew S. Gold and Paul B. Miller (eds), *Philosophical Foundations of Fiduciary Law* (OUP 2014) 410; Antony Anghie, *Imperialism, Sovereignty and the Making of International Law* (CUP 2007) 145–46.

Each Mandate was governed by an international agreement (a 'charter'), which set out the conditions according to which Mandatory Powers were to administer territories for which they assumed responsibility.[41] These charters were confirmed by the Council of the League of Nations, which also monitored the administration of Mandates by Mandatory Powers.[42] The international status of Mandates, and the international agreements governing them, represented an innovation in international law and practice, as observed by Lord McNair in his Separate Opinion in *South West Africa* (1950).[43] In view of the novel character of the treaty arrangements undergirding the Mandate System, the precise status of territories subject to Mandates remained unsettled.[44]

The League of Nations monitored the administration of Mandates in accordance with Article 22 of the Covenant of the League of Nations, which set out the parameters of the Mandate System.[45] Paragraph 1 of Article 22 provided that the 'well-being and development' of the peoples of Mandate Territories is the guiding principle of the Mandate System, and that administration of Mandates is a 'sacred trust of civilisation'.[46] The ICJ would state that 'the ultimate objective of the sacred trust was the self-determination and independence of the peoples concerned'.[47] Paragraph 2 further stipulated that the responsibility of Mandatory Powers to this end takes the form of 'tutelage' of the peoples of Mandate Territories, and that such responsibility is exercised 'on behalf of the League'.[48] Paragraph 3 of Article 22 contemplated that Mandates differed as to the circumstances of the people of a given territory, according to factors including development, geography, and economic conditions. Informed by these factors, paragraphs 4–6 identified three categories into which mandated territories fell, referred to as 'A' Mandates (Syria,

[41] For a compilation of Mandate instruments, see *Terms of League of Nations Mandates* (republished by the United Nations), A/70 (1946).

[42] *South West Africa Cases (Ethiopia v South Africa; Liberia v South Africa)*, Preliminary Objections, Judgment, ICJ Rep 1962, 319 (hereinafter *South West Africa Cases* (1962)) 329.

[43] *South-West Africa* (1950) Sep Op McNair 150.

[44] James Crawford, *The Creation of States in International Law* (2nd edn, OUP 2006) 568–73. Note, however, that the underlying concepts of Mandate, and later Trusteeship, were not themselves without precedent: see Hall (n 32) 93.

[45] Treaty of Versailles, Part I, The Covenant of the League of Nations art 22 (hereinafter League of Nations Covenant).

[46] Hall (n 32) 97–100. See Chapter 7.b.i.1.

[47] *Namibia* (1971) para 53.

[48] See *South West Africa Cases* (1962) 329.

Lebanon, Transjordan, Palestine, and Iraq) 'B' Mandates (the Cameroons, Togoland, Tanganyika, and Ruanda-Urundi), and 'C' Mandates (South West Africa and the Islands of the Pacific).[49] These categories corresponded to the degree of administration by the responsible Mandatory Power, as reflected in the terms of the respective Mandate charters, and their differential trajectories towards realizing independence.[50] Paragraph 7 imposed an annual reporting obligation for Mandatory Powers with respect to each 'territory committed to its charge'. Paragraphs 8 and 9 contemplated the role of the League of Nations in setting terms of Mandates not previously agreed upon and monitoring the administration of Mandate Territories.[51]

Four 'A' Mandates (Syria, Lebanon, Transjordan, and Iraq) were effectively terminated by their achievement of independence.[52] All 'B' Mandates were terminated by transfer to the United Nations Trusteeship System, as were all 'C' Mandates with the exception of South West Africa.[53] The Mandate for the Islands of the Pacific was terminated a result of Japan's violation of its terms during the Second World War, leading to the creation of the strategic Trust Territory of the Pacific Islands following the establishment of the United Nations.[54] Only the Mandates of Palestine and South West Africa continued beyond the dissolution of the League of Nations in April 1946 without coming under the purview of the United Nations Trusteeship System.[55] The UNGA would ultimately assert responsibility for, and terminate, each of those remaining Mandates.[56]

[49] *Mandates System* 24. Mandated territories were not, however, identified in the League of Nations Covenant. On the different categories of Mandates, see Hall (n 32) 149–52.

[50] Hall (n 32) 80–81. These distinctions conceivably reflet corresponding differential degrees of sovereignty retained by the Mandate Territory vis-à-vis a Mandatory Power. See Crawford (n 44) 569–73. The precise terms of the relationships between Mandate Territories and Mandatory Powers were reflected in their respective Mandate instruments.

[51] See *Mandates System* 33–51.

[52] See Crawford (n 44) 596. The process by which Mandates were terminated was not formal and has been characterized as 'haphazard'. Ibid 575–81.

[53] Ibid 580–81. See Chapter 2.b.iii.

[54] Trusteeship agreement for the former Japanese Mandated Islands, Approved by the Security Council on 2 April 1947, 8 UNTS 189 (entered into force 18 July 1947). See Crawford (n 44) 589.

[55] Resolution for the Dissolution of the League of Nations, Doc A.32.(1).1946.X (18 Apr 1946) 12–16, reproduced in (1947) 1(1) *International Organization* 246. See Hans Kelsen, *The Law of the United Nations* (London Institute of World Affairs 1950) 594–95; Hall (n 32) 272. For the transition of Mandates to the Trusteeship System, see ibid 281–94.

[56] On Palestine, see A/Res/181 (II) (29 Nov 1947) (Future Government of Palestine); see also Hall (n 32) 263–65; Crawford (n 44) 580. On South West Africa, see A/Res/2145 (XXI) (27 Oct 1966) (Question of South West Africa); see also John Dugard, 'The Revocation of the Mandate

Although Article 22 does not refer to self-determination explicitly, self-determination was the animating principle of the Mandate System.[57] It has been observed that application of self-determination through the Mandate System was largely possible because the principle offered a solution to the political problem of disposition of the colonies and other territories of the defeated belligerents of the First World War.[58] This circumstance accounts for the limited application of the principle of self-determination to a specific subset of European territories. The limited application of the principle of self-determination through the narrow scope of the Mandate System has, in turn, been regarded as a reason for its success.[59]

The application of self-determination in the League of Nations Covenant, however limited, would influence the subsequent extension of the principle of self-determination to all non-self-governing territories under the UN Charter.[60] This influence is reflected in the specific modalities in Chapters XI and XII of the UN Charter related to decolonization.[61] The Mandate System itself would ultimately be superseded by the International Trusteeship System established by Chapter XII of the UN Charter.[62] In this way, the Mandate System of the League of Nations links the Wilsonian conceptualization of self-determination articulated during the First World War to the application of the principle of self-determination in the UN Charter. Moreover, both Article 22 of the League of Nations Covenant and Chapter XI of the UN Charter invoke a 'sacred trust' undertaken by States responsible for the administration of Non-Self-Governing Territories (NSGTs).[63] The UN Charter expanded the application of the 'sacred trust' defined in the League of Nations Covenant to all NSGTs.[64] Finally, Article 23(b) of the League of

for South West Africa' (1968) 62(1) *AJIL* 78, 78–97. See also *South-West Africa* (1950) 136–37 (affirming the authority of the UNGA to carry out supervisory functions previously exercised by the League of Nations in relation to Mandate Territories).

---

[57] *Namibia* (1971) paras 52–53.

[58] *Mandates System* 7; Hall (n 32) 30.

[59] Hall (n 32) 35.

[60] *Namibia* (1971) para 52.

[61] See Chapter 2.b.

[62] *Namibia* (1971) paras 60, 73, 90. See Kelsen (n 55) 566. For discussion of differences between the Mandate System and Trusteeship system, see Francis B. Sayre, 'Legal Problems Arising from the United Nations Trusteeship System' (1948) 42(2) *AJIL* 263, 265–68.

[63] League of Nations Covenant art 22; Charter of the United Nations art 73, XV UNCIO 335 (26 June 1945, entered into force 24 Oct 1945). See Chapter 7.b.i.1.

[64] *Namibia* (1971) paras 52–53.

Nations Covenant contained a general obligation regarding the treatment of populations of dependent territories:

> Subject to and in accordance with the provisions of international conventions existing or hereafter to be agreed upon, the Members of the League ... undertake to secure just treatment of the native inhabitants of territories under their control[.][65]

Although Article 23(b) remained 'dormant' in the practice of the League of Nations, which would focus principally on the Mandate System under Article 22, it has been suggested that this general obligation under the League of Nations Covenant of Member States concerning the treatment of populations of territories for which they were responsible is the precursor to the general obligations of administering powers of NSGTs under Chapter XI of the UN Charter.[66]

ii. Aaland Islands Dispute

On 12 July 1920, the Council of the League of Nations unanimously adopted a resolution concerning arbitration of a dispute between Finland and Sweden over the Aaland Islands.[67] While the Aaland Islands had historic ties to Sweden, following their annexation by the Russian Empire in the early nineteenth century, the islands were incorporated into Finland under Russian rule.[68] The political status of the Aaland Islands became a point of contention upon Finland's independence from the Russian Empire following the Russian Revolution in 1917. The Aaland Islands dispute centred on whether the inhabitants of the Aaland Islands were free to determine by plebiscite whether to remain under Finish sovereignty or become incorporated by Sweden.[69]

[65] League of Nations Covenant art 23(b).

[66] Hall (n 32) 223–28.

[67] 1920 Aaland Islands Report 1. For general background, see Norman J. Padelford & K. Gösta A. Andersson, 'The Aaland Islands Question' (1939) 33(3) *AJIL* 465, 465–74.

[68] 1920 Aaland Islands Report 9.

[69] Ibid 3. See also Chapter 11.f.i.

The Council of the League of Nations first appointed an International Committee of Jurists to examine whether the League of Nations had jurisdiction over the dispute.[70] In its September 1920 report, the Committee found that the League of Nations had jurisdiction to adjudicate the dispute and rendered conclusions on the applicable law.[71] The Committee observed that, despite the prominence of the principle of self-determination during the period, the principle had not been codified as a rule of positive international law.

> Although the principle of self-determination of peoples plays an important part in modern political thought, especially since the Great War, it must be pointed out that there is no mention of it in the Covenant of the League of Nations. The recognition of this principle in a certain number of international treaties cannot be considered as sufficient to put it upon the same footing as a positive rule of the Law of Nations.[72]

Accordingly, positive international law did not entitle sub-State groups to secession.[73] The Committee considered, however, that 'the formation, transformation and dismemberment of States as a result of revolutions and wars' may present factual circumstances that cannot be resolved through 'the application of the normal rules of positive law'.[74] 'Under such circumstances', which the Committee reasoned applied to Finland upon its emergence from Russian rule, where 'territorial sovereignty[] is lacking',

> the principle of self-determination of peoples may be called into play. . . . The principle recognising the rights of peoples to determine their political fate may be applied in various ways; the most important of these are, on the one hand the formation of an independent State, and on the other hand the right of choice between two existing States.[75]

[70] For discussion of the International Committee of Jurists and its report, see James Brown Scott, 'The Aaland Islands Question' (1921) 15(2) *AJIL* 268, 268–72; Padelford & Andersson (n 67) 474–75.

[71] 1920 Aaland Islands Report 5–6, 14.

[72] Ibid 5.

[73] Ibid.

[74] Ibid 6.

[75] Ibid.

Having recognized the relevance of the principle of self-determination, the Committee then evaluated the relationship between the principle and the protection of minorities.[76] Considering the application of self-determination in that context, the Committee assessed that the principle of self-determination must be balanced against other principles of international law.[77]

After receiving the Committee's report on jurisdiction, the Council of the League of Nations appointed a second body, the Commission of Rapporteurs, to advise on the merits of the dispute.[78] Regarding the applicable law, in its April 1921 report on the merits of the dispute, the Commission followed the Committee regarding the status of the principle of self-determination as falling outside of positive international law.

> This principle is not, properly speaking a rule of international law and the League of Nations has not entered it in its Covenant. This is also the opinion of the International Commission of Jurists. . . . It is a principle of justice and of liberty, expressed by a vague and general formula which has given rise to the most varied interpretations and differences of opinion.[79]

The Commission departed, however, from the reasoning of the Committee regarding whether the dispute was governed by positive international law. Finland, in the view of the Commission, was to be regarded as the former autonomous State of Finland and, as such, subject to positive international law, which rejected an entitlement to secession by sub-State groups.[80] The Commission considered, instead, that the interests of the Aaland Islanders could be adequately safeguarded by Finland and identified the 'most suitable measures for the preservation of its national character for this population'.[81] The Commission identified certain essential 'international guarantees' for the Aaland Islanders in the areas of language teaching, territorial property rights, political participation, and representation.[82] While the Commission

[76] Ibid.

[77] Ibid.

[78] 1921 Aaland Islands Report. For discussion of the Commission of Rapporteurs and its report, see Padelford & Andersson (n 67) 475–76.

[79] 1921 Aaland Islands Report 27.

[80] Ibid 27–28.

[81] Ibid 31.

[82] Ibid 31–34.

did not rule out the possibility of considering the appropriateness of incorporation with Sweden had it been 'the only means of preserving its Swedish language for Aaland', the Commission characterized such a solution as 'exceptional' and 'a last resort'.[83] Finland's readiness to afford guarantees to the Aaland Islanders negated the need for such consideration.[84]

The Council of the League of Nations, after considering the report of the Commission and hearing views of the parties, recognized Finland's sovereignty over the Aaland Islands.[85] Finland and Sweden reached an agreement reflecting the guarantees recommended by the Commission, which was approved by the Council, ending consideration of the case.[86] The underlying dispute is an early illustration of the interplay between the principles of territorial integrity and self-determination, and its treatment by the arbitral bodies constituted by the League of Nations brought to light the contested position of self-determination in international law.[87]

d. Atlantic Charter

The Atlantic Charter, endorsed by most of the States that would comprise the initial membership of the United Nations, is one of the earliest international statements expressing aspects of a universal entitlement to self-determination as the right would develop in international law.[88] US President Franklin Roosevelt and UK Prime Minister Winston Churchill signed the Atlantic Charter on 14 August 1941 as a series of common principles intended to guide international relations following the Second World War.[89] On 1 January 1942, twenty-six States signed the Declaration by United Nations, according to which its signatories committed to the purposes and principles set out in

[83] Ibid 28.
[84] Ibid 29.
[85] Padelford & Andersson (n 67) 476.
[86] Ibid. See Convention relating to the Non-Fortification and Neutralisation of the Aaland Islands, 9 LNTS 213 (20 Oct 1921).
[87] Cf Charles Noble Gregory, 'The Neutralization of the Aaland Islands' (1923) 17(1) *AJIL* 63, 76; Padelford & Andersson (n 67) 477.
[88] Joint declaration by the President of the United States and the Prime Minister of the United Kingdom August 14, 1941, 55 Stat. 1603, Department of State Executive Agreement Series No 236 (hereinafter Atlantic Charter).
[89] Atlantic Charter para 1.

the Atlantic Charter.[90] Twenty-one additional States signed the Declaration by the end of the war, bringing the total number of States committing to the principles contained in the Atlantic Charter to forty-seven.[91]

The Atlantic Charter has been regarded as the first multilateral acceptance of the principle of self-determination.[92] The second and third principles of the Atlantic Charter provide:

> [The signatories] desire to see no territorial changes that do not accord with the freely expressed wishes of the peoples concerned;
>
> [The signatories] respect the right of all peoples to choose the form of government under which they will live; and they wish to see sovereign rights and self-government restored to those who have been forcibly deprived of them[.][93]

These principles articulated in the Atlantic Charter, while not explicitly referring to self-determination, reflect key elements of the right as it would emerge in international law and subsequent practice. Notably, the principles are articulated in reference to peoples as their beneficiaries, a legal subject novel to self-determination as the principle and right would be articulated in the UN Charter and other international instruments.[94] The second principle conditions territorial change on the 'freely expressed wishes of the peoples concerned', the touchstone of the exercise of the right to self-determination as it would emerge in international law.[95] The third principle articulates a right of peoples to self-government and to choose their form of government, which are core elements of the right to self-determination.[96]

The endorsement of elements of what would come to be recognized as the right to self-determination in the Atlantic Charter, an instrument enjoying broad international consensus immediately prior to the establishment of the United Nations, provides a precursor to the subsequent codification of the principle in the UN Charter.

[90] Declaration by United Nations, CCIV LNTS 381 (1 Jan 1942).

[91] 'The Declaration by United Nations' (1947) 1 *Yearbook of the United Nations 1946–47* 1–2 (citing US State Department Bulletin, January 3, 1942, p. 3).

[92] Brownlie (n 9) 97.

[93] Atlantic Charter (Second and Third Principles).

[94] See Chapter 6.a.

[95] See Chapter 7.b.i.2.

[96] See Chapter 7.b; Chapter 8.c. The Third Principle articulated in the Atlantic Charter includes the domestic aspect of self-determination. See Cassese (n 15) 37.

2
International Instruments

a. Overview

Following the Second World War, in October 1945, the United Nations came into operation with the entry into force of the UN Charter.[1] The League of Nations was subsequently dissolved in April 1946.[2] Principal instruments of the United Nations system, the UN Charter and the two human rights covenants, respectively codified the principle of self-determination and the right to self-determination. The prominence of self-determination in each of these instruments—as a principle of friendly relations articulated in Article 1 of the UN Charter, and as right of peoples codified in Article 1 common to the ICCPR and ICESCR—suggests the foundational role that self-determination was viewed to serve in the rules-based international order of the United Nations. The right to self-determination was subsequently codified in various regional human rights instruments.

Treaty-based sources of rights and obligations related to self-determination are evaluated in this chapter. The first section assesses the UN Charter, particularly Articles 1 and 55, Chapter XI on Non-Self-Governing Territories, and Chapters XII and XIII on the International Trusteeship System. The next section considers the two international human rights covenants, with a focus on common article 1 of the ICCPR and ICESCR, which codify the right to self determination. The final section of this chapter addresses regional instruments with provisions on self-determination.

[1] Charter of the United Nations, XV UNCIO 335 (26 June 1945, entered into force 24 Oct 1945) (hereinafter UN Charter).

[2] Resolution for the Dissolution of the League of Nations, Doc A.32(1).1946.X (18 Apr 1946) 12–16, reproduced in (1947) 1(1) *International Organization* 246. See Hans Kelsen, *The Law of the United Nations* (London Institute of World Affairs 1950) 594–95.

The Right to Self-Determination in International Law. Thomas Weatherall, Oxford University Press.
 DOI: 10.1093/9780197798119.003.0003

b. United Nations Charter

The UN Charter is the first multilateral instrument to refer to the principle of self-determination. The League of Nations Covenant did not refer to self-determination and the principle was not regarded as a rule of positive international law in the League of Nations system.[3] The UN Charter contains provisions that explicitly (Articles 1 and 55) and implicitly (Chapters XI and XII) address self-determination.[4]

i. Principle of Self-Determination (Articles 1 and 55)

Articles 1 and 55 of the UN Charter establish 'the principle of equal rights and self-determination of peoples'.

> **Chapter I: Purposes and Principles**
> *Article 1*
> The Purposes of the United Nations are. . . .
>
> 2. To develop friendly relations among nations based on respect for the principle of equal rights and self-determination of peoples, and to take other appropriate measures to strengthen universal peace[.]
>
> . . .
>
> **Chapter IX: International Economic and Social Cooperation**
> *Article 55*
> With a view to the creation of conditions of stability and well-being which are necessary for peaceful and friendly relations among nations based on respect for the principle of equal rights and self-determination of peoples, the United Nations shall promote:

[3] See Chapter 1.c.

[4] Because all former Trust Territories have attained independence, there are no UN Member States subject to the performance of obligations under a Chapter XII Trusteeship Agreement, therefore Chapter XII is not included in its entirety.

a. higher standards of living, full employment, and conditions of economic and social progress and development;
b. solutions of international economic, social, health, and related problems; and international cultural and educational cooperation; and
c. universal respect for, and observance of, human rights and fundamental freedoms for all without distinction as to race, sex, language, or religion.

Article 1 regards the principle of equal rights and self-determination of peoples as the basis of friendly relations among States and establishes the advancement of such friendly relations as a purpose of the United Nations. Article 55, which addresses the promotion by the United Nations of cooperation in the economic, social, and cultural fields, as well as non-discrimination in respect for human rights, situates these ends as conditions for peaceful and friendly relations among States based on respect for the principle of equal rights and self-determination of peoples.[5] In this way, Articles 1 and 55 are directed towards the United Nations as an institution rather than its member States.[6] As a result, neither provision sets out obligations for States in relation to the principle of self-determination.[7]

The *travaux préparatoires* of the Charter, while limited, sheds light on its drafters' understanding of the principle of self-determination.[8] The equal rights of peoples and self-determination of peoples are understood to constitute two components of a single 'standard of conduct' or 'norm'.[9] According

[5] See also UN Charter art 56 ('All Members pledge themselves to take joint and separate action in co-operation with the Organization for the achievement of the purposes set forth in Article 55'). In *Western Sahara* (1975), the ICJ considered Article 56 to be relevant to the references to self-determination in Articles 1 and 55 of the UN Charter, without elaboration. See *Western Sahara*, Advisory Opinion, ICJ Rep 1975, 12 para 54.

[6] Bruno Simma et al (eds), *The Charter of the United Nations: A Commentary* (3rd edn, OUP 2012) vol I 108–09 para 4 (Article 1), vol II 1541 para 19 (Article 55).

[7] Antonio Cassese, *Self-Determination of Peoples: A Legal Reappraisal* (CUP 1995) 43. See Kelsen (n 2) 50–53.

[8] This discussion refers to three reports by Committee I/1: Summary Report of Sixth Meeting of Committee I/1, Doc 343, I/1/16, in (1945) 6 *UN Conference on International Organization* 296 (hereinafter 15 May 1945 Report); Report of Rapporteur, Subcommittee I/1/A, to Committee I/1, June 1, 1945, Doc 723, I/1/A/19, in (1945) 6 *UN Conference on International Organization* 696 (hereinafter 1 June 1945 Report); Report of Rapporteur of Committee 1 to Commission I, Doc 944, I/1/34(l), in (1945) 6 *UN Conference on International Organization* 446 (hereinafter 13 June 1945 Report).

[9] 13 June 1945 Report 455 ('The Committee understands that the principle of equal rights of peoples and that of self-determination are two complementary parts of one standard of conduct'); 1 June 1945 Report 703 ('It was understood: That the principles of equal rights of people and that of self-determination are two component elements or one norm').

to the reports of the relevant drafting committee, 'an essential element of the principle in question is a free and genuine expression of the will of the people', which was set against the examples of annexations by Germany and Italy during the Second World War.[10] Early in the drafting of the Charter, it was understood that self-determination referred in this sense to a right to self-government, but not an entitlement to secession, the latter being incompatible with the purposes of the Charter.[11] Subsequent reports by the drafting committee reflected an understanding of respect for self-determination as 'a basis for the development of friendly relations and [a]s one of the measures to strengthen universal peace',[12] a framing reflected in the text of Articles 1 and 55.

Chapter XI (Non-Self-Governing Territories) and Chapter XII (International Trusteeship System) of the UN Charter set out obligations and objectives for States that may be understood to follow from the principle of self-determination articulated in Articles 1 and 55.

ii. Non-Self-Governing Territories (Chapter XI)

Chapter XI (Articles 73 and 74) of the UN Charter addresses territories whose 'peoples have not yet attained a full measure of self-government', which are regarded under the Charter as Non-Self-Governing Territories (NSGTs).[13] Chapter XI does not extend to all NSGTs the Trusteeship System, which succeeded the League of Nations Mandate System and entailed the conclusion of Trusteeship agreements governing the relationships between Trust Territories and 'administering authorities'.[14] Instead, Chapter XI sets forth general obligations for States with responsibility for the administration of NSGTs as 'administering powers'.[15]

[10] 13 June 1945 Report 455. See also 1 June 1945 Report 704.

[11] 15 May 1945 Report 296.

[12] 13 June 1945 Report 455. See also 1 June 1945 Report 704 (adding: 'It was understood likewise that the principle in question, as a provision of the Charter, should be considered in function of other provisions').

[13] UN Charter arts 73–74. See Kelsen (n 2) 550–65. See also Chapter 10.b.i.

[14] See Chapter 2.b.iii.

[15] The relationship between an administering power and a NSGT is understood as one in which sovereignty is exercised by the administering power over the NSGT. However, this exercise of sovereignty is conditioned by the obligations imposed upon administering powers by

At base, Article 73 of the UN Charter imposes upon administering powers 'the obligation to promote to the utmost, within the system of international peace and security established by the Charter, the well-being of the inhabitants of [Non-Self-Governing] territories'.[16] '[T]o this end', Article 73 enumerates five elements. Article 73(a) sets out a standard of treatment of the peoples of NSGTs by administering powers resembling Article 23(b) of the League of Nations Covenant.[17] Under Article 73(b), administering powers are subject to an obligation 'to develop self-government, to take due account of the political aspirations of the peoples, and to assist them in the progressive development of their free political institutions'. This obligation operates with a view towards the exercise by the people of a NSGT of its right to self-determination.[18] Article 73(b) does not prescribe a timeframe for discharge of the obligations of an administering power in this regard. Instead, Article 73(b) contemplates the development of self-government 'according to the particular circumstances of each territory and its peoples and their varying stages of advancement'. Article 73(c) obligates administering powers to further international peace and security, and Article 73(d) consists of obligations regarding the promotion of social, economic, and scientific aims. Under Article 73(e), administering powers are directed to report to the UN Secretary-General 'statistical and other information of a technical nature relating to economic, social, and educational conditions' of NSGTs under their administration. This reporting requirement is subject to limitations as 'security and constitutional considerations may require'.[19] Article 73 does not address the cessation of obligations of administering powers under Chapter XI.[20]

Article 74 provides that the policy of UN Member States towards NSGTs is to be based on 'the general principle of good-neighbourliness', taking into account the 'interests and well-being of the rest of the world, in social,

the UN Charter. See James Crawford, *The Creation of States in International Law* (2nd edn, OUP 2006) 613–15. See Chapter 9.c.ii.

---

[16] UN Charter art 73.

[17] Cf Treaty of Versailles, Part I, The Covenant of the League of Nations art 23(b).

[18] See Chapter 7.b.i.

[19] A/Res/1541 (XV) (15 Dec 1960) (hereinafter Resolution 1541) Annex, Principle X. See Chapter 3.c.

[20] See Chapter 10.b.ii.

economic, and commercial matters'.[21] There is, however, a dearth of practice interpreting or applying this provision.

In practice, eighty territories formerly subject to Chapter XI of the Charter have emerged into a self-governing status,[22] while seventeen territories continue to be regarded by the UNGA as NSGTs under Chapter XI of the Charter.[23] The performance of the obligations of administering powers in relation to NSGTs is addressed in Chapter 9, and the practice of the United Nations in the field of decolonization is examined in Chapter 10.

iii. International Trusteeship System (Chapters XII and XIII)

The International Trusteeship System under Chapters XII and XIII of the UN Charter succeeded the League of Nations Mandate System.[24] Chapter XII (Articles 75–85) of the UN Charter sets out a framework for obligations of administering authorities of territories to which the Trusteeship System applied. Article 77 provides that the Trusteeship System applied to three categories of territories—territories then held under League of Nations mandate,[25] territories detached from defeated States following the Second World War, and territories voluntarily placed under the system by States responsible for their administration—by operation of Trusteeship agreements.[26]

[21] UN Charter art 74.

[22] Appendix 1: Former Trust Territories and Non-Self-Governing Territories.

[23] Appendix 2: Non-Self-Governing Territories.

[24] *Legal Consequences for States of the Continued Presence of South Africa in Namibia (South West Africa) notwithstanding Security Council Resolution 276 (1970)*, Advisory Opinion, ICJ Rep 1971, 16 (hereinafter *Namibia* (1971)) paras 60, 73, 90. See Kelsen (n 2) 566. For discussion of differences between the Mandate System and Trusteeship System, see Francis B. Sayre, 'Legal Problems Arising from the United Nations Trusteeship System' (1948) 42(2) *AJIL* 263, 265–68. For further discussion of the Trusteeship System, see Chapter 9.c.i; Chapter 10.b.iv.1; Kelsen (n 2) 566–695.

[25] The UN Charter did not provide for the automatic application of the Trusteeship System to League of Nations Mandates. Instead, such territories were brought under Trusteeship System through the subsequent conclusion of Trusteeship agreements between Mandatory Powers and the United Nations. See UN Charter art 77(2). The UN Charter did not impose obligations on Mandatory Powers to conclude Trusteeship agreements. See *International Status of South-West Africa*, Advisory Opinion, ICJ Rep 1950, 128, 139–40.

[26] UN Charter art 77. See Kelsen (n 2) 578–609. No territory has been voluntarily placed under the Trusteeship System by a State responsible for its administration pursuant to Article 77(1)(c).

Trusteeship agreements, concluded pursuant to Article 81 of the UN Charter between the United Nations and respective administering authorities regarding individual Trust Territories, established specific obligations of administering authorities towards implementation of the basic objectives of the Trusteeship System set out in Article 76 of the UN Charter.[27]

Article 76(b) includes, as a basic objective of the Trusteeship System, 'to promote the political, economic, social, and educational advancement of the inhabitants of the trust territories, and their progressive development towards self-government or independence as may be appropriate to the particular circumstances of each territory and its peoples and the freely expressed wishes of the peoples concerned'.[28] As such, Article 76 implicitly limits the scope of the Trusteeship System to territories whose populations have not yet attained 'self-government or independence'.[29] Article 78 expressly excludes territories 'which have become Members of the United Nations' from the Trusteeship System.[30] Other objectives of the Trusteeship System are to further international peace and security (Article 76(a)), encourage respect for human rights and fundamental freedoms without discrimination as well as 'the interdependence of the peoples of the world' (Article 76(c)), and to ensure equal treatment of UN Member States and their nationals in social, economic, and commercial matters, as well as in the administration of justice for the latter (Article 76(d)).

Chapter XIII of the UN Charter provides for the establishment and operation of the Trusteeship Council, a subsidiary body of the UNGA with competence to monitor the administration of Trust Territories by administering authorities.[31] Article 85 of the Charter contemplates the operation of the Trusteeship Council under the authority of the UNGA in order to assist the UNGA in carrying out functions related to Trusteeship agreements, namely, those related to approval and alteration or amendment of such agreements.[32] In 1946, UNGA Resolution 64 (I) was adopted to establish the Trusteeship

[27] UN Charter art 81.
[28] Ibid art 76(b).
[29] Kelsen (n 2) 570, 574–75.
[30] UN Charter art 78.
[31] See Kelsen (n 2) 609–31. See Chapter 10.b.iv.1.
[32] UN Charter art 85. The terms of 'non-strategic' Trusteeship agreements were approved by the UNGA; the terms of the Trust Agreement for the Trust Territory of the Pacific Islands, designated as 'strategic' in character, were approved by the United Nations Security Council (UNSC). See ibid arts 82–83. On approval, to mean conclusion of an agreement, see Kelsen (n 2) 606–09.

Council, consistent with the provisions of Article 86 of the Charter concerning the composition of the Council.[33]

Eleven Trust Territories were subject to the Trusteeship System. Administering authorities of each Trust Territory were subject to obligations under Trusteeship agreements.[34] Each Trust Territory attained self-government, most after a plebiscite conducted under the auspices of the United Nations, following which its respective Trusteeship agreement was terminated by the UNGA.[35] As a result, no UN Member State is subject to the performance of obligations under a Chapter XII Trusteeship agreement. Consequently, on 25 May 1994, the Trusteeship Council adopted a resolution suspending its operation.[36]

[33] UN Charter art 86; A/Res/64 (I) (14 Dec 1946).

[34] Trusteeship agreement for the Territory of Western Samoa (with Annex), 8 UNTS 71 (entered into force 13 Dec 1946); Trusteeship agreement for the Territory of Tanganyika, 8 UNTS 91 (entered into force 13 Dec 1946); Trusteeship agreement for the Territory of Ruanda-Urundi, 8 UNTS 105 (entered into force 13 Dec 1946); Trusteeship agreement for the Territory of the Cameroons under British administration, 8 UNTS 119 (entered into force 13 Dec 1946); Trusteeship agreement for the Territory of the Cameroons under French administration, 8 UNTS 135 (entered into force 13 Dec 1946); Trusteeship agreement for the Territory of Togoland under British administration, 8 UNTS 151 (entered into force 13 Dec 1946); Trusteeship agreement for the Territory of Togoland under French administration, 8 UNTS 165 (entered into force 13 Dec 1946); Trusteeship agreement for the Territory of New Guinea, 8 UNTS 181 (entered into force 13 Dec 1946); Trusteeship agreement for the former Japanese Mandated Islands, 8 UNTS 189 (entered into force 18 July 1947); Trusteeship agreement for the Territory of Nauru, 10 UNTS 3 (entered into force 1 Nov 1947); Trusteeship agreement for the Territory of Somaliland under Italian administration, 118 UNTS 255 (entered into force 8 Jan 1952).

[35] *Case Concerning the Northern Cameroons (Cameroon v United Kingdom)*, Preliminary Objections, Judgment, ICJ Rep 1963, 15 (hereinafter *Northern Cameroons* (1963)) 32 ('Whatever the motivation of the General Assembly in reaching the conclusions [in its Resolution terminating the Trusteeship agreement with respect to the Northern Cameroons] . . . the resolution had definitive legal effect'). See A/Res/1044 (XI) (13 Dec 1956) (Togoland under British Administration); A/Res/1349 (XIII) (13 Mar 1959) (Cameroons under French Administration); A/Res/1416 (XIV) (5 Dec 1959) (Togoland under French Administration); A/Res/1418 (XIV) (5 Dec 1959) (Somaliland under Italian administration); A/Res/1608 (XV) (21 Apr 1961) (Cameroons under British Administration); A/Res/1609 (XV) (21 Apr 1961) (Tanganyika); A/Res/1626 (XVI) (18 Oct 1961) (Western Samoa); A/Res/1642 (XVI) (6 Nov 1961) (Tanganyika); A/Res/1746 (XVI) (27 June 1962) (Ruanda-Urundi); A/Res/2347 (XXII) (19 Dec 1967) (Nauru); A/Res/3284 (XXIX) (13 Dec 1974) (New Guinea). Regarding the strategic Trust Territory of the Pacific Islands, the Federated States of Micronesia, the Marshall Islands, and Palau are States that emerged from this Trust Territory. The Northern Mariana Islands became a commonwealth territory of the United States. The Trusteeship agreement was terminated by the UNSC upon Palau entering into free association with the United States: S/Res/956 (10 Nov 1994). See also S/Res/683 (22 Dec 1990) (change in status of the Federated States of Micronesia, the Marshall Islands, and the Northern Mariana Islands). See also Crawford (n 15) 581–84.

[36] T/Res/2200 (LXI) (25 May 1994).

iv. Self-Determination in the United Nations Charter System

Although neither Chapter XI nor Chapter XII makes express reference to self-determination, the obligations of administering powers under Article 73 and objectives of the Trusteeship System under Article 76 have been linked to the principle of self-determination articulated in Articles 1 and 55 of the UN Charter. For example, during the drafting of the of the human rights covenants, the Commission on Human Rights observed:

> The United Nations could not promote the principle of self-determination of peoples in accordance with Articles 1 and 55 without promoting the right of the peoples of non-self-governing and trust territories to self-government or independence in accordance with Articles 73(b) and 76(b), or vice versa. It would be an absurd interpretation that under the Charter the peoples of non-self-governing and trust territories should have the right to self-government or independence, but not the right to self-determination. The right of self-determination was a universal right; it was a right of all peoples and all nations.[37]

Similarly, the ICJ later considered that 'the legal régime of non-self-governing territories, as set out in Chapter XI of the Charter, was based on the progressive development of their institutions so as to lead the populations concerned to exercise their right to self-determination'.[38] In reference to Trust Territories to which Chapter XII applied, the ICJ observed 'that the ultimate objective of the sacred trust was the self-determination and independence of the peoples concerned'.[39] This same rationale is reflected in the *chapeau* of Article 76, which sets out the objectives of the Trusteeship System 'in accordance with the Purposes of the United Nations laid down in Article 1'. Taken together, obligations and objectives under Chapters XI and XII may

[37] Draft International Covenants on Human Rights: Annotation, Prepared by the Secretary-General, A/2929 (1 July 1955) (hereinafter A/2929) ch IV para 7.

[38] *Legal Consequences of the Separation of the Chagos Archipelago from Mauritius in 1965*, Advisory Opinion, ICJ Rep 2019, 95 (hereinafter *Chagos* (2019)) para 147. See ibid paras 146, 163.

[39] *Namibia* (1971) para 53.

be understood in reference to the principle of self-determination set out in Articles 1 and 55 of the Charter.

The Charter identifies self-determination in relation to *peoples*, rather than nations or States, though the term 'peoples' is not defined in the Charter. However, the term does appear in other parts of the Charter in reference the populations of three distinct territorial delineations: States, NSGTs, and Trust Territories. The Preamble of the Charter begins by referring to its signatories as peoples ('We the peoples of the United Nations determined'), indicating that the populations represented by States acceding to the Charter constitute 'peoples'. Article 73 refers to the populations of NSGTs as 'peoples [that] have not yet attained a full measure of self-government'.[40] Article 76 refers to the populations of Trust Territories as 'peoples' in reference to their progressive development towards self-government or independence in line with 'the freely expressed wishes of the peoples concerned'.[41] The identification and delineation of 'peoples' for purposes of self-determination is addressed in Chapter 6.

c. International Human Rights Covenants

On 4 December 1950, the UNGA adopted Resolution 421 (V), calling upon the Economic and Social Council 'to request the Commission on Human Rights to study ways and means which would ensure the right of peoples and nations to self-determination, and to prepare recommendations for consideration by the General Assembly at its sixth session'.[42] UNGA Resolution 545 (VI), adopted on 5 February 1952, provided a detailed directive on the inclusion of a provision on the right to self-determination in the international covenants on human rights, one intended to reaffirm the principle of self-determination in the UN Charter.[43] The right to self-determination was codified in Article 1 common to both the ICCPR and the ICESCR, adopted by the UNGA Third Committee on 29 November 1955.[44] The final texts of

[40] UN Charter art 73.
[41] Ibid art 76(b); see also arts 80, 83 (referring to such peoples).
[42] A/Res/421 (V) (4 Dec 1950) para 6.
[43] A/Res/545 (VI) (5 Feb 1952).
[44] A/C.3/SR.676 (29 Nov 1955) para 27.

the two covenants were unanimously adopted by the Third Committee and the UNGA in December 1966.[45] Article 1 of the two covenants is as follows:

Article 1

1. All peoples have the right of self-determination. By virtue of that right they freely determine their political status and freely pursue their economic, social and cultural development.
2. All peoples may, for their own ends, freely dispose of their natural wealth and resources without prejudice to any obligations arising out of international economic co-operation, based upon the principle of mutual benefit, and international law. In no case may a people be deprived of its own means of subsistence.
3. The States Parties to the present Covenant, including those having responsibility for the administration of Non-Self-Governing and Trust Territories, shall promote the realization of the right of self-determination, and shall respect that right, in conformity with the provisions of the Charter of the United Nations.

Article 1 common to the ICCPR and the ICESCR is the principal source of treaty-based obligations undertaken by States with respect to the right to self-determination. Together, common Article 1 binds 177 of 197 members of the international community.[46]

Article 1 regards self-determination as a right, in contrast to the UN Charter, which refers to self-determination as a principle.[47] Treatment of self-determination as a right implies at once the imposition of obligations arising from the right and its enforceability as a matter of law.[48] The substantive content of the right to self-determination, and obligations undertaken by States in relation to it, are codified in common Article 1 with high level of

[45] A/Res/2200 (XXI) (16 Dec 1966). See also A/C.3/SR.1451 (7 Dec 1966) paras 8–9 (unanimous vote adopting each covenant by the Third Committee); A/PV.1496 (16 Dec 1966) paras 58–59 (unanimous vote adopting each covenant by the UNGA).

[46] As of the time of writing, 173 States are parties to the ICCPR, and 171 States are parties to the ICESCR.

[47] See Chapter 2.b.iv.

[48] HRC, *CCPR General Comment No. 12: The Right to Self-Determination of Peoples (Art 1)* (1984) (hereinafter HRC GC 12) para 2.

generality.[49] This may be a product of the difficulty of reconciling divergent views of States during the drafting of Article 1.[50]

Although the UN Charter refers to self-determination as a principle, the codification of a right to self-determination was viewed during the drafting of the two human rights covenants to relate to the principle of self-determination articulated in the UN Charter.[51] The HRC, in General Comment No 12 on Article 1 of the ICCPR, similarly identified a linkage between Article 1 and the purposes and principles in Article 1 of the UN Charter.[52]

i. Right to Self-Determination (Article 1(1))

Paragraph 1 of Article 1 provides that self-determination consists of the right of peoples to 'freely determine their political status' and 'freely pursue their economic, social and cultural development'.[53] At base, the meaning of the right as it is defined in Article 1(1) was understood during its drafting to constitute an entitlement of every people 'to establish its own political institutions' and 'to develop its own economic resources, and to direct its own social and cultural evolution, without the interference of other peoples or nations'.[54] The language used in Article 1(1) indicates that this right is of a

[49] Manfred Nowak, *UN Covenant on Civil and Political Rights: CCPR Commentary* (2nd edn, N. P. Engel 2005) para 6.

[50] See e.g. A/2929 ch IV paras 13–15; *Report of the Third Committee*, A/3077 (8 Dec 1955) (Draft International Covenants on Human Rights) (hereinafter A/3077) 27 ff. See also Nowak (n 49) paras 8–13.

[51] A/3077 para 37. See Chapter 5.b.

[52] HRC GC 12 para 1 ('In accordance with the purposes and principles of the Charter of the United Nations, article 1 of the International Covenant on Civil and Political Rights recognizes that all peoples have the right of self-determination').

[53] This definition was criticized during its drafting due to its breadth and lack of clarity: A/2929 ch IV paras 12–13. The term 'development' replaced 'status' in reference to the economic, social, and cultural element: see A/3077 paras 43, 53, 57. The term 'development' has been interpreted to imply a 'more organic and less structured process' by contrast to the term 'status' in reference to the political element. See Ben Saul et al, *The International Covenant on Economic, Social and Cultural Rights: Commentary, Cases, and Materials* (OUP 2014) 55–56.

[54] A/2929 ch IV para 12. Note that early in the drafting of Article 1, the term 'all nations' was added alongside 'all peoples' 'in order to emphasize the universal character of the right'. A/2929 ch IV para 10. Reference to 'nations' was ultimately omitted in the final text because '"peoples" was considered to be the more comprehensive term and was used in the Preamble to the Charter'. See A/3077 para 63.

continuing character ('All peoples *have* the right . . . By virtue of that right *they freely determine . . .* and *freely pursue . . .*').[55]

Paragraph 1 of Article 1 provides that the right to self-determination is enjoyed by *all* peoples and, in this sense, is regarded to be 'universal'.[56] The term 'peoples' is, however, not defined in Article 1. During the drafting of the covenants, the term 'peoples' 'was understood to mean peoples in all countries and territories, whether independent, trust or non-self-governing'.[57] This approach aligns with the use of the term 'peoples' in the UN Charter to refer to the populations of three categories of territorial units (States, Trust Territories, and NSGTs).[58] The term 'peoples' was understood to exclude ethnic, religious, or linguistic minorities as defined in ICCPR Article 27, which separately addresses the individual rights of members of such groups.[59]

The right to self-determination, as one inuring to peoples, is a collective right.[60] The inclusion of a provision on self-determination as Article 1 of the two covenants has been interpreted to reflect the importance of the right as an 'essential condition' to the enjoyment of the human rights enumerated in the two covenants.[61] The corollary was noted by the Third Committee during the drafting of the two covenants: 'To be deprived of the right of self-determination entailed the loss of individual human rights'.[62] In this way self-determination, a collective right belonging to peoples rather than an

[55] Nowak (n 49) paras 18–19; Cassese (n 7) 54. See A/3077 paras 32, 39.

[56] A/2929 ch IV paras 7–8; A/3077 para 39. See HRC GC 12 para 2.

[57] A/2929 ch IV para 9. See also para 17.

[58] See Chapter 2.b.iv; Chapter 6.a.

[59] A/2929 ch IV para 9 ('[T]he right of minorities was a separate problem of great complexity'). See *The Right to Self-Determination: Implementation of United Nations Resolutions* (Study prepared by Héctor Gros Espiell, Special Rapporteur of the Sub-Commission on Prevention of Discrimination and Protection of Minorities), E/CN.4/Sub.2/405/Rev.1 (1980) (hereinafter *Espiell Report* (1980)) para 56. See Nowak (n 49) para 28; Cassese (n 7) 61–62.

[60] A/3077 paras 34, 40. See e.g. *Lubicon Lake Band v Canada*, Communication No 167/1984, CCPR/C/38/D/167/1984 (1990) (hereinafter *Lubicon Lake* (1990)) para 13.3. See Nowak (n 49) paras 15–17.

[61] HRC GC 12 para 1; Committee on Economic, Social and Cultural Rights, *General Comment No. 26 (2022) on land and economic, social and cultural rights*, E/C.12/GC/26 (2023) para 11 (citing HRC GC 12). See A/3077 para 35 ('Those who wanted to include an article on self-determination in the draft covenants insisted that the "right" of self-determination was essential for the enjoyment of all other human rights and must, therefore, appear in the forefront of the covenants. In many cases, individual rights could not be exercised because peoples did not enjoy the right of self-determination'); *Lubicon Lake* (1990) para 13.3; *E.P. et al v Colombia*, Communication No 318/1988, CCPR/C/39/D/318/1988 (1990) para 8.2.

[62] A/3077 para 40.

individual right, nevertheless can be viewed as related to the enjoyment of individual rights. It is in this regard that the right to self-determination is viewed as a 'fundamental human right',[63] a formulation whose implications are discussed in greater detail in Chapter 8.[64] This relationship accounts for the inclusion of a provision on the right of peoples to self-determination as Article 1(1) of the two human rights covenants.

ii. Free Disposal of Natural Wealth and Resources (Article 1(2))

Paragraph 2 of Article 1 provides a corollary of the right to self-determination, and consists of the entitlement of peoples to control over their natural wealth and resources.[65] Article 1(2) is additive to the directive contained in UNGA Resolution 545 (VI) on the inclusion of a provision on self-determination in the two human rights covenants.[66] Early in the drafting of Article 1, reference to the principle of sovereignty over natural resources was introduced following a proposal by Chile.[67] The introduction of the principle in Article 1 was directed towards colonialism and safeguarding the interests of peoples of NSGTs and newly independent territories in the exploitation of their natural resources.[68] As reflected in the *travaux préparatoires*, 'it was stated

[63] *Legal Consequences arising from the Policies and Practices of Israel in the Occupied Palestinian Territory, including East Jerusalem*, Advisory Opinion, ICJ Rep 2024, para 233 (citing *Chagos* (2019) para 144).

[64] Because the subjects of human rights are individuals, characterization of the right to self-determination, a collective right of peoples, as a 'fundamental human right' is problematic as a technical matter. The distinction between individual rights and collective rights is one of practical significance, as illustrated by the HRC. Under its individual complaint mechanism, the HRC has competence to consider communications alleging violations of individual rights under the ICCPR but not the right to self-determination as a collective right. See Chapter 12.b.i.

[65] A/2929 ch IV paras 19–21. For extended commentary, see Saul et al (n 53) 62–123.

[66] A/Res/545 (VI) (5 Feb 1952).

[67] E/CN.4/L.24 (16 Apr 1952). See E/2256 para 70 (adoption by the Commission on Human Rights). See also Nico Schrijver, *Sovereignty over Natural Resources: Balancing Rights and Duties* (CUP 1997) 49–56; Daniëlla Dam-de Jong, *International Law and Governance of Natural Resources in Conflict and Post-Conflict Situations* (CUP 2015) 34. See also A/Res/837 (IX) para 1 (14 Dec 1954).

[68] James N. Hyde, 'Permanent Sovereignty over Natural Wealth and Resources' (1965) 50(4) *AJIL* 854, 855. One court subsequently interpreted the provision to be directed towards the conduct of administering powers vis-à-vis NSGTs: *Western Sahara Campaign UK v Secretary of State for International Trade et al* [2022] EWHC 3108 (Admin) [136].

that the right of self-determination certainly included the simple and elementary principle that a nation or people should be master of its own natural wealth or resources'.[69] It was unclear whether the principle of permanent sovereignty over natural resources, as an attribute of State sovereignty, could adequately address the interests of peoples in relationships of subordination vis-à-vis administering States.[70] During the course of drafting of Article 1, the principle of 'permanent sovereignty over [] natural wealth and resources', as it had initially been incorporated, was amended to refer to an entitlement to 'freely dispose of' natural wealth and resources, thereby broadening application of the concept beyond sovereign States.[71] The drafting history of common Article 1(2) of the two human rights covenants confirms that the entitlement of peoples to freely dispose of their natural wealth and resources derives from the principle of permanent sovereignty over natural resources.[72] Consistent with the *travaux préparatoires* of common Article 1, the scope of Article 1(2) was contemplated by the HRC to be 'universal' in application so as to apply to all peoples.[73]

To this entitlement of peoples to freely dispose of their natural wealth and resources, Article 1(2) adds various qualifying clauses. The entitlement to freely dispose of wealth and natural resources is conditioned by applicable international obligations, i.e. 'without prejudice to any obligations arising out of international economic co-operation, based upon the principle of mutual benefit, and international law'. This clause addresses concerns over possible ramifications of Article 1(2), including its potential invocation as a justification for expropriation and unilateral renunciation of international agreements.[74] Notably, ICCPR Article 47 and ICESCR Article 25 consist of

[69] A/2929 ch IV para 21. Inclusion of 'nations' alongside 'peoples' has been explained to safeguard this entitlement before and after the exercise of self-determination in relation to its international aspect. However, inclusion of 'nations' as a subject of the right to permanent sovereignty over natural resources ultimately receded. See Schrijver (n 67) 10.

[70] Schrijver (n 67) 50, 53; See Karol N. Gess, 'Permanent Sovereignty over Natural Resources: An Analytical Review of the United Nations Declaration and Its Genesis' (1964) 13(2) *ICLQ* 398, 446 (1964).

[71] A/3077 paras 57, 65. See *Report of the Working Party on Article 1* (A/C.3/L.489 and Corr.1 and 2) (continued), General Assembly Official Records (GAOR) Tenth Session, Agenda Item 28, A/C.3/SR/668 (22 Nov 1955) para 5 (El Salvador). Cf A/2929 ch IV para 19. See Nowak (n 49) paras 35–40; Schrijver (n 67) 49–56.

[72] A/3077 paras 57, 65.

[73] HRC GC 12 para 2. See A/2929 ch IV paras 7–8.

[74] A/3077 para 65; A/2929 ch IV para 20. This clause rendered redundant the clause 'on the grounds of any rights that may be claimed by other States', which had been included in the final

safeguard clauses providing that '[n]othing in the present Covenant shall be interpreted as impairing the inherent right of all peoples to enjoy and utilize fully and freely their natural wealth and resources'.[75] These provisions have been interpreted as a limitation on the conditioning of the free disposal of natural wealth and resources by 'any obligations arising out of international economic co-operation'.[76] Finally, Article 1(2) provides that '[i]n no case may a people be deprived of its own means of subsistence'. This language was introduced to discourage damaging economic concessions undertaken with frequency during the nineteenth century.[77] One commentator has observed that Article 1(2) 'was heavily amended to the point that its legal meaning has become extremely unclear'.[78]

iii. Obligations to Promote and Respect the Right (Article 1(3))

Paragraph 3 of Article 1 contains general obligations of all States to promote the realization of the right of self-determination and to respect the right.[79] While Article 1(3) refers to the obligations contained in Chapters XI and XII of the UN Charter, it is expressly not limited to those obligations as they apply to administering States in relation to NSGTs and Trust Territories.[80] Instead, as observed by the HRC in General Comment No 12, Article 1(3) 'imposes specific obligations on States parties, not only in relation to their own peoples but *vis-à-vis* all peoples which have not been able to exercise or have been deprived of the possibility of exercising their right to self-determination'.[81] In

sentence in the draft language introduced by Chile. See Schrijver (n 67) 53. See also Saul et al (n 53) 109–16.

[75] International Covenant on Civil and Political Rights art 47, 999 UNTS 171 (16 Dec 1966, entered into force 23 Mar 1976); International Covenant on Economic, Social and Cultural Rights art 25, 993 UNTS 3 (16 Dec 1966, entered into force 3 Jan 1976).

[76] Saul et al (n 53) 14.

[77] Hyde (n 68) 858; Schrijver (n 67) 55. See *Report of the Working Party on Article 1* (A/C.3/ L.489 and Corr.1 and 2) (continued), A/C.3/SR.672 (25 Nov 1955) para 36 (Saudi Arabia). See also Saul et al (n 53) 116–21.

[78] Nowak (n 49) para 36.

[79] A/2929 ch IV para 17. See Chapter 9.b.

[80] See A/3077 para 66.

[81] HRC GC 12 para 6.

the view of the HRC, Article 1(3) imposes obligations of an extraterritorial character. These obligations are largely framed in progressive terms and require States to 'respect' the right to self-determination and 'promote' its realization.[82] Article 1(3) is silent as to the modalities by which such obligations are to be performed, except to impose a limitation that such actions must be 'in conformity with the provisions of the Charter of the United Nations'. In this regard, the HRC referred specifically to non-interference in the internal affairs of other States, which itself was understood to adversely affect the right to self-determination.[83]

d. Regional Instruments

A number of international instruments of regional scope contain provisions on the right to self-determination. Those instruments—the African Charter on Human and Peoples' Rights (ACHPR) and the Arab Charter on Human Rights—are discussed below. No European Union, Inter-American,[84] or other regional instrument contains a provision on self-determination. However, preambular language in the Additional Protocol to the American Convention on Human Rights in the area of Economic, Social and Cultural Rights ('Protocol of San Salvador') refers to self-determination and is also discussed briefly below.

i. African Charter on Human and Peoples' Rights

The African Charter on Human and Peoples' Rights (ACHPR) entered into force on 21 October 1986, and fifty four States are currently parties to the instrument.[85] The ACHPR contains an operative provision on the right of

[82] As noted during the drafting of Article 1, obligations in Chapters XI and XII are similarly progressive in character: A/3077 para 30.

[83] HRC GC 12 para 6.

[84] The non-binding American Declaration on the Rights of Indigenous Peoples refers to the right of Indigenous Peoples to self-determination. See American Declaration on the Rights of Indigenous Peoples, OAS AG/Res 2888 (XLVI-0/16) (15 June 2016) arts III, XXI(1). See Chapter 8.e.iii.1.

[85] African [Banjul] Charter on Human and Peoples' Rights, OAU Doc CAB/LEG/67/3/Rev.5, 1520 UNTS 217 (27 June 1981, entered into force 21 Oct 1986) (hereinafter ACHPR).

peoples to self-determination at Article 20, as well as other rights of peoples at Articles 19 and 21–24.[86] Article 20 of the ACHPR imposes obligations upon State parties with respect to the right to self-determination.[87]

Article 20

1. All peoples shall have the right to existence. They shall have the unquestionable and inalienable right to self-determination. They shall freely determine their political status and shall pursue their economic and social development according to the policy they have freely chosen.
2. Colonized or oppressed peoples shall have the right to free themselves from the bonds of domination by resorting to any means recognized by the international community.
3. All peoples shall have the right to the assistance of the States parties to the present Charter in their liberation struggle against foreign domination, be it political, economic or cultural.

The right to self-determination is defined in Article 20(1) in terms similar to common Article 1(1) of the two human rights covenants: it consists of a right of peoples to 'freely determine their political status' and to 'pursue their economic and social development according to the policy they have freely chosen'.[88] In the view of the African Court on Human and Peoples' Rights (ACtHPR), the right defined at ACHPR Article 20 is 'broader and stronger' than the corresponding provision of common Article 1 of the two human rights covenants in its linkage of the right to self-determination to a 'right of existence of peoples'.[89] The ACtHPR has contextualized this aspect of the right to self-determination codified in

[86] Richard N. Kiwanuka, 'The Meaning of "People" in the African Charter on Human and Peoples' Rights' (1988) 82(1) *AJIL* 80 (identifying four meanings of 'people' in the ACHPR).

[87] See Rose M. D'Sa, 'Human and Peoples' Rights: Distinctive Features of the African Charter' (1985) 29(1) *Journal of African Law* 72, 77–78; Rachel Murray, *The African Charter on Human and Peoples' Rights: A Commentary* (OUP 2019) 497–507.

[88] Unlike common Article 1 of the two human right covenants, ACHPR Article 20(1) does not include a reference to cultural development. *Cf* ACHPR art 22(1) ('All peoples shall have the right to their economic, social and cultural development').

[89] *Bernard Anbataayela Mornah v Benin et al*, ACtHPR, Application No 028/2018, Judgment (22 Sept 2022) (hereinafter *Mornah v Benin* (2022)) para 295.

Article 20 as a product of 'the continent's history of colonialism and military occupation'.[90]

Paragraphs 2 and 3 of ACHPR Article 20 contain provisions without equivalent in common Article 1 of the two human rights covenants. Article 20(2) provides for a 'right of resistance', specific to 'colonized or oppressed peoples', by 'any means recognized by the international community'.[91] Article 20(3) contemplates an entitlement of all peoples to the 'assistance' of States parties 'in their liberation struggle against foreign domination, be it political, economic or cultural'. Article 20(3) has been interpreted by the ACtHPR as imposing positive duties upon States parties to render assistance to such peoples, 'without geographical or temporal limitations', and in this view, the 'right to the assistance of States parties' defined at Article 20(3) constitutes a corresponding entitlement to receive such assistance.[92] The African Commission on Human and Peoples' Rights has interpreted the provisions of Articles 20(2) and 20(3) to be 'reserved for colonized peoples'.[93]

Taken together, the ACtHPR has described Article 20 as imposing positive and negative obligations upon States parties to the ACHPR.[94] The ACtHPR has observed that the right to self-determination in ACHPR Article 20 'is essentially related to peoples' right to ownership over a particular territory and their political status over that territory'.[95]

The ACHPR provides for the right of peoples to freely dispose of their wealth and natural resources in a separate provision at Article 21.[96] The ACtHPR has found Article 21 to be applicable in cases where the right to self-determination under ACHPR Article 20 is inapplicable.[97] Finally, ACHPR Article 22 contains a right to development that incorporates elements of the right to self-determination at Article 20.[98]

[90] Ibid para 121. See also *Front for the Liberation of the State of Cabinda v Angola*, African Commission on Human and Peoples' Rights (ACommHPR), Communication No 328/06 (2013) (hereinafter *Cabinda v Angola* (2013)) para 124.

[91] See Chapter 7.b.ii.2.

[92] *Mornah v Benin* (2022) paras 151, 299.

[93] *Cabinda v Angola* (2013) para 125.

[94] *Mornah v Benin* (2022) para 297 (citing HRC, *CCPR General Comment No 31 [80]: The Nature of the General Legal Obligation Imposed on States Parties to the Covenant*, CCPR/C/21/Rev.1/Add.13 (2004)).

[95] Ibid para 301.

[96] ACHPR art 21.

[97] *ACHPR v Kenya*, ACtHPR, Application No 006/2012, Judgment (2017) paras 195–201. See Chapter 8.d.i.

[98] ACHPR art 22.

ii. Arab Charter on Human Rights

The Arab Charter on Human Rights was adopted by the Council of the League of Arab States at the Arab Summit on 23 May 2004 and entered into force in 2008.[99] Article 2(1) of the Charter includes a provision on the right of peoples to self-determination:

> All peoples have the right of self-determination and to control over their natural wealth and resources, and the right to freely choose their political system and to freely pursue their economic, social and cultural development.

Like the two human rights covenants, the Arab Charter includes self-determination in its first substantive provision.[100] The Arab Charter defines self-determination among a bundle of rights which, in other instruments, are enumerated as aspects of the right to self-determination (i.e. the right of peoples to freely choose their political system and to freely pursue their economic, social, and cultural development). The right of peoples to control over their natural wealth and resources is enumerated alongside the right to self-determination. Separate paragraphs in Article 2 provide that all peoples have the right to 'national sovereignty and territorial integrity' and the right to 'resist foreign occupation'.[101]

[99] Arab Charter on Human Rights, [ST/HR/]CHR/NONE/2004/40/Rev.1 (22 May 2004, entered into force 15 Mar 2008) (hereinafter Arab Charter on Human Rights). Article 1 of the Arab Charter on Human Rights, adopted by the Council in 1994 but which never entered into force, also contained a provision on self-determination. See Wael Allam, 'The Arab Charter on Human Rights: Main Features' (2014) 28(1) *Arab Law Quarterly* 40, 42.

[100] See Ibid 55–56.

[101] Arab Charter on Human Rights arts 2(2), 2(4). Article 2(3) contains the following provision deeply problematic in its reference to Zionism: 'All forms of racism, Zionism and foreign occupation and domination constitute an impediment to human dignity and a major barrier to the exercise of the fundamental rights of peoples; all such practices must be condemned and efforts must be deployed for their elimination'. See Malcom N Shaw, *International Law* (8th edn, CUP 2017) 286–87 n 590 (discussing concerns raised by the UN Commissioner on Human Rights, including that, by equating Zionism with racism, the Arab Charter is inconsistent with A/Res/46/86 (16 Dec 1991)).

iii. Protocol of San Salvador

The Protocol of San Salvador was signed at San Salvador, El Salvador, on 14 November 1988, at the Eighteenth Regular Session of the OAS General Assembly and entered into force on 16 November 1999.[102] The preamble to the Protocol, an optional protocol to the American Convention on Human Rights, includes a reference to self-determination:

> Bearing in mind that, although fundamental economic, social and cultural rights have been recognized in earlier international instruments of both world and regional scope, it is essential that those rights be reaffirmed, developed, perfected and protected in order to consolidate in America, on the basis of full respect for the rights of the individual, the democratic representative form of government as well as the right of its peoples to development, self-determination, and the free disposal of their wealth and natural resources[.][103]

This preambular language in the Protocol incorporates various aspects of the right to self-determination as it is articulated in common Article 1 of the two human rights covenants, which are referred to alongside (rather than as constituent elements of) self-determination. Because self-determination only appears in the preamble of the instrument, and is not included in an operative provision, it does not appear that the Protocol imposes obligations upon States parties with respect to the right to self-determination as such.

[102] Additional Protocol to the American Convention on Human Rights in the Area of Economic, Social, and Cultural Rights ('Protocol of San Salvador'), OAS Treaty Series No. 69 (17 Nov 1988, entered into force 16 Nov 1999), (1989) reproduced in 28(1) ILM 156. See Domingo E. Acevedo, 'Introductory Note' (1989) 28(1) ILM 156.

[103] Protocol of San Salvador preambular para 7.

3

Resolutions and Declarations

a. Overview

Non-binding resolutions and declarations may provide insight into the views of States as to the content of international law. Under certain circumstances, such resolutions and declarations may contribute to the formation of CIL.[1] As discussed in greater detail in Chapter 5, the right to self-determination has crystalized as a rule of CIL. Accordingly, resolutions and declarations pertaining to self-determination may be of particular relevance to the right as it has developed in CIL.

While it has been observed that there are more UN resolutions referring to self-determination than can be effectively documented,[2] several UNGA resolutions in particular have been identified by the ICJ as contributing to the crystallization and content of the CIL of self-determination.[3] These are Resolution 1514 (1960),[4] Resolution 1541 (1960),[5] and Resolution 2625 (1970) adopting the FRD.[6] While these resolutions are neither the first, nor the only, resolutions to refer to the right to self-determination,[7] they receive detailed treatment in this chapter because of their contribution to the right to self-determination in CIL. In addition, two instruments adopted after the FRD—the Helsinki Final Act (1975),[8] and Vienna Declaration and

[1] See e.g. *Legality of the Threat or Use of Nuclear Weapons*, Advisory Opinion, ICJ Rep 1996, 266 para 70.

[2] *Reference re Secession of Quebec* [1998] 2 SCR 217 para 117.

[3] *Legal Consequences of the Separation of the Chagos Archipelago from Mauritius in 1965*, Advisory Opinion, ICJ Rep 2019, 95 (hereinafter *Chagos* (2019)) paras 148–57.

[4] A/Res/1514 (XV) (14 Dec 1960) (hereinafter Resolution 1514).

[5] A/Res/1541 (XV) (15 Dec 1960) (hereinafter Resolution 1541).

[6] A/Res/2625 (24 Oct 1970) Annex (hereinafter FRD).

[7] Prior to 1960, other UNGA resolutions referred to self-determination as a 'right'. See e.g. A/Res/421 (V) (4 Dec 1950) para 6; A/Res/545 (VI) (5 Feb 1952); A/Res/637 (VII) (16 Dec 1952); A/Res/738 (VIII) (28 Nov 1953); A/Res/1188 (XII) (11 Dec 1957).

[8] Conference on Security and Cooperation in Europe: Final Act (1 Aug 1975), reproduced in (1975) 14(5) ILM 1292 (hereinafter Helsinki Final Act (1975)).

The Right to Self-Determination in International Law. Thomas Weatherall, Oxford University Press.
 DOI: 10.1093/9780197798119.003.0004

Programme of Action (1993)[9]—provide significant insight into the views of States as to the content of the right to self-determination.

b. Resolution 1514

UNGA Resolution 1514, entitled Declaration on the Granting of Independence to Colonial Countries and Peoples, was adopted by a vote of 89–0–9 on 14 December 1960.[10] Resolution 1514 is regarded by the ICJ as having 'provided the basis for the process of decolonization' from 1960 onwards,[11] and as 'a defining moment in the consolidation of State practice on decolonization'.[12]

Self-determination is defined in Resolution 1514 in the same terms as Article 1(1) common to the two human rights covenants: 'All peoples have the right to self-determination; by virtue of that right they freely determine their political status and freely pursue their economic, social and cultural development'.[13] The preamble of Resolution 1514 contains the entitlement of peoples to 'freely dispose of their natural wealth and resources without prejudice to any obligations arising out of international economic co-operation, based upon the principle of mutual benefit, and international law', in terms that correspond to this corollary of self-determination as it appears in Article 1(2) of the two human rights covenants.[14] The touchstone of the exercise of the right to self-determination, as it is articulated in Resolution 1514, is 'the freely expressed will and desire' of the people concerned.[15] This language

[9] United Nations World Conference on Human Rights: Vienna Declaration and Programme of Action (25 June 1993), A/CONF/157/23 (12 July 1993), reproduced in (1993) 32(6) ILM 1661 (hereinafter Vienna Declaration (1993)).

[10] See A/PV.947 (1960) para 34.

[11] *Western Sahara*, Advisory Opinion, ICJ Rep 1975, 12 (hereinafter *Western Sahara* (1975)) para 57.

[12] *Chagos* (2019) para 150.

[13] Resolution 1514 para 2. Cf International Covenant on Civil and Political Rights art 1(1), 999 UNTS 171 (16 Dec 1966, entered into force 23 Mar 1976) (hereinafter ICCPR); International Covenant on Economic, Social and Cultural Rights art 1(1), 993 UNTS 3 (16 Dec 1966, entered into force 3 Jan 1976) (hereinafter ICESCR). See Chapter 2.c.i.

[14] Common Article 1(2) contains the additional proviso, 'In no case may a people be deprived of its own means of subsistence', absent from Resolution 1514. See Chapter 2.c.ii; Chapter 8.d.i.

[15] Resolution 1514 para 5 (continuing: 'without any distinction as to race, creed or colour, in order to enable them to enjoy complete independence and freedom'). See *Western Sahara* (1975) para 55 ('thus confirm[ing] and emphasiz[ing] that the application of the right of self-determination requires a free and genuine expression of the will of the peoples concerned').

parallels Article 76 of the UN Charter, which refers to the objectives of the Trusteeship System.[16]

The focus of Resolution 1514 is the political element of the right to self-determination in reference to decolonization, and the text accordingly contains additional aspects of the realization of the right particular to this context. The preamble refers to 'the necessity of bringing *to a speedy and unconditional end* colonialism in all its forms and manifestations', and the operative text of the resolution provides that '[*i*]*mmediate steps shall be taken* . . . to transfer all powers to the peoples of [non-independent] territories'.[17] In this way, Resolution 1514 introduces an element of timing of particular relevance to the performance of obligations under Chapter XI and realization of the objectives of Chapter XII of the UN Charter.[18] Finally, Resolution 1514 suggests that the outcome of a people's exercise of this aspect of the right to self-determination is independence.[19]

Resolution 1514 contains language addressing territorial implications of the right to self-determination. The preamble of the resolution states that 'all peoples have an inalienable right to complete freedom, the exercise of their sovereignty and the integrity of their national territory', suggesting an overall linkage between the right of peoples to self-determination and sovereignty and territorial integrity. This linkage is refined in operative paragraphs 6 and 7, which contain safeguard clauses reflecting the persistent concern of States over the potentially destabilizing effects of secession and political interference in the internal affairs of other States under the guise of self-determination. Paragraph 6 provides that '[a]ny attempt aimed at the partial or total disruption of the national unity and the territorial integrity of a country is incompatible with the purposes and principles of the Charter of the United Nations'.[20] Although this paragraph has at times been invoked to support claims to retrocession of colonial territories, it is more generally understood to oppose the fragmentation of NSGTs.[21] Paragraph 7

[16] Charter of the United Nations art 76(b), XV UNCIO 335 (26 June 1945, entered into force 24 Oct 1945). See Chapter 7.b.i.2.

[17] Resolution 1514 preambular para 12, para 5 (emphasis added).

[18] See Chapter 9.c.

[19] Resolution 1514 para 5 ('in order to enable them to enjoy complete independence and freedom'). See Chapter 7.b.i.3.

[20] Resolution 1514 para 6.

[21] *Chagos* (2019) para 153; Thomas M. Franck and Paul Hoffman, 'The Right of Self-Determination in Very Small Places' (1976) 8(3) *New York University Journal of International Law and Politics* 331, 370.

more broadly calls on States to observe the provisions of the UN Charter, the Universal Declaration of Human Rights, and Resolution 1514 'on the basis of equality, noninterference in the internal affairs of all States, and respect for the sovereign rights of all peoples and their territorial integrity'.[22]

According to the ICJ in its *Chagos Archipelago* (2019) advisory opinion, Resolution 1514 marked the crystallization of the right to self-determination in CIL.[23]

c. Resolution 1541

UNGA Resolution 1541, entitled Principles Which Should Guide Members in Determining Whether or Not an Obligation Exists to Transmit the Information Called for Under Article 73 e of the Charter, was adopted by a vote of 69–2–21 on 15 December 1960, the day after the adoption of Resolution 1514.[24] The resolution contains an annex which, as its name suggests, sets out a series of principles for States to apply to determine the applicability of the reporting obligation under Article 73(e) of the UN Charter. Insofar as the principles set out in Resolution 1541 identify the circumstances under which the reporting obligations of an administering power under Article 73(e) of the UN Charter would be regarded as having been discharged, as observed by the ICJ, these principles effectively provide for the 'means of implementing' the right to self-determination with respect to NSGTs.[25]

Principles I–III contemplate the legal character of the reporting requirement of Article 73(e) of the UN Charter, and Principles X–XII concern the transmission of information pursuant to that obligation. The intervening principles address the exercise of the international aspect of the right to self-determination in the context of NSGTs. These principles have been viewed as complementary to Resolution 1514.[26]

Principle I refers to a NSGT as one 'known to be of the colonial type'. Principle IV describes a NSGT as 'a territory which is geographically

[22] Resolution 1514 para 7. See Chapter 7.d.1.
[23] *Chagos* (2019) paras 150, 152–53. See Chapter 5.c.ii.
[24] Resolution 1541. See A/PV.948 (1960) para 88.
[25] *Chagos* (2019) para 156. For context, see Chapter 10.b.i.
[26] *Western Sahara* (1975) para 57.

separate and is distinct ethnically and/or culturally from the country administering it', providing in effect a definition of the kind of territory regarded *prima facie* as a NSGT.[27] To that description, Principle V adds other elements 'of an administrative, political, juridical, economic or historical nature' that may be taken into consideration when assessing whether a territory constitutes a NSGT, with a focus on whether such elements indicate a position or status of subordination.

Principle VI provides that a NSGT 'can be said to have reached a full measure of self-government' when it realizes one of three outcomes: (a) emergence as a sovereign independent State, (b) free association with an independent State, or (c) integration with an independent State.[28] Principles VII and IX 'give effect to the essential feature of the right of self-determination established in resolution 1514' by conditioning free association and integration on the freely expressed wishes of the people concerned, expressed through an informed and democratic process.[29] Resolution 1541 provides additional guidance on implementation of the modalities of integration and free association discussed in Chapter 7.[30]

d. Resolution 2625

In 1962, the UNGA resolved to undertake a study of principles of international law concerning friendly relations and cooperation among States 'with a view to their progressive development and codification'.[31] The following year, the Special Committee on Principles of International Law concerning Friendly Relations and Co-Operation among States was established to this end.[32] Between 1964 and 1970, the Special Committee held six sessions during which States negotiated the text of the principles that would ultimately be included in the Declaration on Principles of International Law concerning Friendly Relations and Co-operation among States in accordance with the Charter of the United Nations, or the Friendly Relations Declaration

[27] *Chagos* (2019) para 156. See Chapter 10.b.i.
[28] *Western Sahara* (1975) para 57; *Chagos* (2019) para 156. See Chapter 7.b.i.3.
[29] *Western Sahara* (1975) para 57. See *Chagos* (2019) para 157. See Chapter 8.c.ii.
[30] See Chapter 7.b.i.4.
[31] A/Res/1815 (XVII) (18 Dec 1962) para 2.
[32] A/Res/1966 (XVIII) (16 Dec 1963) para 1.

(FRD).[33] Principle V of the FRD is the 'principle of equal rights and self-determination of peoples', in reference to Article 1 of the UN Charter. The FRD was adopted by consensus with Resolution 2625 on 24 October 1970.[34] While the contribution of the FRD to the content of the international law on self-determination has been contested,[35] the ICJ has repeatedly taken the position that the FRD reflects CIL.[36] In its *Chagos Archipelago* (2019) advisory opinion, the ICJ considered that the FRD reiterated 'the nature and scope' of the right to self-determination, and 'confirmed its normative character under CIL'.[37]

Notwithstanding reference in the UN Charter to self-determination as a principle only, paragraph 1 of Principle V provides that that principle entails a right of peoples to self-determination.[38] The right to self-determination is defined in paragraph 1 in the same terms as Article 1(1) common to the two human rights covenants and Resolution 1514, thereby contributing to a consolidation of the essential elements of the right.[39] This definition, and its appearance in an instrument not focused on decolonization, reinforces the universality of the right as one belonging to all peoples.[40] Paragraph 1 includes the additional proviso that 'every State has the duty to respect this right in accordance with the provisions of the Charter', a provision echoing Article 1(3) common to the two human rights covenants.

Additional duties of States to promote realization of the right to self-determination are set out in paragraph 2, which in this way further aligns with Article 1(3) of the two human rights covenants.[41] Paragraph 2 provides

[33] Robert Rosenstock, 'The Declaration of Principles of International Law Concerning Friendly Relations: A Survey' (1971) 65(5) *AJIL* 713, 714; Piet-Hein Houben, 'Principles of International Law Concerning Friendly Relations and Co-operation Among States' (1967) 61(3) *AJIL* 703, 723–25. See A/6230 (1966) paras 456–521; A/6799 (1967) paras 171–235; A/7326 (1968) paras 135–203; A/7619 (1969) paras 137–92; A/8018 (1970) paras 26–29, 61–78.

[34] A/PV.1883 (24 Oct 1970) para 8.

[35] Cf Gaetano Arangio-Ruiz, *The UN Declaration on Friendly Relations and the System of the Sources of International Law* (Sijthoff & Noordhoff 1979) s 52; Antonio Cassese, *Self-Determination of Peoples: A Legal Reappraisal* (CUP 1995) 120; Rosenstock (n 33) 714–15.

[36] *Military and Paramilitary Activities in and against Nicaragua (Nicaragua v United States of America)*, Merits, Judgment, ICJ Rep 1986, 14 (hereinafter *Nicaragua* (1986)) paras 191–93, 264; *Accordance with International Law of the Unilateral Declaration of Independence in Respect of Kosovo*, Advisory Opinion, ICJ Rep 2010, 403 para 80 (citing *Nicaragua* (1986)).

[37] *Chagos* (2019) para 155.

[38] FRD Principle V, para 1.

[39] See Chapter 5.c.ii.

[40] Rosenstock (n 33) 731; Arangio-Ruiz (n 35) s 76.

[41] FRD Principle V, para 2. See ICCPR art 1(3); ICESCR art 1(3).

that States are to promote such realization 'through joint and separate action', reinforcing the scope of this obligation as extending beyond the obligations of administering States of NSGTs and Trust Territories under the UN Charter.[42] Moreover, paragraph 2 contemplates a duty of States to 'render assistance to the United Nations' in support of implementation of its responsibilities regarding the principle under the Charter. Paragraph 2 identifies two objectives of the duties of States to promote realization of self-determination: to promote friendly relations and co-operation among States and to bring 'a speedy end to colonialism, having due regard to the freely expressed will of the peoples concerned'.[43] Paragraph 2 also suggests that obligations of States arising from the right to self-determination, at least in the context of decolonization, are progressive in character.[44] Finally, paragraph 2 concludes 'that subjection of peoples to alien subjugation, domination and exploitation constitutes a violation of the principle, as well as a denial of fundamental human rights, and is contrary to the Charter', thereby indicating an additional circumstance, beyond colonialism, that implicates the international aspect of self-determination.[45]

The relationship between the right of peoples to self-determination and the enjoyment of human rights and fundamental freedoms is implied by paragraph 3. Paragraph 3 articulates a duty of States to promote universal respect for human rights and fundamental freedoms. Although the paragraph makes no mention of self-determination, its inclusion in Principle V at minimum suggests a relationship between the right to self-determination and respect for human rights and fundamental freedoms.[46] The proposition that the enjoyment of human rights is a condition precedent to the exercise and enjoyment of the right to self-determination is reflected in the *travaux préparatoires*.[47]

[42] See Chapter 2.c.iii.
[43] See also FRD Principle V, para 4.
[44] Rosenstock (n 33) 731.
[45] See similarly Resolution 1514 para 1. See Chapter 7.b.ii.
[46] See Chapter 8.b.
[47] For example, see A/8018 (1970) para 82, Working paper on the final stage of drafting of the Declaration submitted by the delegation of Italy at the 1970 session of the Special Committee, A/AC.125/L.83, 58 ('[T]here is a close interrelationship between th[e] principle [of self-determination] and the promotion of Human Rights. In so far can the exercise of Equal rights and Self-determination of peoples as collective entities can be effectively secured, as the individuals composing those entities are allowed effectively to exercise their rights and fundamental freedoms before, during and after the self-determining process. The very existence and

The touchstone of a people's exercise of its right to self-determination—the freely expressed wishes of the people concerned—is set out in paragraph 4.[48] Paragraph 4 provides that 'modes of implementing' the right of self-determination by a people include independence, free association or integration with an independent State, 'or the emergence into any other political status freely determined by a people'. The inclusion of this catchall renders the FRD less prescriptive than either Resolution 1541 or Resolution 1541.[49] Moreover, paragraph 4 regards the freely expressed wishes of the people concerned, rather than any particular outcome, to be the controlling consideration of a people's exercise of its right to self-determination.[50] If not a departure from Resolutions 1514 and 1541—which also refer to the freely expressed wishes of the people concerned—the FRD at minimum reflects a difference in emphasis in this regard.

Paragraph 5 provides that peoples are entitled, in their action against and resistance to forcible action which deprives a people of its 'right to self-determination and freedom and independence', 'to seek and to receive support in accordance with the purposes and principles of the Charter'. Implicit in such an entitlement is a 'right of resistance' in relation to the duty of States to refrain from any forcible action which deprives a people of its right to self-determination.[51]

Under the UN Charter, according to paragraph 6, the territory of a colony or other NSGT remains 'separate and distinct' from that of the State administering it, which status exists until the people of such NSGT has exercised its right to self-determination.[52] Such separateness follows implicitly from Chapters XI and XII of the Charter. The inclusion of explicit language on this point was intended to discourage 'dissimulation' of a territory's subordinate status so as to undermine the right to self-determination of its people.[53] By operation of paragraph 6, actions to effectuate such incorporation in the absence of a people's exercise of its right to self-determination would

functioning of structures and machineries through which Self-Determination is to be expressed depends upon the possession and effective exercise of individual rights and freedoms').

[48] See Chapter 7.b.i.2.
[49] See Chapter 7.b.i.3.
[50] *Western Sahara* (1975) para 58.
[51] Arangio-Ruiz (n 35) s 79. See Chapter 7.b.ii.2.
[52] See Chapter 7.d.ii.
[53] Arangio-Ruiz (n 35) s 78.

not remove that territory from the decolonization mandate of the United Nations.[54] Conceptually related cases, concerning territorial claims over NSGTs by contiguous States, which in practice have admitted integration by contiguous States without regard for the freely expressed wishes of the populations concerned, are discussed in Chapter 7.[55]

The final two paragraphs of Principle V consist of safeguard clauses concerning territorial integrity and political or national unity.[56] Paragraph 7 states:

> Nothing in the foregoing paragraphs shall be construed as authorizing or encouraging any action which would dismember or impair, totally or in part, the territorial integrity or political unity of sovereign and independent States conducting themselves in compliance with the principle of equal rights and self-determination of peoples as described above and thus possessed of a government representing the whole people belonging to the territory without distinction as to race, creed or colour.[57]

Paragraph 8 contains a corollary, that '[e]very State shall refrain from any action aimed at the partial or total disruption of the national unity and territorial integrity of any other State or country'. This language resembles in part the two safeguard clauses of Resolution 1514,[58] and has been viewed as intended to prevent self-determination from being invoked in such a way as to undermine the territorial integrity of States.[59] In *Chagos Archipelago* (2019), the ICJ referred to paragraph 8 as a reiteration of language concerning national unity and territorial integrity in Resolution 1514, which the court interpreted to oppose the fragmentation of NSGTs.[60] In *Palestine* (2024), the ICJ referred to paragraph 8 when evaluating the effect of the breach of the obligation to respect the right to self-determination on the lawfulness of Israel's presence in the Occupied Palestinian Territory.[61]

54 Rosenstock (n 33) 731–32.
55 See Chapter 7.f.
56 See Chapter 7.d.i.
57 FRD Principle V, para 7.
58 Resolution 1514 paras 6–7.
59 See e.g. A/7619 (1969) paras 178–79. See also Rosenstock (n 33) 732–33; Arangio-Ruiz (n 35) s 80. See Chapter 7.c.
60 *Chagos* (2019) paras 153, 155.
61 *Legal Consequences arising from the Policies and Practices of Israel in the Occupied Palestinian Territory, including East Jerusalem*, Advisory Opinion, ICJ Rep 2024, para 255.

Paragraph 7 also provides a standard of conduct addressing the domestic aspect of respect for the right to self-determination as an entitlement to representative government.[62] A plain reading of this provision indicates that a State conducting itself in compliance with the principle of self-determination is one possessed of a representative government, which represents the entire population of a territory.[63] This interpretation may be understood in the context of the linkage between self-determination and human rights implied by paragraph 3, and refers to the domestic aspect of self-determination as entitling peoples to representative government.[64] Paragraph 7 has at times been invoked to support 'remedial secession', a concept addressed in Chapter 7.[65]

e. Helsinki Final Act

The Conference on Security and Co-Operation in Europe convened in Helsinki on 3 July 1973; from 18 September 1973 to 21 July 1975, the Conference continued in Geneva, then concluded on 1 August 1975 in Helsinki with the adoption of a Final Act by the thirty-five participating States.[66] Although the geographical representation of States participating at the Conference was limited to Europe and North America, the ICJ has looked to the Final Act as evidence of *opinio juris* and, in relation to a different principle, 'inferred that the text testifies to the existence . . . of a customary principle which has universal application'.[67] The *Declaration on Principles Guiding Relations Between Participating States* includes, as its eighth principle, the principle of 'equal rights and self-determination of peoples', in reference to Article 1 of the UN Charter.[68]

VIII. Equal rights and self-determination of peoples
The participating States will respect the equal rights of peoples and their right to self-determination, acting at all times in conformity with the

[62] See Chapter 8.c.i.
[63] Arangio-Ruiz (n 35) s 80. See A/7326 (1968) para 186.
[64] Cassese (n 35) 110–11; Rosenstock (n 33) 732; Arangio-Ruiz (n 35) s 80.
[65] See Chapter 7.c.ii.
[66] Helsinki Final Act (1975).
[67] *Nicaragua* (1986) para 204. See also paras 189, 264.
[68] For historical context, see Boris Meissner, 'The Right to Self-Determination After Helsinki and Its Significance for the Baltic Nations' (1981) 13(2) *Case Western Reserve Journal of International Law* 375–84.

> purposes and principles of the Charter of the United Nations and with the relevant norms of international law, including those relating to territorial integrity of States.
>
> By virtue of the principle of equal rights and self-determination of peoples, all peoples always have the right, in full freedom, to determine, when and as they wish, their internal and external political status, without external interference, and to pursue as they wish their political, economic, social and cultural development.
>
> The participating States reaffirm the universal significance of respect for and effective exercise of equal rights and self-determination of peoples for the development of friendly relations among themselves as among all States; they also recall the importance of the elimination of any form of violation of this principle.[69]

The first paragraph of Principle VIII consists of a safeguard clause, potentially reflecting a principal concern of this constellation of States in reference to the right.[70] This clause may be viewed in light of safeguard clauses in earlier instruments, namely Resolution 1514 and the FRD, which similarly place realization of the right to self-determination within the bounds of the UN Charter and, in particular, preservation of the territorial integrity of States.[71]

The content of the right to self-determination is defined in the second paragraph of Principle VIII. The definition in this paragraph is noteworthy in its treatment of the political element of the right to self-determination, and in particular, the explicit distinction between its internal and external aspects. In Article 1(1) common to the two human rights covenants, Resolution 1514, and the FRD, the political element of self-determination is defined in terms of the right of peoples to 'freely determine their political status'.[72] The domestic aspect of the political element, as an entitlement to representative government,[73] was only referred to in the *travaux préparatoires* of the two human rights covenants, and was later recognized as such

[69] Helsinki Final Act (1975) Principle VIII.

[70] Ibid para 1. See Chapter 7.d.i.

[71] Cf Resolution 1514 paras 6–7; FRD Principle V, paras 7–8. See Chapter 7.d.ii.

[72] ICCPR art 1(1); ICESCR art 1(1); Resolution 1514 para 2; FRD Principle V, para 1 (adding: 'without external interference').

[73] See Chapter 8.c.i.

in the FRD.[74] In the Final Act, however, the political element of the right is defined as an entitlement of peoples to freely determine their '*internal and external* political status',[75] making explicit what had only been implied in the aforementioned instruments.

Moreover, the Final Act defines the exercise of the political element of the right to self-determination in terms that correspond to the touchstone of the 'freely expressed wishes' of peoples reflected in other instruments,[76] and builds upon that standard by adding 'in full freedom, to determine, when and as they wish . . . without external interference'.[77] In this way, the political element of the right to self-determination is explicitly formulated as both a right enjoyed by all peoples and as a continuing right ('when and as they wish'); this framing also incorporates an entitlement to non-interference in the exercise of the right.[78] The Final Act also refers to the right of peoples to pursue their 'political, economic, social and cultural development', thereby adding an element of 'political development' to the element of economic, social, and cultural development included in other definitions of the right to self-determination.[79]

The final paragraph of the principle on self-determination in the Final Act reaffirms the universal character of the right to self-determination and its relevance to friendly relations among all States (not only those participating in the Conference).[80] The final paragraph also recalls the importance of the elimination of any form of violation of the right to self-determination.

f. Vienna Declaration and Programme of Action

On 18 December 1990, the UNGA resolved to convene a World Conference on Human Rights in 1993 with a series of ambitious objectives in the field of human rights.[81] The Vienna Declaration and Programme of

[74] *Report of the Third Committee*, A/3077 (8 Dec 1955) (Draft International Covenants on Human Rights) (hereinafter A/3077) para 32; FRD Principle V, para 7.
[75] Helsinki Final Act (1975) Principle VIII, para 2 (emphasis added).
[76] See Chapter 7.b.i.2.
[77] Helsinki Final Act (1975) Principle VIII, para 2.
[78] See Chapter 8.b.
[79] Helsinki Final Act (1975) Principle VIII, para 2.
[80] Ibid para 3.
[81] A/Res/45/155 (18 Dec 1990).

Action, drafted over several years, is the outcome document of the Second World Conference on Human Rights, held in Vienna in June 1993.[82] The Vienna Declaration was adopted by acclamation on the final day of the conference.[83]

The Preamble of the Vienna Declaration refers to self-determination in the context of 'major changes taking place on the international scene and the aspirations of all the peoples for an international order based on the principles enshrined in the Charter of the United Nations'.[84] The Vienna Declaration includes, as its second section, three paragraphs on the right to self-determination that largely restate aspects of the right articulated in previous instruments, borrowing heavily from the FRD.

> [] All peoples have the right of self-determination. By virtue of that right they freely determine their political status, and freely pursue their economic, social and cultural development.
>
> Taking into account the particular situation of peoples under colonial or other forms of alien domination or foreign occupation, the World Conference on Human Rights recognizes the right of peoples to take any legitimate action, in accordance with the Charter of the United Nations, to realize their inalienable right of self-determination. The World Conference on Human Rights considers the denial of the right of self-determination as a violation of human rights and underlines the importance of the effective realization of this right.
>
> In accordance with the Declaration on Principles of International Law concerning Friendly Relations and Cooperation Among States in accordance with the Charter of the United Nations, this shall not be construed as authorizing or encouraging any action which would dismember or impair, totally or in part, the territorial integrity or political unity of sovereign and independent States conducting themselves in compliance with the principle of equal rights and self-determination of peoples and thus possessed of a Government representing the whole people belonging to the territory without distinction of any kind.[85]

[82] A/CONF/157/24 (Part I) (13 Oct 1993).
[83] Ibid para 88.
[84] Vienna Declaration (1993) preambular para 9.
[85] Ibid part I, s 2.

The first paragraph on self-determination defines the right in the same terms as Article 1(1) of the two human rights covenants, Resolution 1514, and the FRD. The final paragraph on self-determination refers to the FRD and largely restates its safeguard clause addressing territorial integrity and representative government.[86]

The second paragraph on self-determination identifies circumstances implicating the international aspect of self-determination. The paragraph refers in this regard to 'the particular situation of peoples under colonial *or other* forms of alien domination or foreign occupation', and in this way appears to collapse the two circumstances that give rise to the entitlement to exercise the international aspect of the right to self-determination.[87] The reference to 'alien domination or foreign occupation' departs from the corresponding reference to 'alien subjugation, domination and exploitation' in the FRD, though it is unclear whether this difference is material.[88] The relationship between situations of occupation and the right to self-determination is discussed in Chapter 7.[89]

The second paragraph on self-determination expressly articulates a 'right of resistance', i.e. 'the right of peoples to take any legitimate action, in accordance with the Charter of the United Nations, to realize their inalienable right of self-determination'.[90] Unlike the FRD—which refers to an entitlement 'to seek and receive assistance' in support of resistance to 'forcible action' depriving a people subject to alien subjugation, domination, and exploitation of its right to self-determination—the 'right of resistance' articulated in the Vienna Declaration refers more broadly to a right of peoples to take 'any legitimate action' pursuant to realization of the right to self-determination.[91] The Vienna Declaration provides that the UN Charter furnishes limitations on the legitimate action that might be undertaken to this end. This qualification indicates that the Vienna Declaration was not contemplated to be additive to the measures that might otherwise be lawfully undertaken under

[86] Cf FRD Principle V, para 7 (referring specifically to impermissibility of 'distinction as to race, creed or colour'). See Marc Weller, *Escaping the Self-Determination Trap* (Martinus Nijhoff 2008) 62–63. See Chapter 7.d.i.

[87] Vienna Declaration (1993) part I, s 2, para 2 (emphasis added). See Chapter 7.b.

[88] Cf FRD Principle V, para 2. See similarly Resolution 1514 para 1. See Chapter 7.b.ii.

[89] See Chapter 7.b.ii.1.A.

[90] See Chapter 7.b.ii.2.

[91] These differences suggest some shift since 1970 in the direction of proponents of a more forward-leaning 'right of resistance'. See Arangio-Ruiz (n 35) s 79.

the UN Charter pursuant to realization of the right to self-determination. The second paragraph concludes by referring to the denial of the right to self-determination as a violation of human rights, which invokes the interrelation between respect for the right to self-determination and the enjoyment of human rights and fundamental freedoms.[92]

Section eight of the Vienna Declaration addresses democracy in terms that are referential to aspects of the right to self-determination.[93] This relation is discussed in Chapter 8.

[92] See Chapter 8.b. See similarly Resolution 1514 para 1; FRD Principle V, para 2. See also A/3077 para 40.

[93] See Chapter 8.c.i.

4
International Court of Justice Judgments and Opinions

a. Overview

Article 38 of the ICJ Statute identifies judicial decisions as a subsidiary source for the determination of rules of international law.[1] Formally, judgments of the ICJ are binding only in relation to the parties to a contentious case.[2] Even so, statements by the ICJ as to the content of international law are regarded as authoritative and influential.[3] Although international law does not admit the common law concept of *stare decisis* in the form of binding precedent,[4] in practice, international courts and tribunals, in the words of former ICJ President Gilbert Guillaume, 'construct an entire jurisprudence based on their own precedent'.[5] One may therefore expect pronouncements by the ICJ to be regarded as authoritative expressions of the content of international law and applied by the ICJ, as well as other international courts and tribunals, in future cases. This same conclusion would seem to apply with equal force to the legal content of both judgments in contentious cases as well as advisory opinions, even if advisory opinions are not binding on any State.[6]

[1] Statute of the International Court of Justice art 38(1)(d), XV UNCIO 355 (26 June 1945, entered into force 24 Oct 1945).

[2] Ibid art 59.

[3] W. Michael Reisman, 'The Constitutional Crisis in the United Nations' (1993) 87(1) *AJIL* 83, 92. See e.g. Case T-279/19 *Front populaire pour la libération de la Saguia-el-Hamra et du Rio de Oro (Front Polisario) v Council of the European Union*, General Court, Judgment (29 Sept 2021) (hereinafter *Polisario III* (2021)) para 386.

[4] 'Stare decisis', *Black's Law Dictionary* (12th edn 2024).

[5] Gilbert Guillaume, 'The Use of Precedent by International Judges and Arbitrators' (2011) 2(1) *Journal of International Dispute Settlement* 5, 14; Hersch Lauterpacht, *The Development of International Law by the International Court* (CUP 1982) 8–15, 20–22. This practice more closely resembles the concept of *jurisprudence constante* of the civil law tradition. See 'Jurisprudence', *Black's Law Dictionary* (12th edn 2024).

[6] See Richard Falk, 'The *Kosovo* Advisory Opinion: Conflict Resolution and Precedent' (2011) 105(1) *AJIL* 50, 52–54. See e.g. *Polisario III* (2021) para 386; *Dispute Concerning Delimitation*

The Right to Self-Determination in International Law. Thomas Weatherall, Oxford University Press.
 DOI: 10.1093/9780197798119.003.0005

In view of the foregoing, judgments and opinions by the ICJ addressing self-determination are of particular importance to identifying the content of the right to self-determination as it has developed in international law. The ICJ has expressly addressed self-determination on seven occasions: in its *East Timor* (1995) judgment, and advisory opinions in *Namibia* (1971), *Western Sahara* (1975), *The Wall* (2004), *Kosovo* (2010), *Chagos Archipelago* (2019), and *Palestine* (2024). Regional and domestic cases of significance are addressed in Parts II and III.[7]

b. *Namibia* (1971)

The *Namibia* (1971) advisory opinion was issued by the ICJ in response to a request by the UNSC in Resolution 284 (1970).[8] The request arose in the context of South Africa's administration of Namibia under the League of Nations Mandate for South West Africa, for which South Africa was responsible. The manner of South Africa's administration of the territory, including the imposition of apartheid, led the UNGA to terminate the Mandate in 1966.[9] Termination of the Mandate for South West Africa followed an unsuccessful effort spanning two decades by the United Nations seeking performance by South Africa of its obligations under the Mandate, in view of the UN Trusteeship System.[10] The UNSC, in Resolution 276 (1970), declared the continued presence of South Africa in Namibia, following the termination of the Mandate, to be unlawful and called upon States to take certain actions.[11] The UNSC subsequently referred one question to the ICJ: 'What are the legal consequences for States of the continued presence of South Africa in

of the Maritime Boundary Between Mauritius and Maldives in the Indian Ocean (Mauritius / Maldives), ITLOS, Case No 28, Preliminary Objections, Judgment (28 Jan 2021) para 202.

---

[7] Perhaps the most notable treatment of the right to self-determination by a domestic court is *Reference re Secession of Quebec* [1998] 2 SCR 217 (hereinafter *Quebec* (1998)), an advisory opinion of the Supreme Court of Canada. See Chapter 7.c.i.

[8] S/Res/284 (29 July 1970).

[9] A/Res/2145 (XXI) (27 Oct 1966). See also John Dugard, 'The Revocation of the Mandate for South West Africa' (1968) 62(1) *AJIL* 78.

[10] *Legal Consequences for States of the Continued Presence of South Africa in Namibia (South West Africa) notwithstanding Security Council Resolution 276 (1970)*, Advisory Opinion, ICJ Rep 1971, 16 paras 84–86.

[11] S/Res/276 (30 Jan 1970).

Namibia, notwithstanding Security Council resolution 276 (1970)?'.[12] The advisory opinion rendered in 1971 in response to that request was the sixth instance in which the ICJ had opined on the situation in Namibia.[13] Because the UNSC had already determined South Africa's presence in Namibia, following termination of the Mandate by the UNGA, to be unlawful,[14] the ICJ was asked only to identify the legal consequences flowing from that unlawful situation.[15]

Self-determination is expressly identified in *Namibia* (1971) as the common thread running through the League of Nations Mandate System, the subsequent UN Trusteeship System, and obligations of administering powers vis-à-vis NSGTs under Chapter XI of the UN Charter. The ICJ recalled that, in establishing the League of Nations Mandate System, 'two principles were considered to be of paramount importance: the principle of non-annexation and the principle that the well-being and development of such peoples form "a sacred trust of civilization"'.[16] A significant portion of the Advisory Opinion addresses the way in which the League of Nations Mandate System was succeeded by the UN Trusteeship System.[17] The court identified the common purpose underlying these systems and associated obligations under international law. According to the court, the UN Charter 'confirmed and expanded' the concept of sacred trust, the lodestar of the League of Nations Mandate System,[18] to all peoples that had not yet achieved a full measure of self-government.[19] The development of international law in the context of NSGTs 'made the principle of self-determination applicable

[12] S/Res/284 (29 July 1970).

[13] *Namibia* (1971) para 44. For historical background, see John F. Murphy, 'Whither Now Namibia' (1972) 6(1) *Cornell International Law Journal* 1, 4–11.

[14] Neither of these determinations by UN organs was reviewed by the ICJ. See *Namibia* (1971) para 89. For a summary of these aspects of the opinion, and in particular disagreement amongst members of the court on these points, see Antony J. M. Zuijdwijk, 'The International Court and South West Africa: Latest Phase' (1973) 3 *Georgia Journal of International & Comparative Law* 323.

[15] *Namibia* (1971) paras 111–17. While the binding character of UNSC Resolution 276 (1970) upon UN Member States is based in Article 25 of the UN Charter, the ICJ identified the legal consequences arising from the illegal situation as applicable *erga omnes*, extending beyond the UN Charter and its Member States: ibid para 126.

[16] Ibid para 45 (quoting *International Status of South-West Africa*, Advisory Opinion, ICJ Rep 1950, 128). See Chapter 1.c.i.

[17] *Namibia* (1971) paras 60, 73, 90.

[18] Treaty of Versailles, Part I, The Covenant of the League of Nations art 22.

[19] *Namibia* (1971) para 52 (citing UN Charter art 73). See Chapter 7.b.i.1.

to all of them'.[20] And, in light of these developments, the ICJ assessed that 'the ultimate objective of the sacred trust was the self-determination and independence of the peoples concerned'.[21] While the only references to self-determination in the advisory opinion appear in these two paragraphs, the discussion is significant in its orientation of the League of Nations Mandate System, the subsequent UN Trusteeship System, and obligations under the UN Charter related to NSGTs along this common axis.

The operative portion of the *Namibia* (1971) advisory opinion responds directly to the question referred in Resolution 284 (1970) by identifying the consequences of the finding of illegality by the UNSC in Resolution 276 (1970).[22] As a result of South Africa's occupation of the territory of Namibia without title, the ICJ found that South Africa incurred international responsibility for breach of an international obligation of a continuing character, and identified an obligation to bring that breach to an end (i.e. 'to withdraw its administration from the Territory of Namibia').[23] The court also identified three consequences for UN Member States (third-States) arising from the unlawful situation in Namibia. First, third-States were under an obligation of non-recognition, i.e. 'to recognize the illegality and invalidity of South Africa's continued presence in Namibia'.[24] Second, third-States were under an obligation of non-maintenance, i.e. 'to refrain from lending any support or any form of assistance to South Africa with reference to its occupation of Namibia'.[25] Finally, third-States were obligated to cooperate, including through various measures specified by the court, to bring the unlawful situation in Namibia to an end.[26] The court identified the consequences of the illegality of South Africa's continued presence in Namibia as having an *erga omnes* character.[27]

[20] *Namibia* (1971) para 52.
[21] Ibid para 53.
[22] *Namibia* (1971) paras 111–27. See Chapter 9.d.
[23] *Namibia* (1971) para 118.
[24] Ibid para 119.
[25] Ibid.
[26] Ibid paras 120–24.
[27] As a result, the consequences for third-States identified by the ICJ were not limited to UN Member States through applicability of Articles 24 and 25 of the UN Charter: *Namibia* (1971) para 126.

c. *Western Sahara* (1975)

The *Western Sahara* (1975) advisory opinion was issued by the ICJ in response to a request by the UNGA in Resolution 3292 (XXIX) (1974).[28] The request was made in the context of a dispute between Spain, the administering power of Western Sahara within the meaning of Chapter XI of the UN Charter, and Morocco and Mauritania, which each claimed Western Sahara as part of their respective national territories by virtue of purported links at the time of its colonization by Spain beginning in 1884.[29] Morocco invaded Western Sahara in 1975 and, after clashing with Mauritania, assumed sole control over most of the territory.[30] In 1976, Spain informed the UN Secretary-General that it had, inter alia, withdrawn as administering power of Western Sahara and considered itself exempt from associated obligations under the UN Charter.[31]

Prior to Spain's withdrawal from Western Sahara, in 1974, the UNGA submitted two questions to the ICJ. First, '[w]as Western Sahara (Río de Oro and Sakiet El Hamra) at the time of colonization by Spain a territory belonging to no one (*terra nullius*)?'[32] and, if the answer to that question was negative, '[w]hat were the legal ties between this territory and the Kingdom of Morocco and the Mauritanian entity?'[33] In responding to the questions presented by the UNGA, the court did not limit itself to their historic framing, and considered that 'the applicable principles of decolonization call for examination by the Court, in that they are an essential part of the framework of the questions contained in the request'.[34] The court also assessed that '[t]he right of th[e] population [of Western Sahara] to self-determination constitutes [] a basic assumption of the questions put to the Court'.[35]

28 A/Res/3292 (XXIX) (13 Dec 1974).

29 *Western Sahara*, Advisory Opinion, ICJ Rep 1975, 12 (hereinafter *Western Sahara* (1975)) paras 75–77.

30 For background, see Thomas M. Franck, 'The Stealing of the Sahara' (1976) 70(4) *AJIL* 694; Malcolm Shaw, 'The *Western Sahara* Case' (1978) 49(1) *British Yearbook of International Law* 119.

31 *Letter dated 26 February 1967 from the Permanent Representative of Spain to the United Nations addressed to the Secretary-General*, A/31/56, S/11997 (26 Feb 1976) 3. The absence of a *de jure* administering power in Western Sahara has complicated its people's realization of the right to self-determination.

32 *Western Sahara* (1975) para 79.

33 A/Res/3292 (XXIX) (13 Dec 1974).

34 *Western Sahara* (1975) para 52. See Shaw (n 30) 126.

35 *Western Sahara* (1975) para 70.

In response to the first question referred by the UNGA, the court concluded that Western Sahara was not *terra nullius* at the time of its colonization, in light of State practice at the relevant period, according to which 'territories inhabited by tribes or peoples having a social and political organization were not regarded as *terra nullius*'.[36] Given that, the court proceeded to address the second question, finding that neither Morocco nor Mauritania exercised sovereignty over Western Sahara at the time of its colonization by Spain.[37] The court therefore concluded that it had not identified 'legal ties of such a nature as might affect the application of resolution 1514 (XV) in the decolonization of Western Sahara and, in particular, of the principle of self-determination through the free and genuine expression of the will of the peoples of the Territory'.[38]

The discussion of self-determination in the advisory opinion began with a recounting of the principle as it is articulated in the UN Charter, and the way in which Chapter XI 'made the principle applicable' to all NSGTs.[39] Turning to UNGA Resolution 1514, the ICJ assessed that its provisions (in particular paragraph 2) 'confirm and emphasize that the application of the right of self-determination requires a free and genuine expression of the will of the peoples concerned'.[40] The court observed that UNGA Resolution 1514 'provided the basis for the process of decolonization', and is 'complemented in certain of its aspects' by UNGA Resolution 1541.[41] In light of UNGA Resolution 1541, which addresses implementation of the right to self-determination, the court again emphasized the touchstone of the right to self-determination as, inter alia, the freely expressed wishes of the people concerned.[42] The court then recalled UNGA Resolution 2625 (the FRD), which 'reiterates the basic need to take account of the wishes of the people concerned'.[43] On the

[36] Ibid paras 79–83. The ICJ also quoted its advisory opinion in *Reparation for Injuries Suffered in the Service of the United Nations* (ICJ Rep 1949, 178), where it described such a group as 'an entity capable of availing itself of obligations incumbent upon its Members'. Ibid para 149. See Shaw (n 30) 127–34.

[37] *Western Sahara* (1975) paras 105, 150.

[38] Ibid para 162. See Shaw (n 30) 134–44.

[39] *Western Sahara* (1975) para 54 (quoting *Namibia* (1971)).

[40] Ibid para 55. See Chapter 7.b.i.2.

[41] *Western Sahara* (1975) para 57 ('certain of its provisions give effect to the essential feature of the right of self-determination as established in resolution 1514 (XV)').

[42] Ibid. See Chapter 7.b.i.4.

[43] *Western Sahara* (1975) para 58. See Chapter 7.b.i.3.

basis of this survey, the court synthesized what it referred to as a definition of the principle of self-determination as 'the need to pay regard to the freely expressed will of peoples'.[44]

After defining the principle of self-determination, the ICJ addressed various practical aspects of its implementation. The court identified a 'measure of discretion' in the exercise by the UNGA of its responsibilities under the UN Charter regarding the principle of self-determination.[45] Moreover, apparent deviations from the principle of self-determination by the UNGA—namely, instances in which a self-determination process was not administered, and others where the principle was found to be inapplicable as a threshold matter—were explained by the court to be consistent with the principle.[46]

> The validity of the principle of self-determination, defined as the need to pay regard to the freely expressed will of peoples, is not affected by the fact that in certain cases the General Assembly has dispensed with the requirement of consulting the inhabitants of a given territory. Those instances were based either on the consideration that a certain population did not constitute a 'people' entitled to self-determination or on the conviction that a consultation was totally unnecessary, in view of special circumstances.[47]

The first instance identified by the court contemplates situations in which the right to self-determination is not implicated as a threshold matter because the population concerned does not constitute a 'people' entitled to the right.[48] The second instance regards 'special circumstances' in which consultation of

[44] *Western Sahara* (1975) para 59.

[45] Ibid para 71. See Chapter 10.b.

[46] Antonio Cassese, *Self-Determination of Peoples: A Legal Reappraisal* (CUP 1995) 89; Jamie Trinidad, *Self-Determination in Disputed Colonial Territories* (CUP 2018) 56–63.

[47] *Western Sahara* (1975) para 59.

[48] There are exceptionally few cases in which the population of a NSGT may not have been regarded as a 'people' entitled to the right to self-determination. São João Batista de Ajudá, a NSGT administered by Portugal which lacked a civilian population that was annexed by Dahomey (now Benin), and French Establishments in India, a NSGT integrated into India with the consent of France, are referred to in commentary as examples. See Trinidad (n 46) 242. For discussion of 'peoples', see Chapter 6.

the people concerned is unnecessary to ascertain their wishes, though such 'special circumstances' are not defined.[49]

In addition to the measure of discretion and anomalies in the practice of the UNGA, the ICJ contemplated the possibility that 'legal ties' of territorial sovereignty 'might affect' the otherwise applicable right to self-determination.[50] While the questions referred to the court and its responses to those questions were largely historical in nature, the court accepted the potential for historic claims of territorial sovereignty to impact the right to self-determination in the present.[51] The court had already considered, as a threshold matter, that the population of Western Sahara enjoyed the right to self-determination.[52] Nevertheless, in addressing countervailing territorial claims by Mauritius and Mauritania over Western Sahara, the court assessed whether there existed any 'legal tie of territorial sovereignty' that might have qualified application of the right to self-determination of the people of Western Sahara.[53] The treatment of the question of legal ties of territorial sovereignty by the court admits the possibility of a change in the political status of a territory designated as a NSGT under Chapter XI of the UN Charter in the absence of an exercise of self-determination by the people concerned. However, in the absence of such legal ties in the case of Western Sahara, the court did not reach the question of precisely how such ties 'might affect the application' of Resolution 1514 and the right to self-determination. Whatever their impact, the advisory opinion accepted the premise that legal ties of territorial sovereignty may condition the right of a people to self-determination.[54]

The *Western Sahara* (1975) advisory opinion has informed subsequent litigation concerning the territory, discussed in Chapter 11.[55] The political status of Western Sahara remains unsettled.

[49] The ICJ might have contemplated the case of Ifni, which 'having been decolonized by transfer to Morocco, [] no longer appeared in the resolutions of the Assembly': *Western Sahara* (1975) para 63. See Chapter 7.f.

[50] Cf Shaw (n 30) 148.

[51] Ibid; Crawford (n 7) 644; Trinidad (n 46) 50–56.

[52] *Western Sahara* (1975) para 70.

[53] Ibid para 162.

[54] See Chapter 7.f.

[55] See Chapter 11.e.ii.

d. *East Timor* (1995)

East Timor became a colony of Portugal in the sixteenth century,[56] and in the UN system was regarded as a NSGT under the administration of Portugal.[57] Following unrest in East Timor, on 7 December 1975, Indonesia intervened and then occupied the territory; Portugal ultimately withdrew from the territory, which was annexed by Indonesia under Indonesian law on 17 July 1976.[58] Proceedings before the ICJ later instituted by Portugal concerned a 1989 treaty concluded between Indonesia and Australia, which had recognized the de facto incorporation of East Timor as part of Indonesia, for the joint exploration and exploitation of resources in an area of the continental shelf known as the Timor Gap.[59] Portugal instituted proceedings against Australia before the ICJ, alleging, inter alia, that negotiation, conclusion and implementation of the 1989 treaty 'infringed the rights of the people of East Timor to self-determination and to permanent sovereignty over its natural resources, infringed the rights of Portugal as the administering Power, and contravened [two] Security Council resolutions'.[60] Because the gravamen of Portugal's claim was whether Portugal or Indonesia had the authority to conclude a treaty on behalf of East Timor, the ICJ determined that it did not have jurisdiction over the matter because Indonesia was an indispensable third party to the proceeding that had not consented to the jurisdiction of the court to adjudicate the dispute.[61]

[56] For historical background, see Roger S. Clark, 'The "Decolonization" of East Timor and the United Nations Norms on Self-Determination and Aggression' (1980) 7(2) *Yale Journal of World Public Order* 2. For critical commentary, see Catriona Drew, 'The East Timor Story: International Law on Trial' (2001) 12(4) *EJIL* 651.

[57] A/Res/1542 (XV) (15 Dec 1960). See Clark (n 56) 3–5 (on Portugal's recognition of its obligations as an administering power under Chapter XI of the UN Charter).

[58] Peter H. F. Bekker, '*East Timor*' (1996) 90(1) *AJIL* 94, 94–95. See also Clark (n 56) 11–19 (discussing the administration of a purported self-determination process by Indonesia that the UNGA did not recognize as valid).

[59] See Treaty between Australia and the Republic of Indonesia on the Zone of Cooperation in an Area between the Indonesian Province of East Timor and Northern Australia (11 Dec 1989) arts 2.1, 2.2, reproduced in (1990) 29(3) ILM 475.

[60] *East Timor (Portugal v Australia)*, Judgment, ICJ Rep 1995, 90 (hereinafter *East Timor* (1995)) para 19. For discussion, see Bekker (n 58) 94–98.

[61] *East Timor* (1995) paras 27–28, 35. See *Case of the Monetary Gold removed from Rome in 1943 (Italy v France, United Kingdom, and United States of America)*, Preliminary Question, Judgment, ICJ Rep 1954, 19, 32. For discussion of the indispensable third party principle in this case, see Christine M. Chinkin, 'Symposium: The East Timor Case before the International Court of Justice, East Timor Moves into the World Court' (1993) 4(2) *EJIL* 206, 218–22. See also Christian J. Tams, *Enforcing Obligations* Erga Omnes *in International Law* (CUP 2005) 183–85.

Portugal, in attempting to overcome the absence of Indonesia's consent to jurisdiction, argued that the requirement of consent articulated by the ICJ in *Monetary Gold* (1954) was inapplicable where the obligation in question is *erga omnes* in character.[62] The ICJ concluded that 'the *erga omnes* character of a norm and the rule of consent to jurisdiction are two different things', and that the former is insufficient to overcome the requirement of consent to enable the court to exercise jurisdiction over a State without its consent.[63] In reaching that conclusion, the court recognized the *erga omnes* character of the right to self-determination.[64] The court also emphasized that the parties to the case regarded East Timor as a NSGT, and that 'the General Assembly, which reserves to itself the right to determine the territories which have to be regarded as non-self-governing for the purposes of the application of Chapter XI of the Charter, has treated East Timor as such a territory'.[65] The final paragraph of the judgment recalls that, 'for the two Parties, the Territory of East Timor remains a non-self-governing territory and its people has the right to self-determination'.[66]

e. *The Wall* (2004)

The request for an advisory opinion by the UNGA in Resolution ES-10/14 (2003) was submitted to the ICJ in the complex legal and political context of the Israel-Palestine conflict and, in particular, amid criticism of specific actions by Israel in the Occupied Palestinian Territory (OPT).[67] It may be

[62] *East Timor* (1995) para 29.
[63] Ibid. See Chapter 11.b; Chapter 11.c.
[64] *East Timor* (1995) para 29. See Chapter 5.d.
[65] *East Timor* (1995) para 31.
[66] Ibid para 37.
[67] For summary and immediate context, see Geoffrey R. Watson, 'The "Wall" Decisions in Legal and Political Context' (2005) 99(1) *AJIL* 6. For background, see Crawford (n 7) 421–48, especially 428, 434–35 ('Palestine in 1948 constituted a self-determination unit in international law. . . . Israel was effectively and lawfully established as a State by secession from Palestine in the period 1948–1949 . . . leaving its remaining territory subject still to the principles of the mandate. . . . The Balfour Declaration had been accepted as incorporated in the Mandate, and the Jewish people accordingly had a right of self-determination in respect of post-1922 Palestine as a whole. But so too did the Palestinian people. Israel could be regarded as an expression of the principle of self-determination for the Jewish people of Palestine as at 1948, even though the Partition Resolution had not been implemented. But there was no equivalent expression for the Palestinian population. The implementation of their right to self-determination has been, from a legal as well as a political point of view, the key element in the conflict since then').

recalled that Israel, together with the Palestinian territories, had comprised the former League of Nations Mandate of Palestine.[68] The question referred by the UNGA to the court requested advice on the legal consequences arising from the construction of the wall being built by Israel, the occupying Power, in the OPT.[69] Explicit in the question presented by the UNGA, and confirmed by the court, is that a situation of occupation existed in the OPT and that Israel had the status of occupying Power in relation thereto.[70] The situation of occupation is key to the way in which the right to self-determination is implicated and to the performance by Israel of its obligations under the right to self-determination towards the people of Palestine in that context.[71] In response to UNGA Resolution ES-10/14, the court rendered an advisory opinion addressing different areas of international law implicated by the question referred, including international human rights law and international humanitarian law, as well as the right to self-determination.[72]

The treatment of the right to self-determination by the ICJ in *The Wall* (2004) suggests a unitary rule of international law, one which is undifferentiated in its substantive content and distinct from other fields of international law. The discussion of self-determination in the advisory opinion identifies sources of the principle and right, including the FRD and common Article 1 of the two human rights covenants.[73] The court also summarized earlier pronouncements on self-determination and reaffirmed its *erga omnes* character.[74] The court also distinguished obligations arising from the right to self-determination from those under both international human rights law and international humanitarian law.[75]

[68] *Legal Consequences of the Construction of a Wall in the Occupied Palestinian Territory*, Advisory Opinion, ICJ Rep 2004, 136 (hereinafter *Wall* (2004)) paras 70–71. See also A/Res/181 (II) (29 Nov 1947) (recommending partition of the Mandate of Palestine).

[69] A/Res/ES-10/14 (8 Dec 2003).

[70] *Wall* (2004) para 78.

[71] See Chapter 7.b.ii.1.

[72] *Wall* (2004) (this differentiation of different areas of international law is reflected most clearly at para 149). For commentary and a critical assessment of the ICJ in this regard, see Michla Pomerance, 'The ICJ's Advisory Jurisdiction and the Crumbling Wall Between the Political and the Judicial' (2005) 99(1) *AJIL* 26; see also Richard A. Falk, 'Toward Authoritativeness: The ICJ Ruling on Israel's Security Wall' (2005) 99(1) *AJIL* 42.

[73] *Wall* (2004) para 88.

[74] Ibid.

[75] Ibid para 149.

The ICJ found that certain aspects of the occupation of Palestinian territory by Israel breached its obligation to respect the right of the Palestinian people to self-determination. Specifically, the court assessed that construction of the wall—the ways in which it effected de facto annexation of the territory at issue and contributed to alteration of the demographic composition of that territory—breached Israel's obligation to respect the right to self-determination in relation to the Palestinian people.[76] In this way, breaches of the obligation to respect the right to self-determination were defined in relation to substantive elements of the right, i.e. the political status of the territory and its people. Notably, the court did not find occupation *vel non* to breach the obligation to respect the right to self-determination.[77]

Turning to the legal consequences arising from Israel's breach of various international law obligations, the ICJ assessed that 'Israel is bound to comply with its obligation to respect the right of the Palestinian people to self-determination and its obligations under international humanitarian law and international human rights law'.[78] Israel was accordingly under obligations to put an end to its breaches of international law and to make reparation for associated damages.[79] The court also identified third-States obligations to promote the right to self-determination and render assistance to the United Nations in reference to the FRD.[80] In light of 'the character and the importance of the rights and obligations involved', the court concluded that all States were under obligations of non-recognition and to not render aid or assistance in the maintenance of the situation.[81] The court added:

> It is also for all States, while respecting the United Nations Charter and international law, to see to it that any impediment, resulting from the construction of the wall, to the exercise by the Palestinian people of its right to self-determination is brought to an end.[82]

[76] Ibid paras 118–22.
[77] See Chapter 7.b.ii.1.
[78] *Wall* (2004) para 149.
[79] Ibid paras 150–53.
[80] Ibid paras 155–56.
[81] Ibid para 159.
[82] Ibid.

In effect, the court refined and restated earlier articulations of the *erga omnes* character of obligations arising from the right to self-determination, and reiterated the legal consequences for third-States arising from the breach of such obligations previously articulated in *Namibia* (1971).[83]

f. *Kosovo* (2010)

The *Kosovo* (2010) advisory opinion was delivered by the ICJ in response to a request by the UNGA following the declaration of independence by Kosovo on 17 February 2008.[84] The 2008 declaration of independence followed a years-long 'final status process' under the auspices of the United Nations that failed to yield a negotiated outcome regarding the future political status of Kosovo.[85] Following the declaration, the UNGA referred a single question to the court in Resolution 63/3 (2008): 'Is the unilateral declaration of independence by the Provisional Institutions of Self-Government of Kosovo in accordance with international law?'[86] The court construed the scope of the question presented as asking whether international law prohibited the declaration of independence, rather than whether the population of Kosovo was entitled make it.[87] According to this approach, it was possible for a unilateral declaration of independence 'not to be in violation of international law without necessarily constituting the exercise of a right conferred by it'.[88] The court ultimately concluded that the declaration of independence did not violate any applicable rule of international law.[89] In reaching this conclusion,

[83] See ILC Draft Articles on Responsibility of States for Internationally Wrongful Acts art 41 (and associated commentary), A/56/10, Report of the International Law Commission on the Work of its Fifty-Third Session, [2001] II(2) *YbILC* 26 et seq, A/CN.4/SER.A/2001/Add.1 (Part 2) (hereinafter ILC ARSIWA). See Chapter 9.d.ii.

[84] Christian Walter, 'The Kosovo Advisory Opinion: What It Says and What It Does Not Say' in Christian Walter et al (eds), *Self-Determination and Secession in International Law* (OUP 2014) 13; Richard Falk, 'The *Kosovo* Advisory Opinion: Conflict Resolution and Precedent' (2011) 105(1) *AJIL* 50; Ralphe Wilde, '*Accordance with International Law of the Unilateral Declaration of Independence in Respect of Kosovo*' (2011) 105(2) *AJIL* 301, 303–07.

[85] For a summary of this process, see *Accordance with International Law of the Unilateral Declaration of Independence in Respect of Kosovo*, Advisory Opinion, ICJ Rep 2010, 403 (hereinafter *Kosovo* (2010)) paras 57–76.

[86] A/Res/63/3 (8 Oct 2008).

[87] Wilde (n 84) 303.

[88] *Kosovo* (2010) paras 49–56.

[89] Ibid para 122.

the court considered the relationship between independence and the right to self-determination.

Framing the pertinent part of its opinion in historical context, the ICJ took note of the many declarations of independence since the eighteenth century, some of which resulted in the creation of new States. The court further recalled that, in the twentieth century, the international law of self-determination had developed as a 'right to independence' for peoples of NSGTs and peoples subject to 'alien subjugation, domination and exploitation'.

> During the eighteenth, nineteenth and early twentieth centuries, there were numerous instances of declarations of independence, often strenuously opposed by the State from which independence was being declared. Sometimes a declaration resulted in the creation of a new State, at others it did not. In no case, however, does the practice of States as a whole suggest that the act of promulgating the declaration was regarded as contrary to international law. On the contrary, State practice during this period points clearly to the conclusion that international law contained no prohibition of declarations of independence. During the second half of the twentieth century, the international law of self-determination developed in such a way as to create a right to independence for the peoples of non-self-governing territories and peoples subject to alien subjugation, domination and exploitation. A great many new States have come into existence as a result of the exercise of this right. There were, however, also instances of declarations of independence outside this context. The practice of States in these latter cases does not point to the emergence in international law of a new rule prohibiting the making of a declaration of independence in such cases.[90]

On the basis of international practice—particularly the historical frequency of declarations of independence and absence of indicia of their perceived unlawfulness—the court determined that general international

[90] Ibid para 79 (citations omitted).

law contains no prohibition on declarations of independence and is instead neutral.[91] This conclusion was viewed to be consistent with the principle of territorial integrity because the principle is 'confined to the sphere of relations between States', and as such, not opposable internally to cases of secession.[92]

In addition to the neutrality of international law towards declarations of independence, the ICJ recognized an affirmative entitlement to independence that resides exclusively within the right to self-determination. The court further identified the two recognized circumstances in which a people is entitled to exercise the right to self-determination in relation to its international aspect ('the context of non-self-governing territories and peoples subject to alien subjugation, domination and exploitation'),[93] consistent with other instruments addressing the scope of the international aspect of self-determination.[94] Whether the right to self-determination additionally entitles a part of the population of a State to separate from it, and whether international law contains a so-called right of remedial secession, are questions that were acknowledged but not resolved by the court.[95] While the court observed that States participating expressed 'radically different views' and 'sharp differences of views' on these two formulations of secession, the court neither endorsed nor rejected either of them. Because it was not necessary for the court to identify an applicable entitlement to independence in order to determine that the declaration of independence was not prohibited by international law,[96] its pronouncements on self-determination may be viewed as *obiter dictum*.

[91] See also ibid para 81; Christian Walter & Antje von Ungern-Sternberg, 'Introduction: Self-Determination and Secession in International Law Perspectives and Trends with Particular Focus on the Commonwealth of Independent States' in Christian Walter et al (eds), *Self-Determination and Secession in International Law* (OUP 2014) 3. See Chapter 7.c.

[92] *Kosovo* (2010) para 80. See Chapter 7.d.

[93] *Kosovo* (2010) para 82. See Chapter 7.b.

[94] A/Res/1514 (XV) (14 Dec 1960) paras 1, 5; A/Res/2625 (24 Oct 1970) Annex (hereinafter FRD) Principle V, para 2. See also United Nations World Conference on Human Rights: Vienna Declaration and Programme of Action (25 June 1993), A/CONF/157/23 (12 July 1993), reproduced in (1993) 32(6) ILM 1661, part I, s 2, para 2.

[95] *Kosovo* (2010) paras 82–83. See Chapter 7.c.ii.

[96] *Kosovo* (2010) paras 55–56. In this regard, the ICJ distinguished the question referred in relation to Kosovo from the question posed to the Supreme Court of Canada in *Quebec* (1998). See Chapter 7.c.i.

g. *Chagos Archipelago* (2019)

The *Chagos Archipelago* (2019) advisory opinion contains a comprehensive assessment of the crystallization of the right to self-determination in CIL.[97] At the centre of the request for an advisory opinion was the separation of the Chagos Archipelago from Mauritius by the United Kingdom pursuant to the 23 September 1965 'Lancaster House agreement'.[98] Prior to its detachment, the Chagos Archipelago was administered by the United Kingdom as a dependency of Mauritius, a NSGT subject to Chapter XI of the UN Charter.[99] Subsequent to the detachment, on 8 November 1965, the United Kingdom established the British Indian Ocean Territory (BIOT), consisting of the Chagos Archipelago and several other islands.[100] Decades after securing its independence in 1968,[101] Mauritius undertook a series of legal efforts to advance its assertion of sovereignty over the Chagos Archipelago. These efforts included arbitration under Annex VII of the United Nations Convention on the Law of the Sea (UNCLOS),[102] and securing passage of an UNGA resolution requesting an advisory opinion from the ICJ on the Chagos Archipelago.[103] UNGA Resolution 71/292 (2017) sought advice from the court on (a) whether the process of decolonization of Mauritius was lawfully completed when Mauritius gained independence in 1968, and (b) the legal consequences of the continued administration of the Chagos Archipelago by the UK.[104] The court concluded that the detachment of the

[97] For a summary and commentary, see Diane Marie Amann, 'Legal Consequences of the Separation of the Chagos Archipelago from Mauritius in 1965' (2019) 113(4) *AJIL* 784; Stephen Allen, 'Self-Determination, the *Chagos Advisory Opinion* and the Chagossians' (2020) 69(1) *ICLQ* 203. For commentary regarding Chagossians, see Peter Hilpold, '"Humanizing" the Law of Self-Determination—the Chagos Island Case' (2022) 91 *Nordic Journal of International Law* 189.

[98] *Legal Consequences of the Separation of the Chagos Archipelago from Mauritius in 1965*, Advisory Opinion, ICJ Rep 2019, 95 (hereinafter *Chagos* (2019)) paras 32, 108–10. The 'Lancaster House agreement' was concluded between Mauritius and the United Kingdom. In 1966, the United Kingdom then concluded with the United States the 'Agreement Concerning the Availability for Defence Purposes of the British Indian Ocean Territory'. Ibid paras 36–37.

[99] Ibid paras 28–29. See A/Res/66 (I) (14 Dec 1946).

[100] *Chagos* (2019) para 33.

[101] See A/Res/2371 (XXII) (24 Apr 1968).

[102] *Award in the Arbitration regarding the Chagos Marine Protected Area between Mauritius and the United Kingdom of Great Britain and Northern Ireland*, XXXI RIAA 359 (18 Mar 2015). See Chapter 11.e.i.

[103] A/Res/71/292 (22 June 2017).

[104] Ibid. See *Chagos* (2019) para 1.

Chagos Archipelago was unlawful and that, because of its detachment, the decolonization of Mauritius was not completed when it gained independence in 1968.[105]

The ICJ framed the underlying dispute in the context of decolonization and the unique role of the UNGA in that process, rather than as a dispute over territorial sovereignty.[106] The court discussed the particular functions of the UNGA in the context of the work of the United Nations on decolonization, with a particular focus on its oversight over 'the application' of the right to self-determination and supervision of obligations of administering powers under the UN Charter.[107] A relevant part of this practice by the UNGA, according to the court, included calls for administering powers to respect the territorial integrity of NSGTs.[108]

The time period relevant to the questions referred, 1965 to 1968, coincided with the crystallization of the right to self-determination in CIL, meaning that the identification of applicable international law required a granular assessment of State practice and *opinio juris* to determine the point at which the right had crystalized.[109] The methodology applied by the ICJ was to identify the relevant *opinio juris* and confirm its earliest expression in State practice to ascertain when the right to self-determination could be said, in the view of the court, to have emerged in CIL.[110] In so doing, the court undertook an assessment of the content of the right to self-determination, particularly as that right and its aspects have found expression in various international instruments.

The ICJ oriented its assessment of self-determination in the particular context of decolonization, meaning the exercise of the international aspect of the right to self-determination by the peoples of NSGTs.[111] Even so, the survey of sources relied upon by the court indicates its approach to the right to self-determination as a unitary rule of international law, much like its earlier treatment of the right in *The Wall* (2004).[112] The court began by reference to the principle of self-determination as it was codified in the UN Charter and

[105] Ibid para 174.
[106] Ibid paras 83–90. On consent, see Chapter 11.d.
[107] *Chagos* (2019) paras 163, 167. See Chapter 10.b.
[108] *Chagos* (2019) para 168.
[109] Ibid para 142. See Chapter 5.c.ii.
[110] *Chagos* (2019) paras 144–61, especially para 150.
[111] See Chapter 7.b.i.
[112] See Chapter 4.e.

associated obligations of administering powers vis-à-vis NSGTs in Chapter XI of the Charter.[113] The court referred to the right to self-determination 'as a fundamental human right' of 'broad scope of application'.[114] According to the court, UNGA Resolution 1514 marked the crystallization of the right to self-determination in CIL.[115] The court considered that common Article 1 of the two human rights covenants and UNGA Resolution 2625 (the FRD) further evidenced the right to self-determination in CIL.[116] Returning to the particular context of decolonization, the court identified UNGA Resolution 1541 as providing for the modalities of implementation of the right to self-determination in reference to the exercise of its international aspect by the peoples of NSGTs.[117] The court repeated its earlier articulations in *Western Sahara* (1975) of a definition of the principle of self-determination and a margin of appreciation in the performance by the UNGA of its associated functions.[118]

In its survey of the content of the right to self-determination in CIL, the ICJ addressed territorial integrity, which the court characterized as 'a corollary' of the right to self-determination.[119] The court also considered that a people is entitled to exercise its right to self-determination over its territory as a whole, itself a corollary of the premise that the entire people of a territory (i.e. the people as a whole) is entitled to exercise the right to self-determination.[120] Territorial integrity in this sense concerned excision by an administrating power of a part of a NSGT, in contrast to the treatment of the principle (and the right to self-determination more generally) as inapplicable to cases of secession in *Kosovo* (2010).[121] The court did not make express reference to the principle of *uti possidetis*, a complementary application of territorial integrity considered by the ICJ in other judgments.[122] Finally,

113 See Chapter 2.b; Chapter 9.c.ii.
114 *Chagos* (2019) para 144.
115 Ibid paras 148–53. See Chapter 3.b; Chapter 5.c.ii.
116 *Chagos* (2019) paras 154–55. See Chapter 2.c; Chapter 3.d.
117 *Chagos* (2019) paras 156–57. See Chapter 3.c; Chapter 7.b.i.4.
118 *Chagos* (2019) paras 157–58. See Chapter 4.c.
119 *Chagos* (2019) para 160. See Chapter 7.d.
120 *Chagos* (2019) para 160 (citing Resolution 1514 para 6). See Chapter 6.c; Chapter 8.c.i.
121 Cf *Kosovo* (2010) para 80.
122 At least the first question referred to the court might have been approached by reference to *uti possidetis*. See Hilpold (n 97) 198. See also Chapter 7.e.

the court reaffirmed its observation in *Namibia* (1971) that international law affords self-determination to the peoples of all NSGTs.[123]

In light of the applicability of the right to self-determination during the relevant period, the ICJ applied 'heightened scrutiny' to the question of whether Mauritius, while under the administration of the United Kingdom, could be said to have consented to the detachment of the Chagos Archipelago, 'an integral part' of the NSGT, by operation of the Lancaster House agreement.[124] Based on the circumstances under which the Lancaster House agreement was undertaken by Mauritius, the ICJ concluded that detachment of the Chagos Archipelago 'was not based on the free and genuine expression of the will of the people concerned'.[125] The court therefore concluded, in response to question (a) presented by the UNGA, that the detachment of the Chagos Archipelago was unlawful and, because of its detachment and incorporation into a new colony, that the decolonization of Mauritius 'was not lawfully completed' when it gained independence in 1968.[126]

After concluding that 'the decolonization of Mauritius was not conducted in a manner consistent with the right of peoples to self-determination',[127] the ICJ turned to question (b) presented by the UNGA and addressed the legal consequences arising from that situation. The court found that the United Kingdom's continued administration of the Chagos Archipelago constituted an internationally wrongful act of a continuing character, engaging its international responsibility.[128] The United Kingdom was therefore, according to the court, under an obligation to bring its administration of the Chagos Archipelago to an end 'as rapidly as possible, thereby enabling Mauritius to complete the decolonization of its territory in a manner consistent with the right of peoples to self-determination'.[129] Regarding the modalities by which this result was to be achieved, the court deferred to the exercise of the decolonization functions of the UNGA.[130] The court reiterated the *erga omnes*

[123] *Chagos* (2019) para 161. See Chapter 4.b.
[124] *Chagos* (2019) paras 170–72.
[125] Ibid para 172.
[126] Ibid para 174.
[127] Ibid para 177.
[128] Ibid. See Chapter 9.d.i.
[129] *Chagos* (2019) para 178.
[130] Ibid para 179. Relatedly, the ICJ deferred the question of resettlement of Chagossians to the UNGA. Ibid para 181.

character of obligations arising from the right to self-determination, giving rise to consequences for third-States in the event of breach.[131]

While the ICJ identified an obligation of cooperation with the United Nations for third-States in reference to the FRD,[132] it did not refer to additional obligations for third-States of non-recognition and non-maintenance, consequences which it had identified in *Namibia* (1971) and *The Wall* (2004).[133] One possible explanation for this differentiation lies in the character of the specific obligations at issue in *Chagos Archipelago* (2019), namely the positive obligations of administrating powers of NSGTs directed towards winding down relationships of subordination,[134] as distinct from the negative character of general obligations that prohibit the creation of new relationships of subordination.[135] It is also significant that the court did not refer to the right to self-determination as belonging to *jus cogens*, a determination which would have substantively impacted the advisory opinion in view of Articles 53 and 64 of the Vienna Convention on the Law of Treaties (1969),[136] given that the underlying sovereignty dispute over the Chagos Archipelago was predicated upon an international agreement.[137]

The ICJ concluded its advisory opinion by responding to question (b) 'that the United Kingdom has an obligation to bring to an end its administration of the Chagos Archipelago as rapidly as possible, and that all Member States must co-operate with the United Nations to complete the decolonization of Mauritius'.[138]

h. *Palestine* (2024)

The second request for an advisory opinion by the UNGA related to the Israel-Palestine conflict concerned a range of policies and practices of Israel

[131] Ibid para 180. See Chapter 5.d; Chapter 9.d.ii.
[132] See Chapter 9.d.ii.2.
[133] *Namibia* (1971) paras 119–26; *Wall* (2004) para 159. See ILC ARSIWA art 41 (and associated commentary). See Chapter 9.d.ii.1.
[134] See Chapter 9.c.
[135] See Chapter 9.b.
[136] See Chapter 5.e.
[137] This issue was evidently before the court. See *Chagos* (2019) Sep Op Robinson paras 83–88; Sep Op Sebutinde para 45; Sep Op Cançado-Trindade paras 168–69.
[138] *Chagos* (2019) para 182.

in the OPT. In Resolution 77/247 (2022), the UNGA submitted two questions to the court, regarding (a) the legal consequences arising from the 'ongoing violation' by Israel of the right of the Palestinian people to self-determination 'from its prolonged occupation, settlement and annexation' of the OPT, and (b) the impact of these policies and practices on the legal status of the occupation and legal consequences arising therefrom.[139] On 19 July 2024, the ICJ rendered an advisory opinion containing an expansive treatment of the right to self-determination under CIL and its relationship to occupation.

In evaluating question (a), the ICJ considered that the prolonged character of occupation does not affect its status as a situation of occupation under international humanitarian law.[140] 'Instead', 'the legality of the occupying Power's presence in the occupied territory must be assessed in light of other rules', including the right to self-determination.[141]

The ICJ recalled the right of the Palestinian people to self-determination,[142] and the treatment of self-determination in the UN Charter, UNGA Resolution 2625 (the FRD), and UNGA Resolution 1514.[143] The court also restated its earlier affirmation of the right to self-determination as 'one of the essential principles of contemporary international law',[144] as well as its recognition that 'the obligation to respect the right to self-determination is owed *erga omnes* and that all States have a legal interest in protecting that right'.[145] The court took note of common Article 1 of the ICCPR and ICESCR as reflecting the 'centrality of the right to self-determination in international law', and its realization as 'an essential condition' for the enjoyment of human rights.[146] The court also reaffirmed that the right to self-determination is a 'fundamental human right' and took note of its treatment by the UNGA as an 'inalienable right'.[147] While the court regarded the right to self-determination as a peremptory norm 'in

[139] A/Res/77/247 (30 Dec 2022).

[140] *Legal Consequences arising from the Policies and Practices of Israel in the Occupied Palestinian Territory, including East Jerusalem*, Advisory Opinion, ICJ Rep 2024 (hereinafter *Palestine* (2024)) para 109.

[141] Ibid. See Chapter 7.b.ii.1.A.

[142] *Palestine* (2024) para 230 (citing *Wall* (2004) para 118).

[143] Ibid para 231. See Chapter 2.b.i; Chapter 3.b; Chapter 3.d.

[144] *Palestine* (2024) para 232 (citing *East Timor* (1995) para 29). See Chapter 4.d.

[145] *Palestine* (2024) para 232 (citing *Wall* (2004) para 155 and *Chagos* (2019) para 180). See Chapter 4.e; Chapter 4.g.

[146] *Palestine* (2024) para 233 (citing HRC, *CCPR General Comment No. 12: The Right to Self-Determination of Peoples (Art 1)* (1984)). See Chapter 2.c.

[147] *Palestine* (2024) para 233. See Chapter 5.f; Chapter 8.b.

cases of foreign occupation such as the present case', it devoted just a single sentence to the qualified character of the right to self-determination as a peremptory norm.[148] Because this pronouncement was of no legal consequence to the advisory opinion, it may be viewed as *obiter dictum*.

Having addressed the normative status of the right to self-determination, the ICJ recalled that '[t]he right of self-determination of peoples has a broad scope of application'.[149] In order to answer the first question presented by the UNGA, the court was called upon to assess 'whether the policies and practices of Israel, as the occupying Power, in the [OPT] impede the exercise of the right of the Palestinian people to self-determination'.[150] To this end, the court identified four 'elements' of the right to self-determination 'of particular relevance' to the proceeding.[151]

First, the ICJ reiterated 'that the right to territorial integrity is recognized under CIL as "a corollary of the right to self-determination" '.[152] Applying this element of the right to self-determination, the court considered 'that Israel, as the occupying Power, has the obligation not to impede the Palestinian people from exercising its right to self-determination, including its right to an independent and sovereign State, over the entirety of the [OPT]'.[153] In view of its earlier findings on annexation, and its treatment of the OPT as a single territorial unit, the court held that 'Israel's annexation of large parts of the [OPT] violates the integrity of the [OPT], as an essential element of the Palestinian people's right to self-determination'.[154]

Second, the ICJ considered that, 'by virtue of the right to self-determination, a people is protected against acts aimed at dispersing the population and undermining its integrity as a people'.[155] The court referred to its earlier findings in *The Wall* (2004), as well as its conclusions regarding annexation and discriminatory practices and procedures, to inform its determination that Israel had impeded the right to self-determination of the Palestinian people in this regard.[156] The court concluded that 'these policies

[148] See Chapter 5.e.i.
[149] *Palestine* (2024) para 234 (citing *Chagos* (2019) para 144).
[150] Ibid.
[151] Ibid para 236.
[152] Ibid para 237 (citing *Chagos* (2019) para 160). Cf *Kosovo* (2010) para 80. See Chapter 7.d.
[153] *Palestine* (2024) para 237.
[154] Ibid para 238.
[155] Ibid para 239. See Chapter 6.c.
[156] *Palestine* (2024) para 239 (citations omitted).

and practices undermine the integrity of the Palestinian people in the [OPT], significantly impeding the exercise of its right to self-determination'.[157]

Third, the ICJ recalled that 'the right to exercise permanent sovereignty over natural resources, which is a principle of customary international law', is an element of the right to self-determination.[158] Referring to its earlier finding that Israel had breached its obligation to respect the right of the Palestinian people to permanent sovereignty over natural resources, the court held that, '[i]n depriving the Palestinian people of its enjoyment of the natural resources in the [OPT] for decades, Israel has impeded the exercise of its right to self-determination'.[159]

Fourth, the ICJ recognized that 'a key element of the right to self-determination is the right of a people freely to determine its political status and to pursue its economic, social and cultural development'.[160] In relation to the substantive content of the right to self-determination, the court held that 'Israel's policies and practices obstruct the right of the Palestinian people freely to determine its political status and to pursue its economic, social and cultural development'.[161]

In view of the 'prolonged character' of the adverse impacts of Israel's occupation of the OPT on the right to self-determination of the Palestinian people, the ICJ held that Israel had breached its obligation to respect the right to self-determination in relation to the people of Palestine.[162] Having thus answered question (a), the court turned next to the two parts of question (b).

The first part of question (b) called upon the ICJ to assess the effects of unlawful policies and practices of Israel on the legal status of its occupation of the OPT.[163] The court considered the laws and principles governing the use of force, 'together with the right to self-determination', to be relevant to the legality of the occupation of the OPT.[164] The court assessed that the breach of the obligation to respect the right to self-determination by Israel impacted the legality of its continued presence in the OPT, finding that the 'right to

[157] Ibid.

[158] Ibid para 240 (citing *Armed Activities on the Territory of the Congo (Democratic Republic of the Congo v Uganda)*, Judgment, ICJ Rep 2005). See Chapter 8.d.i.1.

[159] *Palestine* (2024) paras 240–41. See Chapter 8.d.i.2.

[160] *Palestine* (2024) para 241. See Chapter 8.d.

[161] *Palestine* (2024) para 242.

[162] Ibid para 243.

[163] Ibid paras 244–64.

[164] Ibid para 251.

self-determination cannot be subject to conditions on the part of the occupying Power, in view of its character as an inalienable right'.[165] The court, in turn, assessed the continued presence of Israel in the OPT to be unlawful on the basis of its impacts on the right to self-determination of the people of Palestine as well as the annexation by Israel of parts of the OPT.[166] In addressing the illegality of Israel's continued presence in the OPT, the court expressly identified the OPT as the 'territorial unit' for purposes of the right to self-determination, whose population constitutes a people entitled to the exercise of the right in relation to the territory as a whole.[167]

The second part of question (b) concerned the legal consequences arising from Israel's unlawful policies and practices and from the illegality of Israel's continued presence in the OPT.[168] The court held that the maintenance of policies and practices referred to in question (a), found to have breached international obligations of Israel, constitutes an unlawful act of a continuing character engaging Israel's international responsibility.[169]

Regarding the legal consequences for Israel in the field of State responsibility,[170] the ICJ first identified an obligation of cessation.[171] The court also identified an obligation of reparation and took note of the three forms of reparation available under international law (restitution, compensation, and satisfaction).[172] Regarding restitution, the court prescribed certain measures, and alternatively, an obligation of compensation should restitution prove 'materially impossible'.[173] Finally, the court recalled that these secondary obligations in the field of State responsibility do not relieve Israel from its performance of the primary obligations breached, including the obligation to respect the right to self-determination.[174]

Regarding the legal consequences for third-States, the ICJ first reiterated that certain obligations breached by Israel, including the obligation to respect the right to self-determination, are obligations *erga omnes*.[175] The court then

[165] Ibid para 257. See Chapter 7.b.ii.1.A.
[166] *Palestine* (2024) para 261.
[167] Ibid para 262. See also ibid para 78. See Chapter 6.c.
[168] *Palestine* (2024) paras 265–81.
[169] Ibid para 265.
[170] See Chapter 9.d.i.
[171] *Palestine* (2024) para 267. See Chapter 9.d.i.1.
[172] *Palestine* (2024) para 269. See Chapter 9.d.i.2.
[173] *Palestine* (2024) para 270–71.
[174] Ibid para 272.
[175] Ibid paras 273–79, especially para 274. See Chapter 9.d.ii.

identified an obligation of cooperation with the United Nations for third-States to 'ensure' an end to Israel's presence in the OPT and 'the full realization of the right of the Palestinian people to self-determination'.[176] The court further identified obligations of non-recognition and non-maintenance for third-States in relation to unlawful policies and practices of Israel,[177] as well as Israel's unlawful presence in the OPT.[178] The court also restated the obligation of cooperation for third-States to bring an end to the breach of the obligation to respect the right to self-determination.[179]

Regarding legal consequences for the United Nations, the ICJ considered that the duty of non-recognition 'also applies to international organizations, including the United Nations, in view of the serious breaches of obligations *erga omnes* under international law'.[180] The conclusion of the advisory opinion referred to 'the realization of the right of the Palestinian people to self-determination' as 'including its right to an independent and sovereign State'.[181]

i. Other Significant Cases

In *Northern Cameroons* (1963), a contentious proceeding was instituted by the Republic of Cameroon against the United Kingdom alleging that the United Kingdom had breached certain obligations under the Trusteeship Agreement for the Cameroons under British Administration.[182] Following plebiscites for Northern Cameroons and Southern Cameroons conducted under the auspices of the United Nations, Southern Cameroons joined the Republic of Cameroon and Northern Cameroons joined the Federation of Nigeria. The UNGA endorsed the plebiscites and terminated the Trusteeship agreement.[183] Because the UNGA terminated the Trusteeship agreement,

[176] *Palestine* (2024) para 275 (quoting FRD). See Chapter 9.d.ii.2.
[177] *Palestine* (2024) para 278 (citing *Namibia* (1971) paras 122, 125–27). See Chapter 9.d.ii.1.
[178] *Palestine* (2024) para 279.
[179] Ibid.
[180] Ibid para 280.
[181] Ibid para 283. See Chapter 7.b.ii.
[182] *Case Concerning the Northern Cameroons (Cameroon v United Kingdom)*, Preliminary Objections, Judgment, ICJ Rep 1963, 15 (hereinafter *Northern Cameroons* (1963)). See 'The Northern Cameroons Case' (1964) 1964(3) *Duke Law Journal* 550; James Crawford, *The Creation of States in International Law* (2nd edn, OUP 2006) 584–86.
[183] UNGA Resolution 1608 (XV) (21 Apr 1961).

the only remedy sought by the Republic of Cameroon was a finding of breach of the Trusteeship agreement no longer in force. The ICJ considered that 'no question of actual legal rights [was] involved' and, in order to preserve its 'judicial integrity', declined to adjudicate the claim despite having jurisdiction.[184] The judgment remains significant for its affirmation of the authority of the UNGA to terminate Trusteeship agreements and recognition of the principle that the exercise of self-determination by the people of a Mandate or Trust Territory is conclusive as to the political status of such territory.

In *Nicaragua* (1986), the ICJ referred to the right to self-determination in reference to 'less grave forms of the use of force' identified in the FRD.[185] The court quoted the FRD: 'Every State has the duty to refrain from any forcible action which deprives peoples referred to in the elaboration of the principle of equal rights and self-determination of that right to self-determination and freedom and independence'.[186]

Finally, *Certain Phosphate Lands* (1992) concerned the administration of the Trust Territory (and former Mandate Territory) Nauru in connection with economic activities undertaken in Nauru and, in particular, failure to remediate certain environmental damage resulting from such activities.[187] The ICJ found that it had jurisdiction and that the application was admissible. However, on 9 September 1993, the parties notified the ICJ that they had reached a settlement in the matter and agreed to discontinue the proceedings before the ICJ reached the merits of the dispute.[188]

[184] *Northern Cameroons* (1963) 29, 37–38.

[185] See *Military and Paramilitary Activities in and against Nicaragua (Nicaragua v United States of America)*, Merits, Judgment, ICJ Rep 1986, 14 para 191.

[186] Ibid. See FRD Principle V, para 5.

[187] *Certain Phosphate Lands in Nauru (Nauru v Australia)*, Preliminary Objections, Judgment, ICJ Rep 1992, 240.

[188] ICJ Pleadings, *Certain Phosphate Lands in Nauru (Nauru v Australia)*, vol III (Joint letter of the Parties notifying the Court that they have agreed to discontinue the proceedings in the case concerning *Certain Phosphate Lands in Nauru (Nauru v Australia)*). See also Antony Anghie, '*Certain Phosphate Lands in Nauru*' (1993) 87(2) *AJIL* 282.

5

Normative Status of Self-Determination

a. Overview

The foregoing chapters in this part illustrated the evolution of self-determination in the post–Second World War international legal order. By virtue of its diversity of sources and uncertainty over its substantive content, the right to self-determination has generated extensive commentary and significant divergences of opinion as to its normative status.[1] To systematically analyse the normative character of self-determination, this chapter assesses in turn specific aspects of the development of self-determination in international law. First, this chapter considers the introduction of self-determination in the UN Charter as a principle and its subsequent emergence as a right. This chapter next distinguishes the ways in which the right to self-determination finds expression—and thereby imposes obligations upon States—under treaty law and CIL. This chapter then assesses the *erga omnes* character of obligations arising from the right to self-determination. Next, this chapter evaluates the right to self-determination as a peremptory norm of general international law (*jus cogens*). Finally, this chapter considers treatment of the right to self-determination as an 'inalienable right'.

b. From Principle to Right

The earliest appearance of self-determination in a formal source of international law took the form of a 'principle' in the UN Charter.[2] The Covenant

[1] For a survey of scholarship, see Matthew Saul, 'The Normative Status of Self-Determination in International Law: A Formula for Uncertainty in the Scope and Content of the Right?' (2011) 11(4) *Human Rights Law Review* 609.
[2] See Chapter 2.b.

The Right to Self-Determination in International Law. Thomas Weatherall, Oxford University Press.
 DOI: 10.1093/9780197798119.003.0006

of the League of Nations did not refer to self-determination and the principle, while recognized in the Aaland Islands arbitration, was not regarded as a rule of positive international law in the League of Nations system.[3] Articles 1 and 55 of the Charter refer to the principle of self-determination together with equal rights, i.e. 'the principle of equal rights and self-determination of peoples'.[4] Articles 1 and 55 address self-determination in relation to the purpose of the United Nations to develop friendly relations among nations. The *travaux préparatoires* of the Charter provides insight, albeit limited, into how drafters of the Charter understood the principle of self-determination.[5] The 1 June 1945 report of the relevant sub-committee of the drafting committee reflects the understanding that 'the principles of equal rights of people and that of self-determination are two component elements or one norm'.[6] The drafting committee, in its subsequent report of 13 June 1945, explained that it 'understands that the principle of equal rights of peoples and that of self-determination are two complementary parts of one standard of conduct'.[7] Description of the principle of self-determination as part of a 'norm' or 'standard of conduct' indicates the role that drafters of the Charter conceived self-determination to play within the UN system. To this description, the reports of the relevant drafting committee and sub-committee added that 'an essential element of the principle in question is a free and genuine expression of the will of the people'.[8] Taken together, the *travaux préparatoires* of the UN Charter indicates that self-determination, as a principle, consists of a norm or standard of conduct concerned with the free and genuine expression of the will of peoples.[9] Recognition of self-determination as a principle raises

[3] *Report submitted to the Council of the League of Nations by the Commission of Rapporteurs*, League of Nations Council Doc B7.21/68/106 (16 Apr 1921) 27; *Report of the International Committee of Jurists entrusted by the Council of the League of Nations with the task of giving an advisory opinion upon the legal aspects of the Aaland Islands Question*, (Oct 1920) *League of Nations Official Journal*, Special Supplement No 3, 5. See Chapter 1.c.

[4] See Chapter 2.b.i.

[5] Summary Report of Sixth Meeting of Committee I/1, Doc 343, I/1/16, in (1945) 6 *UN Conference on International Organization* 296; Report of Rapporteur, Subcommittee I/1/A, to Committee I/1, June 1, 1945, Doc 723, I/1/A/19, in (1945) 6 *UN Conference on International Organization* 696 (hereinafter 1 June 1945 Report); Report of Rapporteur of Committee 1 to Commission I, Doc 944, I/1/34(l), in (1945) 6 *UN Conference on International Organization* 446 (hereinafter 13 June 1945 Report).

[6] 1 June 1945 Report 703.

[7] 13 June 1945 Report 455.

[8] Ibid. See also 1 June 1945 Report 704.

[9] Antonio Cassese, *Self-Determination of Peoples: A Legal Reappraisal* (CUP 1995) 128–29.

the question of whether the principle constitutes a general principle of law within the meaning of Article 38(1)(c) of the ICJ Statute.[10]

In instruments addressing self-determination adopted after the UN Charter,[11] rights-oriented nomenclature took precedence over reference to self-determination as a principle. The drafting and formulation of early post-Charter instruments addressing self-determination—notably the two human rights covenants and the FRD, adopted by UNGA Resolution 2625—reflect the shift towards treatment of self-determination as a right, as distinct from but nevertheless based in self-determination as a principle in the Charter.

Not long after the UN Charter was adopted, work began in the UN Human Rights Commission on drafting the two human rights covenants.[12] UNGA Resolution 545 (VI), adopted on 5 February 1952, provided a prescriptive directive on the inclusion of a provision on the right to self-determination, one intended to reaffirm the principle of self-determination in the Charter.[13] The distinction between the principle of and right to self-determination was identified and debated at the UNGA Third Committee during drafting of the two human rights covenants.

> No attempt was being made to broaden or distort the provisions of the Charter. Self-determination was proclaimed as a principle in the Charter, but it was clear that any Member State which had accepted that *principle* was committed to respect the *right which derived from it*. Member States

[10] Statute of the International Court of Justice art 38(1)(c), XV UNCIO 355 (26 June 1945, entered into force 24 Oct 1945) (hereinafter ICJ Statute). *See* Cassese (n 9) 140; *Reference re Secession of Quebec* [1998] 2 SCR 217 para 114. *But see The Right to Self-Determination: Historical and Current Development on the Basis of United Nations Instruments* (Study prepared by Aureliu Cristescu, Special Rapporteur of the Sub-Commission on Prevention of Discrimination and Protection of Minorities), E/CN.4/Sub.2/404/Rev.1 (1981) (hereinafter *Cristescu Report* (1981)) paras 152–53.

[11] International Covenant on Civil and Political Rights art 1, 999 UNTS 171 (16 Dec 1966, entered into force 23 Mar 1976) (hereinafter ICCPR); International Covenant on Economic, Social and Cultural Rights art 1, 993 UNTS 3 (16 Dec 1966, entered into force 3 Jan 1976) (hereinafter ICESCR). See also A/Res/1514 (XV) (14 Dec 1960) (hereinafter Resolution 1514); A/Res/2625 (24 Oct 1970) Annex (hereinafter FRD) Principle V; Conference on Security and Cooperation in Europe: Final Act (1 Aug 1975), reproduced in (1975) 14(5) ILM 1292, Principle VIII; United Nations World Conference on Human Rights: Vienna Declaration and Programme of Action (25 June 1993), A/CONF/157/23 (12 July 1993), reproduced in (1993) 32(6) ILM 1661 (hereinafter Vienna Declaration (1993)) part I, s 2.

[12] See Chapter 2.c.

[13] A/Res/545 (VI) (5 Feb 1952).

> had already undertaken, therefore, in Articles 1 and 55, to respect the right of self-determination. Under Chapters XI and XII the Administering Powers were obliged to promote self-government or independence by taking into account the freely expressed wishes of the peoples of the Trust and Non-Self-Governing Territories.[14]

The Third Committee, in its treatment of self-determination as a right, contemplated the right as deriving from the principle of self-determination in the UN Charter, and sought to link the legal implications of such a right to relevant obligations already undertaken under the Charter by UN Member States.

A similar methodology—deriving the right to self-determination from the principle contained in the UN Charter—was applied during the drafting of the FRD.[15] The FRD, it may be recalled, was the product of a study of principles of international law concerning friendly relations and cooperation among States in relation to principles contained in the Charter. The principle of self-determination provided for in the Charter entails, according to the FRD, a right of peoples to self-determination. This relationship between the principle and right is explicit in paragraph 1 of Principle V (The principle of equal rights and self-determination of peoples):

> By virtue of the *principle* of equal rights and self-determination of peoples enshrined in the Charter of the United Nations, all peoples have the *right* freely to determine, without external interference, their political status and to pursue their economic, social and cultural development[.][16]

The drafting of common Article 1 of the two human rights covenants, and the text of the FRD, illustrate that the shift towards treatment of self-determination as a right was viewed in reference to, and as derived from, the principle of self-determination contained in the Charter.

[14] *Report of the Third Committee*, A/3077 (8 Dec 1955) (Draft International Covenants on Human Rights) para 37 (emphasis added).

[15] See Chapter 3.d.

[16] FRD Principle V, para 1 (emphasis added).

A corresponding shift in nomenclature is reflected in the jurisprudence of the ICJ. The first advisory opinion of the ICJ to explicitly address self-determination, *Namibia* (1971), referred to self-determination exclusively as a principle.[17] Next, in *Western Sahara* (1975), the ICJ referred to 'the principle of self-determination as a right of peoples'.[18] The usage of both terms by the ICJ in that advisory opinion appears to connote a distinction between the substance of self-determination as a principle (i.e. 'the need to pay regard to the freely expressed will of peoples') and the entitlement of a people to self-determination as a right. From 1995 onwards, ICJ judgments and opinions referring to self-determination more fully adopted a rights-oriented approach that largely superseded reference to the underlying principle. In *East Timor* (1995), the ICJ referred to 'the right of peoples to self-determination, as it evolved from the Charter and from United Nations practice',[19] thereby orienting the right to self-determination in the principle contained in the Charter, a linkage which the court restated in *The Wall* (2004).[20] In *Chagos Archipelago* (2019), the ICJ referred to the right to self-determination as 'a fundamental human right',[21] a formulation repeated in *Palestine* (2024), where the court also referred to the right to self-determination as 'an inalienable right'.[22] It is possible that the emerging status of the right to self-determination as a rule of CIL at the beginning of this period, a right also reflected in treaty law, informed the gradual embrace by the ICJ of a rights-oriented approach to self-determination.[23] In any case, this shift in the approach of the ICJ to self-determination may be

[17] *Legal Consequences for States of the Continued Presence of South Africa in Namibia (South West Africa) notwithstanding Security Council Resolution 276 (1970)*, Advisory Opinion, ICJ Rep 1971, 16 (hereinafter *Namibia* (1971)) para 52. See Chapter 4.b. It may be recalled that, in the arbitration of the Aaland Islands dispute, self determination was also regarded as a principle, albeit one not yet codified in positive international law. See Chapter 1.c.ii.

[18] *Western Sahara*, Advisory Opinion, ICJ Rep 1975, 12 (hereinafter *Western Sahara* (1975)) paras 54–59. See Chapter 4.c.

[19] *East Timor (Portugal v Australia)*, Judgment, ICJ Rep 1995, 90 (hereinafter *East Timor* (1995)) para 29.

[20] *Legal Consequences of the Construction of a Wall in the Occupied Palestinian Territory*, Advisory Opinion, ICJ Rep 2004, 136 (hereinafter *Wall* (2004)) para 156.

[21] *Legal Consequences of the Separation of the Chagos Archipelago from Mauritius in 1965*, Advisory Opinion, ICJ Rep 2019, 95 (hereinafter *Chagos* (2019)) para 144.

[22] *Legal Consequences arising from the Policies and Practices of Israel in the Occupied Palestinian Territory, including East Jerusalem*, Advisory Opinion, ICJ Rep 2024 (hereinafter *Palestine* (2024)) paras 233, 257.

[23] See Chapter 5.c.

viewed in relation to treatment of self-determination as a right in contemporaneous practice.[24]

Treatment of self-determination as a right, in contrast to a principle, is a distinction of legal import: while self-determination qua principle connotes a standard of conduct, self-determination qua right refers to a legal entitlement giving rise to concomitant obligations of States. Aureliu Cristescu, Special Rapporteur of the Sub-Commission on Prevention of Discrimination and Protection of Minorities, in his 1981 study of the right to self-determination in the UN system, took note of this development.

> It is clear that the relevant provisions of the Charter have been interpreted in an increasingly progressive spirit over the years. Today it is generally recognized that the concept of self-determination entails international legal rights and obligations and that a right of self-determination definitely exists.[25]

In 1984, the HRC made a similar observation in General Comment No 12, in reference to Article 1 of the ICCPR on the right to self-determination.[26] Given the legal implications of a distinction between principle and right, and in particular the enhanced legal force of a right as compared to a principle, it is perhaps unsurprising that the principle of self-determination has in practice largely been overtaken by the emergence of a right to self-determination in both treaty law and CIL.

Notwithstanding the emergence and development of self-determination as a right, the principle in the UN Charter is unaffected by the subsequent development of the right in treaty law and CIL.[27] As such, the principle of self-determination remains a 'norm' or 'standard of conduct' underpinning friendly relations amongst States in the UN Charter system and may yet be relevant to situations outside the scope of self-determination qua right.[28]

[24] Cf Stefan Talmon, 'Determining Customary International Law: The ICJ's Methodology between Induction, Deduction and Assertion' (2015) 26(2) *EJIL* 417, 440.

[25] *Cristescu Report* (1981) para 95.

[26] HRC, *CCPR General Comment No. 12: The Right to Self-Determination of Peoples (Art 1)* (1984) (hereinafter HRC GC 12) para 2.

[27] Gaetano Arangio-Ruiz, *The UN Declaration on Friendly Relations and the System of the Sources of International Law* (Sijthoff & Noordhoff 1979) s 52.

[28] See Cassese (n 9) 248–54.

c. Treaty and Customary International Law

The right to self-determination finds expression in both treaty law and CIL. It is axiomatic that, '[w]here a treaty states an obligation which also exists under customary international law, the treaty obligation and the customary law obligation remain separate and distinct'.[29] Accordingly, notwithstanding the crystallization of the right to self-determination in CIL, that source remains separate and distinct from the right to self-determination in treaty law. This distinction between sources of the right to self-determination is one of practical relevance as treaty-based obligations pertaining to the right to self-determination may not be in every instance identical to those arising under CIL.[30]

i. Treaty Law

The principal treaty-based source of the right to self-determination in international law is Article 1 common to the ICCPR and the ICESCR.[31] Together, common Article 1 of the two human rights covenants binds 177 of 197 members of the international community, indicating the significant proportion of States that have undertaken general treaty-based obligations related to the right to self-determination. As discussed above, treatment of self-determination as a right implies at once the imposition of obligations arising from the right and its enforceability as a matter of law.[32] The right to self-determination codified in treaty law provides an unambiguous source of that right, and associated obligations, in positive international law.[33]

[29] *Application of the Convention on the Prevention and Punishment of the Crime of Genocide (Croatia v Serbia)*, Judgment, ICJ Rep 2015, 3 para 88 (citing *Military and Paramilitary Activities in and against Nicaragua (Nicaragua v United States of America)*, Merits, Judgment, ICJ Rep 1986, 14).

[30] This distinction may be particularly relevant where instruments and jurisprudence of a regional character addressing the right to self-determination diverge from international instruments and customary international law.

[31] ICCPR art 1; ICESCR art 1. See Chapter 2.c.

[32] HRC GC 12 para 2.

[33] Regarding obligations, States responsible for the administration of NSGTs and Trust territories are subject to treaty-based obligations under the UN Charter directed towards the realization of self-determination. See Chapter 9.c.

At the regional level, several instruments refer to the right to self-determination.[34] The ACHPR, which at Article 20 imposes obligations upon States parties with respect to the right to self-determination, has generated a substantial jurisprudence owing to the practice of the African Commission on Human and Peoples' Rights and the ACtHPR.[35] At present, fifty-four States are parties to the ACHPR, which thereby provides a significant source of treaty-based obligations related to self-determination for those States. The Arab Charter on Human Rights also imposes obligations under the right to self-determination.[36] Although no Inter-American instrument establishes a right to self-determination as such,[37] Article 21 of the American Convention on Human Rights (ACHR; the Right to Property) has been interpreted to incorporate aspects of self-determination related to economic, social, and cultural development for members of Indigenous and tribal communities.[38] The content of regional instruments addressing self-determination is discussed in Chapter 2.

ii. Customary International Law

While the emergence of a right from the principle of self-determination reflects one shift in international consensus as to the character of self-determination, a second development of significance is the recognition of that right as CIL.[39] Unlike treaty law obligations arising from the right to self-determination, which bind only States that have expressly acceded to international agreements containing those obligations, 'the right to

[34] See Chapter 2.d.

[35] See Chapter 2.d.i; Chapter 12.c.i; Chapter 12.c.ii.

[36] See Chapter 2.d.ii.

[37] However, the Protocol of San Salvador refers to the right to self-determination in its preamble. Additional Protocol to the American Convention on Human Rights in the Area of Economic, Social, and Cultural Rights ('Protocol of San Salvador') preambular para 7, OAS Treaty Series No. 69 (17 Nov 1988, entered into force 16 Nov 1999), reproduced in (1989) 28(1) *ILM* 156. See Chapter 2.d.iii. The non-binding American Declaration on the Rights of Indigenous Peoples refers to the right of Indigenous Peoples to self-determination. See American Declaration on the Rights of Indigenous Peoples arts III, XXI(1), OAS AG/Res 2888 (XLVI-0/16) (15 June 2016). See Chapter 8.e.iii.1.

[38] See Chapter 12.c.iii; Chapter 12.c.iv.

[39] ICJ Statute art 38(1)(b).

self-determination crystalized as a customary rule binding on all States'.[40] While universality is often invoked as a hallmark of self-determination as a right of all peoples,[41] such universality was only realized with the crystallization of the right to self-determination in CIL. The ICJ had long applied the right to self-determination under CIL by implication through the *erga omnes* obligations arising from the right.[42] In *Chagos Archipelago* (2019), the court explicitly confirmed the status of the right to self-determination in CIL.[43] Today, it is beyond question that the right to self-determination has achieved the status of international custom, as evidence of a general practice accepted as law, within the meaning of Article 38(1)(b) of the ICJ Statute.[44]

CIL is the product of *opinio juris sive necessitatis* (belief of law or necessity) evidenced by the practice of States.[45] In *Chagos Archipelago* (2019), the ICJ evaluated the right to self-determination in CIL by identifying expressions of *opinio juris* and looking to its earliest evidence in State practice.[46]

To identify the *opinio juris* of the right to self-determination, the ICJ relied principally on UNGA Resolution 1514 (1960), common Article 1 of the two human rights covenants, and UNGA Resolution 2625 (1970) (the FRD). According to the ICJ, Resolution 1514 'clarifies the content and scope of the right to self-determination' in the field of decolonization.[47] The court referred to the 'declaratory' and 'normative' character of Resolution 1514 in support of its assessment that the resolution reflected the *opinio juris* of States.[48] Common Article 1 of the two human rights covenants, which codified the right to self-determination in treaty law, was regarded as

[40] *Chagos* (2019) para 148.

[41] See e.g. Draft International Covenants on Human Rights: Annotation, Prepared by the Secretary-General, A/2929 (1 July 1955) (hereinafter A/2929) ch IV para 7; HRC GC 12 para 2.

[42] *Wall* (2004) paras 88, 155–56; *East Timor* (1995) para 29; *Namibia* (1971) para 126. See Chapter 5.d.

[43] *Chagos* (2019) paras 144–61, especially para 148. See also *Palestine* (2024) para 237.

[44] Historically, this question has generated debate and uncertainty: see e.g. Stephen Allen, 'Self-Determination, the *Chagos Advisory Opinion* and the Chagossians' (2020) 69(1) *ICLQ* 203, 208–09. Cf C. Don Johnson, 'Toward Self-Determination—A Reappraisal as Reflected in the Declaration on Friendly Relations' (1973) 3 *Georgia Journal of International and Comparative Law* 145, 159; Rupert Emerson, 'Self-Determination' (1971) 65(3) *AJIL* 459, 461–62.

[45] *Nicaragua* (1986) paras 183–86; *North Sea Continental Shelf (Federal Republic of Germany v Denmark; Federal Republic of Germany v Netherlands)*, Judgment, ICJ Rep 1969, 3 para 77.

[46] *Chagos* (2019) paras 144–61, especially para 150.

[47] Ibid. See also *Palestine* (2024) paras 231, 241.

[48] *Chagos* (2019) paras 152–53.

'reaffirm[ing]' the right of all peoples to self-determination.[49] And the FRD, adopted by Resolution 2625, contains a provision on self-determination that, according to the ICJ, 'reiterated' the 'nature and scope of the right' and 'confirmed its normative character under customary international law'.[50] Each indicia of *opinio juris* identified by the ICJ to support its assessment of CIL is itself rooted in the principle of self-determination contained in the UN Charter.[51] The diversity of expressions of *opinio juris* relied upon by the ICJ to identify the right to self-determination in CIL evinces an undifferentiated legal rule of general application, i.e. a rule having 'a broad scope of application'.[52]

State practice immediately following the adoption of Resolution 1514, according to the ICJ, evidenced the crystallization of the right to self-determination in CIL. In the view of the court, Resolution 1514 represented a 'defining moment' with respect to State practice concerning the right to self-determination, in light of the pace at which decolonization progressed following its adoption.[53] Resolution 1514 was thus viewed as the point from which *opinio juris* was evidenced by the practice of States with respect to the right to self-determination, as confirmed in the field of decolonization. While the question of precisely when the right to self-determination crystallized in CIL is primarily historical, such a granular assessment of the formation of CIL was necessitated by the questions placed before the ICJ by the UNGA in reference to the Chagos Archipelago.[54] The inquiry by the ICJ in the *Chagos Archipelago* (2019) advisory opinion therefore offers particular insight into the acceptance by States of the right to self-determination as a rule of CIL.

[49] Ibid para 154. See also *Wall* (2004) para 88; *Palestine* (2024) para 233.

[50] *Chagos* (2019) para 155. See also *Wall* (2004) para 88; *Palestine* (2024) paras 231 ('recognized' the right), 241 ('reflected' the right) 255 ('reaffirmed' the right).

[51] See Resolution 1514 especially preambular para 1, para 1; A/Res/545 (VI) (5 Feb 1952) para 1 ('*Decides* to include in the International Covenant or Covenants on Human Rights an article on the right of all peoples and nations to self-determination in reaffirmation of the principle enunciated in the Charter of the United Nations'); FRD Principle V, para 1.

[52] *Chagos* (2019) para 144. See similarly *Palestine* (2024) para 234 (quoting *Chagos* (2019) para 144).

[53] *Chagos* (2019) para 150.

[54] See Chapter 4.g.

d. Obligations *Erga Omnes*

Obligations *erga omnes* ('towards all') are obligations owed by each State to the international community of States as a whole under CIL.[55] The ICJ first referred to the concept in *Barcelona Traction* (1970) and has since invoked the doctrine repeatedly.[56] In *Barcelona Traction* (1970), the ICJ defined obligations *erga omnes* by contrast to bilateral obligations, and linked such obligations to a limited category of rules of concern to the international community as a whole.

> In particular, an essential distinction should be drawn between the obligations of a State towards the international community as a whole, and those arising vis-à-vis another State in the field of diplomatic protection. By their very nature the former are the concern of all States. In view of the importance of the rights involved, all States can be held to have a legal interest in their protection; they are obligations *erga omnes*.[57]

The *erga omnes* character of an obligation is a function of the importance of the maintenance of the rule from which such an obligation derives and the common interest of States in its performance. The primary legal consequence of the *erga omnes* character of an obligation is a general legal interest in the performance of that obligation. As explained by the International Law Commission (ILC) in its commentary to the Articles on State Responsibility, 'the focus of obligations to the international community as a whole is

[55] Christian J. Tams, *Enforcing Obligations* Erga Omnes *in International Law* (CUP 2005); Maurizio Ragazzi, *The Concept of International Obligations* Erga Omnes (Clarendon Press 1997); André De Hoogh, *Obligations* Erga Omnes *and International Crimes* (Kluwer Law International 1996).

[56] *Barcelona Traction, Light and Power Company, Limited (Belgium v Spain)*, Judgment, ICJ Rep 1970, 3 (hereinafter *Barcelona Traction* (1970)) paras 33–34. See also *Namibia* (1971) para 126; *East Timor* (1995) para 29; *Application of the Convention on the Prevention and Punishment of the Crime of Genocide (Bosnia and Herzegovina v Yugoslavia)*, Preliminary Objections, Judgment, ICJ Rep 1996, 595 para 31; *Wall* (2004) paras 88, 155–56; *Armed Activities on the Territory of the Congo (New Application: 2002) (Democratic Republic of the Congo v Rwanda)*, Jurisdiction and Admissibility, Judgment, ICJ Rep 2006, 6 paras 64, 125; *Application of the Convention on the Prevention and Punishment of the Crime of Genocide (Bosnia and Herzegovina v Serbia and Montenegro)*, Judgment, ICJ Rep 2007, 43 para 147; *Chagos* (2019) para 180; *Palestine* (2024) para 232.

[57] *Barcelona Traction* (1970) para 33. See also para 34.

essentially on the legal interest of all States in compliance'.[58] Each State bound by an obligation *erga omnes* has a legal interest in the performance of such obligation by every other bound State. It is this 'legal indivisibility' of interest in their performance that distinguishes obligations *erga omnes* from other obligations in international law.[59]

The ICJ has on six occasions referred to the *erga omnes* concept in relation to self-determination.[60] The first such reference appeared in *Namibia* (1971), where the ICJ identified the consequences of the illegality of South Africa's presence in Namibia as having an *erga omnes* character.[61] This application of the *erga omnes* concept closely followed its earliest reference in *Barcelona Traction* (1970) and preceded much of the concept's substantive development. These judgments may be viewed as a recalibration by the court following its rejection of claims by Ethiopia and Liberia against South Africa in *South West Africa Cases* (1966). In that judgment, an evenly divided court (with the President casting the deciding vote) found that Ethiopia and Liberia had failed to establish 'any legal right or interest appertaining to them in the subject-matter' of its claims against South Africa concerning its obligations as a Mandatory Power under the Mandate for South West Africa.[62]

A degree of refinement of the *erga omnes* doctrine is clear from the way in which its treatment by the ICJ evolved across its decisions addressing self-determination. The ICJ next referred to the *erga omnes* concept in relation to self-determination in *East Timor* (1995), when confronted with the question of whether the principle requiring consent to the jurisdiction of the ICJ could be overcome by the *erga omnes* character of the rule at issue.[63] Although it responded in the negative, the ICJ viewed the right to self-determination to have an *erga omnes* character.

[58] ILC Draft Articles on Responsibility of States for Internationally Wrongful Acts ch III, Commentary para 7, UN Doc A/56/10, Report of the International Law Commission on the Work of its Fifty-Third Session, [2001] II(2) *YbILC* 26 et seq, UN Doc A/CN.4/SER.A/2001/Add.1 (Part 2) (hereinafter ILC ARSIWA).

[59] *Fourth Report on State Responsibility* (Gaetano Arangio-Ruiz, Special Rapporteur), A/CN.4/444 and Add. 1–3 (1992) para 92; *Fifth Report on State Responsibility* (Robert Ago, Special Rapporteur), A/CN.4/291 and Add.1 and 2 (1976) para 89.

[60] *Namibia* (1971) para 126; *East Timor* (1995) para 29; *Wall* (2004) paras 88, 155–56; *Chagos* (2019) para 180; *Palestine* (2024) paras 232, 274, 280.

[61] *Namibia* (1971) para 126.

[62] *South West Africa Cases (Ethiopia v South Africa; Liberia v South Africa)*, Second Phase, Judgment, ICJ Rep 1966, 6 (hereinafter *South West Africa Cases* (1966)) paras 99–100.

[63] *East Timor* (1995) para 29.

> In the Court's view, Portugal's assertion that the right of peoples to self-determination, as it evolved from the Charter and from United Nations practice, has an *erga omnes* character, is irreproachable. The principle of self-determination of peoples has been recognized by the United Nations Charter and in the jurisprudence of the Court; it is one of the essential principles of contemporary international law.[64]

The ICJ further refined its treatment of the *erga omnes* concept in relation to self-determination in *The Wall* (2004), where it reiterated its earlier conclusion in *East Timor* (1995) and referred to the obligation to respect the right to self-determination as an obligation *erga omnes*.[65]

> [T]the Court has already observed that in the *East Timor* case, it described as 'irreproachable' the assertion that 'the right of peoples to self-determination, as it evolved from the Charter and from United Nations practice, has an *erga omnes* character'.[66]

By the time the ICJ rendered its *Chagos Archipelago* (2019) advisory opinion, the nomenclature around the *erga omnes* concept, as well as its principal legal implication, had stabilized in the jurisprudence of the court. It found: 'Since respect for the right to self-determination is an obligation *erga omnes*, all States have a legal interest in protecting that right'.[67] This legal interest in the performance of obligations arising from the right to self-determination is the distinguishing feature and legal effect of their *erga omnes* character.

Other courts have recognized the *erga omnes* character of obligations arising from the right to self-determination. Pre-Trial Chamber 1 of the ICC, in identifying the right to self-determination as an 'internationally recognized human [right]' within the meaning of Article 21(3) of the ICC Statute, referred to ICJ jurisprudence establishing that 'the right to self-determination is owed *erga omnes*'.[68] The Court of Justice of the European Union (CJEU)

[64] Ibid (internal citations to *South West Africa* (1971) and *Western Sahara* (1975) omitted).
[65] *Wall* (2004) para 88.
[66] Ibid paras 155–56 (citations omitted).
[67] *Chagos* (2019) para 180. See also *Palestine* (2024) para 232.
[68] *Decision on the 'Prosecution request pursuant to article 19(3) for a ruling on the Court's territorial jurisdiction in Palestine'*, PTC I, ICC-01/18-143 (5 Feb 2021) paras 120–23 (citing *East Timor* (1995), *Wall* (2004)). See Chapter 11.e.iii.

referred to self-determination as 'a legally enforceable right *erga omnes* and one of the essential principles of international law'.[69] The ACtHPR has recognized the *erga omnes* character of obligations arising from the right to self-determination as obligations '*on all States*.... As such... all States have a legal interest in protecting that right'.[70] The High Court of Justice of England and Wales recognized the *erga omnes* character of obligations arising under the right to self-determination in litigation concerning Western Sahara.[71] Each court recognizing the *erga omnes* character of obligations arising from the right to self-determination relied upon statements by the ICJ. In this way, recognition of obligations *erga omnes* under the right to self-determination illustrates resonance of the jurisprudence of the ICJ across different judicial fora.

The legal effects and consequences of the *erga omnes* character of obligations arising under the right to self-determination in the areas of State responsibility,[72] and international dispute resolution,[73] are discussed respectively in Chapters 9 and 11.

i. Obligations *Erga Omnes Partes*

The associated concept of obligations *erga omnes partes* ('towards all parties') refers to obligations owed to all parties to a multilateral international agreement.[74] Obligations *erga omnes partes* in the law of treaties are analogous to

[69] Case C-104/16 *Council of the European Union vs Front populaire pour la libération de la saguia-el-hamra et du rio de oro (Front Polisario)*, Grand Chamber, Judgment (21 Dec 2016) para 88 (citing *East Timor* (1995)).

[70] *Bernard Anbataayela Mornah v Benin et al*, ACtHPR, No 028/2018, Judgment, para 298 (22 Sept 2022) (quoting *Chagos* (2019), citing also *Barcelona Traction* (1970), *East Timor* (1995)) (emphasis in original).

[71] *Western Sahara Campaign UK v Secretary of State for International Trade et al* [2022] EWHC 3108 (Admin) (hereinafter *Western Sahara Campaign II* (2022)) [132]–[133] (citing *East Timor* (1995), *Wall* (2004), *Chagos* (2019)).

[72] See Chapter 9.d.

[73] See Chapter 11.b.

[74] *Application of the International Convention on the Elimination of All Forms of Racial Discrimination (Azerbaijan v Armenia)*, Preliminary Objections, Judgment, ICJ Rep 2024, para 48; *Application of the Convention on the Prevention and Punishment of the Crime of Genocide in the Gaza Strip (South Africa v Israel)*, Provisional Measures, Order of 26 January 2024, ICJ Rep 2024, paras 33–34; *Application of the Convention against Torture and Other Cruel, Inhuman or Degrading Treatment or Punishment (Canada and Netherlands v Syrian Arab Republic)*, Provisional Measures, Order of 16 November 2023, ICJ Rep 2023, 587 paras 50–51, 57; *Application of the Convention on the Prevention and Punishment of the Crime of Genocide*

obligations *erga omnes* under CIL.[75] The *erga omnes partes* character of certain treaty-based obligations performs the same function in relation to those treaty obligations as the *erga omnes* character of obligations under CIL. The ICJ explained in *Prosecute or Extradite* (2012) that each State bound by an obligation *erga omnes partes* has a legal interest in the performance of such obligation by every other State subject to it.[76]

No court has squarely addressed whether treaty-based obligations arising from the right to self-determination in common Article 1 of the two human rights covenants constitute obligations *erga omnes partes*. However the HRC, in General Comment No 31, characterized obligations under the ICCPR as obligations *erga omnes partes*.[77] Moreover, common Article 1 reflects a common interest characteristic of obligations *erga omnes*.[78] In particular, the extraterritorial character of obligations under Article 1(3) to respect the right to self-determination and promote its realization implies a common interest in the performance of the obligations in Article 1.[79] During its drafting, Article 1(3) was understood to constitute a general obligation of all States to promote the realization of the right of self-determination and to respect that right.[80] As observed by the HRC in General Comment No 12, Article 1(3) 'imposes specific obligations on States parties, not only in relation to their own peoples but *vis-à-vis* all peoples which have not been able to exercise or have been deprived of the possibility of exercising their right to self-determination'.[81] In this way, common Article 1 of the two human

(The Gambia v Myanmar), Preliminary Objections, Judgment, ICJ Rep 2022, 477 paras 106–14; *Application of the Convention on the Prevention and Punishment of the Crime of Genocide (The Gambia v Myanmar)*, Provisional Measures, Order of 23 January 2020, ICJ Rep 2020, 3 para 41; *Questions relating to the Obligation to Prosecute or Extradite (Belgium v Senegal)*, Judgment, ICJ Rep 2012, 422 (hereinafter *Prosecute or Extradite* (2012)) para 68.

[75] *Fourth Report on State Responsibility* (Gaetano Arangio-Ruiz, Special Rapporteur), A/CN.4/444 and Add.1–3 (1992) para 92.

[76] *Prosecute or Extradite* (2012) para 68.

[77] HRC, *CCPR General Comment No 31 [80]: The Nature of the General Legal Obligation Imposed on States Parties to the Covenant*, CCPR/C/21/Rev.1/Add.13 (2004) para 2.

[78] See Saul (n 1) 632.

[79] See James Crawford, 'Opinion: Third Party Obligations with respect to Israeli Settlements in the Occupied Palestinian Territories' para 31 (24 Jan 2012) (In relation to similar language in Resolution 2625 (The FRD), observing: 'This is simply a statement that the principle of self-determination has an *erga omnes* character').

[80] A/2929 ch IV paras 16–18.

[81] HRC GC 12 para 6.

rights covenants assumes a common interest in the performance of obligations under the right to self-determination.[82] Moreover, the ICJ has regarded common Article 1 of the two human rights covenants to 'reaffirm[]' the right of all peoples to self-determination as evidence of its crystallization as a rule of CIL with an *erga omnes* character.[83] That common Article 1 informs obligations *erga omnes* arising from the right to self-determination under CIL at least implies the *erga omnes partes* character of common Article 1.

With respect to the ACHPR, the ACtHPR invoked the *erga omnes* character of obligations arising from the right to self-determination in the context of Article 20 of the ACHPR.[84]

e. *Jus Cogens*

Jus cogens ('compelling law') consists of peremptory norms of general international law 'accepted and recognized by the international community of States as a whole as [] norm[s] from which no derogation is permitted'.[85] The doctrine of *jus cogens* was codified by Articles 53 and 64 of the Vienna Convention on the Law of Treaties (1969), which established the illegality of treaties conflicting with peremptory norms of general international law. In particular, the 'Vienna Convention effects' of peremptory norms render a treaty null and void upon its conclusion that conflicts with a norm belonging to *jus cogens* and provide that, if a peremptory norm emerges with which a treaty in force conflicts, that treaty 'becomes void and terminates'.[86] The Vienna Convention thereby establishes that there are limits beyond which States may not conclude law. During the drafting of the law of treaties, *jus cogens* was understood to have broader structural implications in international law.[87] This is reflected in subsequent practice, in which there are exceedingly few examples of the invocation of Articles 53 and 64 of the Vienna Convention to invalidate a treaty.[88] Instead, peremptory norms—which

[82] See Chapter 2.c; Chapter 9.b.i.
[83] *Chagos* (2019) para 154. See also *Wall* (2004) para 88.
[84] *Mornah v Benin* (2022) para 298.
[85] Vienna Convention on the Law of Treaties art 53, 1155 UNTS 331 (23 May 1969, entered into force 27 Jan 1980) (hereinafter VCLT).
[86] Ibid arts 53, 64.
[87] Thomas Weatherall, Jus Cogens: *International Law and Social Contract* (CUP 2015) 3–8.
[88] Ibid 86–89.

permit derogation by no subject of international law—are violated as a practical matter by individual conduct rather than international agreements between States.[89]

Jus cogens is closely related to obligations *erga omnes* and it has been observed that obligations *erga omnes* are 'virtually coextensive' with *jus cogens*.[90] Functionally, however, the legal implications of the *erga omnes* character of an obligation and the *jus cogens* status of a norm are distinct. As explained by James Crawford in his capacity as ILC special rapporteur on State responsibility:

> In the context of peremptory norms the emphasis is on the primary rule itself and its non-derogable or overriding status. . . . By contrast, the emphasis with obligations to the international community is on the universality of the obligation and the persons or entities to whom it is owed, specifically all States and other legal entities which are members of that community.[91]

While in practice there appears to be a causal relationship between the category of *jus cogens* and obligations *erga omnes*, such that the former gives rise to the latter, the inverse of this relation does not necessarily follow.[92] It is against this backdrop that the general endorsement of the *erga omnes* character of obligations under the right to self-determination has not been matched by consensus as to the *jus cogens* status of the right.[93]

[89] Alexander Orakhelashvili, *Peremptory Norms in International Law* (OUP 2008) 205–08; Thomas Weatherall, *Duality of Responsibility in International Law: The Individual, the State, and International Crimes* (Brill Nijhoff 2022) 38–46.

[90] *Third Report on State Responsibility* (James Crawford, Special Rapporteur), A/CN.4/507 and Add.1–4 (2000) para 106(a); *Fourth Report on State Responsibility* (James Crawford, Special Rapporteur), A/CN.4/517 and Add.1 (2001) para 49 ('Thus even if the two are not different aspects of the one underlying idea, the two substantially overlap').

[91] *Fourth Report on State Responsibility* (James Crawford, Special Rapporteur), A/CN.4/517 and Add.1 (2001) para 49.

[92] 'Draft conclusions on identification and legal consequences of peremptory norms of general international law (*jus cogens*), with commentaries', A/77/10 (hereinafter ILC *Jus Cogens* Draft Conclusions) Conclusion 17 and Commentary para 3.

[93] Saul (n 1) 635 ('There simply has not been sufficient agreement amongst states to establish this proposal as a point of law'); James J. Summers, 'The Status of Self-determination in International Law: A Question of Legal Significance or Political Importance' (2003) 14 *Finnish Yearbook of International Law* 271, 283–88; James Summers, *Peoples and International Law* (2nd edn, Brill Nijhoff 2014) 78–84. Cf Cassese (n 9) 140; D. W. Greig, 'Reflections on the Role of Consent' (1992) 12(1) *Australian Year Book of International Law* 125, 155–57. Compare James Crawford, *The Creation of States in International Law* (1st edn, OUP 1979) 81 ('[T]he suggestion'

i. The International Court of Justice

One indication of the lack of acceptance and recognition of the *jus cogens* status of the right to self-determination is the jurisprudence of the ICJ.[94] Although the ICJ has repeatedly referred to the *erga omnes* concept in relation to self-determination,[95] in no instance has it referred to the right to self-determination as belonging categorically to *jus cogens*. One UK court has drawn a negative inference from this disparate treatment by the ICJ.[96] The lack of recognition of the *jus cogens* status of the right to self-determination by the ICJ in *Chagos Archipelago* (2019) is of particular significance. Had the right to self-determination been found to belong to *jus cogens*, that finding would have given rise to specific legal consequences under the Vienna Convention that would have substantively impacted the advice of the court, given that the underlying sovereignty dispute over the Chagos Archipelago was predicated upon an international agreement.[97] In subsequent domestic proceedings concerning the Chagos Archipelago, a different UK court took note of the legal import of this omission.[98] The impact of the normative status of the right to self-determination on the advice of the ICJ in *Chagos Archipelago* (2019) was also raised by several judges in their separate opinions.[99]

In *Palestine* (2024), the ICJ stated that it 'considers that, in cases of foreign occupation such as the present case, the right to self-determination constitutes a peremptory norm of international law'.[100] The court devoted only this single line to the peremptory character of the right to self-determination in such cases of foreign occupation. The court did not, however, explain the

that self-determination belongs to *jus cogens* 'is difficult to accept') and James Crawford, *The Creation of States in International Law* (2nd edn, OUP 2006) 101 ('To this list [of *jus cogens* norms] we must now add self-determination').

---

94 Weatherall (n 87) 250–53. Cf *Palestine* (2024) para 233 (discussed infra).

95 See Chapter 5.d.

96 *Western Sahara Campaign II* (2022) [132]–[133], [156] (citing *East Timor* (1995), *Wall* (2004), and *Chagos* (2019)).

97 See Chapter 4.g.

98 *R (Hoareau and Bancoult) v Secretary of State for Foreign and Commonwealth Affairs* [2020] EWCA Civ 1010 [133]–[134].

99 See *Chagos* (2019), Sep Op Robinson paras 83–88; Sep Op Sebutinde para 45; Sep Op Cançado-Trindade paras 168–69. Cf Allen (n 44) 220 (describing this omission as a 'missed opportunity').

100 *Palestine* (2024) para 233. See Chapter 4.h.

meaning of this conditional treatment of the right to self-determination or its implications.[101] Nor did the court ascribe any legal consequence to this consideration in the advisory opinion.[102] These aspects of the statement suggest that it may be viewed as *obiter dictum*.[103] Elsewhere, the court contemplated consequences arising from the right to self-determination 'in view of its character as an inalienable right'.[104]

ii. The International Law Commission

The ILC has referred to self-determination in the context of *jus cogens* on several occasions. One early reference to self-determination appears in commentary to the Draft Articles on the Law of Treaties, where the ILC noted, without apparent endorsement, that 'treaties violating human rights, the equality of States or the principle of self-determination were mentioned as other possible examples' of those conflicting with peremptory norms.[105] During the first session of the UN Conference on the Law of Treaties, Sir Humphry Waldock, the final special rapporteur on the law of treaties then serving as Expert Consultant to the conference, clarified the position of the ILC as viewing self-determination not to belong to *jus cogens*.

> The question of illegality was dealt with in the two articles treating of *jus cogens*. The question of self-determination was also covered in the commentary. In the Commission's view, self-determination was an independent principle which belonged to another branch of international law and which had its own conditions and problems.[106]

[101] *Palestine* (2024) Sep Op Cleveland para 31; Decl Xue para 5.
[102] Ibid Decl Tladi para 28.
[103] See ibid Sep Op Cleveland para 35.
[104] *Palestine* (2024) paras 233, 257. See Chapter 5.f.
[105] Draft Articles on the Law of Treaties with Commentaries, Draft Article 50 Commentary para 3, *Reports of the International Law Commission on the Second Part of its Seventeenth Session (3–28 January 1966) and on its Eighteenth Session (4 May-19 July 1966)*, A/6309/Rev.1, [1966] II *YbILC* 187, 248, A/CN.4/SER.A/1966/Add.1.
[106] United Nations Conference on the Law of Treaties, First Session (Vienna, 26 March–24 May 1968), *Summary records of the plenary meetings and of the meetings of the Committee of the Whole*, A/CONF.39/11 (1969) 381 para 31 (Sixty-Fifth Meeting, 11 May 1968).

In the context of codification of the doctrine of *jus cogens* in the law of treaties, then, the ILC adopted the view that self-determination fell outside the category.

Subsequent projects by the ILC shifted to support the *jus cogens* status of the right to self-determination. In its commentary to the Articles on State Responsibility, the ILC twice referred to self-determination as belonging to *jus cogens* in reference to *East Timor* (1995), although that judgment does not refer to the *jus cogens* status of the right to self-determination.[107] Later, citing this commentary, in its Report of the Study Group on the Fragmentation of International Law, the ILC referred again to the *jus cogens* status of the right to self-determination.[108] Finally, the Draft Conclusions on Peremptory Norms of General International Law (*Jus Cogens*) include an annex consisting of a non-exhaustive list of some of the norms that the ILC previously referred to as belonging to *jus cogens*, which includes the right to self-determination on the basis of the foregoing references.[109] The ILC did not, however, support its assertions of the *jus cogens* status of the right to self-determination by analysing *opinio juris* and State practice indicating that the right had been 'accepted and recognized by the international community of States as a whole as a norm from which no derogation is permitted'.[110]

iii. Other Authorities

Other authorities are mixed on the question of the *jus cogens* status of the right to self-determination. For instance, Héctor Gros Espiell, as Special

[107] ILC ARSIWA art 26, Commentary para 5; ibid art 40, Commentary para 5 ('the obligation to respect the right of self-determination deserves to be mentioned').

[108] Conclusions of the work of the Study Group on the Fragmentation of International Law: Difficulties arising from the Diversification and Expansion of International Law, Conclusion 33, *Report of the International Law Commission on the work of its fifty-eighth session*, para 251, A/61/10, [2006] II(2) *YbILC* 177, 182 (citing ILC ARSIWA, Commentary to Article 40); *Fragmentation of International Law: Difficulties arising from the diversification and expansion of International Law, Report of the Study Group on the Fragmentation of International Law* (finalized by Martti Koskenniemi), para 374, A/CN.4/L.682 (13 Apr 2006) (same).

[109] ILC *Jus Cogens* Draft Conclusions, Annex para h.

[110] VCLT art 53. For critical commentary, see Sean D. Murphy, 'Current Developments: Peremptory Norms of General International Law (*Jus Cogens*) and Other Topics: The Seventy-First Session of the International Law Commission' (2020) 114(1) *AJIL* 68, 71–72.

Rapporteur of the Sub-Commission on Prevention of Discrimination and Protection of Minorities, in his 1980 study *The Right to Self-Determination: Implementation of United Nations Resolutions*, assigned *jus cogens* status to the right to self-determination, but did so on the basis of natural law rather than State practice.[111] By contrast, the following year, Aureliu Cristescu, as Special Rapporteur of the Sub-Commission on Prevention of Discrimination and Protection of Minorities, in his 1981 study *The Right to Self-Determination: Historical and Current Development on the Basis of United Nations Instruments*, concluded that '[n]o United Nations instrument confers such a peremptory character on the right of peoples to self-determination.'[112]

In 2022, the ACtHPR, in a case considering whether admission of Morocco into the African Union violated the right to self-determination of the people of Western Sahara, 'observe[d] that . . . the right to self-determination has achieved the status of *jus cogens* or a peremptory norm', without further analysis or citation to authority.[113] By contrast, the same year, a UK court in a case concerning whether specific economic measures afforded to Morocco violated the right to self-determination of the people of Western Sahara, after consideration of State practice and ICJ jurisprudence regarding the status of the right to self-determination in international law, concluded that 'the right to self-determination is not a *jus cogens* norm.'[114]

These sharp divergences are reflected in scholarship, with corresponding differences in opinion as to whether the right to self-determination or certain of its aspects may properly be regarded as belonging to *jus cogens*.[115]

[111] *The Right to Self-Determination: Implementation of United Nations Resolutions* (Study prepared by Héctor Gros Espiell, Special Rapporteur of the Sub-Commission on Prevention of Discrimination and Protection of Minorities), E/CN.4/Sub.2/405/Rev.1 (1980) paras 70–86. See Saul (n 1) 637.

[112] *Cristescu Report* (1981) para 154.

[113] *Mornah v Benin* (2022) para 298.

[114] *Western Sahara Campaign II* (2022) [132]–[133], [156] (citing *East Timor* (1995), *Wall* (2004), and *Chagos* (2019)). See similarly *R (Hoareau and Bancoult) v Secretary of State for Foreign and Commonwealth Affairs* [2020] EWCA Civ 1010 [133]–[134].

[115] Saul (n 1) 634–41 (surveying scholarship). See supra n 702.

iv. State Practice

The foregoing divergences regarding the *jus cogens* status of the right to self-determination—from assertion, to silence, with a degree of rejection—are similarly reflected in the practice of States. State practice is critical to assessing the *jus cogens* status of a norm because peremptory norms are those 'recognized and accepted' as such 'by the international community *of States* as a whole'.[116] While unanimity is not necessary to satisfy this standard, recognition and acceptance by a very large majority of States is required to establish the *jus cogens* status of a norm.[117] In this regard, it has been observed that 'it cannot be said that there is a sufficient degree of consistent state practice for it to be possible to say that it is *opinio juris* that the right to self-determination is a peremptory norm'.[118] Instances in which States have been provided with clear opportunities to provide views on the *jus cogens* status of the right to self-determination appear to reflect this assessment, though States have become increasingly more willing to express support for the *jus cogens* status of the right to self-determination.[119]

f. An Inalienable Right

The right to self-determination is characterized across a range of authorities as 'an inalienable right'. It has been observed that, '[i]n the context of decolonization, the General Assembly has repeatedly emphasized the significance of the right to self-determination as an "inalienable right"'.[120] The UNGA has adopted a similar formulation outside the context of decolonization.[121] The UNSC has also referred to the right to self-determination as an 'inalienable right'.[122] The corollary entitlement of peoples to freely dispose of their

[116] VCLT art 53 (emphasis added).
[117] ILC *Jus Cogens* Draft Conclusions, Conclusion 7(2). See Weatherall (n 87) 28–29.
[118] *Western Sahara Campaign II* (2022) [137]. See similarly Saul (n 1).
[119] This is reflected in the submissions by States during the drafting of the VCLT, FRD, and ILC *Jus Cogens* Draft Conclusions, as well as to the ICJ in advisory proceedings concerning self-determination.
[120] *Palestine* (2024) para 233 (citing A/Res/40/25 (29 Nov 1985) para 3; A/Res/42/14 (6 Nov 1987) para 4; A/Res/49/40 (9 Dec 1994) para 1). See similarly Resolution 1514 preambular para 11.
[121] See e.g. A/Res/2131 (XX) (21 Dec 1965) paras 5–6.
[122] See e.g. S/Res/384 (22 Dec 1975); S/Res/389 (22 Apr 1976).

natural wealth and resources has similarly been regarded as an inalienable right.[123] The HRC, in General Comment No 12, referred to paragraphs 1 and 2 of Article 1 (the right to self-determination) common to the two human rights covenants as 'enshrin[ing] an inalienable right of all peoples'.[124] The Vienna Declaration (1993) similarly refers to the 'inalienable right of self-determination'.[125] The right of Indigenous Peoples to self-determination has also been regarded as an inalienable right.[126] At the regional level, Article 20 of the ACHPR imposes obligations upon State parties with respect to 'the unquestionable and inalienable right to self-determination'.[127] The ICJ described the right to self-determination as an inalienable right in *Palestine* (2024).[128]

The legal implications of the inalienability of the right to self-determination are underdeveloped in practice. In *Palestine* (2024), the court considered that an effect of this character of the right is that it 'cannot be subject to conditions'.[129] This concept of the inalienability of the right may provide an analog to the non-derogability of the prohibitions recognized and accepted as peremptory norms. Put differently, non-derogability is well-suited to negative rules (i.e. prohibitions) but may conceptually be less suitable for positive rules (i.e. rights). In view of this distinction, the inalienability of the right to self-determination may provide a functional parallel to the non-derogability characteristic of peremptory norms.

[123] Hans Corell, Letter dated 29 January 2002 from the Under-Secretary-General for Legal Affairs, the Legal Counsel, addressed to the President of the Security Council, S/2002/161 (12 Feb 2002) para 22. See e.g. A/Res/61/123 (14 Dec 2006) para 9.

[124] HRC GC 12 para 2.

[125] Vienna Declaration (1993) part 1, s 2, para 2.

[126] *Sanila-Aikio v Finland*, Communication No 2668/2015, CCPR/C/124/D/2668/2015 (20 Mar 2019) para 6.8; *Käkkäläjärvi et al v Finland*, Communication No 2950/2017, CCPR/C/124/D/2950/2017 (18 Dec 2019) para 9.8.

[127] African [Banjul] Charter on Human and Peoples' Rights art 20, OAU Doc CAB/LEG/67/3/Rev.5, 1520 UNTS 217 (27 June 1981, entered into force 21 Oct 1986).

[128] *Palestine* (2024) paras 233, 257.

[129] Ibid para 257.

PART II
CONTENT

Part II surveys the content of the right to self-determination in international law. It contains chapters addressing 'peoples' as the subjects and beneficiaries of the right to self-determination, the international (or 'external') aspect of self-determination, the domestic (or 'internal') aspect of self-determination, and the obligations of States arising from or otherwise related to the right to self-determination.

6

Peoples

Subjects and Beneficiaries of the Right to Self-Determination

a. Overview

Self-determination, as both a principle and right under international law, is defined as applying to 'peoples'.[1] The right to self-determination, as one inuring to peoples, is a collective right.[2] This construct suggests that a people, as

[1] Charter of the United Nations arts 1(2), 55, XV UNCIO 335 (26 June 1945, entered into force 24 Oct 1945) (hereinafter UN Charter); International Covenant on Civil and Political Rights art 1, 999 UNTS 171 (16 Dec 1966, entered into force 23 Mar 1976) (hereinafter ICCPR); International Covenant on Economic, Social and Cultural Rights art 1, 993 UNTS 3 (16 Dec 1966, entered into force 3 Jan 1976) (hereinafter ICESCR). See also African [Banjul] Charter on Human and Peoples' Rights art 20, OAU Doc CAB/LEG/67/3/Rev.5, 1520 UNTS 217 (27 June 1981, entered into force 21 Oct 1986); Arab Charter on Human Rights art 1, [ST/HR/]CHR/NONE/2004/40/Rev.1 (22 May 2004, entered into force 15 Mar 2008); Additional Protocol to the American Convention on Human Rights in the Area of Economic, Social, and Cultural Rights ('Protocol of San Salvador') preambular para 7, OAS Treaty Series No. 69 (17 Nov 1988, entered into force 16 Nov 1999), reproduced in (1989) 28(1) ILM 156; A/Res/1514 (XV) (14 Dec 1960) (hereinafter Resolution 1514) para 2; A/Res/2625 (24 Oct 1970) Annex (hereinafter FRD) Principle V, para 1; Conference on Security and Cooperation in Europe: Final Act (1 Aug 1975), reproduced in (1975) 14(5) ILM 1292 (hereinafter Helsinki Final Act (1975)) Principle VIII para 2; United Nations World Conference on Human Rights: Vienna Declaration and Programme of Action (25 June 1993), A/CONF/157/23 (12 July 1993), reproduced in (1993) 32(6) ILM 1661 (hereinafter Vienna Declaration (1993)) part I, s 2, para 1. See *Legal Consequences of the Separation of the Chagos Archipelago from Mauritius in 1965*, Advisory Opinion, ICJ Rep 2019, 95 (hereinafter *Chagos* (2019)) paras 146–48, 152–55; *Legal Consequences for States of the Continued Presence of South Africa in Namibia (South West Africa) notwithstanding Security Council Resolution 276 (1970)*, Advisory Opinion, ICJ Rep 1971, 16 (hereinafter *Namibia* (1971)) para 52; HRC, *CCPR General Comment No. 12: The Right to Self-Determination of Peoples (Art 1)* (1984) (hereinafter HRC GC 12) paras 1–2.

[2] *Report of the Third Committee*, A/3077 (8 Dec 1955) (Draft International Covenants on Human Rights) (hereinafter A/3077) paras 34, 40. See e.g. *Lubicon Lake Band v Canada*, Communication No 167/1984, CCPR/C/38/D/167/1984 (1990) para 13.3. See similarly *The Social and Economic Rights Action Center for Economic and Social Rights v Nigeria*, ACommHPR, Communication No 155/96 para 40 (2001). See also Manfred Nowak, *UN Covenant on Civil and Political Rights: CCPR Commentary* (2nd edn, N. P. Engel 2005) paras 15–17.

The Right to Self-Determination in International Law. Thomas Weatherall, Oxford University Press.
 DOI: 10.1093/9780197798119.003.0007

the subject of the right to self-determination, enjoys legal personality separate and distinct from that of the individuals that comprise it or the territorial unit (e.g. the State) of whose population it consists.[3] This differentiation of peoples as legal subjects, distinct from both territorial units and individuals for purposes of the right to self-determination, follows from the specific content of the right. It has been observed that the legal personality of peoples in international law is a product of the development of the right to self-determination.[4] The ICJ has considered that, 'by virtue of the right to self-determination, a people is protected against acts aimed at dispersing the population and undermining its integrity as a people'.[5]

This chapter begins by considering the absence of a constitutive definition of 'peoples' in international law. The second section identifies the close relationship between the right to self-determination and sovereignty over territory, and the way in which peoples have, in practice, been defined in relation to territorial units entitled to self-government. The subsequent section assesses the populations of States, and Non-Self-Governing Territories and Trust Territories, as generally accepted categories of peoples for purposes of the right to self-determination. The final section of this chapter addresses the situation of minority groups (i.e. ethnic, religious, and linguistic minorities), which are generally not regarded as peoples for purposes of the right to self-determination, and Indigenous Peoples.

b. Absence of a Definition of 'Peoples'

Despite the clarity with which international law defines self-determination as a right belonging to peoples, no instrument codifying the right to

[3] For an explicit recognition of this distinction, see UNESCO, *Final Report and Recommendations*, International Meeting of Experts on further study of the concept of the rights of peoples (Paris, 27–30 Nov 1989), UNESCO Doc SHS-89/CONF.602/7 (1990) (hereinafter *UNESCO Report*) para 29. This distinct legal personality is reflected in the inability of an individual to bring a claim on behalf of a people against a State before the HRC under ICCPR Article 1 through the individual complaint mechanism of the ICCPR Optional Protocol. See Chapter 12.b.i.

[4] Nico Schrijver, *Sovereignty over Natural Resources: Balancing Rights and Duties* (CUP 1997) 7.

[5] *Legal Consequences arising from the Policies and Practices of Israel in the Occupied Palestinian Territory, including East Jerusalem*, Advisory Opinion, ICJ Rep 2024 (hereinafter *Palestine* (2024)) para 239.

self-determination contains a definition of 'peoples' for purposes of the right.[6] Unsurprisingly, this omission has contributed to 'doctrinal debates . . . [that] have no end in sight'.[7] The breadth of possible meanings that could be ascribed to the term 'peoples' for purposes of the right to self-determination is illustrated by the *travaux préparatoires* of the two human rights covenants.

> With regard to the word 'peoples', it was said that no distinction should be made on the grounds that peoples were under the sovereignty of another country, that they lived in a particular continent, that they were independent territories or were within the territory of a sovereign State.
>
> [] It was also suggested that 'peoples' should be interpreted to mean all peoples that could exercise the right of self-determination, that such a people should inhabit a compact territory and that its members should be related ethnically or in some other way.
>
> [] Other views were that 'peoples' should apply to large compact national groups; that the right of self-determination should be granted only to those who made a conscious demand for it; and that peoples who were politically undeveloped should be placed under the protection of the International Trusteeship System, which would prepare them for the exercise of the right of self-determination.[8]

In the context of the two human rights covenants, it was ultimately 'thought, however, that the term "peoples" should be understood in its most general sense and that no definition was necessary'.[9]

The complexity of the term 'peoples' is further reflected in the *travaux préparatoires* of the FRD, in which different aspects and challenges were identified by representatives at the 1968 session of the Special Committee

[6] *Reference re Secession of Quebec* [1998] 2 SCR 217 (hereinafter *Quebec* (1998)) para 123. See similarly *ACHPR v Kenya*, ACtHPR, Application No 006/2012, Judgment (2017) (hereinafter *ACHPR v Kenya* (2017)) para 196.

[7] Matthew Saul, 'The Normative Status of Self-Determination in International Law: A Formula for Uncertainty in the Scope and Content of the Right?' (2011) 11(4) *Human Rights Law Review* 609, 611.

[8] See Commission on Human Rights, *Report to the Economic and Social Council on the eighth session of the Commission, held in New York, from 14 April to 14 June 1952*, E/2256 paras 41–43.

[9] Draft International Covenants on Human Rights: Annotation, Prepared by the Secretary-General, A/2929 (1 July 1955) (hereinafter A/2929) ch IV para 9.

on Principles of International Law concerning Friendly Relations and Co-Operation among States established by the UNGA.

> Several representatives stressed that difficulties arose in arriving at a precise definition of 'peoples'. The identification of a unique 'people' to whom the principle applied, could present extremely complex problems. The difficulty, one representative said, was easier to settle in a colonial context, where there had never been any difficulty in determining whether a given territory's population could, or could not, be regarded as having sufficient identity to claim the right of self-determination.
>
> [] Some representatives considered that the right of self-determination was reserved to all peoples, since the Charter used the term a number of times, particularly in the preamble, as a synonym for nations or States. Other representatives attached certain qualifications to be fulfilled if an ethnic entity was to be recognized to have an inherent right to exercise equal rights and self-determination. One representative considered a formulation based on the term 'organized people'. Another representative was of the opinion that a rule should be adopted in accordance with which the principle would be presumed to be satisfied by the existence of a sovereign and independent State possessing representative Government, effectively functioning as such to all distinct peoples within its territory. According to another representative, the principle of self-determination should be limited to political units already defined as countries or colonies. In practice, self-determination should not go to the extent of creating an entity without political or economic viability and should not deprive a State of its economic base.
>
> [] Some representatives stated that the principle should serve rather to unite peoples on a voluntary and democratic basis than to dismember existing national entities. Any formulation of the principle should be avoided which might be interpreted as widening the scope of the principle and making it applicable to peoples already forming part of an independent sovereign State.[10]

[10] A/7326 (1968) paras 162–64.

Like the two human rights covenants, the FRD does not include a definition of 'peoples' for purposes of the right to self-determination.

At first blush, the absence of an accepted legal definition of 'peoples' for purposes the right to self-determination seems difficult to reconcile with the extensive treatment of the right in international law and accompanying practice. However, this practice, including the crystallization of the right of peoples to self-determination as a rule of CIL, in the absence of an accepted legal definition of 'peoples' indicates that practice is not dependent upon the application of a constitutive definition to identify the subjects of the right.

c. Peoples as the Populations of Territorial Units

The development of the right to self-determination in international law notwithstanding the absence of a definition of 'peoples' can be explained by the close practical relationship between peoples and territory.[11] UNGA Resolution 1514, which in the view of the ICJ represented a 'defining moment' in the crystallization of the right to self-determination in CIL,[12] includes language addressing the territorial implications of the right to self-determination. Most illustrative for present purposes is the preamble of the resolution, which states that 'all peoples have an inalienable right to complete freedom, the exercise of their sovereignty and the integrity of their national territory', indicating an overarching linkage between peoples and territorial sovereignty. While this approach to the delineation of peoples is not without tensions,[13] practice suggests a complementary relationship between the right to self-determination and the principle of territorial integrity.[14] In *Chagos Archipelago* (2019) and *Palestine* (2024), the ICJ characterized territorial integrity as 'a corollary' of the right to self-determination.[15] In

[11] Rosalyn Higgins, *The Development of International Law Through the Political Organs of the United Nations* (OUP 1963) 104; Malcolm N. Shaw, 'Peoples, Territorialism and Boundaries' (1997) 3 *EJIL* 478, 479; James Crawford, *The Creation of States in International Law* (2nd edn, OUP 2006) 115–27. See Chapter 7.d.ii.

[12] *Chagos* (2019) para 150.

[13] See Chapter 7.d.ii.

[14] See e.g. *Bernard Anbataayela Mornah v Benin et al*, ACtHPR, Application No 028/2018, Judgment (22 Sept 2022) (hereinafter *Mornah v Benin* (2022)) para 301.

[15] *Chagos* (2019) para 160; *Palestine* (2024) para 237 (citing *Chagos* (2019) para 160). See Theodore Christakis, 'Self-Determination, Territorial Integrity and *Fait Accompli* in the Case

particular, the ICJ considered that a people is entitled to exercise its right to self-determination over its territorial unit as a whole, itself a corollary of the proposition that the entire population of a territorial unit (i.e. the people as a whole) is entitled to exercise the right to self-determination.[16] The development of the right to self-determination within the framework of, and in reference to, the principle of territorial integrity accounts for the application of the right in the absence of a definition of 'peoples' in international law through what may be characterized as a territorial approach.[17]

In practice, peoples have been understood in relation to specific categories of 'territorial units'.[18] This approach is based in the principal international instruments—the UN Charter and the two human rights covenants—that respectively codified self-determination as a principle and as a right in international law. While the UN Charter does not define 'peoples' for purposes of the principle of self-determination in Articles 1 and 55, the term 'peoples' appears in the Charter in reference the populations of three distinct categories of territorial units: States,[19] NSGTs,[20] and Trust Territories.[21] Similarly, common Article 1 of the two human rights covenants provides that the right to self-determination is enjoyed by *all* peoples but lacks a definition of 'peoples'.[22] However, during the drafting of the two human right covenants, the

of Crimea' (2015) 75 *Zeitschrift für ausländisches öffentliches Recht und Völkerrecht* 75, 76; Jamie Trinidad, *Self-Determination in Disputed Colonial Territories* (CUP 2018) 239.

[16] See Chapter 8.

[17] Proposed definitions of 'peoples' for purposes of the right to self-determination also reflect a linkage to territory. For one example, see *The Right to Self-Determination: Historical and Current Development on the Basis of United Nations Instruments* (Study prepared by Aureliu Cristescu, Special Rapporteur of the Sub-Commission on Prevention of Discrimination and Protection of Minorities), E/CN.4/Sub.2/404/Rev.1 (1981) (hereinafter *Cristescu Report* (1981)) para 279. See also *UNESCO Report* para 22. The definition of a NSGT necessarily implies its people's linkage to territory: see A/Res/1541 (XV) (15 Dec 1960) (hereinafter Resolution 1541) Annex, Principle IV.

[18] Crawford (n 11) 115–27, especially 126 ('At the root, the question of defining "people" concerns identifying the categories of territory to which the principle of self-determination applies as a matter of right. Practice identifies such categories plainly enough'); Higgins (n 11) 104 ('Self-determination refers to the right of the majority within a generally accepted political unit to the exercise of power'). For use of the term 'territorial unit' in this regard, see e.g. *Palestine* (2024) paras 78, 262.

[19] UN Charter preambular para 1, arts 1(2), 55. See Hans Kelsen, *The Law of the United Nations* (London Institute of World Affairs 1950) 51.

[20] UN Charter art 73.

[21] Ibid arts 76(b), 80.

[22] A/2929 ch IV paras 8–9; A/3077 para 39. See HRC GC 12 paras 1–2.

term 'peoples' 'was understood to mean peoples in all countries and territories, whether independent, trust or non-self-governing',[23] an understanding that aligns with the use of the term 'peoples' in the UN Charter. These categories of territorial units share an entitlement to self-government under the UN Charter.[24]

That peoples are understood in practice in reference to specific categories of territorial units accounts for the absence of a definition of 'peoples' for purposes of the right to self-determination in international law. If peoples constitute the populations of defined territorial units, then the challenge of identifying constitutive features or distinguishing characteristics of peoples is of reduced legal significance for purposes of identifying subjects of the right to self-determination.[25] Codification of the right to self-determination in international law and its crystallization in CIL in the absence of a definition of 'peoples' indicate that the identification of peoples for purposes of the right to self-determination has neither relied on a constitutive definition nor been inhibited by its absence. Instead, practice indicates a deductive exercise closely related to territorial demarcation, such that peoples are defined in the first instance in reference to 'generally accepted political units'.[26] In this way, the inquiry into the 'unit' of self-determination begins with a territorial population rather than application of any socio-political standard to such a group. At base, then, self-determination 'applies as a matter of right only after the unit of self-determination has been determined'.[27] To be sure, the treatment of a given territorial unit as a State, NSGT, or Trust Territory is, to varying degrees, a question of politics as well as law.[28] However, because the right to self-determination operates within a United Nations system that prioritizes preservation of the existing boundaries of territorial units,[29] the

[23] A/2929 ch IV para 9. See also para 17.

[24] Regarding the practical relationship between 'peoples' and territorial units entitled to self-government and the circumstances under which a people is entitled to exercise the international aspect of the right to self-determination: while the circumstance of alien subjugation, domination, and exploitation is one entitling a people to exercise the right to self-determination, unlike the circumstance of the peoples of Trust Territories and NSGTs, the former is not coextensive with a particular category of peoples or their territorial units, and does not separately define a territorial unit or delineate its population as a people for purposes of the right to self-determination. See Chapter 7.b.

[25] Crawford (n 11) 125.

[26] Higgins (n 11) 104.

[27] Crawford (n 11) 127.

[28] Ibid 115.

[29] See Chapter 7.d; Chapter 7.e.

set of peoples entitled to the right to self-determination in contemporary international relations is largely fixed.[30]

d. Populations of Territorial Units regarded as Peoples

States, NSGTs, and Trust Territories are the territorial units whose populations are regarded as peoples for purposes of the right to self-determination. The treatment of the populations of States, NSGTs, and Trust Territories as peoples is considered in the sections that follow.

i. Populations of States

The State is the principal subject of international law, and its population constitutes a people for purposes of the right to self-determination.[31] The Preamble of the UN Charter begins by referring to its signatories as peoples ('We the peoples of the United Nations determined'), indicating that the populations represented by States acceding to the Charter constitute 'peoples', a meaning that may also be ascribed to the term as it appears in reference to friendly relations at Articles 1 and 55.[32] States parties to the ICCPR and ICESCR, in common Article 1, undertook obligations under the right to self-determination towards their own populations as peoples with respect to political participation and economic, social, and cultural development.[33] The FRD further indicates that the population of a State constitutes a people for purposes of self-determination in its standard of representative

[30] This observation is without prejudice to the emergence of new territorial units and their recognition as States. One consequence of such emergence into statehood is that the population of such a State would be regarded as a people entitled to the right to self-determination under international law. See Marcelo G. Kohen, 'Introduction' in Marcelo G. Kohen (ed), *Secession: International Perspectives* (CUP 2006) 12.

[31] *Cristescu Report* (1981) para 58; Antonio Cassese, *Self-Determination of Peoples: A Legal Reappraisal* (CUP 1995) 102–03; Crawford (n 11) 126 ('excluding for the purposes of self-determination those parts of the State that are themselves self-determination units as defined').

[32] UN Charter preambular para 1, arts 1(2), 55. See A/7326 (1968) para 163. See also Kelsen (n 19) 51–52.

[33] ICCPR art 1; ICESCR art 1. See A/2929 ch IV para 17. See also Cassese (n 31) 59. See Chapter 8.

government as one 'representing the whole people belonging to the territory without distinction as to race, creed or colour'.[34] By referring to the right to self-determination as entitling peoples to representative government in such terms,[35] the FRD indicates that the entire population of the State constitutes a people (i.e. the 'whole people belonging to the territory') for purposes of the right to self-determination.[36] The Vienna Declaration (1993) contains a parallel standard of representative government, referring to 'sovereign and independent States conducting themselves in compliance with the principle of equal rights and self-determination of peoples and thus possessed of a Government representing the whole people belonging to the territory without distinction of any kind'.[37] These instruments make clear that the population of a State constitutes a people for purposes of the right to self-determination.

At least one domestic court has raised the possibility that a State, if comprised of more than one 'nation', may thereby contain multiple peoples for purposes of the right to self-determination under international law. In *Quebec* (1998), the Supreme Court of Canada took the position that a 'people' may consist of a portion of the population of a State on this basis.[38] However, there is no indication in the sources of the right to self-determination to suggest that 'nations' constitute 'peoples' or are otherwise distinct subjects of the right to self-determination. To the contrary, the treatment of 'nations' alongside 'peoples' during the drafting of the two human rights covenants suggests that 'nations' are conceptually distinct from 'peoples'. The Commission on Human Rights had initially formulated the right to self-determination as 'a right of all peoples and all nations'.[39] However, the *travaux préparatoires* of the human rights covenants indicates that the words 'and all nations' were added after 'all peoples' in common Article 1, and then subsequently removed during the course of negotiations, as a distinct category of beneficiaries of the right to self-determination.[40] Not only does the juxtaposition of the terms

[34] FRD Principle V, para 7.

[35] Cassese (n 31) 110–11; Robert Rosenstock, 'The Declaration of Principles of International Law Concerning Friendly Relations: A Survey' (1971) 65(5) *AJIL* 713, 732; Gaetano Arangio-Ruiz, *The UN Declaration on Friendly Relations and the System of the Sources of International Law* (Sijthoff & Noordhoff 1979) s 80.

[36] Ibid. See A/8018 (1970) 91 para 150 (France).

[37] Vienna Declaration (1993) part I, s 2, para 3.

[38] *Quebec* (1998) para 124.

[39] A/2929 ch IV para 8. See e.g. A/Res/421 (V) (4 Dec 1950) para 6.

[40] A/2929 ch IV para 10; A/3077 para 63.

'nations' and 'peoples' connote distinct concepts, but omission of 'nations' as subjects of the right to self-determination in common Article 1 suggests that 'nations', however defined, do not enjoy a right to self-determination separate from the population of the territorial unit they inhabit. Even if a single State may be comprised of more than one 'nation', the enjoyment of the right to self-determination by sub-State groups is better understood through representation as part of the population of that State.[41]

ii. Populations of Non-Self-Governing Territories and Trust Territories

The populations of NSGTs and Trust Territories constitute peoples for purposes of the right to self-determination. The UN Charter refers to the populations of such territories as 'peoples' in chapters setting out obligations of States responsible for the administration of such territories. Article 73 refers to NSGTs as 'territories whose peoples have not yet attained a full measure of self-government'.[42] Article 76 refers to the populations of Trust Territories as 'peoples' in reference to their progressive development towards independence or self-government in line with 'the freely expressed wishes of the peoples concerned'.[43] Article 77 extends the Trusteeship System to Mandate Territories under the League of Nations Mandate System, indicating that the populations of Mandate Territories are regarded under the Charter to be situated similarly to the populations of Trust Territories.[44] Identification of the populations of these categories of territories as peoples entitled to self-determination under the Charter is a product of the prioritization of decolonization by the UN system.[45]

Other instruments confirm that the populations of NSGTs and Trust Territories constitute 'peoples' for purposes of the right to self-determination. Common Article 1(3) of the two human rights covenants implies that the

[41] See Chapter 6.e.

[42] UN Charter art 73. See Crawford (n 11) 606. Consequently, uninhabited territories have generally not been regarded as NSGTs under Chapter XI of the UN Charter.

[43] UN Charter arts 76(b). See also ibid art 80.

[44] See Chapter 1.c.i.

[45] A/2929 ch IV para 7 (quoted supra Chapter 2 n 37).

populations of NSGTs and Trust Territories constitute 'peoples' for purposes of the right to self-determination, an interpretation confirmed by the *travaux préparatoires*.[46] The principal UNGA resolutions contributing to the crystallization of the right to self-determination in CIL similarly refer to the populations of NSGTs and Trust Territories as 'peoples' entitled to the right to self-determination.[47]

The ICJ has confirmed that the populations of NSGTs and Trust Territories are peoples entitled to the right to self-determination. In *Namibia* (1971), the ICJ illustrated this point when addressing the common purpose of the League of Nations Mandate System, the United Nations Trusteeship System that succeeded it, and the obligations of administering powers of NSGTs.[48] *Namibia* (1971) is notable not only for the way in which the ICJ treats concepts of territory and people almost interchangeably in the context of NSGTs and Trust Territories, but also in its focus on the territories themselves in relation to self-determination. Similarly, in *Chagos Archipelago* (2019), the ICJ reaffirmed that the populations of NSGTs constitute peoples for purposes of the right to self-determination in markedly territorial terms.[49]

By reference to the practice of the UNGA, the ICJ has indicated that there are cases of NSGTs in which 'a certain population did not constitute a "people" entitled to self-determination'.[50] There are, however, exceptionally few cases in which the population of a NSGT may be said to have been so regarded.[51] Practice regarding the identification of NSGTs,[52] and deviations from the right to self-determination in relation to the populations of NSGTs,[53] are discussed in Chapters 7 and 10.

[46] Ibid para 9. See also HRC GC 12 para 6; Cassese (n 31) 59.

[47] Resolution 1514 para 5; Resolution 1541 Annex, Principles I, II, VII–IX; FRD Principle V, para 6.

[48] *Namibia* (1971) paras 52–53.

[49] *Chagos* (2019) para 160.

[50] *Western Sahara*, Advisory Opinion, ICJ Rep 1975, 12 para 59; *Chagos* (2019) para 158 (quoting *Western Sahara* (1975)).

[51] São João Batista de Ajudá, a NSGT administered by Portugal which lacked a civilian population that was annexed by Dahomey (now Benin), and French Establishments in India, a NSGT administered by France that was integrated by India with the consent of France, are referred to in commentary as examples. See Trinidad (n 15) 242.

[52] See Chapter 10.b.i.

[53] See Chapter 7.f.

e. Groups not Populations of Territorial Units

Minority groups within the populations of territorial units do not enjoy a free-standing entitlement to the right to self-determination under international law, as such groups are not regarded as 'peoples'. This approach is without prejudice to the recognition under international law of the unique status of Indigenous and tribal communities in relation to self-determination as Indigenous Peoples. The treatment of minority groups and Indigenous Peoples under the right to self-determination is considered in the sections that follow.

i. Minority Groups

Implicit in the way 'peoples' are defined in reference to the populations of territorial units is that a minority group within the population of such a territorial unit is not a 'people' for purposes of the right to self-determination in international law.[54]

The distinction between 'peoples' and minority groups is reflected in common Article 1 of the two human rights covenants and other provisions of the ICCPR.[55] The *travaux préparatoires* of common Article 1 of the two human rights covenants indicates that the term 'peoples' was understood to exclude ethnic, religious, or linguistic minority groups as defined in ICCPR Article 27.[56] Article 27 separately addresses the rights of members of such groups.[57] In General Comment No 23, the HRC underscored the distinction between the right of peoples to self-determination under

[54] See *The Right to Self-Determination: Implementation of United Nations Resolutions* (Study prepared by Héctor Gros Espiell, Special Rapporteur of the Sub-Commission on Prevention of Discrimination and Protection of Minorities), E/CN.4/Sub.2/405/Rev.1 (1980) para 56. See also Patrick Thornberry, 'Self-Determination, Minorities, Human Rights: A Review of International Instruments' (1989) 38(4) *ICLQ* 867; Will Kymlicka, *Politics in the Vernacular: Nationalism, Multiculturalism, and Citizenship* (OUP 2001) 127; Christakis (n 15) 85. For a different view, see S. James Anaya, *Indigenous Peoples in International Law* (2nd edn, OUP 2004) 100–03.

[55] Nowak (n 2) para 28; Cassese (n 31) 61–62.

[56] A/2929 ch IV para 9.

[57] ICCPR art 27.

ICCPR Article 1 and the rights of members of minority groups under Article 27.

> The Covenant draws a distinction between the right to self-determination and the rights protected under article 27. The former is expressed to be a right belonging to peoples and is dealt with in a separate part (Part I) of the Covenant. Self-determination is not a right cognizable under the Optional Protocol. Article 27, on the other hand, relates to rights conferred on individuals as such and is included, like the articles relating to other personal rights conferred on individuals, in Part III of the Covenant and is cognizable under the Optional Protocol.[58]

General Comment No 23 identifies a practical aspect of the distinction between the right of peoples to self-determination and the rights of members of minority groups for purposes of the individual complaint mechanism under the Optional Protocol to the ICCPR, and in so doing clarifies that the right of peoples to self-determination falls outside the scope of 'rights of minorities' under Article 27. Consequently, '[t]he enjoyment of the rights to which article 27 relates does not prejudice the sovereignty and territorial integrity of a State party'.[59] A corresponding distinction is reflected in the Helsinki Final Act (1975), which addresses the rights of members of minority groups separately from the principle of equal rights and self-determination of peoples.[60]

Regional practice similarly indicates that minority groups are not regarded as 'peoples' for purposes of the right to self-determination. The Inter-American Commission on Human Rights (IACHR), in *Report on the Situation of Human Rights of a Segment of the Nicaraguan Population of Miskito Origin* (1983), recognized the right to self-determination in international law, but did not consider the right to be applicable to ethnic

[58] HRC, *CCPR General Comment No. 23: Article 27 (Rights of Minorities)*, CCPR/C/21/Rev.1/Add.5 (1994) (hereinafter HRC GC 23) para 3.1.

[59] Ibid para 3.2.

[60] Cf Helsinki Final Act (1975) Principle VII, especially para 4; Principle VIII.

minority groups within a State 'as such'.[61] The ACtHPR has considered that the term 'peoples' for purposes of the ACHPR may refer to minority groups within the population of a State, at least with respect to certain collective rights as defined in the ACHPR.[62] Like other instruments codifying the right to self-determination, the ACHPR lacks a definition of 'peoples', an intentional omission providing for a degree of flexibility in the application of collective rights under the ACHPR.[63] In *ACHPR v Kenya* (2017), the ACtHPR identified the possibility that certain collective rights under the ACHPR may apply to 'sub-state ethnic groups and communities', though it questioned whether the right to self-determination at Article 20(1) could enjoy such application. The ACtHPR explained this relatively narrower application of the right to self-determination, as compared to other collective rights under the ACHPR, on the basis of its implications for sovereignty and territorial integrity.[64] However, the ACtHPR admitted the possibility that a State may be comprised of multiple 'peoples' for purposes of collective rights under the ACHPR.[65] Later, in *Mornah v Benin* (2022), the ACtHPR observed that 'the right to self-determination is essentially related to peoples' right to ownership over a particular territory and their political status over that territory'.[66] Such a territorial approach to self-determination, consistent with the prevailing approach under international law, casts further doubt on whether a sub-State group may be treated as a 'people' for purposes of the right to self-determination under the ACHPR.

[61] *Report on the Situation of Human Rights of a Segment of the Nicaraguan Population of Miskito Origin*, IACHR, OAS Doc OEA/Ser.L/V.II.62, doc 10 rev 3 (29 Nov 1983) part II.B, paras 9–11.

[62] Richard N. Kiwanuka, 'The Meaning of "People" in the African Charter on Human and Peoples' Rights' (1988) 82(1) *AJIL* 80 (identifying four meanings of 'people' in the ACHPR). See *Front for the Liberation of the State of Cabinda v Angola*, ACommHPR, Communication No 328/06 (2013) paras 114–30 (finding the right of peoples to freely dispose of their wealth and natural resources under ACHPR Article 21 applicable to sub-State groups).

[63] *ACHPR v Kenya* (2017) para 196.

[64] Ibid paras 198–99.

[65] The African Commission previously admitted the possibility that a sub-State group may claim a right to self-determination under certain circumstances. See *Mgwanga Gunme et al v Cameroon*, ACommHPR, Communication No 266/2003 (2009) paras 178–203; *Katangese Peoples' Congress v Zaire*, ACommHPR, Communication No 75/92 (1995) paras 2–6. Cf Chapter 7.c.ii.

[66] *Mornah v Benin* (2022) para 301.

ii. Indigenous Peoples

Indigenous and tribal communities enjoy a unique status in relation to self-determination as 'Indigenous Peoples'.[67] 'Indigenous Peoples' are defined in the influential 1986 study by José Martínez Cobo, Special Rapporteur of the Sub-Commission on Prevention of Discrimination and Protection of Minorities, in the following terms:

> Indigenous communities, peoples and nations are those which, having a historical continuity with pre-invasion and pre-colonial societies that developed on their territories, consider themselves distinct from other sectors of the societies now prevailing in those territories, or parts of them. They form at present non-dominant sectors of society and are determined to preserve, develop and transmit to future generations their ancestral territories, and their ethnic identity, as the basis of their continued existence as peoples, in accordance with their own cultural patterns, social institutions and legal systems.[68]

Another definition, which appears alongside a broader term 'Tribal peoples' not defined in historical relation to colonization, is contained in Article 1 of International Labour Organisation (ILO) Convention No 169.[69] The precise legal meaning and scope of application of the term 'Indigenous Peoples' are complex and contested.[70] Such challenges reverberate in the application of the right to self-determination to Indigenous Peoples.[71]

Neither the instruments surveyed in Part I codifying the right to self-determination, nor the relevant *travaux préparatoires*, indicate that Indigenous Peoples have traditionally been considered to enjoy a free-standing claim to the right to self-determination as it is codified in treaty law

[67] Anaya (n 54) 3.

[68] *Study of the Problem of Discrimination against Indigenous Populations* (Final report (last part), submitted by José R. Martínez Cobo, Special Rapporteur of the Sub-Commission on Prevention of Discrimination and Protection of Minorities), E/CN.4/Sub.2/1986/7/Add.4 (1986) para 379.

[69] ILO Convention (No. 169) concerning Indigenous and tribal peoples in independent countries art 1(1), 1650 UNTS 383 (27 June 1989, entered into force 5 Sept 1991). See Chapter 8.e.i.

[70] See Benedict Kingsbury, '"Indigenous Peoples" in International Law: A Constructivist Approach to the Asian Controversy' (1998) 92(3) *AJIL* 414.

[71] Ibid 424–26.

and reflected in CIL. On the one hand, this suggests that Indigenous Peoples are not regarded as 'peoples' as the term is used for purposes of the right to self-determination in international law.[72] On the other, it is argued that such a 'restrictive approach' unduly limits the right to self-determination to 'peoples' entitled to independence through statehood.[73] Some, including Indigenous Peoples themselves, have advocated for the treatment of Indigenous Peoples as 'peoples' for purposes of the right to self-determination in international law.[74] However, the territorial approach to the delineation of peoples for purposes of the right to self-determination in international law,[75] and the international aspect of self-determination as, at base, a 'right to independence',[76] pose challenges to such treatment. Consideration of the international aspect of the right to self-determination, for example, animated qualifications in the provisions on self-determination in the United Nations Declaration on the Rights of Indigenous Peoples (UNDRIP),[77] and led the ACtHPR to question whether the right to self-determination is among the collective rights enjoyed by an Indigenous People under the ACHPR.[78]

Conceptual and definitional issues notwithstanding, the right to self-determination has come to have a particular application as it relates to Indigenous Peoples.[79] Practice indicates that Indigenous Peoples enjoy, as an application of the domestic aspect of the right to self-determination, an entitlement to political autonomy and self-government as well as to freely pursue their economic, social, and cultural development.[80] This conceptualization is closely related to the development of a normative framework concerning

[72] Cassese (n 31) 103; Kohen (n 30) 9.

[73] Anaya (n 54) 100–03.

[74] Such assertions do not necessarily encompass the international aspect of self-determination. See ibid. See also Russel Lawrence Barsh, 'Indigenous Peoples: An Emerging Object of International Law' (1986) 80(2) *AJIL* 369, 375–76; Kingsbury (n 70) 437. See United Nations Declaration on the Rights of Indigenous Peoples art 2, A/Res/61/295 (13 Sept 2007) Annex (hereinafter UNDRIP).

[75] See Chapter 6.c.

[76] *Accordance with International Law of the Unilateral Declaration of Independence in Respect of Kosovo*, Advisory Opinion, ICJ Rep 2010, 403 para 79. See Chapter 7.

[77] UNDRIP arts 4, 46(1). See Karen Engle, 'On Fragile Architecture: The UN Declaration on the Rights of Indigenous Peoples in the Context of Human Rights' (2011) 22(1) *EJIL* 141, 143–48. See Chapter 8.e.ii.

[78] *ACHPR v Kenya* (2017) paras 105–12.

[79] Marc Weller, 'Self-Determination of Indigenous Peoples: Articles 3, 4, 5, 18, 23, and 46(1)' in Jessie Hohmann & Marc Weller (eds), *The UN Declaration on the Rights of Indigenous Peoples: A Commentary* (OUP 2018) 147.

[80] See Chapter 8.e.

the rights of Indigenous Peoples more broadly, within which a right to self-determination for Indigenous Peoples has been articulated.[81] Implicit in such treatment of self-determination relating to Indigenous Peoples is that the human rights that comprise its substance are collectively enjoyed and exercised by members of an Indigenous People and to be respected by the State within which its members reside.[82] In this way, Indigenous Peoples are subjects and beneficiaries of the right to self-determination.

The treatment of Indigenous Peoples under the ICCPR by the HRC, and under the ICESCR by the Committee on Economic, Social and Cultural Rights (CESCR), is instructive in this regard. HRC General Comment No 23 provides that the rights of Indigenous Peoples are safeguarded under the ICCPR through Article 27, which concerns the rights of members of minority groups.[83] In *Sanila-Aikio v Finland* (2019) and *Käkkäläjärvi et al v Finland* (2019), the HRC applied ICCPR Article 1 to interpret Article 27, as well as Article 25, in relation to 'the principle of internal self-determination relating to indigenous peoples'.[84] The views adopted by the HRC concerning those communications illustrate how self-determination relating to Indigenous Peoples may be regarded as the collective exercise of relevant human rights by members of an Indigenous People informed by the right to self-determination.[85] The CESCR similarly recognized this application of the right to self-determination in General Comment No 26 on land and economic, social, and cultural rights, in which ICESCR Article 1 was interpreted in relation to the 'right to internal self-determination' of Indigenous Peoples.[86] Self-determination relating to Indigenous Peoples is addressed in Chapter 8.

81 Weller (n 79) 125–38.

82 HRC GC 23 paras 3.1–3.2. See Shaw (n 11) 488–89.

83 HRC GC 23 paras 3.1–3.2.

84 *Sanila-Aikio v Finland*, Communication No 2668/2015, CCPR/C/124/D/2668/2015 (20 Mar 2019) para 6.10; *Käkkäläjärvi et al v Finland*, Communication No 2950/2017, CCPR/C/124/D/2950/2017 (18 Dec 2019) para 9.10.

85 See also HRC GC 23 para 3.2.

86 Committee on Economic, Social and Cultural Rights, *General Comment No. 26 (2022) on land and economic, social and cultural rights*, E/C.12/GC/26 (2023) para 11.

7

The International Aspect of Self-Determination

a. Overview

The right to self-determination consists of the entitlement of peoples to freely determine their political status and freely pursue their economic, social, and cultural development.[1] The *travaux préparatoires* of the two human rights covenants reflects a general understanding of these elements of the right as an entitlement of every people 'to establish its own political institutions' and 'to develop its own economic resources, and to direct its own social and cultural evolution, without the interference of other peoples or nations'.[2] The exercise of the right to self-determination by a people has both international (or 'external') and domestic (or 'internal') aspects.[3] This chapter addresses the international aspect of the right to self-determination.

The first section of this chapter examines the free determination of political status, which is the core of the international aspect of the right to

[1] International Covenant on Civil and Political Rights art 1(1), 999 UNTS 171 (16 Dec 1966, entered into force 23 Mar 1976) (hereinafter ICCPR); International Covenant on Economic, Social and Cultural Rights art 1(1), 993 UNTS 3 (16 Dec 1966, entered into force 3 Jan 1976) (hereinafter ICESCR); A/Res/1514 (XV) (14 Dec 1960) (hereinafter Resolution 1514) para 2; A/Res/2625 (24 Oct 1970) Annex (hereinafter FRD) Principle V, para 1; United Nations World Conference on Human Rights: Vienna Declaration and Programme of Action (25 June 1993), A/CONF/157/23 (12 July 1993), reproduced in (1993) 32(6) ILM 1661 (hereinafter Vienna Declaration (1993)) part I, s 2, para 1. See *Legal Consequences arising from the Policies and Practices of Israel in the Occupied Palestinian Territory, including East Jerusalem*, Advisory Opinion, ICJ Rep 2024 (hereinafter *Palestine* (2024)) para 241. See also African [Banjul] Charter on Human and Peoples' Rights art 20, OAU Doc CAB/LEG/67/3/Rev.5, 1520 UNTS 217 (27 June 1981, entered into force 21 Oct 1986) (hereinafter ACHPR); Arab Charter on Human Rights art 1, [ST/HR/]CHR/NONE/2004/40/Rev.1 (22 May 2004, entered into force 15 Mar 2008).

[2] Draft International Covenants on Human Rights: Annotation, Prepared by the Secretary-General, A/2929 (1 July 1955) ch IV para 12.

[3] *Report of the Third Committee*, A/3077 (8 Dec 1955) (Draft International Covenants on Human Rights) (hereinafter A/3077) para 32; FRD Principle V, paras 2, 7.

The Right to Self-Determination in International Law. Thomas Weatherall, Oxford University Press.
 DOI: 10.1093/9780197798119.003.0008

self-determination. This section considers the two circumstances under which peoples are generally recognized as entitled to exercise the right to self-determination in relation to its international aspect: peoples of Non-Self-Governing Territories and Trust Territories, and peoples subject to alien subjugation, domination, and exploitation. Next, this chapter addresses the absence of a general entitlement to secession as a component of the right to self-determination and considers the question of 'remedial secession'. This chapter then evaluates the relationship between the right to self-determination and the principle of territorial integrity. The fourth section of this chapter examines the associated principle of *uti possidetis*, which operates to preserve territorial boundaries during changes of sovereignty over territory to a new State, in the international exercise by a people of its right to self-determination. Finally, this chapter addresses deviations from the international aspect of the right to self-determination.

b. Free Determination of Political Status

The political element of the right to self-determination illustrates the dual nature of the right: it comprises an 'internal', or domestic aspect addressing self-government, and an 'external' aspect concerned with the political status of a people at the international level.[4] The Helsinki Final Act is notable in this regard by expressly defining the political element of the right to self-determination as an entitlement of peoples to freely determine their 'internal and external political status'.[5] It has been observed that the right to self-determination is exercised in the normal course through the domestic aspect of the right, and that the international aspect of the political element is implicated only under specific circumstances.

[4] A/3077 para 32; FRD Principle V, paras 2, 7; A/7326 (1968) para 167 ('It was observed that the principle contained two basic rights of States, the right to self-government and internal sovereignty and the right to independence and external sovereignty. The latter right, although limited by the concept of interdependence, excluded any subordination of one State by another'). See also Committee on the Elimination of Racial Discrimination, General Recommendation XXI (48), adopted at the 1147th meeting, 8 March 1996, in *Report of the Committee on the Elimination of Racial Discrimination*, Annex VIII.B 125, A/51/18 (hereinafter CERD General Recommendation No 21) para 9.

[5] Conference on Security and Cooperation in Europe: Final Act (1 Aug 1975), reproduced in (1975) 14(5) ILM 1292 (hereinafter Helsinki Final Act (1975)) Principle VIII, para 2.

> The recognized sources of international law establish that the right to self-determination of a people is normally fulfilled through internal self-determination—a people's pursuit of its political, economic, social and cultural development within the framework of an existing state. A right to external self-determination . . . arises in only the most extreme of cases and, even then, under carefully defined circumstances.[6]

The entitlement of a people to exercise the right to self-determination in relation to its international aspect is exceptional and arises only under 'carefully defined' circumstances. In particular, the circumstances of two categories of peoples are generally recognized as giving rise to an entitlement to exercise of the right to self-determination in this sense: (1) peoples of NSGTs and Trust Territories,[7] and (2) peoples 'subject to alien subjugation, domination and exploitation'.[8] These two circumstances are reflected in instruments considered to reflect CIL regarding the right to self-determination.[9] The ICJ confirmed this scope of the international aspect of the right to self-determination in its *Kosovo* (2010) advisory opinion, in terms of what it characterized as a 'right to independence'.

> During the second half of the twentieth century, the international law of self-determination developed in such a way as to create a right to independence for the peoples of non-self-governing territories and peoples subject to alien subjugation, domination and exploitation. A great many new States have come into existence as a result of the exercise of this right.[10]

[6] *Reference re Secession of Quebec* [1998] 2 SCR 217 (hereinafter *Quebec* (1998)) para 126 (emphasis in original). See similarly *Reference by the Lord Advocate of devolution issues under paragraph 34 of Schedule 6 to the Scotland Act 1998* [2022] UKSC 31 (hereinafter *Scotland* (2022)) [89].

[7] *Legal Consequences of the Separation of the Chagos Archipelago from Mauritius in 1965*, Advisory Opinion, ICJ Rep 2019, 95 (hereinafter *Chagos* (2019)) para 144.

[8] *Palestine* (2024) para 233.

[9] See Resolution 1514 paras 1, 5; FRD, Principle V, para 2. See also Vienna Declaration (1993) part I, s 2, para 2.

[10] *Accordance with International Law of the Unilateral Declaration of Independence in Respect of Kosovo*, Advisory Opinion, ICJ Rep 2010, 403 (hereinafter *Kosovo* (2010)) para 79 (citing *Legal Consequences for States of the Continued Presence of South Africa in Namibia (South West Africa) notwithstanding Security Council Resolution 276 (1970)*, Advisory Opinion, ICJ Rep 1971, 16 (hereinafter *Namibia* (1971)); *East Timor (Portugal v Australia)*, Judgment, ICJ Rep 1995, 90 (hereinafter *East Timor* (1995)); *Legal Consequences of the Construction of a Wall in the Occupied Palestinian Territory*, Advisory Opinion, ICJ Rep 2004, 136 (hereinafter *Wall* (2004))).

The following subsections consider the two circumstances under which peoples are entitled to freely determine their political status through the exercise of the right to self-determination in relation to its international aspect.

i. Non-Self-Governing Territories and Trust Territories

The first circumstance, or category of peoples generally recognized as entitled to exercise the right to self-determination in relation to its international aspect, consists of peoples of NSGTs and Trust Territories.[11] It has been observed that '[t]he right of colonial peoples to exercise their right to self-determination by breaking away from the "imperial" power is now undisputed'.[12] In this context, the circumstance of non-self-governing political status is coextensive with the category of peoples defined as populations of territorial units entitled to self-government.[13] Put differently, peoples of NSGTs and Trust Territories are, as such, entitled to exercise the right to self-determination to freely determine their political status pursuant to the international aspect of the right.

The foundations of such an entitlement in the United Nations system are Chapter XI (Non-Self-Governing Territories) and Chapter XII (International Trusteeship System) of the UN Charter.[14] Chapter XI of the Charter sets forth obligations for administering powers vis-à-vis NSGTs, while Chapter XII of the Charter sets out a framework for obligations of administering authorities of territories to which the Trusteeship System applied. The ICJ observed that 'the legal régime of non-self-governing territories, as set out in Chapter XI of the Charter, was based on the progressive development of their institutions so as to lead the populations concerned to exercise their right to self-determination'.[15] In reference to territories to which the Trusteeship

[11] The entitlement to self-determination addressed in this section applies equally to the peoples of NSGTs and Trust Territories. Instruments contemplating the entitlement of the right to self-determination for such peoples refer in some instances only to NSGTs. It has been suggested that all Trust Territories are NSGTs and as such, for instance, the provisions of Chapter XI are applicable in relation to Trust Territories. See Hans Kelsen, *The Law of the United Nations* (London Institute of World Affairs 1950) 632. Because all Trust Territories have attained self-government, no UN Member State is subject to the performance of obligations under a Chapter XII Trusteeship agreement, rendering this question moot.

[12] *Quebec* (1998) para 132.

[13] See Chapter 6.d.ii.

[14] *Namibia* (1971) paras 52–53. See Chapter 2.b.

[15] *Chagos* (2019) paras 146–47.

System applied, the ICJ similarly observed 'that the ultimate objective of the sacred trust was the self-determination and independence of the peoples concerned'.[16] These aspects of self-determination build in various ways upon the Mandate System of the League of Nations.[17]

Several UNGA resolutions in particular have been identified by the ICJ as having contributed to the crystallization and content of the CIL of self-determination, which resolutions specifically address the exercise of the right to self-determination by peoples of NSGTs.[18]

1. Concept of the Sacred Trust

The administration of territories whose peoples have not yet attained a full measure of self-government is regarded as a 'sacred trust'.[19] In *Namibia* (1971), the ICJ observed that the sacred trust is a common feature of the League of Nations Mandate System and the administration of NSGTs under the UN Charter.[20] The concept of the sacred trust appears in Article 22 of the League of Nations Covenant, which provided that, in reference to peoples of territories subject to the Mandate System, 'there should be applied the principle that the well-being and development of such peoples form a sacred trust of civilisation'.[21] In *South-West Africa* (1950), the ICJ observed that a Mandate 'was created, in the interest of the inhabitants of the territory, and of humanity in general, as an international institution with an international object—a sacred trust of civilization'.[22] The League of Nations Covenant characterized the provisions of Article 22 as 'securities for the performance of this trust'.[23] In *Namibia* (1971), the ICJ framed these securities as a 'corollary' of 'the assumption of obligations not only of a moral but also of a binding legal character' under a trust.[24]

[16] *Namibia* (1971) para 53.

[17] See Chapter 1.c.i.

[18] *Chagos* (2019) paras 144–62. See Resolution 1514 preambular para 12, para 5; Chapter 3.b; Chapter 3.c. See also FRD Principle V, para 2; Chapter 3.d.

[19] H. Duncan Hall, *Mandates, Dependencies and Trusteeship* (Stevens & Sons Ltd 1948) 97–100. Cf Evan J. Criddle, 'A Sacred Trust of Civilization' in Andrew S. Gold and Paul B. Miller (eds), *Philosophical Foundations of Fiduciary Law* (OUP 2014) 406–12.

[20] *Namibia* (1971) paras 45, 52–53.

[21] Treaty of Versailles, Part I, The Covenant of the League of Nations art 22.

[22] *International Status of South-West Africa*, Advisory Opinion, ICJ Rep 1950, 128, 132.

[23] See Chapter 1.c.i.

[24] *Namibia* (1971) paras 46–47 (internal citation omitted).

While the concept of the sacred trust was limited in its application to Mandates under the League of Nations Covenant, the UN Charter applies the concept to NSGTs more broadly. Article 73 of the UN Charter provides that Member States responsible for the administration of territories whose peoples have not yet attained a full measure of self-government 'accept as a sacred trust the obligation to promote to the utmost . . . the well-being of the inhabitants of these territories'.[25] The UN Charter orients the provisions of Article 73 'to this end'. In this way, Article 73 'confirmed and expanded' the concept of the sacred trust to all peoples that had not yet achieved a full measure of self-government.[26] Article 73 expressly formulates the sacred trust as an obligation of administering States, and has in this regard been considered a 'more precise' framing than Article 22 of the League of Nations Covenant.[27] As noted above, the ICJ observed that 'the ultimate objective of the sacred trust was the self-determination and independence of the peoples concerned'.[28]

2. Freely Expressed Wishes of the People Concerned

The touchstone of the exercise of the right to self-determination, in relation to its international aspect, is the freely expressed wishes of the people concerned.[29] This language parallels the objective of the Trusteeship System, at Article 76 of the UN Charter, to facilitate development towards self-government or independence of peoples of Trust Territories, as appropriate to their particular circumstances 'and the freely expressed wishes of the peoples concerned'.[30] UNGA Resolution 1514 articulates this standard in relation to NSGTs as 'the freely expressed will and desire' of the people concerned.[31] UNGA Resolution 2625 (the FRD) sets out the touchstone of a people's exercise of its right to self-determination in substantively similar terms: 'the freely expressed will of the people concerned'.[32] In *Chagos*

[25] Charter of the United Nations art 73, XV UNCIO 335 (26 June 1945, entered into force 24 Oct 1945) (hereinafter UN Charter).
[26] *Namibia* (1971) para 52.
[27] Kelsen (n 11) 557.
[28] *Namibia* (1971) para 53.
[29] *Western Sahara*, Advisory Opinion, ICJ Rep 1975, 12 (hereinafter *Western Sahara* (1975)) paras 54–59.
[30] UN Charter art 76(b).
[31] Resolution 1514 para 5. See *Western Sahara* (1975) para 55.
[32] FRD Principle V, para 2.

Archipelago (2019), the ICJ recalled the touchstone of the exercise of the right to self-determination as, inter alia, the freely expressed wishes of the people concerned, as previously identified in *Western Sahara* (1975) and reflected in various instruments addressing self-determination.[33] The practical modalities by which a people freely expresses its wishes pursuant to the determination of its political status are discussed in Chapter 10.

3. Forms of Self-Government

International law recognizes at least three options for the political status of a territory resulting from its people's achievement of self-government through the exercise of the right to self-determination: (1) establishment of a sovereign and independent State, (2) free association with an independent state, or (3) integration with an independent State.[34] While Resolution 1541 identifies these options as a closed set,[35] UNGA Resolution 2625 (the FRD) provides that 'modes of implementing the right of self-determination' by a people include independence, free association or integration with an independent State, 'or the emergence into any other political status freely determined by a people'.[36] The inclusion of this catchall renders UNGA Resolution 2625 more flexible, at least in theory, than UNGA Resolution 1541 in its treatment of the possible political status resulting from a people's exercise of the right to self-determination.[37] Moreover, UNGA Resolution 2625 regards the freely expressed wishes of the people concerned, rather than any particular outcome, to be the controlling consideration of the result of a people's exercise of its right to self-determination.[38] While the ICJ has identified UNGA Resolution 1541 as providing for the modalities of implementation of the right to self-determination in specific reference to the exercise of self-determination by the people of a NSGT, it has also contemplated UNGA Resolution 2625 to 'reiterate' CIL in reference to the right to self-determination.[39]

[33] *Chagos* (2019) paras 157–60.
[34] For disposition of former Trust Territories and NSGTs, see Appendix 1.
[35] A/Res/1541 (XV) (15 Dec 1960) (hereinafter Resolution 1541) Annex, Principle VI.
[36] FRD Principle V, para 4. It has been suggested that maintaining a dependent colonial status quo, by rejecting other outcomes, may be considered a 'fourth option'. James Crawford, *The Creation of States in International Law* (2nd edn, OUP 2006) 636–37.
[37] See also Resolution 1514 para 5 (referring to 'complete independence and freedom').
[38] *Western Sahara* (1975) para 58.
[39] *Chagos* (2019) paras 155–57.

Article 73 of the UN Charter contemplates the development of 'self-government' of peoples of NSGTs, while Article 76 refers to the development of 'self-government or independence' of peoples of Trust Territories.[40] It has been suggested that the distinction between self-government and independence in the UN Charter is intended to connote sovereignty in reference to independence only.[41] The express reference to independence in Article 76 might signal an expectation that the peoples of Trust Territories, including former Mandates, would realize a final political status of independence.[42] Practice indicates no substantive distinction among the available options for the political status of a NSGT as compared to a Trust Territory.[43]

4. Further Aspects of Implementation

UNGA Resolution 1541 provides additional guidance on implementation of the modalities of integration and free association. As a general matter, Principles VII and IX condition free association and integration on the freely expressed wishes of the people concerned, expressed through an informed and democratic process.[44] Principle IX also contemplates the possibility of UN supervision of such a process.[45] Regarding integration, Principle VIII prescribes the relation between peoples entering into integration to be one characterized by 'complete equality'. This Principle is drafted in terms that suggest the integrating people retains its identity as a people vis-à-vis the people of the independent State with which it integrates.[46] Regarding free association, Principle VII not only indicates such separation explicitly, but further indicates that the people associating with an independent State 'should . . . retain . . . the freedom to modify the status of that territory through the expression of their will by democratic means and through constitutional processes', suggesting an entitlement by the associated people to revisit its political status vis-à-vis the independent State.[47] Principle VII

40 Cf UN Charter arts 73(b), 76(b).

41 Kelsen (n 11) 559.

42 See *Namibia* (1971) para 53.

43 See Appendix 1.

44 See *Western Sahara* (1975) para 57; *Chagos* (2019) para 157.

45 Ibid. See Chapter 10.a.

46 Resolution 1541 Annex, Principle VIII.

47 See also A/Res/742 (VIII) (27 Nov 1953) Annex, Third Part, s A para 2 (referring to '[t]he freedom of the population of a Non-Self-Governing Territory which has associated itself with the metropolitan country as an integral part of that country or in any other form to modify this status through the expression of their will by democratic means'). Puerto Rico offers an example

also contemplates that the freely associated territory retains its entitlement to self-government. UNGA Resolution 1541 contemplates a gradation of consent across these potential outcomes at its strongest in cases of integration: free association should be subject to heightened criteria while integration should be limited to certain circumstances.[48] Principle IX also suggests the possibility of UN supervision in cases of integration.[49]

The United Nations, and in particular the UNGA, has historically played 'a crucial role' in implementing the exercise of self-determination by peoples of NSGTs through what have been described by the ICJ as 'functions assigned to it to oversee the application of the right to self-determination'.[50] The practice of the UNGA in relation to NSGTs and Trust Territories is addressed in detail in Chapter 10.

In practice, the people of a NSGT or Trust Territory enjoys a single opportunity to determine its political status through its exercise of the right to self-determination, by which it achieves self-government. However, the right to self-determination is a continuing right and as such is not extinguished by the achievement of self-government.[51] Put differently, the continuing character of the right to self-determination is distinct from the circumstances entitling a people to its exercise in relation to its international aspect. The continuing character of the right to self-determination is reflected in the language used in common Article 1 of the two human rights covenants,[52] as

in this regard. See A/Res/748 (VIII) (27 Nov 1953) para 9 ('*Expresses its assurance* that . . . due regard will be paid to the will of both the Puerto Rican and American peoples in the conduct of their relations under their present legal statute, and also in the eventuality that either of the parties to the mutually agreed association may desire any change in the terms of this association'); 'Memorandum of November 30, 1992: Memorandum for the Heads of Executive Departments and Agencies' (1992) 57 *Federal Register* 57093 (2 Dec 1992) ('As long as Puerto Rico is a territory, however, the will of its people regarding their political status should be ascertained periodically by means of a general right of referendum or specific referenda'); 'Executive Order 13183 of December 23, 2000: Establishment of the President's Task Force on Puerto Rico's Status' (2000) 65 *Federal Register* 82889 (29 Dec 2000). See also *Statement of Administration Policy, H.R. 8393—Puerto Rico Status Act* (15 Dec 2022).

---

48 Resolution 1541 Annex, Principles VII–IX.

49 See *Western Sahara* (1975) para 71; *Chagos* (2019) para 157 (quoting *Western Sahara* (1975)). See Chapter 10.a.

50 *Chagos* (2019) para 167.

51 Crawford (n 36) 126. Cf Antonio Cassese, *Self-Determination of Peoples: A Legal Reappraisal* (CUP 1995) 72–73, 101.

52 ICCPR art 1(1); ICESCR art 1(1). See Manfred Nowak, *UN Covenant on Civil and Political Rights: CCPR Commentary* (2nd edn, N. P. Engel 2005) paras 18–19; Cassese (n 51) 54.

well as UNGA Resolutions 1514 and 2625.[53] This continuing character is explicitly reflected in the Helsinki Final Act (1975), which refers to the right of peoples to freely determine their political status 'when and as they wish'.[54] This is to say that the political element of the right, by which peoples 'freely determine their political status', is not exhausted by its exercise, for example, in a given plebiscite.[55] Thus, the people of a NSGT or Trust Territory continues to enjoy the right to self-determination, to include its political element, even after achieving self-government through independence. Once the circumstance (i.e. a non-self-governing status) entitling a people to exercise the right to self-determination in relation to its international aspect has been extinguished by achieving self-government, the subsequent exercise of the political element of the right will in the normal course be expressed through the domestic aspect of the right.[56]

ii. Alien Subjugation, Domination, and Exploitation

The second circumstance recognized to entitle a people to the exercise of the right to self-determination in relation to its international aspect is 'alien subjugation, domination and exploitation'. It has been observed that this circumstance, which is distinct from the situation of peoples of NSGTs and Trust Territories in the colonial context, is '[t]he other clear case where a right to external self-determination accrues'.[57] The identification by the ICJ in *Kosovo* (2010) of an entitlement of peoples subject to alien subjugation, domination, and exploitation to exercise the right to self-determination as a 'right to independence' confirms this proposition.[58]

The concept of alien subjugation, domination, and exploitation is not well defined, making it difficult to draw clear conclusions about the parameters of the exercise of the right to self-determination under this circumstance. UNGA Resolution 2625 provides that 'subjection of peoples to alien subjugation, domination and exploitation constitutes a violation of the principle

[53] Resolution 1514 para 2; FRD Principle V, para 1.
[54] Helsinki Final Act (1975) Principle VIII, para 2.
[55] Nowak (n 52) para 19.
[56] See A/3077 para 32; see also para 39.
[57] *Quebec* (1998) para 133.
[58] *Kosovo* (2010) para 79. See also *Palestine* (2024) paras 237, 283.

[of self-determination], as well as a denial of fundamental human rights, and is contrary to the [UN] Charter'.[59] However, 'alien subjugation, domination and exploitation' is not defined in UNGA Resolution 2625 or other instruments referring to the circumstance.[60] Moreover, unlike the circumstance of peoples of NSGTs and Trust Territories, which is coextensive with categories of defined territorial units, alien subjugation, domination, and exploitation is not similarly circumscribed. Therefore, any people may be subject to alien subjugation, domination, and exploitation, and so entitled to exercise the right to self-determination in relation to its international aspect in the form of a 'right to independence'.[61] A paucity of authoritative guidance is compounded by limited practice regarding this aspect of the right to self-determination.

1. Occupation

One situation that implicates the right to self-determination in relation to alien subjugation, domination, and exploitation is occupation. Courts considering the international aspect of the right to self-determination outside the context of decolonization obligations have done so in relation to situations regarded as occupation.[62] In this way, practice suggests some degree of correspondence between situations of occupation and the subjection of a people to alien subjugation, domination, and exploitation.[63] At minimum, the law of occupation offers a point of reference for a situation that implicates the right to self-determination. The complicated relationship between

[59] FRD Principle V, para 2.

[60] See also Resolution 1514 para 1; Vienna Declaration (1993) part I, s 2, para 2.

[61] See e.g. A/8018 (1970) 114 para 233 (United Kingdom) ('[T]he phrase concerning subjection of peoples to alien subjugation, domination and exploitation governed and coloured the whole of what preceded it. The subjection of peoples to alien subjugation, within the framework of a principle which was of universal application could take many forms, but whatever form it took, it was, his delegation was sure, abhorrent to all members of the Committee').

[62] See Chapter 7.b.ii.1.A.

[63] See Antonio Cassese, 'Wars of National Liberation and Humanitarian Law' in Antonio Cassese (ed), *The Human Dimension of International Law: Selected Papers of Antonio Cassese* (OUP 2008) 103; Malcolm N. Shaw, 'Peoples, Territorialism and Boundaries' (1997) 3 *EJIL* 478, 481; Cassese (n 51) 90–99, especially 99. See e.g. *Quebec* (1998) para 138 ('where a people is oppressed, as for example under foreign military occupation'); *Scotland* (2022) [89] ('situations . . . involving foreign occupation'). See also Protocol additional to the Geneva Conventions of 12 August 1949, and Relating to the Protection of Victims of International Armed Conflicts (Protocol I) art 1(4), 1125 UNTS 3 (8 June 1977, entered into force 7 Dec 1978) (hereinafter Additional Protocol I) ('alien occupation'). Cf Nowak (n 52) para 31.

occupation and self-determination was noted by Judge Iwasawa in *Palestine* (2024):

> The determination of whether the obligation to respect the right to self-determination has been violated is complex in situations of occupation. Occupation in all its forms, by its very nature, affects the exercise of the right to self-determination of the people living in the occupied territory. Thus, occupation itself cannot constitute a violation of the obligation to respect the right to self-determination.[64]

Occupation may—but does not necessarily—constitute alien subjugation, domination, and exploitation, and thereby breach the obligation to respect the right to self-determination.[65]

Occupation 'consists of the exercise by a State of effective control in foreign territory'.[66] In particular, occupation refers to a legal status arising where armed forces gain effective control over foreign territory without consent.[67] The 1907 Hague Regulations provide that 'Territory is considered occupied when it is actually placed under the authority of the hostile army'.[68] The law of occupation applies to situations of occupation to impose obligations upon an occupying power.[69] It has been observed that the law of occupation, in effect, regards the occupying power as a 'trustee'.[70] The ICJ explained this

64 *Palestine* (2024) Sep Op Iwasawa para 16.

65 A tension has been identified in the interplay between the lawfulness of a situation of occupation governed by the law of occupation and the right of the people of an occupied territory to self-determination. See Eliav Lieblich & Eyal Benvenisti, *Occupation in International Law* (OUP 2022) 9 n 1, 220.

66 *Palestine* (2024) para 109. See also ibid paras 91–92.

67 Lieblich & Benvenisti (n 65) 9.

68 Hague Convention (IV) respecting the Laws and Customs of War on Land and its annex: Regulations concerning the Laws and Customs of War on Land, Regulations art 42, 36 Stat. 2277, 1 Bevans 631 (18 Oct 1907, entered into force 26 Jan 1910), reproduced in (1908) 2(Supp) *AJIL* 90 (hereinafter 1907 Hague Regulations).

69 1907 Hague Regulations arts 42–56; Geneva Convention Relative to the Protection of Civilian Persons in Time of War arts 27–34, 47–78, 75 UNTS 287 (12 Aug 1949, entered into force 21 Oct 1950). See *Prosecutor v Naletilić & Martinović*, IT-98-34-T, Judgment (31 Mar 2003) para 217.

70 Lieblich & Benvenisti (n 65) 9–10. See also Orna Ben-Naftali et al, 'Illegal Occupation: Framing the Occupied Palestinian Territory' (2005) 23(3) *Berkeley Journal of International Law* 551, 575–79; Ralph Wilde, 'From Trusteeship to Self-Determination and Back again: The Role of the Hague Regulations in the Evolution of International Trusteeship, and the Framework of Rights and Duties of Occupying Powers' (2009) 31(1) *Loyola of Los Angeles International and Comparative Law Review* 85; Aeyal Gross, *The Writing on the Wall: Rethinking*

relation in *Palestine* (2024): 'The occupying Power bears a duty to administer the territory for the benefit of the local population'.[71] 'Conceptually, occupation is neutral', insofar as the law of occupation is neither a source of rights for an occupying power nor an indication of the lawfulness of its presence in an occupied territory.[72]

Notwithstanding the neutrality of occupation, abuse by the occupying power of its authority 'might taint its continuing presence in the occupied territory with illegality'.[73] As the ICJ reasoned in *Palestine* (2024), 'the legality of the occupying Power's presence in the occupied territory must be assessed in light of other rules', including the right to self-determination.[74] Occupation is not regarded as a violation of the right to self-determination *vel non*.[75] In *The Wall* (2004) and *Palestine* (2024), the ICJ did not regard occupation to categorically breach the obligation to respect the right to self-determination under CIL.[76] Instead, as discussed further below, the ICJ considered certain aspects of the conduct of Israel in the Occupied Palestinian Territory (OPT) to breach its obligations under international law, including its obligation to respect the right to self-determination. The relation between the law of occupation and the right to self-determination is such that, where an occupying power has breached its obligation to respect the right to self-determination in relation to the occupied population, the occupation becomes unlawful and that people is entitled to the exercise of self-determination as a 'right to independence'.[77] In *Palestine* (2024), the ICJ considered that, 'in cases of foreign occupation such as the [the occupation of the OPT by Israel], the right to self-determination constitutes a peremptory norm of international law'.[78]

the International Law of Occupation (CUP 2017) 28. Cf Chapter 7.b.i.1 (The Concept of the Sacred Trust).

[71] *Palestine* (2024) para 105.
[72] Eyal Benvenisti, *The International Law of Occupation* (OUP 2012) 15–16.
[73] Ibid 17. See Ben-Naftali et al (n 70) 551–614.
[74] *Palestine* (2024) para 109.
[75] Benvenisti (n 72) 17–18.
[76] *Wall* (2004) paras 118–22; *Palestine* (2024) paras 245–58. See Ben-Naftali et al (n 70) 552.
[77] See *Palestine* (2024) paras 237, 283 (referring to 'the realization of the right of the Palestinian people to self-determination' as 'including its right to an independent and sovereign State').
[78] Ibid para 233. See Chapter 5.e.

A. Situations of Occupation Implicating Self-Determination

Three advisory opinions of the ICJ—*Namibia* (1971), *The Wall* (2004), and *Palestine* (2024)—address the breach of obligations under the right to self-determination in circumstances characterized by the court as situations of occupation.[79] Additionally, the African Commission on Human and Peoples' Rights and the ACtHPR have respectively addressed the right to self-determination in the context of what they regarded to be situations of occupation in *Democratic Republic of Congo v Burundi, Rwanda and Uganda* (2003) and *Mornah v Benin* (2022). Each case is considered in turn.

In *Namibia* (1971), the ICJ addressed the legal consequences of the continued presence of South Africa in Namibia following termination of the Mandate for South West Africa by the UNGA.[80] Under those circumstances, South Africa had no legal basis to justify its continued presence in Namibia: its presence was no longer founded on a Mandate charter, and South Africa was no longer regarded as an administering authority of a Mandate Territory. The ICJ advised the UNSC 'that, the continued presence of South Africa in Namibia being illegal, South Africa is under obligation to withdraw its administration from Namibia immediately and thus put an end to its occupation of the Territory'.[81] Moreover, the ICJ recognized obligations of third-States of non-recognition and non-assistance towards 'South Africa with reference to its occupation of Namibia', legal consequences also identified in *The Wall* (2004) and *Palestine* (2024), discussed below.[82] The position of the ICJ in *Namibia* (1971) may therefore be understood to implicate South Africa's general obligation to respect the right to self-determination, in relation to the people of Namibia, in a situation of occupation.[83] This understanding is reflected in UNSC Resolution 301 (1971), adopted in response to the advisory opinion, in which the UNSC 'recogniz[ed] the legitimacy

[79] Note that the cases of South Africa / Namibia and Israel / Palestine have been identified as the impetus for Article 1(4) of Additional Protocol I, which addresses resistance by a people pursuant to exercising the right to self-determination. See Cassese (n 63) 103. Cf Stefan Oeter, 'Terrorism and "Wars of National Liberation" from a Law of War Perspective: Traditional Patterns and Recent Trends' (1989) 49 *Zeitschrift für ausländisches öffentliches Recht und Völkerrecht* 445, 472. See Chapter 7.b.ii.3.

[80] See Chapter 4.b.

[81] *Namibia* (1971) para 133.

[82] Ibid para 119. The court also identified an obligation to cooperate to bring the unlawful situation to an end, a consequence identified outside the context of occupation. Ibid paras 119–24. See Chapter 9.d.ii.2.

[83] Ben-Naftali et al (n 70) 576–77. See Chapter 9.

of the movement of the people of Namibia against the illegal occupation of their Territory by the South African authorities and their right to self-determination and independence'.[84]

In *The Wall* (2004), the ICJ identified legal consequences of the construction of a security wall in Palestinian territory occupied by Israel.[85] In its advisory opinion, the ICJ regarded the Palestinians as a people entitled to the right to self-determination and assessed that certain aspects of the occupation of Palestinian territory by Israel breached its obligation to respect the right of the Palestinian people to self-determination.[86] The ICJ therefore did not regard occupation to categorically breach the obligation to respect the right to self-determination, but rather, identified particular aspects of the wall at issue to give rise to a breach of that obligation.[87] Specifically, the ICJ assessed that construction of the wall, in light of its territorial implications and potential to impact the demographic composition of the OPT, breached Israel's obligation to respect the right to self-determination in relation to the Palestinian people.[88] These effects of the wall (permanence of physical control and its impact on the demographic composition of the people of the territory) were defined in terms of the substantive features of the right to self-determination, i.e. the territory and its people.

In *Palestine* (2024), the ICJ examined certain policies and practice of Israel in the OPT and evaluated their impact on the lawfulness of Israel's continued presence in the OPT.[89] As in *The Wall* (2004), the *Palestine* (2024) advisory opinion identified aspects of policies and practices of Israel in connection with its occupation of the OPT that breached its obligation to respect the right to self-determination of the people of Palestine. In particular, the court identified specific effects of these policies and practices that obstructed the exercise of self-determination by the people of Palestine: territorial annexation and fragmentation, undermining the integrity of the Palestinian people, deprivation of the enjoyment of natural resources, and impairment of the pursuit of economic, social, and cultural development.[90] Obstruction of the

[84] S/Res/301 (20 Oct 1971) preambular para 7; see also para 6. See Chapter 7.b.ii.2.
[85] See Chapter 4.e.
[86] *Wall* (2004) paras 118–22.
[87] Ben-Naftali et al (n 70) 552.
[88] See Lieblich & Benvenisti (n 65) 11. See also Gross (n 70) 18.
[89] See Chapter 4.h.
[90] *Palestine* (2024) paras 230–43, 256.

exercise of self-determination by the people of Palestine, in turn, impacted the legality of Israel's occupation of the OPT.[91] Israel's breach of its obligation to respect the right to self-determination thereby contributed to the unlawfulness of its continued presence in the OPT.[92] The court affirmed that the realization of the right of the Palestinian people to self-determination 'include[es] its right to an independent and sovereign State'.[93]

At the regional level, the African Commission on Human and Peoples' Rights, in *Democratic Republic of Congo v Burundi, Rwanda and Uganda* (2003), considered an inter-State petition by the DRC alleging breach of provisions of the ACHPR by Burundi, Rwanda, and Uganda through their armed activities in the DRC.[94] The African Commission regarded the situation in the eastern provinces of DRC during the relevant period to be one of occupation, and found 'the conduct of the Respondent States in occupying territories of the Complainant State to be a flagrant violation of the rights of the peoples of the Democratic Republic of Congo to their unquestionable and inalienable right to self-determination provided for by Article 20 of the African Charter'.[95] The African Commission regarded occupation of provinces of the DRC to breach the obligations of Burundi, Rwanda, and Uganda under ACHPR Article 20. The African Commission did not indicate that any specific aspects of the occupation gave rise to the breach of the obligations of Burundi, Rwanda, and Uganda to respect the right to self-determination of the people of the DRC.

The ACtHPR, in *Mornah v Benin* (2022), considered the entitlement of the Sahrawi people to self-determination in relation to Morocco's control over portions of Western Sahara.[96] The case concerned an Application based on 'the right to self-determination, particularly, the right of the Sahrawi people

[91] Ibid para 257.
[92] Ibid para 261.
[93] Ibid paras 237, 283.
[94] *Democratic Republic of Congo v Burundi, Rwanda and Uganda*, ACommHPR, Communication No 227/99 (2003) paras 1–11.
[95] Ibid paras 69, 77.
[96] *Bernard Anbataayela Mornah v Benin et al*, ACtHPR, Application No 028/2018, Judgment (22 Sept 2022) (hereinafter *Mornah v Benin* (2022)). Other authorities have similarly regarded Morocco's presence in Western Sahara to constitute occupation. See *Saharawi Arab Democratic Republic and Another v Owner and Charterers of the MV 'NM Cherry Blossom' and Others*, High Court of South Africa, [2017] ZAECPEH 31 paras 29, 38; *Western Sahara Campaign UK, R (on the application of) v HR Revenue and Customs* [2015] EWHC 2898 (Admin) [18]. See also A/Res/34/37 (21 Nov 1979); A/Res/35/19 (11 Nov 1980). For background see Chapter 4.c.

to obtain assistance in their struggle for freedom from foreign occupation' under the ACHPR.[97] While the case concerned the application of Article 20 of the ACHPR, the ACtHPR also looked to other sources of the right to self-determination in international law, and in so doing, regarded what it characterized as a situation of occupation as one thereby implicating the right to self-determination.[98] Although the claim before the ACtHPR was based on the right of all peoples to the assistance of States parties to the ACHPR 'in their liberation struggle against foreign domination' under ACHPR Article 20,[99] the ACtHPR considered the occupation of Western Sahara by Morocco to be 'incompatible' with the right of its people to self-determination.[100] The ACtHPR did not, however, identify specific conditions under which it viewed occupation to give rise to a breach of a State's obligations under the right to self-determination.[101]

B. Occupation and 'De Facto' Administration

Practice indicates that a NSGT or Trust Territory may be subject to occupation. Accordingly, irrespective of whether a situation of occupation gives rise to a distinct entitlement to exercise the right to self-determination in relation to its international aspect, the law of occupation may overlap at points with the entitlement of the people of a NSGT or Trust Territory to exercise the right to self-determination. As noted above, the obligations of an occupying power reflect a form of trusteeship, a relationship also characterizing the position of an administering State in relation to the people of a NSGT or Trust Territory.[102] One specific point of convergence reflected in practice in this regard concerns the exploitation of the natural resources of such a territory.[103]

Where a situation of occupation constitutes alien subjugation, domination, and exploitation, its distinction from the non-self-governing status of the people concerned may be without a difference from the perspective of the

[97] *Mornah v Benin* (2022) para 285.

[98] Ibid para 303.

[99] The ACtHPR ultimately concluded that the support of AU member States for the membership of Morocco into the AU did not constitute a breach of their obligations under Article 20(3) of the ACHPR: ibid paras 314–22.

[100] Ibid para 303.

[101] See ibid para 288.

[102] Lieblich & Benvenisti (n 65) 9–10; Ben-Naftali et al (n 70) 575–79; Wilde (n 70) 85–142. See also Gross (n 70) 28. See Chapter 7.b.i.1.

[103] See Chapter 8.d.i.2.

entitlement of that people to a 'right to independence' (i.e. exercise the right to self-determination in relation to its international aspect).[104] However, the potential for overlap between legal regimes applicable to situations of occupation and the administration of NSGTs has unsettled implications for the obligations of an occupying power, and may inform the legal consequences arising from such a situation.[105] For example, as discussed above, Western Sahara, as NSGT, has at times been referred to as an occupied territory,[106] while Morocco has been regarded in relation to Western Sahara as akin to an administering power 'de facto'.[107] The ACtHPR, in *Mornah v Benin* (2022), described control of portions of Western Sahara by Morocco as a situation of occupation of a territory in which decolonization has not yet been completed.[108] Similar issues were surfaced, but not resolved, in *East Timor* (1995) concerning the obligations of Indonesia arising from its control of East Timor, a NSGT, and the right of its people to self-determination.[109] Where an occupying power displaces an administering power and assumes control over a NSGT, practice is inconclusive as to whether respect for the right to self-determination requires such occupying power to perform the obligations of the administering power.[110] Although the presence of an occupying

[104] *Kosovo* (2010) para 79.

[105] See Chapter 9.

[106] Supra n 96.

[107] Case C-266/16 *Western Sahara Campaign UK v Commissioners for Her Majesty's Revenue and Customs, Secretary of State for Environment, Food and Rural Affairs*, Grand Chamber, Judgment (27 Feb 2018) para 72; *Western Sahara Campaign UK v Secretary of State for International Trade et al* [2022] EWHC 3108 (Admin) [29]. See also Hans Corell, 'The Legality of Exploring and Exploiting Natural Resources in Western Sahara' (2008) *Western Sahara Conference Proceedings* 231, 238.

[108] *Mornah v Benin* (2022) para 301.

[109] *East Timor* (1995) paras 12–16. See Chapter 4.d. Note that the exercise by the people of East Timor of its right to self-determination was administered by the United Nations, following agreements between and with Indonesia and Portugal, rather than by an administering power performing obligations under Chapter XI of the UN Charter. See *Question of East Timor: Report of the Secretary-General*, A/53/951, S/1999/513 (5 May 1999) (attaching agreements concerning modalities for the exercise of self-determination by the people of East Timor); S/Res/1264 (15 Sept 1999) (taking note of the outcome of the UN-facilitated referendum through which the people of East Timor achieved self-government through independence); S/Res/1272 (25 Oct 1999) (establishing the United Nations Transitional Administration in East Timor (UNTAET)). See Benvenisti (n 72) 172–77.

[110] See Chapter 9.c. For example, S/Res/384 (22 Dec 1975), which recognized 'the inalienable right of the people of East Timor to self-determination and independence', called on Indonesia to withdraw from East Timor and Portugal 'as administering Power to co-operate fully with the United Nations so as to enable the people of East Timor to exercise freely their right to self-determination'. S/Res/389 (22 Apr 1976) called on Indonesia to withdraw from East Timor yet omitted reference to Portugal as administering power.

power in a NSGT is distinguishable from the relation between an administering power and a NSGT, there are obvious benefits to the people concerned in the performance of the decolonization obligations of the erstwhile administering power by such an occupying power.[111]

2. Resistance

There is a degree of support for an entitlement to resistance by peoples subjected to alien subjugation, domination, and exploitation pursuant to their exercise of the right to self-determination.[112]

UNGA Resolution 2625 (the FRD) provides that peoples are entitled 'to seek and to receive support in accordance with the purposes and principles of the Charter' in their action against and resistance to forcible action depriving them of their right to self-determination.[113] Implicit in such an entitlement is what has been referred to as a 'right of resistance' in relation to the duty of States to refrain from any forcible action which deprives a people of its right to self-determination and freedom and independence.[114] This provision of UNGA Resolution 2625 is triggered by 'forcible action' which deprives a people of the right to self-determination.[115] Despite the element of 'forcible action', however, the provision is not framed in terms of 'self-defense' and makes no reference to the use of force, although the *travaux préparatoires* reflects extensive debate on these subjects.[116] The entitlement to 'seek and receive support' in UNGA Resolution 2625 is conditioned by

[111] There is, in this regard, a possible tension between the law of occupation and decolonization obligations under the UN Charter. The law of occupation aims to preserve the status quo ante during occupation 'unless absolutely prevented'. 1907 Hague Regulations art 43; see Lieblich & Benvenisti (n 65) 14, 25. By contrast, obligations under Chapters XI and XII of the UN Charter are directed towards promoting self-government in NSGTs and Trust Territories and, in this way, mandate departure from the status quo. Cf ibid 118–33 (discussing the concept of 'transformative occupation'); Benvenisti (n 72) 197–99.

[112] Whether this same entitlement applies in the colonial context is more controversial and unsettled. Gaetano Arangio-Ruiz, *The UN Declaration on Friendly Relations and the System of the Sources of International Law* (Sijthoff & Noordhoff 1979) s 79. Cf Cassese (n 51) 153–54. Some UNGA resolutions refer to resistance in the context of colonial situations. See e.g. A/Res/3103 (XXVIII) (12 Dec 1973) preambular para 4; A/Res/2383 (XXIII) (7 Nov 1968) para 1. See also S/Res/301 (20 Oct 1971) preambular para 7.

[113] FRD Principle V, para 5.

[114] Arangio-Ruiz (n 112) s 79.

[115] Cassese (n 51) 99; Shaw (n 63) 481.

[116] A/7326 (1968) paras 174–77; A/7619 (1969) paras 166–68. See C. Don Johnson, 'Toward Self-Determination—A Reappraisal as Reflected in the Declaration on Friendly Relations' (1973) 3 *Georgia Journal of International and Comparative Law* 145, 150–51.

the UN Charter ('in accordance with the purposes and principles of the Charter').

The Vienna Declaration (1993) refers to 'the right of peoples to take any legitimate action, in accordance with the Charter of the United Nations, to realize their inalienable right of self-determination'.[117] Unlike the way in which UNGA Resolution 2625 contemplates resistance in relation to 'forcible action' depriving a people subjected to alien subjugation, domination, and exploitation of its right to self-determination, the 'right of peoples to take any legitimate action' articulated in the Vienna Declaration (1993) is not so limited to responding to 'forcible action' and refers more broadly to actions pursuant to realization of the right to self-determination. Moreover, the Vienna Declaration (1993) extends this 'right' to colonial situations, which it regards as a form of 'alien domination or foreign occupation'. The Vienna Declaration (1993) contemplates that the UN Charter furnishes limitations on the 'legitimate action' that might be undertaken pursuant to this 'right'. This qualification indicates that the Vienna Declaration (1993) was not contemplated to be additive to the measures that might otherwise be lawfully undertaken under international law pursuant to realization of the right to self-determination.

At the regional level, the ACHPR, at Article 20, contains both a 'right of resistance' and a 'right to assistance' to this end. Article 20(2) contains a right, of colonized and oppressed peoples, 'to free themselves from the bonds of domination' by 'any means recognized by the international community'.[118] While Article 20(2) imposes a limitation upon the available means of resistance to those 'recognized by the international community', this formulation differs from the safeguard clauses contained in UNGA Resolution 2625 (the FRD) and the Vienna Declaration (1993), wherein the respective entitlement 'to seek and receive support' and 'right of peoples to take any legitimate action' are qualified by the UN Charter. Article 20(3) further contemplates an entitlement of all peoples to the 'assistance' of States parties 'in their liberation struggle against foreign domination, be it political, economic or cultural'. Article 20(3) has been interpreted by the ACtHPR as imposing positive duties upon States parties to the ACHPR to render assistance to such peoples, 'without geographical or temporal limitations', and in this view, the

[117] Vienna Declaration (1993) part 1, s 2, para 2.
[118] ACHPR art 20(2). See Chapter 2.d.i.

'right to the assistance of States parties' defined at Article 20(3) constitutes an entitlement to receive such assistance.[119] The African Commission on Human and Peoples' Rights has interpreted Articles 20(2) and 20(3) to be 'reserved for colonized peoples'.[120]

3. Additional Protocol I to the 1949 Geneva Conventions (Article 1(4))

Resistance by a people pursuant to exercising the right to self-determination may trigger the application of international humanitarian law. Additional Protocol I to the 1949 Geneva Conventions, at Article 1(4), refers to

> armed conflicts in which peoples are fighting against colonial domination and alien occupation and against racist régimes in the exercise of their right of self-determination, as enshrined in the Charter of the United Nations and the Declaration on Principles of International Law concerning Friendly Relations and Co-operation among States in accordance with the Charter of the United Nations.[121]

The International Committee of the Red Cross (ICRC) Commentary to Article 1(4) clarifies that this provision consists of two distinct elements: (1) 'there must be an armed conflict in which a people is struggling against colonial domination, alien occupation or a racist régime', and (2) 'the struggle of that people must be in order to exercise its right to self-determination'.[122] This distinction is consistent with UNGA Resolution 2625 (the FRD), which frames a 'right of resistance' in terms of 'actions against, and resistance to, such forcible action in pursuit of the exercise of their right to self-determination'.[123] In this way, the applicability of international humanitarian

[119] *Mornah v Benin* (2022) paras 151, 299.

[120] *Front for the Liberation of the State of Cabinda v Angola*, ACommHPR, Communication No 328/06 (2013) (hereinafter *Cabinda v Angola* (2013)) para 125 ('[I]n post-colonial Africa, the right to self[-]determination can be enjoyed within the existing territories and with full respect for the sovereignty and territorial integrity of State Parties to the Charter. The Commission also believes that the right to pursue economic and social development is attainable within the framework of an existing state insofar as different groups and communities are represented in decision-making institutions of the given state').

[121] Additional Protocol I art 1(4). See Oeter (n 79) 469–73.

[122] Yves Sandoz et al (eds), *Commentary on the Additional Protocols of 8 June 1977 to the Geneva Conventions of 12 August 1949* (ICRC / Martinus Nijhoff 1987) (hereinafter *ICRC Commentary*) para 107.

[123] FRD Principle V, para 5.

law is referential to the entitlement of a people to exercise the international aspect of the right to self-determination,[124] but Article 1(4) is not understood to imply that the use of force is itself an exercise of the right to self-determination.

Article 96(3) of Additional Protocol I contains a procedure by which an 'authority representing a people' engaged in an armed conflict contemplated by Article 1(4) against a State Party may bring the Geneva Conventions and Additional Protocol I into application to that conflict.[125] It has been suggested that Article 1(4) may primarily be of 'political and ideological importance', in view of the practical unlikelihood that the requirements of Article 96(3) would be satisfied by parties to such an armed conflict.[126] By contemplating the applicability of international humanitarian law to armed conflicts in which peoples resort to force in order to exercise their right to self-determination, Article 1(4) has been interpreted to confer a degree of legitimacy to such armed conflicts, by regarding them as international in character, and to peoples and persons resorting to force under such circumstances, recognized under international humanitarian law as belligerents and combatants.[127] The procedure under Article 96(3) was invoked for the first time in June 2015 by the *Front Polisario*, representing the people of Western Sahara, upon its deposit of a unilateral declaration of adherence to the 1949 Geneva Conventions and Additional Protocol I.[128] The declaration was notified to States parties by Switzerland, the depository, as having the effects of Article 96(3) of Additional Protocol I as of 23 June 2015.[129]

[124] Interpretation of the terms 'colonial domination', 'alien occupation', and 'racist régimes' varies. See *ICRC Commentary* para 112. Cf Cassese (n 63) 103; Benvenisti (n 72) 17; Oeter (n 79) 470. Even if the first two scenarios enumerated in Article 1(4) overlap with the two generally recognized circumstances under which a people is entitled to exercise self-determination in relation to its international aspect as a 'right to independence', the third scenario is distinct as it is not predicated on the existence of 'distinct peoples' and is therefore not a situation implicating the international aspect of the right to self-determination.

[125] Additional Protocol I art 96(3). See *ICRC Commentary* paras 3758–75.

[126] Oeter (n 79) 472–73; Cassese (n 63) 109.

[127] Oeter (n 79) 470; Cassese (n 63) 99–100.

[128] Swiss Confederation Federal Department of Foreign Affairs, *Notification to the Governments of the States parties to the Geneva Conventions of 12 August 1949 for the Protection of War Victims*, Doc 242.512.0—GEN 4/15 (26 June 2015).

[129] Ibid. See Dominic Gattuso, 'The Polisario Front and the Future of Article 1(4)' (2021) 99 *Texas Law Review* 1201. Morocco became party to Additional Protocol I on 3 June 2011. See https://ihl-databases.icrc.org/en/ihl-treaties/api-1977/state-parties.

c. Secession

The foregoing sections analysed the two recognized circumstances in which peoples are entitled to exercise the right to self-determination in such a way as to 'separate from' another State.[130] Implicit in the exceptional nature of these two circumstances is the absence of a general entitlement to effectuate secession as a component of the right to self-determination under international law.[131] Secession refers to the separation of part of a State,[132] and may be understood as the 'creation of a new independent entity through the separation of part of the territory and population of an existing State, without the consent of the latter'.[133]

Early in the drafting of the UN Charter, it was understood that the principle of self-determination was not intended to give rise to an entitlement to secession, which would be incompatible with the purposes of the Charter.

> Concerning the principle of self-determination, it was strongly emphasized on the one side that this principle corresponded closely to the will and desires of peoples everywhere and should be clearly enunciated in the Chapter; on the other side, it was stated that the principle conformed to the purposes of the Charter only insofar as it implied the right of self-government of peoples and not the right of secession.[134]

In response to concerns over secession, instruments referring to the right to self-determination expressly condition the right and associated conduct of States by provisions safeguarding territorial integrity.[135]

[130] *Kosovo* (2010) para 82.

[131] See (1970) 7 *U.N. Monthly Chronicle* 36 (Former UN Secretary-General U Thant, on the attitude of UN Member States towards secession pursuant to the right to self-determination, remarked: 'As an international organization, the United Nations has never accepted and does not accept and I do not believe it will ever accept the principle of secession of a part of its Member State').

[132] Vienna Convention on Succession of States in respect of Treaties arts 34–37, 1946 UNTS 3 (23 Aug 1978, entered into force 6 Nov 1996).

[133] Marcelo G. Kohen, 'Introduction' in Marcelo G. Kohen (ed), *Secession: International Perspectives* (CUP 2006) 3. See Crawford (n 36) 375–448.

[134] Summary Report of Sixth Meeting of Committee I/1, Doc 343, I/1/16, in (1945) 6 *UN Conference on International Organization* 296.

[135] Resolution 1514 paras 6–7; FRD Principle V, paras 7–8; Helsinki Final Act (1975) Principle VIII, para 1; Vienna Declaration (1993) part I, s 2, para 3. See also ICCPR art 1(3); ICESCR art 1(3). See Chapter 7.d.i.

The following sections consider the absence of a general entitlement to secession under the right to self-determination and assess the specific question of 'remedial secession'.

i. Absence of an Entitlement to Secession

International law has consistently denied a general entitlement to secession as a component of the right to self-determination. An early expression, from the League of Nations period, of the absence of an entitlement to secession in international law is the Aaland Islands dispute.[136] In that context, the International Committee of Jurists appointed by the Council of the League of Nations to examine jurisdiction observed:

> Positive International Law does not recognise the right of national groups, as such, to separate themselves from the State of which they form part by the simple expression of a wish, any more than it recognises the right of other States to claim such a separation. Generally speaking, the grant or refusal of the right to a portion of its population of determining its own political fate by plebiscite or by some other method, is, exclusively, an attribute of the sovereignty of every State which is definitively constituted.[137]

The Committee similarly considered that, even under circumstances where the principle of self-determination may apply outside of positive international law (i.e. to entities lacking territorial sovereignty), the principle would not entitle a national group to secession.[138] The Commission of Rapporteurs, appointed to advise on the merits of the dispute, also rejected an entitlement to secession under positive international law.[139]

[136] *Report of the International Committee of Jurists entrusted by the Council of the League of Nations with the task of giving an advisory opinion upon the legal aspects of the Aaland Islands Question*, (Oct 1920) *League of Nations Official Journal*, Special Supplement No 3 (hereinafter 1920 Aaland Islands Report) 5; *Report submitted to the Council of the League of Nations by the Commission of Rapporteurs*, League of Nations Council Doc B7.21/68/106 (16 Apr 1921) (hereinafter 1921 Aaland Islands Report) 27. See Chapter 1.c.ii.

[137] 1920 Aaland Islands Report 5.

[138] Ibid 6.

[139] Because the Commission viewed Finland to be the former autonomous State of Finland and, as such, subject to positive international law, unlike the Committee, it did not address

> To concede to minorities, either of language or religion, or to any fractions of a population the right of withdrawing from the community to which they belong, because it is their wish or their good pleasure, would be to destroy order and stability within States and to inaugurate anarchy in international life; it would be to uphold a theory incompatible with the very idea of the State as a territorial and political unity.[140]

Nearly a century later, in *Kosovo* (2010), the ICJ considered whether the right to self-determination contains an entitlement to secession.[141] Following a declaration of independence by Kosovo on 17 February 2008, the UNGA sought from the ICJ an advisory opinion on whether 'the unilateral declaration of independence' was 'in accordance with international law'.[142] In its response to the UNGA, the ICJ did not identify an entitlement to exercise the international aspect of the right to self-determination beyond the circumstances of peoples of NSGTs and peoples subject to alien subjugation, domination, and exploitation.[143] The ICJ framed the question referred to it by the UNGA in such a way that identifying an affirmative entitlement to secession fell beyond the scope of the referral.[144] Instead, the ICJ addressed whether the declaration of independence was prohibited,[145] and concluded that the declaration did not violate any applicable rule of international law.[146] The absence of a prohibition of secession under international law was viewed by the ICJ as a product of international practice, in which a number of States had gained independence outside the context of the exercise of the right to self-determination (and its limited entitlement to 'separate from' a State as a 'right to independence').[147] *Kosovo* (2010) indicates that international law

the operation of the principle of self-determination in relation to entities lacking territorial sovereignty.

---

[140] 1921 Aaland Islands Report 28.
[141] See Chapter 4.f.
[142] A/Res/63/3 (8 Oct 2008).
[143] *Kosovo* (2010) para 82.
[144] Ralphe Wilde, 'Accordance with International Law of the Unilateral Declaration of Independence in Respect of Kosovo' (2011) 105(2) *AJIL* 301, 303.
[145] *Kosovo* (2010) paras 55–56.
[146] Ibid para 122.
[147] Ibid para 79 (quoted supra Chapter 4 n 90).

is neutral towards secession, supplying neither a general entitlement nor a prohibition.[148]

Prior to the *Kosovo* (2010) Advisory Opinion, the Committee on the Elimination of Racial Discrimination adopted a General Recommendation on the right to self-determination, in view of what it referred to as the frequent reference by minority groups to the right to self-determination as a basis for an entitlement to secession. The Committee took the position that the right to self-determination does not contain an entitlement to unilateral secession.[149] In reaching this conclusion, the Committee addressed sources of international law referring to self-determination and identified various aspects of the right.[150]

Assertions of an entitlement to secession by sub-State groups have been uniformly rejected by domestic courts. The leading domestic authority concerning a claim to secession is the advisory opinion rendered by the Supreme Court of Canada in *Quebec* (1998).[151] The relevant question before the court concerned whether the right to self-determination under international law conferred upon the population of the province of Quebec or its representative institutions a positive entitlement to 'effect' secession.[152] The court observed that, as a general matter, the right to self-determination is ordinarily fulfilled through its domestic aspect, and that the right had evolved in international law 'within a framework of respect for the territorial integrity of existing states'.[153] The court identified the two recognized 'exceptional circumstances' under which peoples are entitled to exercise the international aspect of the right to self-determination and noted that a denial of a general entitlement to secession may be inferred therefrom.[154] After

[148] See Christian Walter & Antje von Ungern-Sternberg, 'Introduction: Self-Determination and Secession in International Law—Perspectives and Trends with Particular Focus on the Commonwealth of Independent States' in Christian Walter et al (eds), *Self-Determination and Secession in International Law* (OUP 2014) 3.

[149] CERD General Recommendation No 21 para 11.

[150] Ibid paras 7–9.

[151] *Quebec* (1998). See Patrick Dumberry, 'Lessons Learned from the *Quebec Secession Reference* before the Supreme Court of Canada' in Marcelo G. Kohen (ed), *Secession: International Perspectives* (CUP 2006) 416–52.

[152] *Quebec* (1998) para 2. In *Kosovo* (2010), the ICJ distinguished this question posed to the Supreme Court of Canada in its reference on Quebec from the question referred in the Kosovo situation. See *Kosovo* (2010) paras 55–56.

[153] *Quebec* (1998) paras 126–27, 131.

[154] Ibid paras 112, 132–33.

acknowledging that commentators have asserted a third circumstance justifying secession—where a people is denied 'the meaningful exercise of its right to self-determination internally'—the court concluded that, '[w]hile it remains unclear whether this third proposition actually reflects an established international law standard, it is unnecessary for present purposes to make that determination' because Quebec would not meet that standard.[155]

The influence of *Quebec* (1998) is reflected in *Scotland* (2022).[156] In *Scotland* (2022), the UK Supreme Court addressed whether the right to self-determination contains a general entitlement to secession. The question arose as a matter of interpretation of the Scotland Act, which created and established the powers of the Scottish parliament, and its compatibility with international law, in particular the right to self-determination.[157] In line with *Quebec* (1998) and *Kosovo* (2010), the UK Supreme Court concluded that the right to self-determination does not contain a general entitlement to secession.[158]

A pair of cases, decided respectively by the first and second Russian Constitutional Courts in the 1990s, similarly rejected an entitlement to secession by sub-State groups as a component of the right to self-determination. The first case, decided in 1992 by *Decree of the Constitutional Court of the RSFSR*, addressed various actions of the Supreme Soviet of the Republic of Tatarstan, a constituent republic of the Soviet Federative Socialist Republic (RSFSR), including in relation to a political status referendum.[159] The Constitutional Court found aspects of the laws in question to be unconstitutional, including action taken based on the referendum to effectuate the unilateral secession of Tatarstan.[160] The second case, decided by *Decree No 10-P of the Constitutional Court of the Russian Federation*, concerned the constitutionality of four decisions by the Russian president concerning the

155 Ibid paras 134–35. See Chapter 7.c.ii.

156 *Scotland* (2022).

157 Ibid [84]–[91].

158 The court also rejected a second argument that the allocation of powers in the Scotland Act 'infringes any principle of self-determination'. Ibid [90].

159 Decree of the Constitutional Court of the RSFSR, 13 March 1992, in (1994) 30(3) *Statutes & Decisions: The Laws of the USSR and its Successor States* 32 (hereinafter *Decree* (1994)). For discussion see James Summers, *Peoples and International Law* (2nd edn, Brill Nijhoff 2014) 402–03.

160 *Decree* (1994) 43–44.

situation in the Chechen Republic.[161] The right to self-determination in international law did not, in the view of the Constitutional Court, provide a basis for the Chechen Republic to effectuate unilateral secession from the Russian Federation.[162]

Finally, the decision of the Supreme Court of Sri Lanka in *Chandrasoma v Senathirajah et al* (2017) further reflects the exclusion of secession as a component of the right to self-determination.[163] In *Chandrasoma v Senathirajah et al* (2017), the petitioner sought a declaration that the *Illankai Thamil Arasu Kachchi* (ITAK) political party sought to establish a separate State within the territory of Sri Lanka.[164] The constitution of Sri Lanka prohibits political parties with such aims or objects.[165] Because the right to self-determination in international law does not contain a general entitlement to secession, its invocation by a sub-State group was not understood by the Supreme Court of Sri Lanka to contemplate secession. Instead, in view of the content of the right to self-determination in international law, the claim to self-determination by the ITAK was framed in reference to the domestic aspect of the right to self-determination.[166]

At the regional level, the ACtHPR and the African Commission on Human and Peoples' rights have indicated that the right to self-determination under Article 20(1) of the ACHPR does not contain an entitlement to secession. In *Katangese Peoples' Congress v Zaire* (1995) and *Mgwanga Gunme et al v Cameroon* (2009), the African Commission assessed that 'secession is not recognised as a variant of the right to self[-]determination within the context of the African Charter'.[167] In *ACHPR v Kenya* (2017), the ACtHPR identified the possibility that certain collective rights under the ACHPR may apply to

[161] Decree No 10-P of the Constitutional Court of the Russian Federation, 31 July 1995, in (1995) 31(5) *Statutes & Decisions: The Laws of the USSR and its Successor States* 48 (hereinafter *Decree* (1995)). For discussion see Summers (n 159) 403–04.

[162] *Decree* (1995) 51–52.

[163] For context see Kalana Senaratne, *Internal Self-Determination in International Law: History, Theory and Practice* (CUP 2021) 228–35.

[164] *Hikkadu Koralage Don Chandrasoma v Mawai S. Senathirajah et al*, SC SPL 03/2014 (2017) 3.

[165] Ibid 4–5.

[166] Ibid 17.

[167] *Mgwanga Gunme et al v Cameroon*, ACommHPR, Communication No 266/2003 (2009) (hereinafter *Mgwanga Gunme v Cameroon* (2009)) para 200. See also *Katangese Peoples' Congress v Zaire*, ACommHPR, Communication No 75/92 (1995) (hereinafter *Katangese Peoples' Congress v Zaire* (1995)) para 6. See Chapter 7.c.

'sub-state ethnic groups and communities', though it questioned whether the right to self-determination codified in Article 20(1) could enjoy such application in view of its implications for secession:

> It would in fact be difficult to understand that the States which are the authors of the Charter intended, for example, to automatically recognise for the ethnic groups and communities that constitute their population, the right to self-determination and independence guaranteed under Article 20 (1) of the Charter, which in this case would amount to a veritable right to secession.[168]

Even if the right to self-determination does not contain an entitlement to secession, it remains the case that international law is neutral towards secession.[169] In *Quebec* (1998), the Supreme Court of Canada articulated one consequence of this neutrality by distinguishing the absence of a legal entitlement to secede 'in advance' from how 'the law will respond after the fact to a then existing political reality'.[170] In this way, secession may be formulated as a question of the creation of States in international law rather than an aspect of the right to self-determination. However, because peoples are defined coextensively with territorial units, to include the populations of States,[171] one consequence of the emergence into statehood of a political entity through secession is that its population would come to be regarded as a people entitled to the right to self-determination in international law.[172]

ii. Remedial Secession

Notwithstanding the absence of a general entitlement to secession as a component of the right to self-determination, a number of authorities have considered whether an entitlement to exercise self-determination in relation

[168] *ACHPR v Kenya*, ACtHPR, Application No 006/2012, Judgment (2017) (hereinafter *ACHPR v Kenya* (2017)) paras 198–99.
[169] *Kosovo* (2010) paras 79, 122. See Walter & von Ungern-Sternberg (n 148) 3; Malcolm N. Shaw, 'The Heritage of States: The Principle of *Uti Possidetis Juris* Today' (1996) 67(1) *British Yearbook of International Law* 75, 144.
[170] *Quebec* (1998) para 110.
[171] See Chapter 6.
[172] Kohen (n 133) 12.

to its international aspect arises in the specific circumstance in which a sub-State group has been denied participation in the exercise of the right to self-determination at the domestic level.[173] This concept is referred to as 'remedial secession'.[174] Remedial secession has been described as a 'drastic remedy',[175] and while the concept has been embraced in scholarship, it remains contested.[176] Although it is unclear whether an entitlement to remedial secession is supported by international law, particularly as a component of the right to self-determination,[177] authorities have cautiously avoided foreclosing the possibility.[178]

The concept of remedial secession was raised in the context of the Aaland Islands dispute.[179] While the International Committee of Jurists appointed by the League of Nations in 1920 did not opine on the question of remedial secession at the jurisdictional phase,[180] the Commission of Rapporteurs appointed to advise on the merits of the dispute did not deny the possibility of remedial secession:

> The separation of a minority from the State of which it forms a part and its incorporation in another State can only be considered as an altogether exceptional solution, a last resort when the State lacks either the will or the power to enact and apply just and effective guarantees.[181]

[173] *Quebec* (1998) para 134 (describing the concept of remedial secession where 'a people is blocked from the meaningful exercise of its right to self-determination internally'). For another definition, see Marc Weller, *Contested Statehood: Kosovo's Struggle for Independence* (OUP 2009) 239.

[174] See *Kosovo* (2010) paras 82–83.

[175] Rupert Emerson, 'Self-Determination' (1971) 65(3) *AJIL* 459, 475. See also Martti Koskenniemi, 'National Self-Determination Today: Problems of Legal Theory and Practice', (1994) 43(2) *ICLQ* 241 (referring in this context to a 'romantic' notion of self-determination).

[176] Marc Weller, *Escaping the Self-Determination Trap* (Martinus Nijhoff 2008) 64. Cf Cassese (n 51) 119–20; Christian Tomuschat, 'Secession and Self-Determination' in Marcelo G. Kohen (ed), *Secession: International Perspectives* (CUP 2006) 35–36; Crawford (n 36) 119, Theodore Christakis, 'Self-Determination, Territorial Integrity and *Fait Accompli* in the Case of Crimea' (2015) 75 *Zeitschrift für ausländisches öffentliches Recht und Völkerrecht* 75, 88 ('[T]he "remedial secession" theory is highly controversial and it is still not clearly established that it is accepted by positive law').

[177] *Kosovo* (2010) para 82. See Thomas M. Franck, 'The Emerging Right to Democratic Governance' (1992) 86(1) *AJIL* 46, 59; Shaw (n 63) 483.

[178] *Kosovo* (2010) paras 82–83; *Quebec* (1998) para 138. See also *Scotland* (2022) [88] (citing with approval *Quebec* (1998)).

[179] See Chapter 1.c.ii.

[180] See 1920 Aaland Islands Report.

[181] 1921 Aaland Islands Report 28.

Remedial secession was regarded to be an 'exceptional' remedy, and it was not recommended in the case of the Aaland Islanders. This language predated the codification of self-determination in treaty law and crystallization of the right in CIL.

Textual support for the concept of remedial secession may derive in the first instance from the Preamble to the Universal Declaration of Human Rights (UDHR), which states:

> Whereas it is essential, if man is not to be compelled to have recourse, as a last resort, to rebellion against tyranny and oppression, that human rights should be protected by the rule of law[.][182]

Arguably, this language contemplates the possibility of resistance in response to human rights violations and abuses as a last resort, which might conceptually be exercised pursuant to an entitlement to remedial secession. However, even if this language is consistent with the concept of remedial secession, its presence in the preambular text of the non-binding UDHR does not evince a legal entitlement to remedial secession.

Language in the safeguard clauses of UNGA Resolution 2625 (the FRD) has been interpreted to suggest that the concept of remedial secession is at least implicitly authorized as a component of the right to self-determination. The FRD states:

> Nothing in the foregoing paragraphs shall be construed as authorizing or encouraging any action which would dismember or impair, totally or in part, the territorial integrity or political unity of sovereign and independent States conducting themselves in compliance with the principle of equal rights and self-determination of peoples as described above and thus possessed of a government representing the whole people belonging to the territory without distinction as to race, creed or colour.[183]

It is argued, as a corollary, that the FRD implicitly contemplates the availability of remedial secession where a State is not in compliance with the

[182] A/Res/217 A (III) (10 Dec 1948) (Universal Declaration of Human Rights) preambular para 3.
[183] FRD Principle V, para 7.

principle of self-determination.[184] However, an interpretation of this provision as implicitly contemplating any form of secession, however narrowly circumscribed, is difficult to reconcile with the *travaux préparatoires* of the FRD, which indicates that the safeguard clauses manifest a concern over secession.[185] It is doubtful that an entitlement or authorization of remedial secession can be said to have been introduced in such a way.[186]

Judicial authorities addressing the question of remedial secession have declined to endorse the concept as one established in international law, though the possibility of such an entitlement has not been foreclosed. In *Kosovo* (2010), the ICJ briefly addressed the concept of remedial secession.[187] The court concluded that '[d]ebates regarding the extent of the right of self-determination and the existence of any right of "remedial secession", however, concern the right to separate from a State', which fell beyond the scope of the question referred by the UNGA.[188] In its references to remedial secession, the court appeared to contemplate the possibility of any such right to be distinct from the right to self-determination. The court also took note that States participating expressed 'radically different views' on this matter, calling into question whether CIL could be said to sustain such a proposition.[189]

Prior to *Kosovo* (2010), the Supreme Court of Canada considered the question of remedial secession in *Quebec* (1998) and similarly identified no such entitlement in international law.[190] The parameters of the right to self-determination were later articulated by the UK Supreme Court in *Scotland* (2022), in reference to *Quebec* (1998) and without mention of remedial secession.[191]

At the regional level, the ACtHPR has contemplated the possibility that minority groups within the population of a State may constitute 'peoples' for

[184] See e.g. Cassese (n 51) 118–20; John Dugard and David Raič, 'The role of recognition in the law and practice of secession' in Marcelo G. Kohen (ed), *Secession: International Perspectives* (CUP 2006) 103–10, 134–37 (referring in this regard to a 'qualified secession doctrine').

[185] Robert Rosenstock, 'The Declaration of Principles of International Law Concerning Friendly Relations: A Survey' (1971) 65(5) *AJIL* 713, 732–33; Arangio-Ruiz (n 112) s 80; Weller (n 176) 62.

[186] Shaw (n 63) 483.

[187] *Kosovo* (2010) paras 82–83.

[188] Ibid para 83.

[189] Walter & von Ungern-Sternberg (n 148) 3.

[190] *Quebec* (1998) paras 134–35, 138. See Dumberry (n 151) 416–52. See Chapter 7.c.i.

[191] *Scotland* (2022) [88].

purposes of certain collective rights under the ACHPR, yet it has questioned whether the right to self-determination codified in Article 20(1) could enjoy such application.[192] However, in two earlier decisions by the African Commission on Human and Peoples' Rights—*Katangese Peoples' Congress v Zaire* (1995) and *Mgwanga Gunme et al v Cameroon* (2009)—the African Commission considered the possibility that remedial secession may be available in cases of 'concrete evidence of violations of human rights to the point that the territorial integrity of the State Party should be called to question, coupled with the denial of the people, their right to participate in the government as guaranteed by Article 13(1)' of the ACHPR.[193] Even so, the Commission declined to endorse remedial secession as an available option in either case as the criteria of 'oppression and domination' under Article 20(2) were not satisfied.[194]

The practice surveyed above, like the textual sources preceding them, does not provide strong support for the proposition that international law admits an entitlement to remedial secession as a component of the right to self-determination. This conclusion is consistent with the more general concern of States, evidenced throughout the emergence of the right to self-determination in international law, over the possibility that any entitlement to secession could be found to flow from the right, and the emphasis accordingly placed on the principle of territorial integrity in relation to the right to self-determination.[195]

Where authorities have expressly contemplated the possibility of remedial secession under international law, its beneficiaries are generally not defined in terms of 'peoples', the subjects of the right to self-determination. Rather, remedial secession has been contemplated, for example, in relation to 'a minority',[196] 'a definable group',[197] or 'part of the population' of a State,[198] whose

[192] *ACHPR v Kenya* (2017) paras 198–99. See also *Cabinda v Angola* (2013) para 126. See Chapter 6.e.i.

[193] *Mgwanga Gunme v Cameroon* (2009) para 194. See also *Katangese Peoples' Congress v Zaire* (1995) para 6.

[194] *Mgwanga Gunme v Cameroon* (2009) paras 190, 197 (Reference to ACHPR Article 20(2) appears to be intended to orient the criteria previously identified in *Katangese Peoples' Congress v Zaire* (1995) in the ACHPR). See *Katangese Peoples' Congress v Zaire* (1995) para 5.

[195] See Chapter 7.d.

[196] 1921 Aaland Islands Report 28.

[197] *Quebec* (1998) para 138.

[198] *Kosovo* (2010) para 82.

participation, inter alia, in the domestic aspect of self-determination has been denied. Put differently, remedial secession is contemplated in terms of sub-State groups within the population of a territorial unit (i.e. a people). Because peoples are defined in relation to certain categories of territorial units for purposes of the right to self-determination,[199] conceptualizing an entitlement to remedial secession in terms of 'peoples' would render the concept a practical nullity.[200] Definition of remedial secession in terms of sub-State groups suggests a concept distinct from the right to self-determination, which applies only to peoples.[201]

Even if the right to self-determination does not entail an entitlement to remedial secession, it remains the case, as discussed above, that international law is neutral towards secession.[202] Where a sub-State group attempts to secede in response to mistreatment by its State, that basis upon which such a group pursues secession may impact its ultimate success in achieving independence through recognition as an independent State.[203] The recognition of a political entity as an independent State emerging under such circumstances may be related to or even driven by human rights considerations.[204] It is in this sense that the secession of Kosovo has been regarded as the first case of remedial secession,[205] even if the ICJ did not identify remedial secession as a component of the right to self-determination in *Kosovo* (2010). As noted above, one consequence of the emergence into statehood of such a political entity is that its population would come to be regarded as a people entitled to the right to self-determination under international law.

199 See Chapter 6.c.

200 Crawford proposes to overcome this challenge by identifying the possibility of remedial secession in cases where territorial entities are governed in such a way as to render them, in effect, non-self-governing. Cf Crawford (n 38) 126, 611–12. However, there is presently no practice to support such a theory.

201 Otherwise an entitlement to 'remedial secession' under the right to self-determination would 'transform' such a sub-State group into a people upon its denial of participation in the domestic aspect of self-determination. See Kohen (n 133) 12.

202 *Kosovo* (2010) paras 79, 122. See Walter & von Ungern-Sternberg (n 148) 3; Shaw (n 169) 144.

203 Shaw (n 63) 483; Weller (n 176) 65.

204 Ralphe Wilde, 'International Recognition and Human Rights Treaties' in Edward Newman et al (eds), *Routledge Handbook of State Recognition* (Taylor & Francis 2019).

205 Weller (n 173) 239.

d. Principle of Territorial Integrity

The absence of a general entitlement to secession as a component of the right to self-determination is a product of the operation of the right alongside the principle of territorial integrity. The principle of territorial integrity protects territorial boundaries.[206] In *Quebec* (1998), it was observed that '[t]he international law principle of self-determination has evolved within a framework of respect for the territorial integrity of existing states'.[207] The territorial approach to the delineation of peoples for purposes of the right to self-determination may be viewed in light of this interrelation.[208] This section considers the treatment of the principle of territorial integrity in the context of self-determination, and assesses the way territorial integrity has come to be regarded as a corollary of the right to self-determination.

i. Safeguard Clauses

Concerns over interpretation of the right to self-determination as condoning secession animated the drafting of instruments addressing the right, some of which expressly condition the right to self-determination by provisions safeguarding territorial integrity.[209] The *travaux préparatoires* of these instruments indicates that such provisions were included primarily to mollify the perceived risk of the potentially destabilizing effects of self-determination on the territorial integrity of States. In this regard, safeguard clauses address both the exercise of self-determination by peoples as well as actions by States in relation to the right to self-determination.

UNGA Resolution 1514 contains language addressing the territorial implications of the right to self-determination. Paragraph 6 provides that '[a]ny attempt aimed at the partial or total disruption of the national unity and the territorial integrity of a country is incompatible with the purposes and principles of the Charter of the United Nations'.[210] Although this

[206] See UN Charter art 2(4). See also Shaw (n 169) 110.
[207] *Quebec* (1998) para 127. See also *Scotland* (2022) [88]–[89] (citing *Quebec* (1998) with approval).
[208] See Chapter 6.c.
[209] Resolution 1514 paras 6–7; FRD Principle V, paras 7–8; Helsinki Final Act (1975) Principle VIII, para 1; Vienna Declaration (1993) part I, s 2, para 3.
[210] Resolution 1514 para 6.

paragraph has at times been invoked to support claims to retrocession of decolonized territories, it has been understood by the ICJ to preserve the territorial integrity of NSGTs by opposing their fragmentation.[211] Paragraph 7 calls on States to observe the provisions of the UN Charter, the Universal Declaration of Human Rights, and UNGA Resolution 1514 'on the basis of equality, non-interference in the internal affairs of all States, and respect for the sovereign rights of all peoples and their territorial integrity'.[212] This additional safeguard clause addresses the conduct of States and the potentially broader implications of the right to self-determination beyond NSGTs.

UNGA Resolution 2625 (the FRD) contains safeguard clauses at paragraphs 7 and 8 of its Principle V on self-determination, which address territorial integrity in relation to the right to self-determination and associated conduct of States.[213] In *Chagos Archipelago* (2019), the ICJ considered that the FRD 'reiterated' 'the nature and scope of the right to self-determination of peoples, including respect for "the national unity and territorial integrity of a State or country"', an element which the court interpreted in reference to UNGA Resolution 1514 as opposing the fragmentation of NSGTs.[214] These provisions reflect concerns, captured in the *travaux préparatoires*, over self-determination being understood as 'a licence for dangerous secessionist movements' and the possibility of actions by States to undermine the 'national unity and territorial integrity' of other States pursuant to the right to self-determination.[215] Paragraphs 7 and 8 are intended to prevent self-determination from being invoked in such a way as to undermine the territorial integrity of States and other territories.[216]

In the Vienna Declaration (1993), the final paragraph of its section on self-determination refers to the FRD and largely restates its safeguard clauses addressing territorial integrity.[217]

The Helsinki Final Act (1975) contains a safeguard clause in the first paragraph of its principle on self-determination. The first paragraph of Principle

[211] *Chagos* (2019) para 153. See Thomas M. Franck and Paul Hoffman, 'The Right of Self-Determination in Very Small Places' (1976) 8(3) *New York University Journal of International Law and Politics* 331, 370.

[212] Resolution 1514 para 7.

[213] See Chapter 3.d.

[214] *Chagos* (2019) paras 153, 155.

[215] See A/7619 (1969) paras 178–79. See Chapter 7.c.

[216] See Rosenstock (n 185) 732–33; Arangio-Ruiz (n 112) s 80.

[217] Vienna Declaration (1993) part I, s 2, para 3.

VIII commits participating States to respect the right to self-determination 'in conformity with the purposes and principles of the Charter of the United Nations and with the relevant norms of international law, including those relating to territorial integrity of States'.[218] The specific identification of territorial integrity among the 'relevant norms of international law' in the safeguard clause, as well as its placement in the first paragraph of the principle on self-determination, suggests its perceived importance.

While common Article 1 of the two human rights covenants does not contain a safeguard clause expressly addressing territorial integrity, Article 1(3) provides that States parties 'shall promote the realization of the right of self-determination, and shall respect that right, in conformity with the provisions of the Charter of the United Nations'.[219] In the view of the HRC, the UN Charter thereby limits the actions that may be taken by States in performance of obligations of an extraterritorial character to respect the right to self-determination and promote is realization. The HRC referred specifically in this regard to non-interference in the internal affairs of other States; such interference was itself understood to adversely affect the exercise of the right to self-determination.[220]

Instruments addressing the self-determination of Indigenous Peoples also contain safeguard clauses addressing territorial integrity.[221] ILO Convention No 169 Concerning Indigenous and Tribal Peoples in Independent Countries includes preambular language that frames the autonomy and self-government of Indigenous Peoples 'within the framework of the States in which they live'.[222] The UN Declaration on the Rights of Indigenous Peoples (UNDRIP) contains a safeguard clause at Article 46 that explicitly refers to territorial integrity.[223] Like other safeguard clauses, this provision was intended to assuage concerns over territorial integrity in relation to the right to self-determination of Indigenous Peoples, addressed in Articles 3 and 4

[218] Helsinki Final Act (1975) Principle VIII, para 1.

[219] ICCPR art 1(3); ICESCR art 1(3).

[220] HRC, *CCPR General Comment No. 12: The Right to Self-Determination of Peoples (Art 1)* (1984) para 6.

[221] See Chapter 8.e.

[222] ILO Convention (No. 169) concerning Indigenous and tribal peoples in independent countries preambular para 5, 1650 UNTS 383 (27 June 1989, entered into force 5 Sept 1991). See Chapter 8.e.i.

[223] UNDRIP art 46(1). See Chapter 8.e.ii.

of the UNDRIP.[224] Article 46 is notable in expressly addressing a range of actors, i.e. 'any State, people, group or person', underscoring the broad applicability of the safeguard clause. A corresponding safeguard clause appears in Article IV of the American Declaration on the Rights of Indigenous Peoples (ADRIP), a non-binding instrument that parallels the UNDRIP in its treatment of the right to self-determination of Indigenous Peoples.[225]

ii. Territorial Integrity as a Corollary of the Right to Self-Determination

In practice, the principle of territorial integrity has shaped the right to self-determination only indirectly, through the *ex ante* identification of 'peoples' in relation to territorial units, rather than by restricting the exercise by peoples of the right to self-determination *ex post*.[226] Territorial considerations inform the threshold question of which populations are peoples entitled to exercise the right to self-determination. In this regard, the ACtHPR observed in *Mornah v Benin* (2022) that

> the right to self-determination is essentially related to peoples' right to ownership over a particular territory and their political status over that territory. It is inconceivable to materialise the free enjoyment of the right to self-determination in the absence of any territory that peoples could call their homeland.[227]

In light of the practical reality that the delineation of a people, for purposes of the right to self-determination, is inextricably linked to a territorial unit, the ICJ has identified a complementary relationship between the operation of the principle of territorial integrity and the right to self-determination. In *Chagos Archipelago* (2019) and *Palestine* (2024), the ICJ regarded the principle of territorial integrity as 'a corollary' of the right to

[224] Karen Engle, 'On Fragile Architecture: The UN Declaration on the Rights of Indigenous Peoples in the Context of Human Rights' (2011) 22(1) *EJIL* 141, 146–48.

[225] American Declaration on the Rights of Indigenous Peoples, OAS AG/Res 2888 (XLVI-0/16) (15 June 2016) art IV.

[226] See Chapter 6.c.

[227] *Mornah v Benin* (2022) para 301.

self-determination.[228] In both cases, the court found that a people is entitled to exercise its right to self-determination over its territorial unit as a whole. In *Chagos Archipelago* (2019), the court considered 'that the peoples of non-self-governing territories are entitled to exercise their right to self-determination in relation to their territory as a whole, the integrity of which must be respected by the administering Power'.[229] In *Palestine* (2024), the court addressed the requirement of an occupying power to respect the territorial integrity of an occupied territory in relation to the OPT:

> This is the territorial unit across which Israel has imposed policies and practices to fragment and frustrate the ability of the Palestinian people to exercise its right to self-determination. . . . The entirety of the [OPT] is also the territory in relation to which the Palestinian people should be able to exercise its right to self-determination, the integrity of which must be respected.[230]

The entitlement of a people to exercise self-determination relative to its entire territorial unit corresponds to the entitlement of the entire population of a territory (i.e. the people as a whole) to participate in the domestic aspect the right to self-determination.[231]

The circumstances giving rise to an entitlement to exercise the right to self-determination in relation to its international aspect are consistent with the principle of territorial integrity. As discussed above, international law generally admits two discrete circumstances under which peoples are entitled to exercise the right to self-determination in such a way as to 'separate from' another State.[232] In either instance, the right to self-determination concerns the political status of a previously defined, separate and distinct territorial unit in relation to another, and in this way the exercise of the right accords with the principle of territorial integrity.[233] The right of peoples of

[228] *Chagos* (2019) para 160; *Palestine* (2024) para 237.
[229] *Chagos* (2019) para 160.
[230] *Palestine* (2024) para 262.
[231] See Chapter 8.c.i. In *Kosovo* (2010), the court considered that the principle of territorial integrity (and the right to self-determination more generally) was not appliable internally to cases of secession. Cf *Kosovo* (2010) para 80.
[232] Ibid para 82.
[233] Emerson (n 175) 464–65; Cassese (n 51) 334.

NSGTs and Trust Territories to self-determination creates the possibility of severance of the connection between a metropolitan power and its overseas colony, identifiable as a discrete territorial unit under international law (i.e. a NSGT or Trust Territory).[234] The right of peoples subject to alien subjugation, domination, and exploitation to self-determination provides for a return to an *ex ante* territorial sovereignty arrangement as between one State and another discrete territorial unit in international law.[235] In either circumstance, the right to self-determination authorizes a change in the political relationship between separate and distinct territorial units (which, at least in the circumstance of alien subjugation, domination, and exploitation, constitutes restoration of an earlier political relationship as between separate and distinct territorial units).[236] In effect, international law operates to reinforce the territorial integrity of separate and distinct territorial units, and the right to self-determination is exercised within the parameters of those territorial units.[237]

Some have identified an ostensible tension in the interrelation between the right to self-determination and the principle of territorial integrity.[238] Notably, in his Separate Opinion in *Western Sahara* (1975), Judge Dillard critically observed that, '[i]t is for the people to determine the destiny of the territory and not the territory the destiny of the people'.[239] However, practice indicates that this is a false dichotomy.[240] Even if territory defines the parameters within which a people determines its 'destiny', it remains that a people determines 'the destiny of the territory' through its right to self-determination.[241]

234 See e.g. FRD Principle V, para 6.

235 See Chapter 7.b.ii.

236 The same may also be said for the circumstance of decolonization: see Emerson (n 174) 465.

237 See e.g. *Quebec* (1998) para 131.

238 Steven R. Ratner, 'Drawing a Better Line: *Uti Possidetis* and the Borders of New States' (1996) 90(4) *AJIL* 590.

239 *Western Sahara* (1975) Sep Op Dillard 122. This statement has been repudiated: see Weller (n 176) 30; Jamie Trinidad, *Self-Determination in Disputed Colonial Territories* (CUP 2018) 71.

240 Christakis (n 176) 76.

241 For a related discussion of the way secession claims are better understood as disputed territorial claims, rather than assertions of the right to self-determination, see Lea Brilmayer, 'Secession and Self-Determination: A Territorial Interpretation' (1991) 16(1) *Yale Journal of International Law* 177.

e. *Uti Possidetis*

A general principle of international law directly relevant to the international aspect of the right to self-determination is *uti possidetis* ('as you possess').[242] *Uti possidetis* operates to preserve territorial boundaries during changes of sovereignty over territory to a new State.[243] As described by the ICJ, '[t]he essence of the principle lies in its primary aim of securing respect for the territorial boundaries at the moment when independence is achieved'.[244] This moment constitutes the 'critical date', at which point former administrative boundaries become international frontiers.[245] Such frontiers reflect a 'photograph of the territory' in reference to boundaries existing at that critical date, and in this way, '[t]he principle of *uti possidetis* freezes the territorial title; it stops the clock but does not put back the hands'.[246] As applied in the context of decolonization, *uti possidetis* may be understood in relation to the 'principle of the intangibility of frontiers inherited from colonization'.[247] To be sure, *uti possidetis* does not preclude the modification of international boundaries, including by consent or acquiescence of the parties concerned.[248] Moreover, the United Nations may endorse the modification of territorial

[242] *Frontier Dispute (Burkina Faso v Mali)*, Judgment, ICJ Rep 1986, 554 (hereinafter *Frontier Dispute (Burkina Faso v Mali)* (1986)) para 20.

[243] Shaw (n 169) 76.

[244] *Frontier Dispute (Burkina Faso v Mali)* (1986) para 23. See *Territorial and Maritime Dispute between Nicaragua and Honduras in the Caribbean Sea (Nicaragua v Honduras)*, Judgment, ICJ Rep 2007, 659 (hereinafter *Territorial and Maritime Dispute (Nicaragua v Honduras)* (2007)) para 152.

[245] *Frontier Dispute (Benin v Niger)*, Judgment, ICJ Rep 2005, 90 (hereinafter *Frontier Dispute (Benin v Niger)* (2005)) para 46. To be sure, the point at which independence is achieved may not be clear in every instance: see *Frontier Dispute (Burkina Faso v Mali)* (1986) para 33; Ratner (n 238) 608. Similarly, territorial boundaries may also be unclear or ambiguous at independence: see *Land, Island and Maritime Frontier Dispute (El Salvador v Honduras: Nicaragua Intervening)*, Judgment, ICJ Rep 1992, 351 (hereinafter *Land, Island and Maritime Frontier Dispute (El Salvador v Honduras: Nicaragua Intervening)* (1992)) para 41 (referring to 'unsettled' boundaries, with respect to which *uti possidetis* 'speaks for once with an uncertain voice'); Shaw (n 169) 130–31.

[246] *Frontier Dispute (Burkina Faso v Mali)* (1986) para 30. See also *Frontier Dispute (Benin v Niger)* (2005) paras 26, 46; *Land, Island and Maritime Frontier Dispute (El Salvador v Honduras: Nicaragua Intervening)* (1992) para 50.

[247] *Frontier Dispute (Burkina Faso v Mali)* (1986) para 20.

[248] *Land, Island and Maritime Frontier Dispute (El Salvador v Honduras: Nicaragua Intervening)* (1992) para 80. See e.g. A/Res/1608 (XV) (21 Apr 1961) (endorsing plebiscites by which the Northern and the Southern Cameroons, parts of the Trust Territory of Cameroons under British administration, decided to integrate with Nigeria and the Republic of Cameroon, respectively). See Shaw (n 169) 141–47.

boundaries,[249] as reflected in the exceptional cases of Israel / Palestine[250] and Rwanda / Burundi.[251] Modification of territorial boundaries by an administering power, including through agreement with a NSGT, may be subject to 'heightened scrutiny', as reflected in *Chagos Archipelago* (2019).[252] Such departures from the ordinary application of the *uti possidetis* principle are exceptional.[253] The ICJ has 'recognized that "the principle of *uti possidetis* has kept its place among the most important legal principles" regarding territorial title and boundary delimitation at the moment of decolonization'.[254]

i. Origins and Development

Uti possidetis derives from Roman Law, in which the principle operated to preserve the status quo in property disputes and conferred upon the possessor of property the advantaged position of defendant in a dispute to determine ownership.[255] The *uti possidetis* principle was transferred into international law as a means to determine title over territory following a cessation of hostilities.[256] In this way, the principle was adapted, from its private law origin to its application in public international law, as one that operated not merely to recognize possession, but to establish an entitlement to sovereignty.[257] From these origins, the applicability of *uti possidetis* to the process of decolonization may be viewed as an extension of the way in which the

[249] Shaw (n 169) 147–50.

[250] A/Res/181 (II) (29 Nov 1947) (endorsing partition of the Mandate of Palestine into separate Israeli and Palestinian territories).

[251] A/Res/1746 (XVI) (27 June 1962) (recognizing culmination of UN-mediated process by which former Belgian Trust Territory Ruanda-Urundi attained independence as separate States of Rwanda and Burundi on 1 July 1962).

[252] *Chagos* (2019) para 172. Cf *Arbitration Tribunal for the Determination of the Maritime Boundary, Guinea-Bissau / Senegal, Award of 31 July 1989* para 68, reproduced in (1990) 83 ILR 8 (hereinafter *Guinea-Bissau / Senegal Award* (1989)) 39.

[253] Trinidad (n 239) 91–102.

[254] *Territorial and Maritime Dispute (Nicaragua v Honduras)* (2007) para 151 (citing *Frontier Dispute (Burkina Faso v Mali)* (1986)).

[255] John Bassett Moore, *Costa Rica—Panama Arbitration: Memorandum on Uti Possidetis* (The Commonwealth Co., Printers 1913) 5–8. See Shaw (n 169) 98.

[256] Ibid 8–11. See William Edward Hall, *International Law* (Clarendon Press 1880) 494–95; Shaw (n 169) 98.

[257] Moore (n 255) 8; Shaw (n 169) 98.

principle had been incorporated into international law as a means by which to link title to territory with possession.

The application of *uti possidetis* to the process of decolonization first emerged with the independence of former Spanish colonies in Central and South America, as a means to promote stability by safeguarding the boundaries of newly independent territories emerging from Spanish sovereignty.[258] The principle of *uti possidetis* was subsequently applied to decolonization in Africa.[259] In *Frontier Dispute (Burkina Faso v Mali)* (1986), a Chamber of the ICJ observed that, by the point of decolonization in Africa, the principle had emerged as one of general application.[260] Additionally, there is support in practice for the application of the *uti possidetis* principle in the context of former French colonies in south-east Asia, which is reflected in *Temple of Preah Vihear* (1962).[261]

The ICJ has referred to *uti possidetis* as a general principle 'logically connected with the phenomenon of the obtaining of independence, wherever it occurs', and the principle has been invoked beyond the context of decolonization in cases of State succession.[262] Applicability of the principle was articulated by the European Community in its *Declaration on the 'Guidelines on the Recognition of New States in Eastern Europe and in*

[258] *Frontier Dispute (Burkina Faso v Mali)* (1986) paras 20, 23; *Land, Island and Maritime Frontier Dispute (El Salvador v Honduras: Nicaragua Intervening)* (1992) paras 41–42. See Arbitral Award of the Swiss Federal Council, *Affaire des frontières Colombo-vénézuéliennes (Colombie contre Vénézuéla)* (24 March 1922), (1949) I RIAA 228. See also Moore (n 255) 14–19; Shaw (n 169) 98–100; Frida Armas Pfirter and Silvina Gonzáles Napolitano, 'Secession and international law: Latin American practice' in Marcelo G. Kohen (ed), *Secession: International Perspectives* (CUP 2006) 380–81.

[259] *Frontier Dispute (Burkina Faso v Mali)* (1986) para 21; *Frontier Dispute (Benin v Niger)* (2005) para 23. See Boarder Disputes Among African States, AGH/Res 16(I) (1964) para 2; Constitutive Act of the African Union art 4(b), 2158 UNTS 3 (11 July 2000, entered into force 26 May 2001). See also Shaw (n 169) 100–04.

[260] *Frontier Dispute (Burkina Faso v Mali)* (1986) para 20. See *Frontier Dispute (Benin v Niger)* (2005) para 23. See Shaw (n 63) 498. See also *Land, Island and Maritime Frontier Dispute (El Salvador v Honduras: Nicaragua Intervening)* (1992) para 42 (referring to 'the meaning of the principle' of *uti possidetis* in *Frontier Dispute (Burkina Faso v Mali)* (1986) as 'authoritatively stated').

[261] *Case concerning the Temple of Preah Vihear (Cambodia v Thailand)*, Merits, Judgment, ICJ Rep 1962, 6, 16. See Shaw (n 169) 104–05.

[262] *Frontier Dispute (Burkina Faso v Mali)* (1986) para 20. See Shaw (n 63) 499–501; Ratner (n 238) 590 (discussing dissolution of the former Soviet Union, Yugoslavia, and Czechoslovakia). For a critique of application of the principle beyond decolonization, see Peter Radan, 'Post-Secession International Borders: A Critical Analysis of the Opinions of the Badinter Arbitration Commission' (2000) 24(1) *Melbourne University Law Review* 50.

the Soviet Union', which provides for 'respect for the inviolability of all frontiers which can only be changed by peaceful means and by common agreement'.[263] One application of the principle of *uti possidetis* in this broader context appears in relation to the dissolution of Yugoslavia.[264] The principle was expressly invoked in several opinions of the Arbitration Commission on Yugoslavia, created by members of the European Community when convening a peace conference on Yugoslavia.[265] In relation to the breakup of the USSR, the substance of the *uti possidetis* principle is reflected in agreements adopted by former Soviet republics affirming the territorial integrity and inviolability of the existing boundaries of newly independent political entities.[266] Finally, the succession of the Czech Republic and Slovakia from the Czech and Slovak Federal Republic (i.e. Czechoslovakia) along the boundaries of the former States established by 1919 peace treaties provides another illustration of the principle's application in the context of State succession.[267]

ii. Relation to Self-Determination

The interplay of *uti possidetis* and the right to self-determination may be viewed in reference to the complementary relationship between the right to self-determination and the principle of territorial integrity.[268] The principle of *uti possidetis* is not viewed to be adverse to the right to self-determination.

[263] 'Declaration on the "Guidelines on the Recognition of New States in Eastern Europe and in the Soviet Union"' (16 Dec 1991), 31(6) ILM 1485, 1487 (1992).

[264] Marc Weller, 'The International Response to the Dissolution of the Socialist Federal Republic of Yugoslavia' (1992) 86(3) *AJIL* 569, 580; Shaw (n 169) 106–09.

[265] 'Joint Statement' (28 Aug 1991), (1991) 24(7/8) *Bulletin of the European Communities* 115 (1.4.25). See Opinion No 2 s 1, reproduced in *Conference on Yugoslavia Arbitration Commission: Opinions on Questions arising from the Dissolution of Yugoslavia [January 11 and July 4, 1992]*, 31(6) ILM 1488, 1498 (1992); Opinion No 3 s 2, reproduced in *Conference on Yugoslavia Arbitration Commission: Opinions on Questions arising from the Dissolution of Yugoslavia [January 11 and July 4, 1992]*, 31(6) ILM 1488, 1500 (1992). See Chapter 11.f.ii.

[266] Agreement establishing the Commonwealth of Independent States (8 Dec 1991) art 5, reproduced in (1992) 31(1) ILM 138; The Alma Ata Declaration (21 Dec 1991) preambular para 3, reproduced in (1992) 31(1) ILM 148.

[267] Shaw (n 169) 111.

[268] Marc Weller, 'Self-Determination of Indigenous Peoples: Articles 3, 4, 5, 18, 23, and 46(1)' in Jessie Hohmann & Marc Weller (eds), *The UN Declaration on the Rights of Indigenous Peoples: A Commentary* (OUP 2018) 118. See Shaw (n 63) 501–07.

The ICJ elaborated on this aspect of *uti possidetis* in *Frontier Dispute (Burkina Faso v Mali)* (1986).

> At first sight this principle conflicts outright with another one, the right of peoples to self-determination. In fact, however, the maintenance of the territorial status quo in Africa is often seen as the wisest course, to preserve what has been achieved by peoples who have struggled for their independence, and to avoid a disruption which would deprive the continent of the gains achieved by much sacrifice. The essential requirement of stability in order to survive, to develop and gradually to consolidate their independence in all fields, has induced African States judiciously to consent to the respecting of colonial frontiers, and to take account of it in the interpretation of the principle of self-determination of peoples.[269]

The application of *uti possidetis* in the context of decolonization was to deny the possibility that former colonial territories could be regarded as *terra nullius* by colonizing powers and to promote stable relations amongst former colonial territories emerging into independence.[270] In this way, *uti possidetis* can be seen to contribute to geopolitical conditions necessary for peoples to exercise the right to self-determination, especially those emerging into independence from a non-self-governing status.[271]

The operation of the principle of *uti possidetis* alongside the right to self-determination does not imply a favourable view of historic boundaries themselves, particularly those inherited from colonialism. It is without question that administrative boundaries established by colonial powers were often drawn with little or no regard for historic, ethnic, or other demographic characteristics of the groups upon whom they were imposed.[272] The preservation of such boundaries may be viewed as an injustice to groups who, if given the choice, might select different territorial boundaries.[273] To some extent, boundaries of present-day States are political creations that are artificial

[269] *Frontier Dispute (Burkina Faso v Mali)* (1986) para 25.

[270] Ibid para 23; *Territorial and Maritime Dispute (Nicaragua v Honduras)* (2007) paras 152–53.

[271] Shaw (n 169) 123–24 (describing the relationship between self-determination and *uti possidetis* as 'a crucial one for the international community').

[272] Ratner (n 238) 603.

[273] Crawford (n 36) 153. Malcolm Shaw, 'The *Western Sahara* Case' (1978) 49(1) *British Yearbook of International Law* 119, 120 ('This has not unnaturally generated tensions').

and, to varying degrees, arbitrary.[274] Such frontiers may be modified through the mutual consent of the States concerned, however such change cannot be effectuated unilaterally by the wishes of the people of a single State or territory,[275] illustrating one reason the exercise of the right to self-determination is bound by *uti possidetis* and does not contain an entitlement to the modification of boundaries. Respect for such boundaries, however unsatisfactory, promotes international peace and security, essential preconditions to the exercise and enjoyment of the right to self-determination.

f. Deviations from the International Aspect of Self-Determination

Practice evinces a limited number of exceptional cases in which the population of a territory designated as a NSGT under Chapter XI of the UN Charter has not been afforded the opportunity to exercise its right to self-determination to freely determine its political status. Instances in which territories designated as NSGTs have been integrated by contiguous States without regard for the freely expressed wishes of the population concerned include the Panama Canal Zone, Hong Kong, Macao, French Establishments in India, São João Batista de Ajudá, Goa and dependencies, and Ifni.[276] Such exceptional cases involve competing territorial claims and divergence from

[274] J. R. V. Prescott, *The Geography of Frontiers and Boundaries* (Routledge 2015) 41.

[275] See Chapter 7.e.i.

[276] Crawford (n 36) 624. See Appendix 1. See also Crawford (n 36) 624 n 86 (suggesting that West Irian (Papua New Guinea) and Walvis Bay may be similarly regarded); John Dugard, 'Walvis Bay, Decolonization and International Law (Book Review)' (1991) 85(4) *AJIL* 751. Walvis Bay was not, however, designated as a NSGT subject to Chapter XI of the UN Charter but was instead viewed as an integral part of Namibia: see S/Res/432 (27 July 1978); A/Res/32/9 D (4 Nov 1977) para 7. See also Agreement between the Government of the Republic of Namibia and the Government of the Republic of South Africa on the Joint Administration of Walvis Bay and the Off-Shore Islands, reproduced in (1993) 32(4) ILM 1152 (placing Walvis Bay under a Joint Administrative Authority); Treaty between the Government of the Republic of South Africa and the Government of the Republic of Namibia with respect to Walvis Bay and the Off-Shore Islands (28 Feb 1994, entered into force 1 Mar 1994), reproduced in (1994) 33(6) ILM 1526 (transferring Walvis Bay and the Off-Shore Islands to Namibia). Similarly, Mayotte, which France had attempted to fragment from the rest of the territory of Comoros on the basis of referendums, was treated as an integral part of Comoros: see A/Res/31/4 (21 Oct 1976). See Trinidad (n 239) 74–80; Crawford (n 36) 645–46. The Chagos Archipelago was similarly regarded as an integral part of Mauritius: *Chagos* (2019) para 170.

the general alignment of the principle of territorial integrity and the right to self-determination.[277]

Several anomalous cases—the Panama Canal Zone, Hong Kong, and Macao—may be explained by the operation of legal principles based in territorial sovereignty. The ICJ has contemplated that a 'legal tie of territorial sovereignty' may be sufficient to qualify application of the principle of self-determination in the context of decolonization.[278] Following submission of information on the Panama Canal Zone by the United States pursuant to Article 73(e) of the UN Charter, in 1946, Panama protested before the UNGA Fourth Committee treatment of the Panama Canal Zone as a NSGT on the basis that Panama had not relinquished sovereignty over the territory under the Hay-Bunau-Varilla Treaty, which established the territory.[279] Reporting on the Panama Canal Zone under Article 73(e) ceased and, in 1947, the territory no longer appeared on the registry of territories subject to Chapter XI of the UN Charter, without a political process to ascertain the freely expressed wishes of the population concerned. Similarly China, in a 1972 letter to the Chairman of the Special Committee on Decolonization, objected to treatment of Hong Kong and Macao as NSGTs subject to Chapter XI of the UN Charter on the basis that China retained sovereignty over those territories 'occupied' by their respective administering powers.[280] Later that year, Hong Kong and Macao were removed by the UNGA from the registry of territories subject to Chapter XI of the UN Charter, each in

[277] See Alejandro Schwed, 'Territorial Claims as a Limitation to the Right of Self-determination in the Context of the Falkland Islands Dispute' (1982) 6(3) *Fordham International Law Journal* 443, 467.

[278] *Western Sahara* (1975) paras 129, 150, 162.

[279] A/C.4/SR.13–27 (Part I) 113–14 (UNGA Fourth Committee, Summary Record of Meetings 1 November–12 December 1946). See also Convention between the United States and the Republic of Panama for the construction of a ship canal to connect the waters of the Atlantic and Pacific oceans, 33 Stat. (pt 2) 2234, Treaty Series No 431 (18 Nov 1903, entered into force 26 Feb 1904) (establishing the Panama Canal Zone).

[280] A/AC.109/396 (Letter Dated 8 March 1972 from the Permanent Representative of China to the United Nations Addressed to the Chairman of the Special Committee). Regarding treaty arrangements between China and the United Kingdom concerning Hong Kong, see Treaty between Great Britain and China—Signed at Nanking (29 Aug 1842) art III, (1858) 30 *British and Foreign State Papers* 389 (Honk Kong Island 'cede[d] . . . in perpetuity'); Convention of Friendship, between Great Britain and China—Signed at Pekin (24 Oct 1860) art VI, (1867) 50 *British and Foreign State Papers* 10 (Ceding territory); Convention between Great Britain and China, respecting an Extension of Hong Kong Territory—Signed at Peking (9 June 1898), (1898) 90 *British and Foreign State Papers* 17 (Ninety-nine year lease of additional territory from 1 July 1898).

the absence of a political process to ascertain the freely expressed wishes of the populations concerned.[281] Claims to territorial sovereignty by each contiguous third-State—Panama over the Panama Canal Zone,[282] and China over Hong Kong[283] and Macao[284]—were subsequently recognized by international agreements with the respective administering power of each territory. The Panama Canal Zone was integrated into the territory of Panama, and Hong Kong and Macao were integrated into the territory of China. In each instance, a successful assertion of legal ties of territorial sovereignty accounts for a change in the political status of a territory designated as a NSGT under Chapter XI of the UN Charter in the absence of an exercise of self-determination by the population concerned. It has been suggested that the disposition of West Irian (Papua New Guinea), a NSGT subject to Chapter XI of the UN Charter, may similarly be understood in terms of the assertion of territorial sovereignty by a contiguous State.[285]

Other departures from the ordinary operation of the right to self-determination in relation to the populations of NSGTs include the exceptional cases of French Establishments in India, São João Batista de Ajudá, Goa and dependencies, and Ifni. In these cases, the political status of small,

[281] A working group of the Special Committee on Decolonization recommended, in consideration of the letter, that the Special Committee recommend to the UNGA that Hong Kong and Macau and dependencies be excluded from the list of territories subject to Chapter XI of the UN Charter. A/AC.109/L.795 (25 May 1972) 1–2 (Sixty-Sixth Report of the Working Group). The Special Committee approved that recommendation. A/AC.109/PV.873 (6 June 1972) 19–20 (Record of the 873rd Meeting of the Special Committee). The Special Committee included that recommendation in its 1972 report. See A/8723/Rev.1[Vol.I] para 183 (1972). The UNGA approved the report of the Special Committee. A/Res/2908 (XXVII) para 3 (2 Nov 1972).

[282] Panama Canal Treaty, 1280 UNTS 4 (7 Sept 1977, entered into force 1 Oct 1979) (recognizing territorial sovereignty of Panama over the Panama Canal Zone).

[283] Joint Declaration on the Question of Hong Kong (with annexes), 1399 UNTS 33 (19 Dec 1984, entered into force 27 May 1985) (recognizing China 'resuming the exercise of sovereignty' over Hong Kong).

[284] Joint Declaration on the Question of Macao, 1498 UNTS 228 (13 Apr 1987, entered into force 15 Jan 1988) (recognizing China 'resuming the exercise of sovereignty' over Macao).

[285] Crawford (n 36) 624 n 86; A. Rigo Sureda, *The Evolution of the Right of Self-Determination: A study of United Nations Practice* (A. W. Sijthoff 1973) 143–51. See Agreement (with annexes) concerning West New Guinea (West Irian), 437 UNTS 273 (15 Aug 1962, entered into force 21 Sept 1962). See also A/Res/1752 (XVII) (21 Sept 1962) (taking note of the agreement); *Agreement Between the Republic of Indonesia and the Kingdom of the Netherlands concerning West New Guinea (West Irian): Report of the Secretary-General regarding the act of self-determination in West Irian*, A/7723 (6 Nov 1969); A/Res/2504 (XXIV) (19 Nov 1969). For critique, see Thomas D. Musgrave, 'An analysis of the 1969 Act of Free Choice in West Papua' in Christine Chinkin and Freya Baetens (eds), *Sovereignty, Statehood and State Responsibility: Essays in Honour of James Crawford* (CUP 2015) 209, especially 227; Cassese (n 51) 82–86.

disputed colonial territories subject to Chapter XI of the UN Charter was determined by transfer of sovereignty through negotiation or force. Changes in the political status of these territories did not result from political processes based in the freely expressed wishes of the populations concerned. French Establishments in India were transferred by France to the sovereignty of India with little, if any, regard for the wishes of the populations concerned or involvement by the United Nations.[286] São João Batista de Ajudá, a NSGT administered by Portugal lacking a civilian population, was annexed by Benin (then Dahomey).[287] Goa and dependencies, a NSGT also administered by Portugal, was annexed by India in the absence of a political process and Portugal ultimately recognized Indian sovereignty over the territory.[288] Finally, Ifni, a NSGT administered by Spain, was transferred to Morocco without regard for the wishes of the population concerned.[289] Although the UNGA had affirmed the entitlement of the people of Ifni to self-determination,[290] the UNGA also recognized a 'difference in nature of the legal status' of Ifni as compared to Western Sahara, another

[286] Agreement by Exchange of Notes Regarding the Cession of the French Loges in India to the Government of India (annex enclosed), 12 August–30 September 1947, French Diplomatic Archives, Agreement No 19470025; Agreement by Exchange of Notes Regarding the Date of the Cession of the French Loges to the Government of India, 3 October–4 October 1947, French Diplomatic Archives, Agreement No 19470031 (cited by Trinidad (n 239) 181). See also Treaty of cession of the territory of the Free Town of Chandernagore (with Protocol), 203 UNTS 155 (2 Feb 1951, entered into force 9 June 1952); Indo-French Treaty ceding the French Establishments of Pondicherry, Karikal, Mahe and Yanam to India, with Protocol and Exchange of Notes—New Delhi (28 May 1956), (1965) 162 *British and Foreign State Papers* 848.

[287] A/Res/1542 (XV) (15 Dec 1960); *Report of the Special Committee on Territories under Portuguese Administration*, A/5160 (25 Aug 1962) para 6 (Referring to São João Batista de Ajudá as 'having been nationally united with Dahomey'). See Trinidad (n 239) 186–88. To be sure, designation of São João Batista de Ajudá by the UNGA notwithstanding the absence of a stable civilian population calls into question whether the territory was appropriately regarded as a NSGT in the first instance, and whether it is appropriately regarded as an exceptional instance in which the population of a NSGT did not constitute a 'people', a circumstance contemplated by the ICJ. See *Chagos* (2019) paras 157–58 (quoting *Western Sahara* (1975)); Trinidad (n 239) 242.

[288] A/Res/1542 (XV) (15 Dec 1960); *Report of the Special Committee on Territories under Portuguese Administration*, A/5160 (25 Aug 1962) para 6 (Referring to Goa and dependencies as 'having been nationally united with . . . India'). See Treaty on recognition of India's sovereignty over Goa, Daman, Diu, Dadra and Nagar Haveli and related matters, 982 UNTS 153 (31 Dec 1974, entered into force 3 June 1975).

[289] *Western Sahara* (1975) para 63. See Tratado por el que el Estado Español retrocede al Reino de Marruecos el territorio de Ifni (Fez, 4 Jan 1969), *Repertorio Cronológico de Legislación* (Pamplona, Aranzadi 1969) 1008. See also A/7753 (7 Nov 1969) Annex, 2 n f. The UNGA Fourth Committee approved the 'retrocession' and recommended the UNGA take note of it: A/C.4/SR.1865 (9 Dec 1969) para 52.

[290] See e.g. A/Res/2229 (XXI) (20 Dec 1966) para 1; A/Res/2354 I (XXII) (19 Dec 1967) para 1.

Spanish-administered NSGT,[291] and contemplated decolonization of Ifni through transfer to Morocco.[292]

Legal principles based in territorial sovereignty have been invoked by contiguous States in the unresolved cases of Gibraltar, the Falkland Islands / Malvinas, and Western Sahara, each designated as a NSGT subject to Chapter XI of the UN Charter.[293] Regarding the status of Gibraltar, Spain maintains a disputed claim of territorial sovereignty on the contested theory that it did not cede sovereignty over the territory to the United Kingdom under the 1713 Treaty of Utrecht, an assertion rejected by the United Kingdom.[294] The UNGA has emphasized the importance of negotiation between Spain and the United Kingdom over the status of Gibraltar and denounced a 1967 referendum held by the United Kingdom, suggesting that the UNGA might view the situation principally as a territorial dispute and calling into question the entitlement of the population of Gibraltar to the right to self-determination.[295] The dispute between Argentina and the United Kingdom over the Falkland Islands / Malvinas may also be approached as a situation of contested territorial sovereignty.[296] The UNGA has similarly emphasized the importance of negotiations between Argentina and the United Kingdom to resolve the political status of the Falkland Islands / Malvinas, again suggesting that the UNGA may regard the situation in the first instance as a territorial dispute, which again calls into question the entitlement of the population concerned to the right to self-determination.[297] Finally, regarding Western Sahara, assertions of legal ties of territorial sovereignty over the territory by

[291] A/Res/2428 (XXIII) (18 Dec 1968) preambular para 10.

[292] A/Res/2354 I (XXII) (19 Dec 1967). See Schwed (n 277) 464.

[293] Guatemala had maintained an analogous territorial claim over the former NSGT Belize. The UNGA, however, was unequivocal about the entitlement of the people of Belize to self-determination. A/Res/3432 (XXX) (8 Dec 1975). Guatemala ultimately abandoned its claim over Belize. See Heads of Agreement (11 Mar 1981) paras 1, 16, reproduced in (1981) 52(1) *British Yearbook of International Law* 380. Belize was subsequently admitted to the United Nations. A/Res/36/3 (25 Sept 1981). See Crawford (n 36) 637–38; Trinidad (n 239) 215–20.

[294] Treaty of Peace and Friendship between Great Britain and Spain, signed at Utrecht art X (13 July 1713, entered into force 4 Aug 1713), 28 *Consolidated Treaty Series* 295. See Trinidad (n 239) 120–33; Rigo Sureda (n 285) 183–98.

[295] See e.g. A/Res/2353 (XXII) (19 Dec 1967); A/Res/2429 (XXIII) (18 Dec 1968). See Rigo Sureda (n 285) 197–98; Thomas M. Franck, '*Dulce et Decorum Est*: The Strategic Role of Legal Principles in the Falklands War', (1983) 77(1) *AJIL* 109, 121; Crawford (n 36) 643.

[296] Trinidad (n 239) 133–52; Schwed (n 277) 469–71.

[297] See e.g. A/Res/2065 (XX) (16 Dec 1965); A/Res/3160 (XXVIII) (14 Dec 1973) (characterizing the dispute as a 'conflict of sovereignty'). See Franck (n 295) 116, 121; Schwed (n 277) 443.

Morocco and Mauritania were authoritatively assessed and rejected by the ICJ in *Western Sahara* (1975).[298]

i. Theory of Colonial Enclaves

The foregoing cases of exception expose a political element to the treatment of territories as NSGTs, a status conferring upon their populations an entitlement to the exercise of the right to self-determination.[299] A theoretical explanation advanced to rationalize exceptional cases, in which the population of a territory designated as a NSGT under Chapter XI of the UN Charter has not been afforded the opportunity to freely determine its political status pursuant to the right to self-determination, contemplates a rule of exception for 'colonial enclaves'.[300] Colonial enclaves have been defined as 'minute territories which approximate to "enclaves" of the claimant State, which are ethnically and economically parasitic upon or derivative of that State, and which cannot constitute separate territorial units'.[301] The colonial enclaves theory proposes a rule of exception according to which the right to self-determination does not apply to the populations of such NSGTs, which are instead properly integrated into a contiguous State pursuant to the restoration of claimed historical territorial boundaries. In effect, the theory of colonial enclaves would suspend the application of the principles of territorial integrity and *uti possidetis* to so-called colonial enclaves in favour of integration with a claimant State.[302]

The colonial enclaves theory is not, however, based in a formal source of international law and its parameters as a proposed exception to the normal

[298] For discussion of territorial claims by Morocco and Mauritania, see *Western Sahara* (1975) paras 84–150. For disposition of claims as lacking legal ties of territorial sovereignty, see ibid paras 129, 150, 162. See Thomas M. Franck, 'The Stealing of the Sahara' (1976) 70(4) *AJIL* 694, 710–11; Cassese (n 51) 214–18.

[299] See Chapter 10.b.

[300] Rigo Sureda (n 285) 174–77, 196–98; Shaw (n 273) 123; Crawford (n 36) 637–47 (categorizing the Panama Canal Zone, Hong Kong, Macao, French Establishments in India, São João Batista de Ajudá, Goa and dependencies, and Ifni as colonial enclaves, suggesting that West Irian (Papua New Guinea) and Walvis Bay may also be so regarded, and noting that the Falkland Islands / Malvinas and Gibraltar 'arguably' fall into that category). See also Trinidad (n 239) 157–238.

[301] Crawford (n 36) 646–47 (citation omitted). See also Franck and Hoffman (n 211) 369.

[302] Crawford (n 36) 618.

operation of rules of international law are ill-defined.[303] It has been suggested that the colonial enclaves theory is borne from a desire to reconcile deviations from the right to self-determination with assertions of its peremptory (i.e. non-derogable) character by removing such exceptional cases from the scope of the right altogether rather than admitting derogation from the rule.[304] It is unclear whether deviations from the ordinary operation of international legal rules in cases of small, disputed colonial territories may be explained by attaching legal significance to the unique, complicated factual circumstances of such territories.[305] A comprehensive evaluation of practice regarding colonial enclaves found a lack of support for a categorical exception to the application of the right to self-determination to the populations of such territories.[306] That assessment suggests instead that deviations from the international aspect of the right to self-determination, while exceptional, are best regarded as derogations on the basis of political considerations.

[303] Trinidad (n 239) 159, 164.

[304] Ibid 235–36; D. W. Greig, 'Reflections on the Role of Consent' (1992) 12(1) *Australian Year Book of International Law* 125, 155. Notably, the principal exponent of the colonial enclaves theory as a theory of exception was also responsible, in his capacity as the final ILC special rapporteur for State responsibility, for inclusion of reference to the right to self-determination as a peremptory norm in the commentary to the ILC Articles on State Responsibility. See Crawford (n 36) 637–47 (outlining the colonial enclaves doctrine), 101 ('To this list [of *jus cogens* norms] we must now add self-determination'). See similarly ILC Draft Articles on Responsibility of States for Internationally Wrongful Acts art 40, Commentary para 5, UN Doc A/56/10, Report of the International Law Commission on the Work of its Fifty-Third Session, [2001] II(2) *YbILC* 26 et seq, UN Doc A/CN.4/SER.A/2001/Add.1 (Part 2) ('[T]he obligation to respect the right to self-determination deserves to be mentioned'). Cf Chapter 5.e.

[305] Trinidad (n 239) 235–38; Greig (n 304) 155–57.

[306] Trinidad (n 239) 157–238.

8 The Domestic Aspect of Self-Determination

a. Overview

The right to self-determination consists of the entitlement of peoples to freely determine their political status and freely pursue their economic, social, and cultural development.[1] The *travaux préparatoires* of the two human rights covenants reflects a general understanding of these elements of the right as an entitlement of every people 'to establish its own political institutions' and 'to develop its own economic resources, and to direct its own social and cultural evolution, without the interference of other peoples or nations'.[2] The exercise of the right to self-determination by a people has both international (or 'external') and domestic (or 'internal') aspects.[3] The previous chapter addressed the way in which the right to self-determination, and in particular its political element, may under specific circumstances be exercised in relation to its international aspect. It has been rightly observed, however, that

[1] International Covenant on Civil and Political Rights art 1(1), 999 UNTS 171 (16 Dec 1966, entered into force 23 Mar 1976) (hereinafter ICCPR); International Covenant on Economic, Social and Cultural Rights art 1(1), 993 UNTS 3 (16 Dec 1966, entered into force 3 Jan 1976) (hereinafter ICESCR); A/Res/1514 (XV) (14 Dec 1960) (hereinafter Resolution 1514) para 2; A/Res/2625 (24 Oct 1970) Annex (hereinafter FRD) Principle V, para 1; United Nations World Conference on Human Rights: Vienna Declaration and Programme of Action (25 June 1993), A/CONF/157/23 (12 July 1993), reproduced in (1993) 32(6) ILM 1661 (hereinafter Vienna Declaration (1993)) part I, s 2, para 1. See *Legal Consequences arising from the Policies and Practices of Israel in the Occupied Palestinian Territory, including East Jerusalem*, Advisory Opinion, ICJ Rep 2024 (hereinafter *Palestine* (2024)) para 241. See also African [Banjul] Charter on Human and Peoples' Rights art 20, OAU Doc CAB/LEG/67/3/Rev.5, 1520 UNTS 217 (27 June 1981, entered into force 21 Oct 1986) (hereinafter ACHPR); Arab Charter on Human Rights art 1, [ST/HR/]CHR/NONE/2004/40/Rev.1 (22 May 2004, entered into force 15 Mar 2008) (hereinafter Arab Charter on Human Rights).

[2] Draft International Covenants on Human Rights: Annotation, Prepared by the Secretary-General, A/2929 (1 July 1955) (hereinafter A/2929) ch IV para 12.

[3] *Report of the Third Committee*, A/3077 (8 Dec 1955) (Draft International Covenants on Human Rights) (hereinafter A/3077) para 32; FRD Principle V, paras 2, 7.

The Right to Self-Determination in International Law. Thomas Weatherall, Oxford University Press.
 DOI: 10.1093/9780197798119.003.0009

the right to self-determination is exercised in the normal course through the domestic aspect of the right.[4] This chapter addresses the exercise of the right to self-determination at the domestic level.

This chapter begins by addressing general features of the domestic aspect of self-determination. The second section of this chapter revisits the free determination of political status, which in relation to the domestic aspect of self-determination consists of an entitlement to representative government. In this context, this section also considers obligations of States responsible for the administration of NSGTs and Trust Territories to promote self-government therein. The third section of this chapter assesses the entitlement of peoples to freely pursue their economic, social, and cultural development and the associated entitlement of peoples to freely dispose of their natural wealth and resources. The final section of this chapter examines the self-determination of Indigenous Peoples.

b. General Features

The right to self-determination is a universal right of a continuing character.[5] The domestic aspect of the right to self-determination reflects these aspects of the right. Common Article 1 of the two human rights covenants provides that the right to self-determination is enjoyed by *all* peoples and is, in this sense, 'universal'.[6] As reflected in the *travaux préparatoires*, '[t]he right would be proclaimed in the covenants as a universal right and for all time'.[7] UNGA Resolution 2625 (the FRD) similarly defines the right to self-determination in terms that indicate the universality of the right as one belonging to all peoples.[8] The Helsinki Final Act (1975), in reference to the political element of the right to self-determination, provides that '*all peoples always* have the right, in full freedom, to determine, *when and as they wish*, their internal and

[4] *Reference re Secession of Quebec* [1998] 2 SCR 217 para 126.

[5] See Chapter 7.b.i.4.

[6] A/2929 ch IV paras 7–8; A/3077 para 39. See HRC, *CCPR General Comment No. 12: The Right to Self-Determination of Peoples (Art 1)* (1984) (hereinafter HRC GC 12) paras 1–2.

[7] A/3077 para 39.

[8] See A/7619 (1969) para 180. See also Robert Rosenstock, 'The Declaration of Principles of International Law Concerning Friendly Relations: A Survey' (1971) 65(5) *AJIL* 713, 731; Gaetano Arangio-Ruiz, *The UN Declaration on Friendly Relations and the System of the Sources of International Law* (Sijthoff & Noordhoff 1979) s 76.

external political status, without external interference'.[9] The universal and continuing character of the right to self-determination is a presupposition of the domestic aspect of the right.

Respect for the right to self-determination is closely related to the enjoyment of human rights and fundamental freedoms. This relationship is central to the domestic aspect of the right to self-determination and, in particular, the obligations owed by a State towards its people. The inclusion of a provision on self-determination as common Article 1 of the two human rights covenants is understood to reflect the importance of the right as an 'essential condition' to the enjoyment of the human rights enumerated therein.[10] The corollary was noted by the Third Committee during the drafting of the two covenants, where it observed that, '[t]o be deprived of the right of self-determination entailed the loss of individual human rights'.[11] Non-binding instruments similarly regard the violation of the right to self-determination as a violation of human rights.[12] The relationship between self-determination and human rights is implied in the FRD. The *travaux préparatoires* reflects the understanding that the enjoyment of human rights is a condition precedent to the exercise of the right to self-determination.[13] Accordingly, the provision on self-determination in the FRD contains a duty of States to promote universal respect for human rights and fundamental freedoms.[14] In this way self-determination, a collective right belonging to peoples,[15] can be viewed as related to the enjoyment of individual rights. The domestic-facing obligations of States arising from the right to

[9] Conference on Security and Cooperation in Europe: Final Act (1 Aug 1975), reproduced in (1975) 14(5) ILM 1292 (hereinafter Helsinki Final Act (1975)) Principle VIII, para 2 (emphasis added) (adding: 'and to pursue as they wish their political . . . development').

[10] HRC GC 12 para 1; Committee on Economic, Social and Cultural Rights, *General Comment No. 26 (2022) on land and economic, social and cultural rights*, E/C.12/GC/26 (2023) (hereinafter CESCR GC 26) para 11. See A/3077 para 35; *Lubicon Lake Band v Canada*, Communication No 167/1984, CCPR/C/38/D/167/1984 (1990) para 13.3; *E.P. et al v Colombia*, Communication No 318/1988, CCPR/C/39/D/318/1988 (1990) para 8.2.

[11] A/3077 para 40. See Antonio Cassese, *Self-Determination of Peoples: A Legal Reappraisal* (CUP 1995) 53.

[12] FRD Principle V, para 2; Vienna Declaration (1993) part I, s 2, para 2. See also Resolution 1514 para 1.

[13] See e.g. A/8018 (1970) para 82, Working paper on the final stage of drafting of the Declaration submitted by the delegation of Italy at the 1970 session of the Special Committee, A/AC.125/L.83, 58 (quoted supra Chapter 3 n 47).

[14] FRD Principle V, para 3.

[15] See Chapter 6.a.

self-determination are interrelated with its human rights obligations. It is in this sense that the ICJ has regarded the right to self-determination as 'a fundamental human right'.[16]

Also essential to the domestic aspect of the right to self-determination is the entitlement of peoples to exercise the right without interference by other States.[17] The FRD provides that, '[b]y virtue of the principle of equal rights and self-determination of peoples enshrined in the Charter of the United Nations, all peoples have the right freely to determine, without external interference, their political status and to pursue their economic, social and cultural development'.[18] This same linkage between self-determination and non-interference is contained in UNGA Resolution 1514 (1960) and the Helsinki Final Act (1975).[19] As noted above, the *travaux préparatoires* of common Article 1 of the two human rights covenants reflects an understanding of an entitlement to exercise the right to self-determination 'without the interference of other peoples or nations'.[20] Similarly, in General Comment No 12, the HRC referred in this context specifically to non-interference in the internal affairs of other States; such interference was itself understood to adversely affect the exercise of the right to self-determination.[21] In this way, respect for the right to self-determination by States calls for non-interference in the exercise of the right to self-determination by the peoples of other States.[22] This element of non-interference is a condition of the enjoyment and exercise of human rights and fundamental freedoms through which the right to self-determination is realized.

Having identified these general features of the right to self-determination, the following sections consider the constitutive elements of the right in relation to its domestic aspect.

[16] *Palestine* (2024) para 233 (citing *Legal Consequences of the Separation of the Chagos Archipelago from Mauritius in 1965*, Advisory Opinion, ICJ Rep 2019, 95 (hereinafter *Chagos* (2019)) para 144).

[17] See e.g. A/Res/2131 (XX) (21 Dec 1965) paras 5–6.

[18] FRD Principle V, para 1.

[19] Resolution 1514 para 7; Helsinki Final Act (1975) Principle VIII, para 2.

[20] A/2929 ch IV para 12.

[21] HRC GC 12 para 6.

[22] James Crawford, *The Creation of States in International Law* (2nd edn, OUP 2006) 126. For discussion of how the domestic aspect of the right to self-determination may have implications for the lawfulness of intervention, see Oliver Corten, *The Law Against War: The Prohibition on the Use of Force in Contemporary International Law* (Bloomsbury 2021) 274–78.

c. Free Determination of Political Status

The first element of the right to self-determination is the entitlement of a people to freely determine its political status.[23] At base, the domestic aspect of this political element of the right to self-determination is an entitlement to representative government. Sir Ian Brownlie observed that this entitlement is at the heart of self-determination: 'the right of a community which has a distinct character to have this character reflected in the institutions of government under which it lives'.[24]

i. Entitlement to Representative Government

Treaty-based obligations of States related to self-determination indicate that the domestic aspect of the political element of the right constitutes an entitlement to representative government. Article 1(1) common to the two human rights covenants consists of a right of all peoples to self-determination which entails, in relevant part, an entitlement to 'freely determine their political status'.[25] Article 1(1) is thereby a source of corresponding obligations of States parties to respect the political element of the right to self-determination vis-à-vis the peoples within their territories.[26] The *travaux préparatoires* of common Article 1 of the two human rights covenants reflects an understanding of political element of the right to self-determination as an entitlement of every people 'to establish its own political institutions'.[27]

[23] ICCPR art 1(1); ICESCR art 1(1); Resolution 1514 para 2; FRD Principle V, para 1; Vienna Declaration (1993) part I, s 2, para 1. See *Palestine* (2024) para 241. See also ACHPR art 20; Arab Charter on Human Rights art 1.

[24] Ian Brownlie, 'The Rights of Peoples in Modern International Law' in James Crawford (ed), *The Rights of Peoples* (Clarendon Press 1988) 5.

[25] ICCPR art 1(1); ICESCR art 1(1).

[26] This understanding of common Article 1 follows from the territorial scope of treaties. See Vienna Convention on the Law of Treaties art 29, 1155 UNTS 331 (23 May 1969, entered into force 27 Jan 1980) (Territorial scope of treaties). This rule is expressly reflected in the ICCPR itself. See ICCPR art 2(1). Only paragraph 3 of common Article 1 has been interpreted to impose obligations of an extraterritorial character. See HRC GC 12 para 6; James Crawford, 'Democracy and International Law' (1993) 64(1) *British Yearbook of International Law* 113, 116. See also Chapter 2.c.iii.

[27] A/2929 ch IV para 12.

Other international instruments, which have contributed to the crystallization of the right to self-determination in CIL, similarly reflect an entitlement to representative government. The FRD includes a standard of conduct reflecting an entitlement to representative government within the domestic aspect of the right to self-determination. Specifically, paragraph 7 of the principle on self-determination refers to States 'conducting themselves in compliance with the principle of equal rights and self-determination of peoples as . . . thus possessed of a government representing the whole people belonging to the territory without distinction as to race, creed or colour'.[28] This standard of conduct indicates that a State in compliance with its obligations under the right to self-determination is one possessed of a government that represents the entire population of its territory (i.e. its people as a whole).[29] This interpretation is informed by the relationship between self-determination and respect for human rights articulated in paragraph 3 of the same principle, and links the compliance of States with the principle of equal rights and self-determination of peoples in Articles 1 and 55 of the UN Charter to representative government.[30]

The Vienna Declaration (1993) expresses the relationship between a State's compliance with the right to self-determination and representative government in reference to, and in terms that mirror, the FRD.[31] In addition, the Vienna Declaration (1993) includes a section on democracy, which is described in terms that invoke elements of the right to self-determination:

> Democracy, development and respect for human rights and fundamental freedoms are interdependent and mutually reinforcing. Democracy is based on the freely expressed will of the people to determine their own political, economic, social and cultural systems and their full participation in all aspects of their lives.[32]

The basis of democracy is defined in this paragraph in terms that parallel the touchstone of the exercise of the right to self-determination in relation to its international aspect: 'the freely expressed will of the people'.[33] Moreover,

[28] FRD Principle V, para 7.
[29] Arangio-Ruiz (n 8) s 80.
[30] Cassese (n 11) 110–11; Rosenstock (n 8) 732; Arangio-Ruiz (n 8) s 80.
[31] Vienna Declaration (1993) part I, s 2, para 3.
[32] Ibid s 8.
[33] See Chapter 7.b.i.2.

the purpose of democracy is described in terms that correspond to the constituent elements of self-determination as the right of peoples to freely determine their political status and freely pursue their economic, social, and cultural development. At minimum, these parallels between elements of the right to self-determination and the description of democracy in the Vienna Declaration (1993) imply a practical relationship between the right to self-determination and democracy.

In practice, the entitlement to representative government as a component of the right to self-determination has been understood in terms of the collective exercise by a people of human rights and fundamental freedoms through democratic processes. The *travaux préparatoires* of common Article 1 of the two human rights covenants expresses this relationship in the following terms:

> If self-determination constituted a collective right, it nevertheless affected each individual. To be deprived of the right of self-determination entailed the loss of individual human rights. [Draft] Article 23 of the draft Covenant on Civil and Political Rights guaranteed the free expression of the will of the electors in elections. The same idea was expressed in paragraph 3 of article 21 of the Universal Declaration of Human Rights. There was little difference between voting in an election and voting in a plebiscite.[34]

Article 21(3) of the UDHR, it may be recalled, provides that '[t]he will of the people shall be the basis of the authority of government; this will shall be expressed in periodic and genuine elections which shall be by universal and equal suffrage and shall be held by secret vote or by equivalent free voting procedures'.[35] The *travaux préparatoires* of common Article 1 indicates that the right to self-determination is operationalized by the same democratic element expressed in the UDHR. Similar views are reflected in the *travaux préparatoires* of the FRD.[36]

Guidance by the HRC as to the reporting requirement of the ICCPR further indicates that States perform their obligations under Article 1 through

34 A/3077 para 40.
35 A/Res/217 A (III) art 21(3) (10 Dec 1948) (Universal Declaration of Human Rights).
36 A/7326 (1968) para 186.

democratic processes. Under Article 40(1) of the ICCPR, States parties 'undertake to submit reports on the measures they have adopted which give effect to the rights recognized' in the ICCPR.[37] In relation to this reporting requirement, in General Comment No 12, the HRC provided guidance that, '[w]ith regard to paragraph 1 of article 1, States parties should describe the constitutional and political processes which in practice allow the exercise of this right'.[38] States that have addressed Article 1 in their periodic reporting under the ICCPR have focused on the political element of the right to self-determination.[39]

The exercise of particular human rights and fundamental freedoms codified in the ICCPR may be viewed as integral to representative government and associated democratic processes. These include freedoms of expression (Article 19), peaceful assembly (Article 21), and association (Article 22), as well as the right to vote and participate in public affairs (Article 25).[40] The HRC expressly identified such a linkage between ICCPR Article 1 and Article 25 in General Comment No 25:

> The rights under article 25 are related to, but distinct from, the right of peoples to self-determination. By virtue of the rights covered by article 1(1), peoples have the right to freely determine their political status and to enjoy the right to choose the form of their constitution or government. Article 25 deals with the right of individuals to participate in those processes which constitute the conduct of public affairs.[41]

In this way, particular human rights and fundamental freedoms are understood to operationalize the right to self-determination by providing

[37] ICCPR art 40(1).

[38] HRC GC 12 para 4.

[39] Ibid para 3. See Paul M. Taylor, *A Commentary on the International Covenant on Civil and Political Rights: The UN Human Rights Committee's Monitoring of ICCPR Rights* (CUP 2020) 55–56.

[40] ICCPR arts 19, 21, 22, and 25. See Manfred Nowak, *UN Covenant on Civil and Political Rights: CCPR Commentary* (2nd edn, N.P. Engel 2005) para 34; Cassese (n 11) 53 (referring to the domestic aspect of self-determination 'as a manifestation of the totality of rights embodied in the Covenant'); Malcolm N. Shaw, 'Peoples, Territorialism and Boundaries' (1997) 3 *EJIL* 478, 484.

[41] HRC, *CCPR General Comment No. 25: Article 25 (Participation in Public Affairs and the Right to Vote), The Right to Participate in Public Affairs, Voting Rights and the Right of Equal Access to Public Service*, CCPR/C/21/Rev.1/Add.7 (1996) para 2. See also para 1 ('Article 25 lies at the core of democratic government based on the consent of the people and in conformity with the principles of the Covenant').

the mechanism for peoples to exercise the right. From this perspective of process, the domestic aspect of self-determination evinces a democratic entitlement in international law.[42]

At the regional level, Article 20(1) of the ACHPR has been interpreted to impose obligations upon States parties with respect to representative government as a component of the right to self-determination.[43] In *Jawara v The Gambia* (2000), the African Commission considered a communication by the former head of State of the Gambia alleging a range of violations of the ACHPR by the military government that overthrew his government in 1994.[44] The African Commission determined, in relevant part, that the forcible takeover of the Gambia's government by its military violated 'the right of the Gambian people to freely choose their government as entrenched in Article 20(1) of the Charter'.[45] In *Katangese Peoples' Congress v Zaire* (1995),[46] and *Mgwanga Gunme et al v Cameroon* (2009),[47] the African Commission considered forms of governance consistent with the right to self-determination under Article 20(1) and expressly linked representative government to democratic processes.[48] Moreover, in contemplating the possibility of remedial secession pursuant to the right to self-determination under ACHPR Article 20, the Commission considered as a threshold question whether the group in question had been denied 'their right to participate in the government as guaranteed by Article 13(1)', articulating a linkage between political participation and the right to self-determination.[49] Taken together, the African Commission has identified an entitlement to representative government within the right to

[42] Thomas M. Franck, 'The Emerging Right to Democratic Governance' (1992) 86(1) *AJIL* 46, 46–91. See also Nowak (n 40) para 34; Shaw (n 40) 484; Cassese (n 11) 53; Crawford (n 22) 126 n 108.

[43] See Chapter 2.d.i.

[44] *Jawara v The Gambia*, ACommHPR, Communications Nos 147/95 & 149/96 (2000) paras 1–10.

[45] Ibid paras 72–73.

[46] *Katangese Peoples' Congress v Zaire*, ACommHPR, Communication No 75/92 (1995) (hereinafter *Katangese Peoples' Congress v Zaire* (1995)).

[47] *Mgwanga Gunme et al v Cameroon*, ACommHPR, Communication No 266/2003 (2009) (hereinafter *Mgwanga Gunme v Cameroon* (2009)).

[48] *Mgwanga Gunme v Cameroon* (2009) para 199. See also *Katangese Peoples' Congress v Zaire* (1995) para 4.

[49] *Mgwanga Gunme v Cameroon* (2009) para 194; *Katangese Peoples' Congress v Zaire* (1995) para 6.

self-determination under ACHPR Article 20, and has linked the domestic aspect of self-determination to political participation under Article 13 of the ACHPR.

ii. Promotion of Self-Government

States responsible for the administration of NSGTs and Trust Territories are under complementary obligations to promote self-government with respect to the peoples of those territories. Under Article 73(b) of the UN Charter, States responsible for the administration of NSGTs are obligated 'to develop self-government, to take due account of the political aspirations of the peoples, and to assist them in the progressive development of their free political institutions'.[50] Article 76(b) of the UN Charter provides a corresponding objective of the Trusteeship System.[51] States responsible for the administration of NSGTs and Trust Territories are therefore under obligations under the UN Charter to promote representative government with respect to the peoples of those territories that are complementary to obligations owed by States towards the peoples within their territories. In this way, peoples entitled to the exercise of the right to self-determination in relation to its international aspect remain entitled to corresponding respect for and promotion of their right to self-determination at the domestic (or 'internal') level.

The reporting requirement of administering powers under Article 73(e) regarding 'economic, social and educational conditions' has been conditioned in practice by the realization of a degree of self-government by the people of a NSGT in relation to its administering power.[52] This conditioning of Article 73(e) reflects the purposiveness of self-government in the performance of an administering power's obligations vis-à-vis the people of a NSGT.

The role of self-government and democratic decision-making in the exercise of self-determination is further reflected in UNGA Resolution 1541,

[50] Charter of the United Nations art 73(b), XV UNCIO 335 (26 June 1945, entered into force 24 Oct 1945) (hereinafter UN Charter).

[51] Ibid art 76(b). See Chapter 9.c.i (discussing incorporation of Article 76 objectives into Trusteeship agreements).

[52] UN Charter art 73(e). See Resolution 1541 Annex, Principle XI. See also Chapter 9.c.ii (discussing the reporting requirement).

which provides guidance to States on whether obligations exist to transmit information regarding NSGTs under Article 73(e) of the UN Charter.[53] Regarding free association, UNGA Resolution 1541 provides that such status 'should be the result of a free and voluntary choice by the peoples of the territory concerned expressed through informed and democratic processes'.[54] Similarly, integration of a territory with an independent State 'should be the result of the freely expressed wishes of the territory's peoples . . . their wishes having been expressed through informed and democratic processes'.[55] In such cases of integration, the peoples of both territories should have 'equal rights and opportunities for representation and effective participation at all levels in the executive, legislative and judicial organs of government'.[56] In practice, the UNGA has exercised 'a measure of discretion' in its supervision of the exercise of self-determination by the peoples of NSGTs and Trust Territories.[57] However, the obligations of administering States related to the development of representative political institutions, and expectations for democratic decision-making regarding political status, may be viewed as manifestations of the right to self-determination of the peoples of NSGTs and Trust Territories.

d. Free Pursuit of Economic, Social, and Cultural Development

The second element of the right to self-determination is the entitlement of a people to freely pursue its economic, social, and cultural development.[58]

[53] See Chapter 3.c.

[54] Resolution 1541 Annex, Principle VII.

[55] Ibid Principle IX(b).

[56] Ibid Principle VIII.

[57] *Western Sahara*, Advisory Opinion, ICJ Rep 1975, 12 para 71; *Chagos* (2019) paras 157–58. See *The Right to Self-Determination: Implementation of United Nations Resolutions* (Study prepared by Héctor Gros Espiell, Special Rapporteur of the Sub-Commission on Prevention of Discrimination and Protection of Minorities), E/CN.4/Sub.2/405/Rev.1 (1980) paras 251–61. See also Cassese (n 11) 74–85; Crawford (n 22) 620.

[58] ICCPR art 1(1); ICESCR art 1(1); Resolution 1514 para 2; FRD Principle V, para 1; Vienna Declaration (1993) part I, s 2, para 1. See *Palestine* (2024) para 241. See also ACHPR art 20; Arab Charter on Human Rights art 1.

If the domestic aspect of the right to self-determination is understood in terms of the collective exercise by a people of human rights and fundamental freedoms associated with its respective elements, then the economic, social, and cultural (ESC) element of the right to self-determination may be understood in reference to the collective exercise of economic, social, and cultural rights.[59] As a result, the ESC element of the right to self-determination is inherently more progressive in character than its political element, whose demands can be defined with greater precision.[60] This distinction is reflected in the differentiated elements of the right of peoples to self-determination: to freely *determine* their political *status* and freely *pursue* their economic, social, and cultural *development*.[61] In contrast to the political element of the right to self-determination, there is relatively little practice regarding its ESC element.[62]

In *Palestine* (2024), the ICJ regarded the human rights obligations of Israel to extend to the Occupied Palestinian Territory (OPT) and considered the way in which human rights violations in the OPT impacted the right of the Palestinian people to self-determination in relation to pursuit of their economic, social, and cultural development.[63] The court found that policies and practices impacting aspects of the economic, social, and cultural life of Palestinians—including their dependence on Israel for the provision of basic goods and services—contributed to the breach of Israel's obligation to respect the right to self-determination of the people of Palestine in connection with its occupation of the OPT.[64]

[59] See e.g. Committee on Economic, Social and Cultural Rights, *General Comment No. 21: Right of everyone to take part in cultural life (art 15, para. 1 (a), of the International Covenant on Economic, Social and Cultural Rights)*, E/C.12/GC/21 (2009) para 2; CESCR GC 26 paras 4, 11.

[60] See Ben Saul et al, *The International Covenant on Economic, Social and Cultural Rights: Commentary, Cases, and Materials* (OUP 2014) 134. See Chapter 9 n 17 (discussing different standards of performance under the ICCPR and ICESCR).

[61] See A/3077 paras 43, 53, 57. See also Saul (n 60) 55–56.

[62] Ibid 56, 60. This disparity in practice has led one court to question the normative status of the right to self-determination beyond its political element: see *Western Sahara Campaign UK v Secretary of State for International Trade et al* [2022] EWHC 3108 (Admin) (hereinafter *Western Sahara Campaign II* (2022)) [134], [137].

[63] *Palestine* (2024) paras 99–100, 241–42.

[64] Ibid paras 241–43. See Chapter 4.h.

i. Entitlement to Freely Dispose of Natural Wealth and Resources

The entitlement of peoples to freely dispose of their natural wealth and resources is closely related to the right to self-determination.[65] Article 1(2) common to the two human rights covenants, immediately following the definition of the right to self-determination at Article 1(1), provides for the entitlement of peoples to control over their natural wealth and resources:[66]

> All peoples may, for their own ends, freely dispose of their natural wealth and resources without prejudice to any obligations arising out of international economic co-operation, based upon the principle of mutual benefit, and international law. In no case may a people be deprived of its own means of subsistence.[67]

The entitlement of peoples to freely dispose of their natural wealth and resources is generally regarded as a corollary of the right to self-determination.[68] The HRC, in General Comment No 12 on the right to self-determination, characterized Article 1(2) as affirming 'a particular aspect of the economic content' of the right to self-determination as one that 'entails corresponding duties for all States and the international community'.[69] According to this view, the entitlement of peoples to freely dispose of their natural wealth and resources is an aspect of the right to self-determination that entitles peoples to freely pursue their economic development.[70] In this regard, the UK High Court of Justice, in a 2022 decision concerning import regulations impacting Western Sahara, characterized what it referred to as

[65] Nico Schrijver, *Sovereignty over Natural Resources: Balancing Rights and Duties* (CUP 1997) 36–56; Daniëlla Dam-de Jong, *International Law and Governance of Natural Resources in Conflict and Post-Conflict Situations* (CUP 2015) 34–57.

[66] See Chapter 2.c.ii.

[67] See similarly Resolution 1514 preambular para 8.

[68] James Crawford, 'Opinion: Third Party Obligations with respect to Israeli Settlements in the Occupied Palestinian Territories' para 64 (24 Jan 2012). See also Cassese (n 11) 99–100.

[69] HRC GC 12 para 5.

[70] See A/Res/1314 (XIII) (12 Dec 1958) para 1; A/Res/1803 (XVII) (14 Dec 1962) preambular para 2 (referring to permanent sovereignty over natural wealth and resources as a 'basic constituent' of the right to self-determination); see also Saul et al (n 60) 62.

'the right to control natural resources' as a 'corollary' or 'sub-rule' of the right to self-determination.[71]

Several regional instruments refer to the entitlement of peoples to freely dispose of their natural wealth and resources.

Article 21 of the ACHPR, separate from Article 20 on self-determination, provides that '[a]ll peoples shall freely dispose of their wealth and natural resources'.[72] The African Commission on Human and Peoples' Rights has explained that, unlike the right to self-determination under Article 20, the rights in Article 21 'are still applicable in post-colonial Africa'.[73] In *Cabinda v Angola* (2013), the African Commission described this right as one 'held in trust for the people' and identified associated duties of States regarding the management of resources.[74] Article 21, in the view of the African Commission, imposes an obligation on States parties to the ACHPR 'to ensure that resources are effectively managed for the sole and equal benefit of the entire peoples [sic] of the state'.[75] Article 21 has been applied by the African Commission in the inter-State context as well as to claims by sub-State groups, including Indigenous Peoples.[76] The ACtHPR, in *ACHPR*

[71] *Western Sahara Campaign II* (2022) [134], [137]. See similarly Joined Cases C-779/21 P and C-799/21 P *European Commission and Council of the European Union v Front populaire pour la libération de la Saguia el-Hamra et du Rio de oro (Front Polisario)*, Grand Chamber, Judgment (4 Oct 2024) (hereinafter *Polisario VI* (2024)) para 156; Joined Cases C-778/21 P and C-798/21 P *European Commission and Council of the European Union v Front populaire pour la libération de la Saguia el-Hamra et du Rio de oro (Front Polisario)*, Grand Chamber, Judgment (4 Oct 2024) (hereinafter *Polisario V* (2024)) para 184 (referring to 'self-determination or the permanent sovereignty over natural resources which derives from that right and from Article 73 of the Charter of the United Nations'). See Chapter 11.e.ii.

[72] ACHPR art 21. See Chapter 2.d.i. See also Rachel Murray, *The African Charter on Human and Peoples' Rights: A Commentary* (OUP 2019) 508–20.

[73] *Front for the Liberation of the State of Cabinda v Angola*, ACommHPR, Communication No 328/06 (2013) (hereinafter *Cabinda v Angola* (2013)) para 129. See also *ACHPR v Kenya*, ACtHPR, Application No 006/2012, Judgment (2017) (hereinafter *ACHPR v Kenya* (2017)) paras 198–99.

[74] *Cabinda v Angola* (2013) paras 127–32.

[75] Ibid para 131. See also *The Social and Economic Rights Action Center for Economic and Social Rights v Nigeria*, ACommHPR, Communication No 155/96 (2001) (hereinafter *Social and Economic Rights Action Center v Nigeria* (2001)) paras 57–60. See Ben Saul, *Indigenous Peoples and Human Rights: International and Regional Jurisprudence* (Bloomsbury 2016) 159–60.

[76] See e.g. *Social and Economic Rights Action Center v Nigeria* (2001) paras 57–60; *Centre for Minority Rights Development (Kenya) & Minority Rights Group International on behalf of Endorois Welfare Council v Kenya*, ACommHPR, Communication No 276/2003 (2010) (hereinafter *Endorois v Kenya* (2010)) paras 252–68; *Democratic Republic of Congo v Burundi, Rwanda and Uganda*, ACommHPR, Communication No 227/99 (2003) (hereinafter *DRC v Burundi, Rwanda and Uganda* (2003)) paras 90–94; *Cabinda v Angola* (2013) paras 127–32.

v Kenya (2017), contemplated the violation of Article 21 of the ACHPR in relation to the Ogiek Community of Kenya notwithstanding the inapplicability of the right to self-determination to that group under Article 20, illustrating the separability of the entitlement of peoples to freely dispose of their natural wealth and resources from the right to self-determination under the ACHPR.[77]

The Arab Charter on Human Rights, at Article 2(1), refers to the right of all peoples 'of self-determination and to control over their natural wealth and resources', and identifies the political and ESC elements of the right to self-determination as flowing therefrom.[78]

Just as no Inter-American instrument establishes a right to self-determination as such, no regional instrument establishes a right of peoples to freely dispose of their natural wealth and resources. The preamble of the Protocol of San Salvador, however, refers to the 'right of [] peoples' to 'free disposal of their wealth and natural resources' alongside the right to self-determination.[79] In *Saramaka People v Suriname* (2007), the Inter-American Court of Human Rights (IACtHR) interpreted Article 21 of the ACHR (Right to Property) to incorporate elements of self-determination related to economic, social, and cultural development for members of Indigenous and tribal communities, including 'the right to enjoy their particular spiritual relationship with the territory they have traditionally used and occupied'.[80]

1. Permanent Sovereignty over Natural Resources

The entitlement of peoples to freely dispose of their natural wealth and resources, articulated at common Article 1(2) of the two human rights

[77] *ACHPR v Kenya* (2017) paras 195–201. See similarly *Endorois v Kenya* (2010) paras 252–68.

[78] Arab Charter on Human Rights art 2(1). See Chapter 2.d.ii.

[79] Protocol of San Salvador preambular para 7. See Chapter 2.d.iii.

[80] *Saramaka People v Suriname*, Judgment (Preliminary Objections, Merits, Reparations, and Costs), 2007 IACtHR (Ser C) No 172 (28 Nov 2007) (hereinafter *Saramaka People v Suriname* (2007)) paras 93–95. For earlier application, see e.g. *Mayagna (Sumo) Awas Tingni Community v Nicaragua*, Judgment (Merits, Reparations, and Costs), 2001 IACtHR (Ser C) No 79 (31 Aug 2001) (hereinafter *Mayagna (Sumo) Awas Tingni Community v Nicaragua* (2001)) paras 142–49; *Yakye Axa Indigenous Community v Paraguay*, Judgment (Merits, Reparations, and Costs), 2005 IACtHR (Ser C) No 125 (17 June 2005) (hereinafter *Yakye Axa Indigenous Community v Paraguay* (2005)) paras 123–56. For subsequent treatment, see e.g. *Kaliña and Lokono Peoples v Suriname*, Judgment (Merits, Reparations and Costs), 2015 IACtHR (Ser C) No 309 (25 Nov 2015) (hereinafter *Kaliña and Lokono Peoples v Suriname* (2015)) paras 122–25.

covenants, has its origins in the principle of permanent sovereignty over natural resources.[81] In this way, the entitlement of peoples to freely dispose of their natural wealth and resources represents a point of contact between the right to self-determination and the principle of permanent sovereignty over natural resources.

The principle of permanent sovereignty over natural resources refers to an attribute of the sovereignty of the State.[82] To the extent that the beneficiaries of the principle are peoples, the principle provides that exploitation of the natural resources of a territory should inure to the benefit of the people of that territory. This proposition is expressed in UNGA Resolution 1803 (1952) (Permanent Sovereignty over Natural Resources).[83] UNGA Resolution 1803 provides that '[t]he right of peoples and nations to permanent sovereignty over their natural wealth and resources must be exercised in the interest of their national development and of the wellbeing of the people of the State concerned'.[84] In *Armed Activities* (2005) and *Palestine* (2024), the ICJ recognized the principle of permanent sovereignty over natural resources as CIL.[85] The relation between the principle of permanent sovereignty over natural resources and the right to self-determination was expressed in UNGA Resolution 1803, which characterized 'permanent sovereignty over natural wealth and resources as a basic constituent of the right to self-determination'.[86]

The principle of permanent sovereignty over natural resources was incorporated and amended in common Article 1 of the two human rights covenants as an entitlement of peoples to freely dispose of their natural wealth and resources in relation to the right to self-determination.[87]

[81] A/2929 ch IV paras 19–21. See Schrijver (n 65) 49–56; Dam-de Jong (n 65) 34–36.

[82] See e.g. A/Res/626 (VII) (21 Dec 1952); A/Res/1515 (XV) (15 Dec 1960). See A/2929 ch IV para 20.

[83] A/Res/1803 (XVII) (14 Dec 1962). See also A/Res/523 (VI) (12 Jan 1952); A/Res/626 (VII) (21 Dec 1952); A/Res/1314 (XIII) (12 Dec 1958). See Karol N. Gess, 'Permanent Sovereignty over Natural Resources: An Analytical Review of the United Nations Declaration and Its Genesis' (1964) 13(2) *ICLQ* 398 (1964).

[84] A/Res/1314 (XIII) (12 Dec 1958) para 1.

[85] *Armed Activities on the Territory of the Congo (Democratic Republic of the Congo v Uganda)*, Judgment, ICJ Rep 2005 (hereinafter *Armed Activities* (2005)) para 244; *Palestine* (2024) paras 125, 240.

[86] A/Res/1803 (XVII) (14 Dec 1962) preambular para 2. See also A/Res/1314 (XIII) (12 Dec 1958) para 1. See Petra Gümplová, 'Sovereignty over natural resources—A normative reinterpretation' (2020) 9(1) *Global Constitutionalism* 7 (examining the relationship between the concepts).

[87] See Chapter 2.c.ii.

In *Palestine* (2024), the ICJ regarded permanent sovereignty over natural resources itself to be an 'element' of the right to self-determination.[88] In this way, the court appears to have collapsed the distinction between the entitlement of peoples to freely dispose of their natural wealth and resources as a component of the right to self-determination and the principle of permanent sovereignty over natural resources from which the entitlement derives, reflecting substantive correspondence between the two concepts.[89]

2. Application of the Entitlement and its Correlates

Economic activities in relation to NSGTs and Trust Territories and occupied territories may implicate the entitlement of peoples to freely dispose of their natural wealth and resources. *Certain Phosphate Lands in Nauru* (1992)[90] and *East Timor* (1995)[91] concerned economic activities in light of the entitlement of the peoples of a Trust Territory and a NSGT, respectively, to permanent sovereignty over natural resources, though neither case reached the merits phase.[92] Even so, in neither case was it alleged that the exploitation of natural resources by an administering State was categorically prohibited. Relatedly, in *Namibia* (1971), the ICJ noted that the third-State obligation of non-recognition of South Africa's unlawful presence in Namibia 'should not result in depriving the people of Namibia of any advantages derived from international co-operation'.[93] This so-called *Namibia* exception has been identified as allowing an 'element of flexibility' permitting certain economic activities notwithstanding the obligation of non-recognition.[94]

[88] *Palestine* (2024) para 240 (citing *Armed Activities* (2005)).
[89] See similarly *Polisario VI* (2024) para 156; *Polisario V* (2024) para 184. See Chapter 8.d.i.2.
[90] *Certain Phosphate Lands in Nauru (Nauru v Australia)*, Preliminary Objections, Judgment, ICJ Rep 1992, 240 para 5.
[91] *East Timor (Portugal v Australia)*, Judgment, ICJ Rep 1995, 90 para 19.
[92] Litigation involving agreements between the EU (and UK) and Morocco regarding the exploitation of the resources of Western Sahara also concerns the entitlement of the people of a NSGT to permanent sovereignty over natural resources. While controlling judgments in this litigation have turned on the right to self-determination, they were not decided on the basis of the entitlement of peoples to freely dispose of their natural wealth and resources. See Chapter 11.e.ii. Cf *Saharawi Arab Democratic Republic and Another v Owner and Charterers of the MV 'NM Cherry Blossom' and Others*, High Court of South Africa, [2017] ZAECPEH 31 (hereinafter '*NM Cherry Blossom*' (2017)) para 32.
[93] *Legal Consequences for States of the Continued Presence of South Africa in Namibia (South West Africa) notwithstanding Security Council Resolution 276 (1970)*, Advisory Opinion, ICJ Rep 1971, 16 para 125. See Chapter 9.d.ii.1.
[94] Crawford (n 68) paras 48–51.

International law permits the exploitation of the natural resources of a NSGT by an administering power for the benefit of the people of that territory, on their behalf or in consultation with such people.[95] The leading expression of this position is a 2002 legal opinion by the Legal Counsel of the UNSC, Hans Corell, provided at the request of the president of the UNSC, concerning contracts for mineral resource exploitation in Western Sahara concluded by Morocco.[96] On the basis of a survey of practice, the relevant rule of CIL was stated in the following terms:

> [] The recent State practice, though limited, is illustrative of an opinio juris on the part of both administering Powers and third States: where resource exploitation activities are conducted in Non-Self-Governing Territories for the benefit of the peoples of those Territories, on their behalf or in consultation with their representatives, they are considered compatible with the Charter obligations of the administering Power and in conformity with the General Assembly resolutions and the principle of 'permanent sovereignty over natural resources' enshrined therein.[97]

This rule was identified in part on the basis of a consistent series of UNGA resolutions, which affirmed the right of peoples of NSGTs to the benefit of their natural resources, and distinguished natural resource exploitation undertaken to benefit such peoples from activities detrimental to their interests.[98] As applied to the contracts concerning Western Sahara that prompted the opinion, because the contracts entailed no physical exploitation or accrual of benefits, they were not viewed to be unlawful.[99] The Corell Opinion noted, however, that 'if further exploration and exploitation activities were to proceed in disregard of the interests and wishes of the people of Western Sahara, they would be in violation of the principles of international law applicable to mineral resource activities in Non-Self-Governing Territories'.[100]

[95] *'NM Cherry Blossom'* (2007) para 47.

[96] Hans Corell, Letter dated 29 January 2002 from the Under-Secretary-General for Legal Affairs, the Legal Counsel, addressed to the President of the Security Council, S/2002/161 (12 Feb 2002) (hereinafter Corell Opinion (2002)) para 1.

[97] Ibid para 24.

[98] Ibid para 10 (and sources cited therein). See also A/Res/61/123 (14 Dec 2006) (Economic and other activities which affect the interests of the peoples of the Non-Self-Governing Territories).

[99] Corell Opinion (2002) para 25.

[100] Ibid.

While the Corell Opinion continues to inform consideration of the conditions under which the natural resources of a NSGT may be exploited, because Morocco is not the *de jure* administering power of Western Sahara, whether resource exploitation by an administering power provides the appropriate frame of reference for activities of Morocco in relation to Western Sahara has been questioned.[101]

The law of occupation provides a distinct source of obligations concerning natural resource exploitation that limits the ability of an occupying power to exploit the natural resources of an occupied territory.[102] The 1907 Hague Regulations provide that an occupying power is subject to an obligation to administer property, including natural resources, according to the principle of usufruct.[103] The ICJ addressed this obligation in *Palestine* (2024):

> The Court recalls that, under the principle of customary international law contained in Article 55 of the Hague Regulations, the occupying Power shall be regarded only as administrator and usufructuary of natural resources in the occupied territory, including but not limited to forests and agricultural estates, and it shall 'safeguard the capital' of these resources. Therefore, the use by the occupying Power of natural resources must not exceed what is necessary for the purposes of the occupation.[104]

[101] See e.g. *Polisario VI* (2024) paras 137–38; *Polisario V* (2024) paras 166–67; Joined Cases T-344/19 and T-356/19 *Popular Front for the Liberation of Saguia el-Hamra and Rio de Oro (Front Polisario) v Council of the European Union*, General Court, Judgment (29 Sept 2021) para 362; Case T-279/19 *Front populaire pour la libération de la Saguia-el-Hamra et du Rio de Oro (Front Polisario) v Council of the European Union*, General Court, Judgment (29 Sept 2021) paras 385–90; *'NM Cherry Blossom'* (2017) paras 45, 47; Case T-512/12 *Front populaire pour la libération de la saguia-el-hamra et du rio de oro (Front Polisario) v Council of the European Union*, General Court, Judgment (10 Dec 2015) paras 207–10, 222, 229. Various authorities have regarded Morocco's presence in Western Sahara to constitute occupation: see Chapter 7 n 96. See also Chapter 7.b.ii.1.B.

[102] Hague Convention (IV) respecting the Laws and Customs of War on Land and its annex: Regulations concerning the Laws and Customs of War on Land, Regulations art 55, 36 Stat. 2277, 1 Bevans 631 (18 Oct 1907, entered into force 26 Jan 1910), reproduced in (1908) 2(Supp) *AJIL* 90 (hereinafter 1907 Hague Regulations). See also ibid art 47 (prohibiting pillage); Geneva Convention Relative to the Protection of Civilian Persons in Time of War art 33, 75 UNTS 287 (12 Aug 1949, entered into force 21 Oct 1950) (prohibiting pillage).

[103] 1907 Hague Regulations art 55. See A/38/265 / E/1983/85 (21 June 1983) para 29. See Crawford (n 68) paras 52–63.

[104] *Palestine* (2024) para 124.

In *Armed Activities* (2005), although the ICJ considered the principle of permanent sovereignty over natural resources inapplicable to the situation in question, without elaboration, the court nevertheless acknowledged that international humanitarian law permits the exploitation of natural resources for the benefit of the local population.[105] International law permits an occupying power to undertake certain economic activities, including resource exploitation in an occupied territory provided the population of the territory is the primary beneficiary of such activities.[106]

It has been suggested that the permissible activities of an occupying power as administrator and usufructuary of natural resources in an occupied territory largely align in practice with the permissible activities of an administering State under the principle of permanent sovereignty over natural resources in relation to resource exploitation in a NSGT.[107] The ICJ took note of the overlap between the regime of resource exploitation under the law of occupation and the principle of permanent sovereignty over natural resources in *Palestine* (2024):

> Where [] an occupying Power pursues a policy of exploitation of natural resources in the occupied territory contrary to the law of occupation, this policy could be contrary to the principle of permanent sovereignty over natural resources.[108]

[105] *Armed Activities* (2005) paras 222–50 (Finding Uganda responsible under international humanitarian law for acts of looting, plundering and exploitation of DRC's natural resources). See also *DRC v Burundi, Rwanda and Uganda* (2003) (Finding 'the illegal exploitation/looting of the natural resources of the complainant state in contravention of Article 21 of the African Charter', which consists of the right of peoples to freely dispose of their wealth and natural resources).

[106] Institut de Droit International, *Bruges Declaration on the Use of Force* (2 Sept 2003) 3. See also Crawford (n 68) paras 52–63; Eugene Kontorovich, 'Economic Dealings with Occupied Territories' (2015) 53(3) *Columbia Journal of Transnational Law* 584, 603; Cedric Ryngaert & Rutger Fransen, 'EU extraterritorial obligations with respect to trade with occupied territories: Reflections after the case of *Front Polisario* before EU courts' (2018) 2(1) *Europe and the World: A law review* 1, 17; Pål Wrange, 'Self-determination, occupation and the authority to exploit national resources—trajectories from four European judgments on Western Sahara' (2019) 52 *Israel Law Review* 3, 11, 24.

[107] Kontorovich (n 106) 603. See also Ryngaert & Fransen (n 106) 17 (Noting parallels between the '*Namibia* exception' and principle of usufruct in the law of occupation); Wrange (n 106) 11, 24.

[108] *Palestine* (2024) para 125.

In *Palestine* (2024), the court addressed Israel's exploitation of natural resources in the OPT, particularly its diversion of water resources for the benefit of the population of Israel and its settlers in the OPT.[109] The court held that Israel breached 'its obligation to act as administrator and usufructuary' and also that this practice 'is inconsistent with its obligation to respect the Palestinian people's right to permanent sovereignty over natural resources'.[110] The court thereby found that Israel had exploited natural resources in the OPT in such a way as to breach both its obligation as an occupying power in relation to resource exploitation and its obligation to respect the right to permanent sovereignty over natural resources, a component of the right to self-determination.[111]

e. Self-Determination and Indigenous Peoples

Indigenous and tribal communities have been recognized across a range of fora as Indigenous Peoples entitled to self-determination.[112] This conceptualization is closely related to the development of a normative framework concerning the rights of Indigenous Peoples, within which a right to self-determination has been recognized. The relation of self-determination to Indigenous Peoples may be understood in reference to the domestic aspect of the right to self-determination, to include both its political and ESC elements. Practice indicates that Indigenous Peoples enjoy, as an application of the domestic aspect of the right to self-determination, an entitlement to political autonomy and self-government as well as to freely pursue their economic, social, and cultural development as a form of 'internal self-determination of indigenous peoples'.[113] Implicit in such treatment of self-determination relating to Indigenous Peoples is that the human rights that comprise the substance of self-determination are collectively enjoyed and

[109] Ibid paras 124–33.
[110] Ibid para 133.
[111] See ibid para 240.
[112] See Chapter 6.e.ii.
[113] *Sanila-Aikio v Finland*, Communication No 2668/2015, CCPR/C/124/D/2668/2015 (20 Mar 2019) (hereinafter *Sanila-Aikio v Finland* (2019)) para 6.10; *Käkkäläjärvi v Finland*, Communication No 2950/2017, CCPR/C/124/D/2950/2017 (18 Dec 2019) (hereinafter *Käkkäläjärvi v Finland* (2019)) para 9.10; CESCR GC 26 para 11.

exercised by members of an Indigenous People and to be respected by the State within which its members reside.[114]

Recognition of the right to self-determination of Indigenous Peoples under the ICCPR by the HRC is instructive in this regard. HRC General Comment No 23 provides that the rights of Indigenous Peoples are safeguarded under the ICCPR through Article 27, which concerns the rights of members of minority groups, rather than through Article 1, which codifies the right to self-determination.[115] In *Sanila-Aikio v Finland* (2019) and *Käkkäläjärvi et al v Finland* (2019), the HRC looked to ICCPR Article 1 to interpret Article 27 as well as Article 25, which contains the right to vote and participate in public affairs, in relation to the self-determination of Indigenous Peoples.[116] The cases concerned communications brought by members of the Indigenous Sami alleging violations of the ICCPR by Finland through measures impacting eligibility to participate in elections to the Sami parliament.[117] Although the HRC found the authors' claims under Article 1 to be inadmissible,[118] the HRC considered that Finland violated Article 25 and Article 27 of the ICCPR.[119] In so finding, the HRC interpreted ICCPR Article 27 to include 'the principle of internal self-determination relating to indigenous peoples' in reference to Article 1:[120]

> The Committee further observes that article 27 of the Covenant, interpreted in the light of the United Nations Declaration on the Rights of Indigenous Peoples and article 1 of the Covenant, enshrines an inalienable right of indigenous peoples to freely determine their political status and freely pursue their economic, social and cultural development. Article 1 of the Covenant and the corresponding obligations concerning its implementation are interrelated with other provisions of the Covenant and rules of international law.[121]

[114] HRC, *CCPR General Comment No. 23: Article 27 (Rights of Minorities)*, CCPR/C/21/Rev.1/Add.5 (1994) (hereinafter HRC GC 23) paras 3.1–3.2. See Shaw (n 40) 488–89.

[115] HRC GC 23 paras 3.1–3.2.

[116] *Sanila-Aikio v Finland* (2019); *Käkkäläjärvi v Finland* (2019). See CJ Iorns Magallanes, 'Introductory Note' (2020) 59(2) ILM 302.

[117] *Sanila-Aikio v Finland* (2019) para 1.2; *Käkkäläjärvi v Finland* (2019) para 3.1.

[118] *Sanila-Aikio v Finland* (2019) para 1.4; *Käkkäläjärvi v Finland* (2019) para 8.6.

[119] *Sanila-Aikio v Finland* (2019) para 7; *Käkkäläjärvi v Finland* (2019) para 10.

[120] *Sanila-Aikio v Finland* (2019) para 6.10; *Käkkäläjärvi v Finland* (2019) para 9.10.

[121] *Sanila-Aikio v Finland* (2019) para 6.8; *Käkkäläjärvi v Finland* (2019) para 9.8 (citations to UNDRIP arts 3–4 and HRC GC 12 omitted).

The HRC thereby contemplated the elements of the self-determination of Indigenous Peoples to be cognizable under ICCPR Article 27. The HRC further considered that restrictions on representation in the Sami Parliament, pursuant to ICCPR Article 25, 'must have a reasonable and objective justification and be consistent with the other provisions of the Covenant, including the principle of internal self-determination relating to indigenous peoples'.[122] In the view of the HRC, actions at issue by the Supreme Administrative Court of Finland failed to satisfy that standard, resulting in 'a violation of the authors' rights under article 25, read alone and in conjunction with article 27, as interpreted in the light of article 1 of the Covenant'.[123] The HRC concluded that Finland was obligated to review its impugned law to ensure respect for the right of the Indigenous Sami 'to exercise their internal self-determination, in accordance with articles 25 and 27 of the Covenant'.[124] The HRC, in interpreting ICCPR Article 25 and Article 27 in view of Article 1, addressed the collective exercise of individual rights by members of an Indigenous People in light of the right to self-determination.[125] In this way, the views adopted by the HRC illustrate how the right to self-determination of Indigenous Peoples may be conceived through the domestic aspect of the right to self-determination.[126]

The CESCR has similarly recognized the right to self-determination of Indigenous Peoples under the ICESCR in General Comment No 26 on land and economic, social, and cultural rights.[127] CESCR General Comment No 26 provides guidance on ICESCR obligations relating to land, including Article 1 (the right to self-determination).[128] The CESCR explained the linkage between the domestic aspect of the right to self-determination and land rights, with particular relevance to the self-determination of Indigenous Peoples:

> [L]and is also closely linked to the right to self-determination, enshrined in article 1 of the Covenant, the importance of which was emphasized

[122] *Sanila-Aikio v Finland* (2019) para 6.10; *Käkkäläjärvi v Finland* (2019) para 9.10.
[123] *Sanila-Aikio v Finland* (2019) para 6.11; *Käkkäläjärvi v Finland* (2019) para 9.11.
[124] *Sanila-Aikio v Finland* (2019) para 8; *Käkkäläjärvi v Finland* (2019) para 11.
[125] *Sanila-Aikio v Finland* (2019) para 6.9; *Käkkäläjärvi v Finland* (2019) para 9.9.
[126] See HRC GC 23 para 3.2.
[127] CESCR GC 26.
[128] Ibid para 4.

> in Declaration on the Right to Development (1986). The realization of self-determination is an essential condition for the effective guarantee and observance of individual human rights and for the promotion and strengthening of those rights. Indigenous Peoples can freely pursue their political, economic, social and cultural development and dispose of their natural wealth and resources for their own ends only if they have land or territory in which they can exercise their self-determination. The present general comment deals only with the internal self-determination of Indigenous Peoples, which has to be exercised in accordance with international law and respecting the territorial integrity of States. Thus, according to their right to internal self-determination, the collective ownership of lands, territories and resources of Indigenous Peoples shall be respected, which implies that these lands and territories shall be demarcated and protected by States parties.[129]

Although the CESCR made a general statement about the practical relevance of self-determination to the enjoyment of human rights, General Comment No 26 focuses on the relevance of land to 'the internal self-determination of Indigenous Peoples', i.e. the domestic aspect of the right to self-determination as applied in relation to Indigenous Peoples.

The sections that follow consider the self-determination of Indigenous Peoples across international, regional, and State practice. First, efforts to codify the rights of Indigenous Peoples have contributed to a normative framework that informs the right to self-determination of Indigenous Peoples.[130] In this regard, ILO Convention No 169 Concerning Indigenous and Tribal Peoples in Independent Countries and the UN Declaration on the Rights of Indigenous Peoples (UNDRIP) receive careful consideration. The second section considers regional practice in the Inter-American and African human rights systems, which has shaped the contours of the right to self-determination of Indigenous Peoples within those regional systems. Finally, respect for the self-determination of Indigenous Peoples is ultimately contingent upon the domestic implementation of laws and policies by States

[129] Ibid para 11 (internal citations to HRC GC 12, UNDRIP, and *Käkkäläjärvi v Finland* (2019) omitted).

[130] Marc Weller, 'Self-Determination of Indigenous Peoples: Articles 3, 4, 5, 18, 23, and 46(1)' in Jessie Hohmann & Marc Weller (eds), *The UN Declaration on the Rights of Indigenous Peoples: A Commentary* (OUP 2018) 126–34.

in relation to their Indigenous populations. Examples of the ways in which the right to self-determination of Indigenous Peoples may inform—and may be shaped by—State practice regarding the autonomy and self-government of Indigenous Peoples are considered in the final section below.

i. International Labour Organisation Convention No 169

ILO Convention (No. 169) Concerning Indigenous and Tribal Peoples in Independent Countries is the sole binding international instrument addressing the rights of Indigenous Peoples.[131] The instrument revised the earlier ILO Convention (No. 107) on Indigenous and Tribal Populations, the first international instrument addressing the rights of Indigenous Peoples, which was problematic for its focus on the integration of Indigenous Peoples.[132] Although ILO Convention No 169 presently has only twenty-four States parties, and makes no express reference to self-determination, its provisions offer some guidance on the treatment of Indigenous Peoples in international law. The Convention contains a definition of Indigenous Peoples at Article 1(1):

> *Article 1*
>
> 1. This Convention applies to:
>   (a) Tribal peoples in independent countries whose social, cultural and economic conditions distinguish them from other sections of the national community, and whose status is regulated wholly or partially by their own customs or traditions or by special laws or regulations;

[131] ILO Convention (No. 169) concerning Indigenous and tribal peoples in independent countries, 1650 UNTS 383 (27 June 1989, entered into force 5 Sept 1991) (hereinafter ILO Convention No 169).

[132] ILO Convention (No. 107) concerning the protection and integration of Indigenous and other tribal and semi-tribal populations in independent countries, 328 UNTS 247 (26 June 1957, entered into force 2 June 1959). See Russel Lawrence Barsh, 'Revision of ILO Convention No. 107' (1987) 81(3) *AJIL* 756.

(b) Peoples in independent countries who are regarded as indigenous on account of their descent from the populations which inhabited the country, or a geographical region to which the country belongs, at the time of conquest or colonisation or the establishment of present State boundaries and who, irrespective of their legal status, retain some or all of their own social, economic, cultural and political institutions.[133]

This definition is significant in light of the absence of an accepted definition of 'Indigenous Peoples' in other instruments addressing the rights of Indigenous Peoples. In application of this definition, the Convention articulates self-identification as the 'fundamental criterion' for determining the scope of the Convention.[134]

The Convention also includes two key caveats relevant to self-determination in relation to Indigenous Peoples. The first is set out at Article 1(3), which provides that '[t]he use of the term "peoples" in this Convention shall not be construed as having any implications as regards the rights which may attach to the term under international law'.[135] This caveat is consistent with the absence of indicia that Indigenous and tribal communities were intended to be included within the scope of the term 'peoples' as that term is used in international instruments addressing the right to self-determination.[136] The second caveat, included in the Convention's preamble, frames aspects of autonomy and self-government that comprise the self-determination of Indigenous Peoples within the bounds of the territorial unit in which an Indigenous People resides:

> Recognising the aspirations of these peoples to exercise control over their own institutions, ways of life and economic development and to maintain and develop their identities, languages and religions, *within the framework of the States in which they live*[.][137]

[133] ILO Convention No 169 art 1(1).
[134] Ibid art 1(2).
[135] Ibid art 1(3).
[136] See Chapter 6.e.ii.
[137] ILO Convention No 169 preambular para 5 (emphasis added).

This safeguard language is consistent with the relationship between the right to self-determination and the principle of territorial integrity.[138] And, in this way, the Convention indicates that the elements the self-determination of Indigenous Peoples are exercised within the parameters of the domestic aspect of self-determination. The Convention also contains substantive provisions pertaining to the autonomy and self-government of Indigenous Peoples.

ii. United Nations Declaration on the Rights of Indigenous Peoples

The UN Declaration on the Rights of Indigenous Peoples (UNDRIP) is the principal expression of the entitlement of Indigenous Peoples to self-determination. The non-binding instrument was adopted in 2007 as an annex to UNGA Resolution 61/295 (2007), which was approved by an overwhelming majority of the UNGA.[139] The four States that voted against Resolution 61/295 (Australia, Canada, New Zealand, and the United States) subsequently issued statements in support of the UNDRIP.[140] The UNDRIP, which was negotiated over two decades with the involvement of representatives of Indigenous Peoples, represents a significant achievement in advancing the aspirations of Indigenous Peoples towards recognition of their rights, including the right to self-determination.[141]

The UNDRIP contains several express references to self-determination. The preamble of the UNDRIP refers to the 'fundamental importance of the

[138] See Chapter 7.d.

[139] A/61/PV.107 (13 Sept 2007) 19 (143 votes in favour, 4 votes against, 11 abstentions).

[140] Australia: *Permanent Forum on Indigenous Issues: Report on the eighth session (18–29 May 2009)*, Economic and Social Council Official Records, 2009, Supplement No 23, E/2009/43 / E/C.19/2009/14 (2009) para 39; New Zealand: *Permanent Forum on Indigenous Issues: Report on the ninth session (19–30 April 2010)*, Economic and Social Council Official Records, 2010, Supplement No 23, E/2010/43 / E/C.19/2010/15 (2010) para 16; United States: Ibid; see also *Announcement of U.S. Support for the United Nations Declaration on the Rights of Indigenous Peoples* (12 Jan 2011) (available at https://2009-2017.state.gov/s/srgia/154553.htm); Canada: *Permanent Forum on Indigenous Issues: Report on the fifteenth session (9–20 May 2016)*, Economic and Social Council Official Records, 2016, Supplement No 23, E/2016/43 / E/C.19/2016/11 (2016) para 18.

[141] See Weller (n 130) 127–34; Karen Engle, 'On Fragile Architecture: The UN Declaration on the Rights of Indigenous Peoples in the Context of Human Rights' (2011) 22(1) *EJIL* 141, 143–48.

right to self-determination of all peoples, by virtue of which they freely determine their political status and freely pursue their economic, social and cultural development'.[142] In this way, the UNDRIP orients its treatment of the self-determination of Indigenous Peoples within the broader international legal framework of self-determination. Moreover, the preamble states that nothing in the UNDRIP 'may be used to deny any peoples their right to self-determination, exercised in conformity with international law',[143] which indicates that the provisions of the UNDRIP are intended to operate within the parameters of the right to self-determination 'as classically understood'.[144]

Three operative paragraphs of the UNDRIP—Articles 3, 4, and 46(1)—relate specifically to the self-determination of Indigenous Peoples. Article 3 refers to the right of Indigenous Peoples to self-determination and defines that right in the general terms with which it is articulated in international law.[145]

> *Article 3*
> Indigenous peoples have the right to self-determination. By virtue of that right they freely determine their political status and freely pursue their economic, social and cultural development.

Article 4 defines the exercise of the right to self-determination by Indigenous Peoples in reference to autonomy and self-government.

> *Article 4*
> Indigenous peoples, in exercising their right to self-determination, have the right to autonomy or self-government in matters relating to their internal and local affairs, as well as ways and means for financing their autonomous functions.

[142] United Nations Declaration on the Rights of Indigenous Peoples, A/Res/61/295 (13 Sept 2007) Annex (hereinafter UNDRIP) preambular para 17.

[143] Ibid preambular para 18.

[144] Weller (n 130) 137.

[145] See ICCPR art 1(1); ICESCR art 1(1); Resolution 1514 para 2; FRD Principle V, para 1; Vienna Declaration (1993) part I, s 2, para 1. See *Palestine* (2024) para 241. See also ACHPR art 20; Arab Charter on Human Rights art 1.

This provision, which was moved from Article 31 during the course of drafting to immediately follow Article 3 in the final text, appears to qualify Article 3 in such a way as to present the self-determination of Indigenous Peoples as an application of the domestic aspect of the right to self-determination.[146] The final provision of the UNDRIP, Article 46, reinforces this interpretation.

> *Article 46*
>
> 1. Nothing in this Declaration may be interpreted as implying for any State, people, group or person any right to engage in any activity or to perform any act contrary to the Charter of the United Nations or construed as authorizing or encouraging any action which would dismember or impair, totally or in part, the territorial integrity or political unity of sovereign and independent States.

Article 46(1) consists of a safeguard clause that parallels the way in which other instruments addressing the right to self-determination expressly condition its exercise by the principle of territorial integrity.[147] Like those other safeguard clauses, Article 46(1) was intended to assuage concerns about the international exercise of self-determination by Indigenous Peoples and, in so doing, orients the right to self-determination of Indigenous Peoples in the UNDRIP within the domestic aspect of self-determination.[148] Article 46(1) is notable in expressly addressing a range of actors, i.e. 'any State, people, group or person' in its provision on territorial integrity, underscoring the broad applicability of the safeguard clause.

Taken together, the provisions of the UNDRIP conceive of the right to self-determination of Indigenous Peoples as an application of the domestic aspect of self-determination, which entitles Indigenous Peoples to political autonomy and self-government as well as the pursuit of their economic, social, and cultural development. The substance of such an entitlement is borne out in other provisions of the UNDRIP, including those

[146] Weller (n 130) 134, 136.
[147] See Chapter 7.d.i.
[148] Engle (n 141) 146–48.

referring to self-government through institutions established by Indigenous Peoples,[149] and provisions concerning consultation and the free, prior and informed consent of Indigenous Peoples in matters affecting them.[150] This approach is analogous to the way in which the elements of the right to self-determination in the two human rights covenants are given effect through the collective exercise of human rights and fundamental freedoms enumerated in those instruments.[151] It should be noted that the treatment of self-determination in the UNDRIP is viewed as a compromise formulation, one that may be explained by a shift away from advocacy favouring a right to self-determination in the fullest sense for Indigenous Peoples (i.e. to include the international aspect of self-determination) towards a human-rights-oriented approach situated within the domestic aspect of self-determination.[152]

iii. Regional Practice

A substantial body of regional practice has addressed the right to self-determination of Indigenous Peoples. The following sections consider the treatment of the right to self-determination of Indigenous Peoples in the Inter-American human rights system and under the African Charter on Human and Peoples' Rights.

1. Inter-American Human Rights System

While no Inter-American instrument establishes a right to self-determination as such, both the IACHR and the IACtHR have identified protections for Indigenous Peoples, including under the ACHR, to safeguard their right to self-determination. In addition, the American Declaration on the Rights of Indigenous Peoples (ADRIP), adopted in 2016, parallels the UNDRIP in its approach to the self-determination of Indigenous Peoples and replicates key provisions to that end.

[149] UNDRIP arts 5, 20(1), 33(2), 34.
[150] Ibid arts 18, 19. See also CESCR GC 26 para 21.
[151] See Chapter 8.b.
[152] Engle (n 141) 143–48.

An early statement by the IACHR on the question of the self-determination of Indigenous Peoples is found in *Report on the Situation of Human Rights of a Segment of the Nicaraguan Population of Miskito Origin* (1983), which concerned the treatment of Indigenous Miskitos by Nicaragua.[153] In its Report, the IACHR recognized the right to self-determination in international law, but did not consider the right to be applicable to minority groups within a State, including Indigenous groups.[154] Nevertheless, the IACHR recognized 'special legal protection' for the preservation of the cultural identity of the Indigenous groups at issue, including in relation to language, religion, and ancestral land.[155]

Later, in *Saramaka People v Suriname* (2007), the IACtHR referred to the right to self-determination in its judgment concerning an application arising from violations by Suriname of the rights of members of the Indigenous Saramaka community, particularly relating to land they traditionally used and occupied.[156] The IACtHR identified the right to self-determination in international law and interpreted Article 21 of the ACHR (Right to Property) to incorporate elements of self-determination related to economic, social, and cultural development for members of Indigenous and tribal communities.[157] The IACtHR found the right to property under ACHR Article 21—interpreted in light of Articles 1 and 27 of the ICCPR—to encompass protections related to the economic, social, and cultural development of Indigenous Peoples. In interpreting substantive provisions of the ACHR to this effect, the IACtHR considered the human rights of members of the Saramaka community in reference to the right to self-determination, and found that members of such a group 'enjoy and exercise certain rights, such as the right to property, in a distinctly collective manner'.[158] The IACtHR has applied this interpretation of ACHR Article 21 in subsequent cases.[159]

153 *Report on the Situation of Human Rights of a Segment of the Nicaraguan Population of Miskito Origin*, IACHR, OAS Doc OEA/Ser.L/V.II.62, doc 10 rev 3 (29 Nov 1983).

154 Ibid para 9. See also para 10.

155 Ibid para 15. See also para 11.

156 *Saramaka People v Suriname* (2007) para 2. See Saul et al (n 60) 93–97; Saul (n 75) 156–59.

157 *Saramaka People v Suriname* (2007) paras 93–95.

158 Ibid para 164.

159 See e.g. *Kaliña and Lokono Peoples v Suriname* (2015) paras 122–25. For earlier application of Article 21 to Indigenous property, prior to its linkage to the right to self-determination, see *Mayagna (Sumo) Awas Tingni Community v Nicaragua* (2001) paras 142–49; *Yakye Axa Indigenous Community v Paraguay* (2005) paras 123–56.

In *Rama and Kriol Peoples et al v Nicaragua* (2024), the IACtHR addressed the right to self-determination in relation to the political representatives of Indigenous and tribal communities. The IACtHR considered that the exercise of the right to self-determination by Indigenous and tribal communities, within the framework of the State, entitles such groups to elect their authorities and representatives and to participate in decision-making processes that may affect them.[160] In this context, the IACtHR considered that ACHR Article 23 (Right to Participate in Government) and Article 26 (Progressive Development)—the latter regarded as incorporating a 'right to cultural identity'—operate to safeguard this entitlement individually and collectively.[161] The IACtHR found that States parties to the ACHR are, accordingly, under a positive duty to adopt special measures necessary to enable such participation in the context of the exercise of self-determination.[162] By adversely interfering in the appointment of Indigenous authorities, the IACtHR found that Nicaragua violated ACHR Articles 23(1) and 26, in conjunction with Article 1(1), in relation to both affected individuals and communities.[163]

In *Huilcamán Paillama et al v Chile* (2024), a case concerning the conviction of Indigenous individuals for protesting, the IACtHR oriented the protection of the right to self-determination of Indigenous Peoples under the ACHR in the 'right to cultural identity' safeguarded by Article 26.[164] The IACtHR reiterated that the right to self-determination includes the right of Indigenous and tribal groups to elect their own authorities and representatives and to participate in decision-making processes that may affect them.[165] As a prerequisite to such participation, the IACtHR considered that the right to self-determination safeguards the ability of Indigenous and tribal groups to express their opinions.[166] Accordingly, the IACtHR found in relevant part

[160] *Rama and Kriol Peoples, the Black Creole Indigenous Community of Bluefields et al v Nicaragua* (Merits, Reparations and Costs), 2024 IACtHR (Ser C) No 552 (1 Apr 2024) para 124.
[161] Ibid para 133.
[162] Ibid para 127.
[163] Ibid para 147.
[164] *Huilcamán Paillama et al v Chile* (Merits, Reparations and Costs), 2024 IACtHR (Ser C) No 527 (18 June 2024) (hereinafter *Paillama et al v Chile* (2024)) para 252.
[165] Ibid paras 254–55 (Curiously, the IACtHR referred here to the 'external' aspect of self-determination).
[166] Ibid para 255. See also *Maya Kaqchikel Indigenous Peoples of Sumpango et al v Guatemala*, Judgment (Merits, Reparations and Costs), 2021 IACtHR (Ser C) No 440 (6 Oct 2021) para 95.

that impermissible restrictions by Chile in connection with protests violated the right to self-determination of the Indigenous Mapuche People.[167]

In June 2016, the OAS General Assembly adopted the American Declaration on the Rights of Indigenous Peoples (ADRIP), a non-binding instrument that parallels the UNDRIP in its treatment of the right to self-determination of Indigenous Peoples.[168] Article III of the ADRIP refers to the right of Indigenous Peoples to self-determination and defines that right in the general terms with which the right to self-determination is articulated in international law, just as Article 3 of the UNDRIP.[169] Like Article 4 of the UNDRIP, Article XXI(1) of the ADRIP provides for a 'right to autonomy or self-government' that similarly appears to qualify Article III in such a way as to situate the self-determination of Indigenous Peoples within the domestic aspect of self-determination.[170] Finally, Article IV of the ADRIP, which immediately follows its provision on self-determination, consists of a safeguard clause that parallels UNDRIP Article 46(1), a provision concerning territorial integrity understood in the UNDRIP to orient the right to self-determination of Indigenous Peoples within the domestic aspect of self-determination.[171] Like the way the implementation of the right to self-determination of Indigenous Peoples is borne out in other provisions of the UNDRIP, the ADRIP also includes provisions referring to aspects of self-government through institutions established by Indigenous Peoples,[172] and provisions concerning consultation and the free, prior and informed consent of Indigenous Peoples in matters affecting them.[173]

2. African Charter on Human and Peoples' Rights

The ACHPR contains an operative provision on the right of peoples to self-determination at Article 20, as well as other rights of peoples at Articles 19 and 21–24.[174] Both the African Commission on Human and Peoples' Rights

[167] *Paillama et al v Chile* (2024) para 261.

[168] American Declaration on the Rights of Indigenous Peoples, OAS AG/Res 2888 (XLVI-0/16) (15 June 2016).

[169] Ibid art III.

[170] Ibid art XXI(1).

[171] Ibid art IV.

[172] Ibid arts XXI(2), XXII(1), XXX(2).

[173] Ibid art XXIII (Note that other provisions of the ADRIP also refer to free, prior and informed consent).

[174] See Chapter 2.d.i.

and the ACtHPR have applied the ACHPR to Indigenous Peoples in such a way as to safeguard their economic, social, and cultural development in relation to their ancestral lands. Neither treaty body framed its approach in terms of self-determination under ACHPR Article 20, but focused instead on the right of peoples to freely dispose of their wealth and natural resources under Article 21 and the right to economic, social, and cultural development under Article 22.

The African Commission on Human and Peoples' Rights, in *Endorois v Kenya* (2010), considered a complaint against Kenya on behalf of Indigenous Endorois forcibly removed from their ancestral land.[175] In evaluating the complaint, the African Commission assessed that the Endorois constitute a people for purposes of the ACHPR in reference to what it regarded to be 'objective features' of peoples, including those related to rights that a people collectively enjoys.[176] The African Commission concluded that Kenya had violated various provisions of the ACHPR addressing individual and collective rights in relation to the Endorois, rights implicated by the claims of the Endorois related to their ancestral land.[177] In particular, the African Commission found Kenya to have breached its obligations under Article 21 (the right of peoples to freely dispose of wealth and natural resources), by failing to provide the Endorois adequate compensation or restitution for their land,[178] as well as Article 22 (right to economic, social, and cultural development).[179] However, the right to self-determination did not feature in the analysis of the African Commission and Article 20 of the ACHPR (the right to self-determination) was not found to have been violated.

In *ACHPR v Kenya* (2017), the ACtHPR addressed an Application by the African Commission concerning the Indigenous Ogiek community, which faced removal from its ancestral land by Kenya.[180] The ACtHPR considered that the term 'peoples' for purposes of the ACHPR may refer to 'sub-state ethnic groups and communities' that are part of the population of a given State, including Indigenous Peoples.[181] The ACtHPR assessed that the

[175] *Endorois v Kenya* (2010). See John Cerone, 'Introductory Note' (2010) 49(3) ILM 858; Saul et al (n 60) 97–99; Saul (n 75) 160–63.

[176] *Endorois v Kenya* (2010) para 151.

[177] Ibid Recommendations para 1 (Articles 1, 8, 14, 17, 21 and 22).

[178] Ibid paras 252–68.

[179] Ibid paras 269–98.

[180] *ACHPR v Kenya* (2017). See Philip C. Aka, 'Introductory Note' (2017) 56(4) ILM 726.

[181] *ACHPR v Kenya* (2017) paras 198–99.

Indigenous Ogiek community constitutes a 'people' for purposes of certain rights under the ACHPR, one 'deserving special protection deriving from their vulnerability'.[182] However, while the ACtHPR identified collective rights under the ACHPR that may be recognized to apply to such sub-State groups, it questioned whether the right to self-determination under Article 20(1) could enjoy such application.[183] Much like the earlier finding of the African Commission in relation to the Endorois, the ACtHPR found Kenya to have violated various individual and collective rights under the ACHPR in relation to the Ogiek community.[184] The ACtHPR found that Kenya breached its obligations under Article 21, in relation to the right of the Ogiek to freely dispose of their wealth and natural resources because removal from their ancestral land deprived the Ogiek of their traditional food resources,[185] and Article 22 (right to economic, social, and cultural development), due to their eviction from their ancestral land without consultation and lack of involvement in development programs affecting them.[186] The ACtHPR did not, however, find a violation of the right to self-determination (Article 20).

iv. Implementation by States

Realization of the right to self-determination of Indigenous Peoples is dependent upon its implementation by States in consultation and cooperation with Indigenous Peoples. Respect for the self-determination of Indigenous Peoples is therefore a function of domestic legal arrangements shaped by the complex historical and political relationships between States and their Indigenous populations.[187] By their nature, rights of Indigenous Peoples

[182] Ibid paras 105–12.
[183] Ibid paras 198–99.
[184] Ibid para 227.
[185] Ibid paras 195–201.
[186] Ibid paras 207–11.
[187] See Claire Charters, 'Comparative constitutional law and Indigenous peoples: Canada, New Zealand and the USA' in Tom Ginsburg and Rosalind Dixon (eds), *Comparative Constitutional Law* (Edward Elgar 2011); Matthew S. R. Palmer, 'Indigenous Rights: New Zealand' in David S. Law (ed), *Constitutionalism in Context* (CUP 2022) 306. For a survey of such challenges in Asia, see Benedict Kingsbury, '"Indigenous Peoples" in International Law: A Constructivist Approach to the Asian Controversy' (1998) 92(3) *AJIL* 414. By way of further illustration, a number of national constitutions of Central and South American States contain provisions applying self-determination in relation to Indigenous Peoples. See Bolivia (2009) arts 2, 30(II); Ecuador (2008) art 57; Mexico (1917) art 2. See also South Africa (1996) art 235

are collective in character,[188] presenting challenges to domestic legal systems and international law, which generally contemplate individuals rather than groups to be the bearers of rights.[189] Such challenges are inherent to the concept of self-determination, which is something of an outlier in international law as a collective right belonging to peoples.[190] Moreover, just as attention towards respect for the rights of Indigenous Peoples is only a relatively recent focus of international action—as evinced by the adoption of the UNDRIP by the UNGA in 2007 and the ADRIP by the OAS General Assembly in 2016—respect for Indigenous rights in domestic legal systems may also be characterized as both a recent and evolving development, as illustrated by the practice of leading Commonwealth countries.[191] The upshot of these parallel trends is that State practice may inform expectations for the self-determination of Indigenous Peoples just as expressions of the self-determination of Indigenous Peoples may shape State practice.

Implementation of the self-determination of Indigenous Peoples is necessarily informed by the historical relationships between States and their Indigenous populations. The interpretation of the right to self-determination of Indigenous Peoples by the United States in reference to the autonomy and self-government of American Indian Tribes under US law is illustrative in this regard. Before colonization of what would become the United States, Indian Tribes existed as 'self-governing sovereign political communities'.[192] At its founding, the United States regarded Indian Tribes as separate sovereigns akin to foreign nations, a relation reflected in various provisions of the US Constitution, statutes, and regulations.[193] As a result, the United States 'recognizes the right of Indian tribes to self-government and supports tribal

(Permitting 'recognition of the notion of the right to self-determination' to sub-State groups under domestic law).

---

[188] UNDRIP preambular para 22.

[189] Cf *Sanila-Aikio v Finland* (2019) para 6.9; *Käkkäläjärvi v Finland* (2019) para 9.9.

[190] See Chapter 6.a.

[191] See e.g. *Calder v British Columbia (AG)* [1973] SCR 313 (31 Jan 1973) (recognition of aboriginal title rights by the Supreme Court of Canada); *Mabo v Queensland (No 2) ('Mabo case')* [1992] HCA 23, (1992) 175 CLR 1 (3 June 1992) (recognition of aboriginal title rights by the High Court of Australia). See also Palmer (n 187) 318 ff (discussing contemporary treatment of the 1840 Treaty of Waitangi between the British Crown and Māori chiefs, which established the terms of shared power in New Zealand).

[192] *United States v Wheeler*, 435 US 313, 322–23 (1978).

[193] For a comprehensive review of Tribal sovereignty in US law, see *Haaland, et al v Brackeen, et al*, 599 US 255, 308–31 (2023) (Gorsuch, J, Concurring).

sovereignty and self-determination'.[194] When the United States announced its support for the UNDRIP in 2010, it understood the right to self-determination of Indigenous Peoples through the lens of these attributes of Tribal sovereignty and self-determination under US law.[195] The way in which the self-determination of Indigenous Peoples is given effect in the United States is a product of the historic relationship between the United States and American Indian Tribes, underscoring a contextual dimension to the implementation of the right to self-determination of Indigenous Peoples.

Conversely, the right to self-determination of Indigenous Peoples may inform the practice of States in relation to their Indigenous populations. The practice of Canada offers an illustration of such influence in its implementation of self-determination for its Indigenous population. After announcing its support for the UNDRIP in 2016,[196] Canada enacted the *United Nations Declaration on the Rights of Indigenous Peoples Act* (UNDRIP Act).[197] The UNDRIP Act provides for implementation of the UNDRIP in Canadian law by the government of Canada 'in consultation and cooperation with Indigenous peoples' in Canada.[198] Regarding self-determination in particular, the UNDRIP Act 'recognizes that all relations with Indigenous peoples must be based on the recognition and implementation of the inherent right to self-determination, including the right of self-government'.[199] As contemplated by Section 6 of the UNDRIP Act, the Canadian government released a UN Declaration Act Action Plan in 2023, developed in consultation and cooperation with First Nations, Inuit, and Métis, to achieve the objectives of the UNDRIP.[200] The Action Plan details priorities in the areas of self-determination and self-government specific to each of those Indigenous groups. Steps taken to implement the UNDRIP in Canada illustrate how the

194 'Executive Order No 13175 of November 6, 2000: Consultation and Coordination with Indian Tribal Governments', 65 *Federal Register* 67249 (9 Nov 2000) s 2(c).

195 *Announcement of U.S. Support for the United Nations Declaration on the Rights of Indigenous Peoples* (12 Jan 2011) (available at https://2009-2017.state.gov/s/srgia/154553.htm).

196 See *Permanent Forum on Indigenous Issues: Report on the fifteenth session (9–20 May 2016)*, Economic and Social Council Official Records, 2016, Supplement No 23, E/2016/43 / E/C.19/2016/11 (2016) para 18.

197 *United Nations Declaration on the Rights of Indigenous Peoples Act*, SC 2021, c 14.

198 Ibid ss 4–5.

199 Ibid preambular para 12.

200 United Nations Declaration on the Rights of Indigenous Peoples Act Implementation Secretariat, Department of Justice Canada, *United Nations Declaration on the Rights of Indigenous Peoples Act Action Plan* (2023).

right to self-determination of Indigenous Peoples may shape State practice in relation to Indigenous populations.

The right to self-determination of Indigenous Peoples faces unique implementation challenges where an Indigenous people spans inter-State boundaries. The Sami people, who inhabit a territory spanning parts of Norway, Sweden, and Finland, as well as a portion of Russia, is illustrative in this regard.[201] In 2005, Norway, Sweden, and Finland agreed on a draft text for a regional treaty concerning the Sami people, the first such multilateral agreement.[202] The Nordic Sami Convention, which has been signed by the three Nordic States, contains a provision on the right of the Sami people to self-determination at Article 3. The substantive focus of Article 3 is the economic, social, and cultural element of the right to self-determination and the associated entitlement to freely dispose of natural wealth and resources.[203] While the autonomy and self-government of the Sami are advanced through the Sami parliament in each Nordic State, the regional framework contemplated by the Nordic Sami Convention promotes the rights of the Sami people, including the right to self-determination, at the regional level.

Recognition of the right to self-determination of Indigenous Peoples, and its implementation by States with Indigenous populations, provide important contributions to the advancement of the rights of Indigenous Peoples. To be sure, just as the right to self-determination is ill-suited 'to "undo" history and "right historical wrongs"';[204] so too is the right to self-determination of Indigenous Peoples insufficient to right historical wrongs or undo histories painfully punctuated by dark moments and injustices.[205] The right to self-determination offers a legal framework for States to empower their Indigenous populations by respecting the autonomy and self-government

201 See Report of the Special Rapporteur on the rights of indigenous peoples, James Anaya, Addendum: The situation of the Sami people in the Sápmi region of Norway, Sweden and Finland, A/HRC/18/35/Add.2 (6 June 2011) (hereinafter Anaya Report (2011)). See also Malgosia Fitzmaurice, 'The New Developments Regarding the Saami Peoples of the North' (2009) 16(1) *International Journal on Minority and Group Rights* 67.

202 Anaya Report (2011) paras 11–13, 33–36. See also Fitzmaurice (n 201) 115–27.

203 Nordic Saami Convention art 3 (The right of self-determination) (available at https://www.regjeringen.no/globalassets/upload/aid/temadokumenter/sami/sami_samekonv_engelsk.pdf).

204 Theodore Christakis, 'Self-Determination, Territorial Integrity and *Fait Accompli* in the Case of Crimea' (2015) 75 *Zeitschrift für ausländisches öffentliches Recht und Völkerrecht* 75, 85; Jamie Trinidad, *Self-Determination in Disputed Colonial Territories* (CUP 2018) 56.

205 S. James Anaya, *Indigenous Peoples in International Law* (2nd edn, OUP 2004) 110.

to which they are entitled as well as the freedom to pursue their economic, social, and cultural development. The right to self-determination in international law provides support for the collective enjoyment and exercise of human rights and fundamental freedoms by the members of Indigenous Peoples to this end.

9
Obligations of States under the Right to Self-Determination

a. Overview

International law is generally understood to consist of rules and obligations created by and for sovereign States.[1] Even if contemporary international law admits legal subjects in addition to States—notably for present purposes, 'peoples', the subjects of the right to self-determination—international law remains defined by the parameters of legal positivism with States as the principal subjects of international law.[2] Because States are the authors of international law, it follows that the principal subjects of obligations under international law are also States.[3] As a result, realization and enjoyment by peoples of the right to self-determination is dependent upon the performance by States of corresponding obligations in relation to the right. While the ICJ has concluded that the right to self-determination is 'a customary rule binding on all States', and that 'respect for the right to self-determination is an obligation *erga omnes*',[4] the practical significance of these developments is a function of the general and specific obligations of States related to self-determination.

Obligations of States give effect to the right to self-determination. Obligations of States related to the right to self-determination may be distinguished between those that apply territorially and those of an extraterritorial character. Territorial obligations of States to promote the

[1] This is a function of a positivist approach to international law. See Mark W. Janis, 'Jeremy Bentham and the Fashioning of "International Law"' (1984) 78(2) *AJIL* 405.

[2] See Chapter 1.b.

[3] See e.g. Clyde Eagleton, *The Responsibility of States in International Law* (New York University Press 1928) 5.

[4] *Legal Consequences of the Separation of the Chagos Archipelago from Mauritius in 1965*, Advisory Opinion, ICJ Rep 2019, 95 (hereinafter *Chagos* (2019)) paras 148, 180.

The Right to Self-Determination in International Law. Thomas Weatherall, Oxford University Press.
 DOI: 10.1093/9780197798119.003.0010

realization of the right to self-determination and to respect the right correspond to the domestic aspect of the right.[5] Extraterritorial obligations of States to promote the realization of the right to self-determination and to respect the right generally relate to the international aspect of the right.[6] In practice, compliance by States with their obligations under the right to self-determination is informed by corresponding aspects of the right. The performance by States of obligations under the right to self-determination is therefore the counterpart to the domestic and international aspects of the right to self-determination.

Underlying this correspondence between the right to self-determination and associated obligations of States is significant complexity. The complexity of obligations of States arising in relation to the right to self-determination is at least in part a product of the prevalence of relationships of subordination (i.e. colonialism) in international relations at the time that self-determination emerged, first as a principle, and then as a right, in the postwar period. While international law did not apply retroactively to render then-existing subordinate relationships unlawful,[7] the UN Charter imposed specific, affirmative obligations upon States responsible for the administration of non-self-governing territories designed to unwind such relationships of subordination and bring about an end to colonialism and realization of self-determination for all peoples. Looking forward, however, international law would impose negative obligations upon States prohibiting new subordinate relationships through alien subjugation, domination, and exploitation comparable to colonial relationships, thereby safeguarding the right of all peoples to self-determination.

This chapter begins by identifying the general obligations of States arising in relation to self-determination under both treaty law and CIL. Next, this chapter discusses the specific obligations of administering States arising relation to Trust Territories and NSGTs. Finally, this chapter identifies obligations under the law of State responsibility for breach of obligations under the

[5] See Chapter 8.

[6] See Chapter 7. As illustrated in Chapter 8, the domestic aspect of self-determination may be implicated in the context of extraterritorial obligations of States. See Chapter 8.c.ii; Chapter 8.d.i.2.

[7] James J. Summers, 'The Status of Self-determination in International Law: A Question of Legal Significance or Political Importance' (2003) 14 *Finnish Yearbook of International Law* 271, 281.

right to self-determination, arising with respect to both responsible States and third-States.

b. General Obligations under the Right to Self-Determination

States are subject to general obligations in relation to the right to self-determination under both treaty law and CIL.[8] The general, treaty-based obligations of States related to the right to self-determination may be distinguished between those that apply territorially and those of an extraterritorial character. Obligations arising under CIL, while informed by treaty-based obligations, represent a separate source of legal obligations and are therefore considered separately.

i. Treaty-Based Obligations

The principal source of obligations under the right to self-determination in treaty law is common Article 1 of the two human rights covenants.[9] Paragraph 1 of common Article 1 provides that self-determination consists of the right of peoples to 'freely determine their political status' and to 'freely pursue their economic, social and cultural development'.[10] The *travaux préparatoires* of common Article 1 indicates an understanding, reflected in subsequent practice, that self-determination has a 'dual nature' consisting of domestic and international aspects.[11] These aspects of the right to self-determination are relevant not only to the subjects of the right, but also to identifying the 'corresponding obligations' of States 'concerning its implementation'.[12] Obligations of States under common Article 1 correspond to

[8] See Chapter 5.c.

[9] See Chapter 2.c.

[10] International Covenant on Civil and Political Rights art 1(1), 999 UNTS 171 (16 Dec 1966, entered into force 23 Mar 1976) (hereinafter ICCPR); International Covenant on Economic, Social and Cultural Rights art 1(1), 993 UNTS 3 (16 Dec 1966, entered into force 3 Jan 1976) (hereinafter ICESCR).

[11] *Report of the Third Committee*, A/3077 (8 Dec 1955) (Draft International Covenants on Human Rights) para 32.

[12] HRC, *CCPR General Comment No. 12: The Right to Self-Determination of Peoples (Art 1)* (1984) (hereinafter HRC GC 12) para 2.

different aspects and elements of the right to self-determination under that provision.[13]

1. Territorial Obligations

Under common Article 1, States parties to the ICCPR and ICESCR are subject to obligations towards their own populations, as peoples, with respect to political participation and economic, social, and cultural development under the right to self-determination.[14] The scope and nature of obligations under common Article 1 are reflected in paragraph 3:[15]

> The States Parties to the present Covenant, including those having responsibility for the administration of Non-Self-Governing and Trust Territories, shall promote the realization of the right of self-determination, and shall respect that right, in conformity with the provisions of the Charter of the United Nations.[16]

Common Article 1 imposes obligations to 'promote the realization of the right of self-determination' and to 'respect that right'.[17] These negative and

[13] Territorial and extraterritorial obligations under regional instruments are also considered below.

[14] ICCPR art 1; ICESCR art 1. See Draft International Covenants on Human Rights: Annotation, Prepared by the Secretary-General, A/2929 (1 July 1955) (hereinafter A/2929) ch IV paras 9, 17. See e.g. Antonio Cassese, *Self-Determination of Peoples: A Legal Reappraisal* (CUP 1995) 59. See Chapter 2.c.i; Chapter 8.

[15] Article 1(3) clarifies the intent of the parties as to the application of Article 1, and the extraterritorial application of obligations under Article 1 by paragraph (3) is additive to the territorial application of obligations under Article 1. See Vienna Convention on the Law of Treaties art 29, 1155 UNTS 331 (23 May 1969, entered into force 27 Jan 1980) (Territorial scope of treaties). See also HRC GC 12 para 6 (art 1(3) 'imposes specific obligations on States parties, not only in relation to their own peoples but vis-à-vis all peoples which have not been able to exercise or have been deprived of the possibility of exercising their right to self-determination').

[16] ICCPR art 1(3); ICECSR art 1(3).

[17] HRC GC 12 para 6. The obligations of States to 'promote the realization of the right of self-determination' and to 'respect that right' incorporates aspects of the standards of performance of human rights obligations under the ICCPR and ICESCR. Article 2 of the ICCPR requires States parties 'to respect and to ensure to all individuals within its territory and subject to its jurisdiction the rights recognized in the present Covenant'. Article 2 of the ICESCR requires States parties 'to take steps, individually and through international assistance and co-operation, especially economic and technical, to the maximum of its available resources, with a view to achieving progressively the full realization of the rights recognized in the [ICESCR] by all appropriate means'. Common Article 1(3) incorporates aspects of each standard of performance in setting forth the obligation to 'promote the realization of the right of self-determination' (which reflects Article 2 of the ICESCR) and to 'respect that right' (which reflects Article 2 of the ICCPR).

positive aspects of obligations under Article 1 reflect the observation in HRC General Comment No 31 that obligations under the ICCPR are 'both negative and positive in nature', and that 'State Parties must refrain from violation of the rights recognized by the Covenant' and 'adopt . . . appropriate measures in order to fulfill their legal obligations'.[18] Article 1(3) is framed in such a way as to clarify that obligations under the right to self-determination are not limited to administering States of NSGTs and Trust Territories.

The performance of obligations under common Article 1 is informed by the substantive content of the right to self-determination. In relation to the reporting requirement under ICCPR Article 40(1),[19] the HRC provided guidance in General Comment No 12 that informs the performance by States of their obligations under Article 1. The HRC advised that, '[w]ith regard to paragraph 1 of article 1, States parties should describe the constitutional and political processes which in practice allow the exercise of this right'.[20] The HRC further advised that States should provide information on each paragraph of article 1 in their periodic reporting under Article 40(1).[21] Common Article 1(2), it may be recalled, provides an entitlement of peoples to freely dispose of their natural wealth and resources.[22] The HRC advised that '[t]his right entails corresponding duties for all States and the international community'.[23] The entitlement at Article 1(2) may be understood as giving rise to a corresponding obligation of States to exercise their permanent sovereignty over natural resources 'in the interest of the[] national development and of the wellbeing of the people of the State concerned'.[24] To this end, the HRC advised that 'States should indicate any factors or difficulties which prevent the free disposal of their natural wealth and resources contrary to the provisions of this paragraph and to what extent that affects the enjoyment of other rights set forth in the Covenant'.[25] Article 1(3) provides that obligations

[18] HRC, *CCPR General Comment No 31 [80]: The Nature of the General Legal Obligation Imposed on States Parties to the Covenant*, CCPR/C/21/Rev.1/Add.13 (2004) (hereinafter HRC GC 31) paras 6–7.

[19] ICCPR art 40(1).

[20] HRC GC 12 para 4.

[21] Ibid para 3.

[22] See Chapter 2.c.ii.

[23] HRC GC 12 para 5.

[24] A/Res/1803 (XVII) (14 Dec 1962) para 1. See Chapter 8.d.i. See also Daniëlla Dam-de Jong, *International Law and Governance of Natural Resources in Conflict and Post-Conflict Situations* (CUP 2015) 58. Cf A/2929 ch IV para 21.

[25] HRC GC 12 para 5.

under the right to self-determination are to be performed 'in conformity with the provisions of the Charter of the United Nations'.[26]

At the regional level, ACHPR Article 20 imposes obligations upon States parties with respect to the right to self-determination.[27] Article 20(1) of the ACHPR imposes territorial obligations upon States parties to the Charter with respect to the right to self-determination.[28] Like the obligations under common Article 1, which have both positive and negative aspects, the ACtHPR has interpreted obligations under ACHPR Article 20 in corresponding terms.[29] Article 21 separately provides that '[a]ll peoples shall freely dispose of their wealth and natural resources'.[30] The African Commission on Human and Peoples' Rights has identified associated obligations of States parties regarding the management of natural resources pursuant to Article 21.[31]

The Arab Charter on Human Rights also imposes obligations under the right to self-determination, though there is insufficient practice to draw conclusions about its application.[32]

2. Extraterritorial Obligations

Under common Article 1, the ICCPR and ICESCR impose extraterritorial obligations upon States parties in relation to the right to self-determination.[33] As discussed above, Article 1(3) contains a general obligation of States parties to promote the realization of the right to self-determination and to respect that right.[34] Article 1(3) is expressly not limited to obligations in Chapters XI and XII of the UN Charter as they apply to administering States vis-à-vis

[26] See ibid para 6.

[27] African [Banjul] Charter on Human and Peoples' Rights art 20, OAU Doc CAB/LEG/67/3/Rev.5, 1520 UNTS 217 (27 June 1981, entered into force 21 Oct 1986) (hereinafter ACHPR). See Chapter 2.d.i.

[28] For discussion of cases applying Article 20(1) in relation to the domestic aspect of the right to self-determination under the ACHPR, see Chapter 12.c.

[29] *Bernard Anbataayela Mornah v Benin et al*, ACtHPR, Application No 028/2018, Judgment, para 297 (22 Sept 2022). Notably, the ACtHPR referred to HRC GC 12 and HRC GC 31 to support this assessment: see paras 297 n 63, 299 n 66.

[30] ACHPR art 21. See Chapter 2.d.i. See also Rachel Murray, *The African Charter on Human and Peoples' Rights: A Commentary* (OUP 2019) 508–20.

[31] See *Front for the Liberation of the State of Cabinda v Angola*, ACommHPR, Communication No 328/06 (2013) paras 129–31.

[32] See Chapter 2.d.ii.

[33] ICCPR art 1(3); ICESCR art 1(3).

[34] A/2929 ch IV para 17.

NSGTs and Trust Territories. Instead, as observed by the HRC in General Comment No 12, Article 1(3) 'imposes specific obligations on States parties, *not only in relation to their own peoples* but *vis-à-vis all peoples* which have not been able to exercise or have been deprived of the possibility of exercising their right to self-determination'.[35] The HRC continued:

> The obligations exist irrespective of whether a people entitled to self-determination depends on a State party to the Covenant or not. It follows that all States parties to the Covenant should take positive action to facilitate realization of and respect for the right of peoples to self-determination. Such positive action must be consistent with the States' obligations under the Charter of the United Nations and under international law: in particular, States must refrain from interfering in the internal affairs of other States and thereby adversely affecting the exercise of the right to self-determination.[36]

Article 1(3) is silent as to the modalities by which the positive obligation to promote the right to self-determination is to be performed extraterritorially, suggesting that the performance of such obligations is subject to the discretion of States parties.[37] Article 1(3) imposes a limitation on such positive actions, which must be 'in conformity with the provisions of the Charter of the United Nations'. Extraterritorial obligations of States appear to more typically be implicated in this sense of the negative obligation to respect the right of peoples to self-determination.[38]

At the regional level, the ACHPR imposes obligations of an extraterritorial character upon States parties with respect to the right to self-determination under Article 20.[39] As a general matter, the ACtHPR has defined this extraterritorial character in terms that parallel the description by the HRC of the scope of obligations under ICCPR Article 1(3): 'Obligations resulting from the right to self-determination are owed by States not only towards those who are under their jurisdiction but also to all other peoples who are not able

[35] HRC GC 12 para 6 (emphasis added).
[36] Ibid.
[37] See Ben Saul et al, *The International Covenant on Economic, Social and Cultural Rights: Commentary, Cases, and Materials* (OUP 2014) 129–30.
[38] See Chapter 9.b.ii.
[39] See Chapter 2.d.i.

to exercise or have been deprived of their right to self-determination'.[40] 'In line with this' scope of obligations under the right to self-determination,[41] Article 20(3) provides that '[a]ll peoples shall have the right to the assistance of the States parties to the present Charter in their liberation struggle against foreign domination, be it political, economic or cultural'.[42] The ACtHPR has interpreted this provision to impose positive duties upon States parties to render assistance to such peoples, 'without geographical or temporal limitations'.[43] In *Democratic Republic of Congo v Burundi, Rwanda and Uganda* (2003), the African Commission on Human and Peoples' Rights found the respondent States to have breached their obligations under ACHPR Article 20 (the right to self-determination) and Article 21 (the right to freely dispose of wealth and natural resources) through their armed activities in the DRC, indicating the extraterritorial application of obligations under each provision.[44]

ii. Obligations under Customary International Law

The principal obligation of States related to the right to self-determination under CIL has been identified by the ICJ as 'respect for the right to self-determination'.[45] To identify the CIL obligation of States to respect the right to self-determination, the ICJ has looked in particular to common Article 1 of the two human rights covenants and UNGA Resolution 2625 (the FRD), whose Principle V addresses the right to self-determination in reference to the principle of self-determination as it appears in the UN Charter.[46] The reliance by the ICJ on these two sources may be explained by the widespread

[40] *Mornah v Benin* (2022) para 299 (citing HRC GC 12); see also paras 150–51.
[41] Ibid para 299.
[42] ACHPR art 20(3).
[43] *Mornah v Benin* (2022) para 299.
[44] *Democratic Republic of Congo v Burundi, Rwanda and Uganda*, ACommHPR, Communication No 227/99 (2003) paras 68, 94.
[45] *Chagos* (2019) para 180. See also *Legal Consequences arising from the Policies and Practices of Israel in the Occupied Palestinian Territory, including East Jerusalem*, Advisory Opinion, ICJ Rep 2024 (hereinafter *Palestine* (2024)) para 232; *Legal Consequences of the Construction of a Wall in the Occupied Palestinian Territory*, Advisory Opinion, ICJ Rep 2004, 136 (hereinafter *Wall* (2004)) para 155. See Chapter 5.c.ii.
[46] See *Wall* (2004) para 88 (also citing the UN Charter); *Chagos* (2019) paras 150–55; *Palestine* (2024) paras 231, 233, 241, 255 (also citing the UN Charter and UNGA Resolution 1514).

accession of States to the two human rights covenants,[47] and the position of the ICJ that the FRD itself reflects CIL.[48]

In practice, compliance with the obligation to respect the right to self-determination under CIL is informed by corresponding aspects of the right. This approach is reflected in *The Wall* (2004), *Chagos Archipelago* (2019), and *Palestine* (2024), wherein the ICJ identified breaches of the obligation to respect the right to self-determination under CIL in relation to substantive aspects of the right.[49] This treatment suggests that the ICJ, as well as other courts, will likely continue to look to the substance of the right to self-determination—particularly in reference to common Article 1 of the two human rights covenants and the FRD—to assess performance by States of the obligation to respect the right to self-determination under CIL. Analogously, both the IACtHR,[50] and the ACtHPR,[51] have looked to common Article 1 of the two human rights covenants when addressing the right to self-determination and evaluating the performance by States of corresponding obligations.[52]

Various aspects of the FRD bear on the performance by States of the obligation to respect the right to self-determination under CIL.[53] Like common Article 1 of the two human rights covenants, the FRD addresses negative and positive aspects of obligations under the right to self-determination.

The FRD refers to negative duties of States in relation to the right to self-determination that relate to the international aspect of the right. Paragraph 1 of the self-determination provision of the FRD sets out a basic duty of States

[47] See Chapter 2.c.

[48] *Military and Paramilitary Activities in and against Nicaragua (Nicaragua v United States of America)*, Merits, Judgment, ICJ Rep 1986, 14 (hereinafter *Nicaragua* (1986)) paras 191–93, 264; *Accordance with International Law of the Unilateral Declaration of Independence in Respect of Kosovo*, Advisory Opinion, ICJ Rep 2010, 403 (hereinafter *Kosovo* (2010)) para 80 (citing *Nicaragua* (1986)).

[49] See Chapter 4.e; Chapter 4.g; Chapter 4.h.

[50] *Saramaka People v Suriname* (2007) paras 93–96.

[51] *Mornah v Benin* (2022) paras 150–51, 297, 299.

[52] For other decisions looking to these instruments to identify the content of customary international law related to the right to self-determination, see e.g. *Decision on the 'Prosecution request pursuant to article 19(3) for a ruling on the Court's territorial jurisdiction in Palestine'*, PTC I, ICC-01/18-143 (5 Feb 2021) para 120; *Reference re Secession of Quebec* [1998] 2 SCR 217 paras 118–19, 126, 128, 133 (the Supreme Court of Canada also referred to Articles 1 and 55 of the UN Charter (paras 115–16), the Vienna Declaration (1993) (paras 120, 128), and the Helsinki Final Act (1975) (para 121)).

[53] See Chapter 3.d.

in relation to self-determination: 'Every State has the duty to respect this right in accordance with the provisions of the Charter'.[54] The ICJ invoked this same language in identifying the *erga omnes* obligation of States under CIL to respect the right to self-determination.[55] Paragraph 2 provides 'that subjection of peoples to alien subjugation, domination and exploitation constitutes a violation of the principle, as well as a denial of fundamental human rights, and is contrary to the Charter'.[56] The ICJ has referred to this circumstance as giving rise to a corresponding 'right to independence' for such a people under the right to self-determination.[57] A related negative duty is articulated in paragraph 5: 'Every State has the duty to refrain from any forcible action which deprives peoples . . . of their right to self-determination and freedom and independence'.[58] Finally, a safeguard clause at Paragraph 8 provides that '[e]very State shall refrain from any action aimed at the partial or total disruption of the national unity and territorial integrity of any other State or country'.[59] This duty may be viewed as one of non-interference in relation to the exercise of the right to self-determination by peoples of other States.[60] This duty has been interpreted by the ICJ as corresponding to the 'right to territorial integrity' as 'a corollary of the right to self-determination'.[61]

Additionally, the FRD refers to several positive duties of States in relation to the right to self-determination, which align with common Article 1 of the two human rights covenants and relate primarily to the domestic aspect of self-determination. A positive duty of States to promote the realization of the principle of equal rights and self-determination 'through joint and separate action', and 'to render assistance to the United Nations in carrying out' its associated responsibilities, is set out in paragraph 2.[62] This positive duty

[54] A/Res/2625 (24 Oct 1970) Annex (hereinafter FRD) Principle V, para 1. See similarly ICCPR art 1(3); ICESCR art 1(3).

[55] *Palestine* (2024) para 232; *Chagos* (2019) para 180; *Wall* (2004) para 156.

[56] FRD Principle V, para 2. See Chapter 7.b.ii.

[57] *Kosovo* (2010) paras 79, 82. See A/Res/1514 (XV) (14 Dec 1960) (hereinafter Resolution 1514) para 1; *Chagos* (2019) para 153 (citing UNGA Resolution 1514, para 1). See also *Palestine* (2024) paras 237, 283 (Referring to the 'right of the Palestinian people to self-determination [as] including its right to an independent and sovereign State').

[58] FRD Principle V, para 5.

[59] Ibid para 8. See similarly UNGA Resolution 1514 para 7.

[60] See Chapter 8.b. As safeguarding the territorial integrity of NSGTs, see *Chagos* (2019) paras 153, 155.

[61] *Palestine* (2024) para 237; *Chagos* (2019) para 160.

[62] FRD Principle V, para 2. See similarly ICCPR art 1(3); ICESCR art 1(3).

to promote the realization of self-determination has been cited on several occasions by the ICJ, including in reference to the *erga omnes* obligation to respect the right to self-determination under CIL.[63] Paragraph 3 articulates a positive duty of States to promote universal respect for and observance of human rights and fundamental freedoms, which corresponds to the interrelation between self-determination and the enjoyment of human rights, and reflects the domestic aspect of self-determination as the collective exercise of human rights and fundamental freedoms.[64] Finally, paragraph 7 provides that representative government is an aspect of 'compliance with the principle of equal rights and self-determination of peoples'.[65]

The duties of States articulated in the FRD, understood to reflect CIL,[66] inform the performance by States of the obligation to respect the right to self-determination under CIL. Similarly, common Article 1 of the two human rights covenants provides a point of reference for the performance by States of the obligation to respect the right to self-determination under CIL.[67] The performance by States of their obligations under the right to self-determination is the counterpart to the right to self-determination under CIL, and compliance with those obligations is informed by corresponding aspects of the right.

c. Specific Obligations in relation to Trust Territories and Non-Self-Governing Territories

States responsible for the administration of Trust Territories and NSGTs are subject to specific obligations that are additive to general obligations arising from the right to self-determination. Chapter XI (Non-Self-Governing Territories) and Chapter XII (International Trusteeship System) of the UN Charter set out obligations and objectives for States that are understood to follow from the principle of self-determination articulated in Articles 1

[63] *Palestine* (2024) para 275; *Chagos* (2019) para 180; *Wall* (2004) para 156; *Western Sahara*, Advisory Opinion, ICJ Rep 1975, 12 para 58.

[64] FRD Principle V, para 3. See Chapter 8.b.

[65] FRD Principle V, para 7. See Gaetano Arangio-Ruiz, *The UN Declaration on Friendly Relations and the System of the Sources of International Law* (Sijthoff & Noordhoff 1979) s 80. See also Chapter 8.c.i.

[66] *Nicaragua* (1986) paras 191–93, 264; *Kosovo* (2010) para 80 (citing *Nicaragua* (1986)).

[67] See Chapter 9.b.i.

and 55 of the Charter.[68] Such obligations are distinguishable from the general obligations described above not only by virtue of their source—the UN Charter—but also as obligations of administering States towards the peoples of distinct territorial units. In both instances, such obligations are directed towards promoting self-government with respect to the peoples of those distinct territorial units, and in this way may be viewed as complementary to obligations owed by States to the peoples within their territories under the general obligation to respect the right to self-determination. Again, these obligations correspond to aspects of the right to self-determination.[69]

i. Obligations of Administering Authorities of Trust Territories

The UN Charter established the International Trusteeship System, which succeeded the League of Nations Mandate System.[70] Chapter XII (Articles 75–85) of the Charter sets out a framework for the administration of territories to which the Trusteeship System applied. Trusteeship agreements, concluded pursuant to Article 81 of the Charter between the United Nations and respective administering authorities, established specific obligations of administering authorities towards implementation of the basic objectives of the Trusteeship System set out in Article 76 of the Charter. The Charter also contains obligations of administering authorities regarding the maintenance of international peace and security (Article 84) and an annual reporting requirement (Article 88).[71]

Administering authorities of Trust Territories subject to the Trusteeship System were subject to obligations under trusteeship agreements.[72] These

[68] See Chapter 2.b.

[69] See Chapter 7.b.i.

[70] *Legal Consequences for States of the Continued Presence of South Africa in Namibia (South West Africa) notwithstanding Security Council Resolution 276 (1970)*, Advisory Opinion, ICJ Rep 1971, 16 (hereinafter *Namibia* (1971)) paras 60, 73, 90. See Chapter 2.b.iii; Chapter 1.c.i.

[71] Hans Kelsen, *The Law of the United Nations* (London Institute of World Affairs 1950) 641–49.

[72] See Charter of the United Nations art 85, XV UNCIO 335 (26 June 1945, entered into force 24 Oct 1945) (hereinafter UN Charter); A/Res/64 (I) (14 Dec 1946) (Establishment of the Trusteeship Council). See also supra Chapter 2 n 34 (citing Trusteeship agreements).

trusteeship agreements incorporated the basic objectives of the Trusteeship System under Article 76 of the UN Charter as obligations undertaken by administering authorities. Each trusteeship agreement was subsequently terminated following attainment of self-government by its respective Trust Territory.[73] All former Trust Territories have attained self-government and no UN Member State is subject to obligations under a Chapter XII trusteeship agreement.[74]

ii. Obligations of Administering Powers of Non-Self-Governing Territories

Territories 'whose peoples have not yet attained a full measure of self-government' are regarded as Non-Self-Governing Territories (NSGTs) under Chapter XI (Articles 73 and 74) of the UN Charter.[75] Chapter XI sets forth obligations of administering powers of NSGTs. Article 73 of the Charter provides that UN Member States responsible for the administration of NSGTs:

> recognize the principle that the interests of the inhabitants of these territories are paramount, and accept as a sacred trust the obligation to promote to the utmost, within the system of international peace and security established by the present Charter, the well-being of the inhabitants of these territories[.][76]

Article 73 enumerates five elements 'to this end'.[77] In practice, the elements articulated at Article 73(b) and Article 73(e) have been of greatest importance to the performance by administering powers of their obligations under Article 73. Under Article 73(b) of the UN Charter, States responsible for the

[73] See supra Chapter 2 n 35 (citing relevant resolutions).
[74] T/Res/2200 (LXI) (25 May 1994) (suspending operation of the Trusteeship Council).
[75] UN Charter art 73. See Chapter 2.b.ii.
[76] UN Charter art 73. See Chapter 7.b.i.1.
[77] UN Charter art 73.

administration of NSGTs are obligated to develop self-government with respect to the peoples of those territories.[78] It is in this sense that administering powers are under obligations that may be viewed as complementary to obligations owed by States towards their own peoples under general obligations to respect and promote the realization of the right to self-determination.[79] Under Article 73(e) of the UN Charter, administering powers are directed to report 'statistical and other information of a technical nature relating to economic, social, and educational conditions' of NSGTs under their administration to the UN Secretary-General.[80]

The obligations of an administering power under Article 73 of the UN Charter cease upon the attainment of the people of a NSGT of 'a full measure of self-government'.[81] Article 73 does not prescribe a timeframe for discharge of the obligations of an administering power in relation to the exercise of self-determination by the people of a NSGT to attain self-government. Article 73(b) instead contemplates the development of self-government 'according to the particular circumstances of each territory and its peoples and their varying stages of advancement'. Other authorities counsel that this result should be affirmatively pursued by administering powers with alacrity. UNGA Resolution 1514, in its preamble, refers to 'the necessity of bringing *to a speedy and unconditional end* colonialism in all its forms and manifestations', and the operative text of the resolution provides that '[*i*]*mmediate steps shall be taken* ... to transfer all powers to the peoples of [non-independent] territories'.[82] UNGA Resolution 2625 (the FRD) similarly identifies one objective of the realization of self-determination to 'bring *a speedy end* to colonialism, having due regard to the freely expressed will of the peoples concerned', but makes no reference to 'immediate steps'.[83] In *Chagos Archipelago* (2019), the ICJ considered that the United Kingdom was under an obligation to bring its administration of the Chagos Archipelago to an end 'as rapidly as possible'.[84]

[78] Ibid art 73(b). See *Chagos* (2019) para 146.
[79] See Chapter 7.b.i.
[80] UN Charter art 73(e). See A/Res/1541 (XV) (15 Dec 1960) Annex, Principle XI.
[81] See Chapter 10.b.ii.
[82] Resolution 1514 preambular para 12, para 5 (emphasis added).
[83] FRD Principle V, para 2 (emphasis added).
[84] *Chagos* (2019) para 178. However, this guidance must be viewed in the context of a breach of the obligation to respect the right to self-determination. See Chapter 4.g.

d. Obligations under the Law of State Responsibility

The law of State responsibility provides a source of secondary obligations for States in relation to the right to self-determination where a State breaches its primary obligations arising from the right. The ICJ applied the law of State responsibility in relation to the right to self-determination in *Namibia* (1971), *The Wall* (2004), *Chagos Archipelago* (2019), and *Palestine* (2024). These advisory opinions by the ICJ provide a survey of potential legal consequences arising from breach of obligations under the right to self-determination. The legal consequences identified by the ICJ in different situations are informed by the particular relationship between the breaching State and the territory at issue and, therefore, the particular obligations implicated in each case. The operation of the law of State responsibility in each case is therefore shaped by the underlying legal relationships between responsible States and the peoples and territories concerned, and the specific aspects of the right to self-determination at issue. The following sections examine the consequences for responsible States and third-States arising from breaches of obligations in relation to the right to self-determination.

i. Obligations of the Responsible State

The primary consequences for a State responsible for an internationally wrongful act are obligations of cessation of the wrongful conduct and reparation for such wrongful conduct.[85] These obligations reflect the purposes of State responsibility to restore the lawful position of a State in breach of its international obligations,[86] and to 'wipe out' the consequences of an internationally wrongful act so as to establish the situation that would have existed

[85] ILC Draft Articles on Responsibility of States for Internationally Wrongful Acts art 28, Commentary para 2, UN Doc A/56/10, Report of the International Law Commission on the Work of its Fifty-Third Session, [2001] II(2) *YbILC* 26 et seq, UN Doc A/CN.4/SER.A/2001/Add.1 (Part 2) (hereinafter ILC ARSIWA). See e.g. Clyde Eagleton, *The Responsibility of States in International Law* (New York University Press 1928) 182.

[86] See e.g. *Case concerning the difference between New Zealand and France concerning the interpretation or application of two agreements, concluded on 9 July 1986 between the two States and which related to the problems arising from the* Rainbow Warrior *Affair*, Decision of 30 April 1990, XX RIAA 215 (hereinafter *Rainbow Warrior* (1990)) s 114. See Chapter 9.d.i.1.

in the absence of the unlawful conduct.[87] The breaching State remains subject to a continued duty of performance of its international obligations.[88] International law at present does not give rise to other, specific consequences for a State responsible for breach of an obligation *erga omnes*, however serious the breach.[89] The ILC Articles on State Responsibility, at Article 41(3), contemplate the breach of an obligation *erga omnes* to give rise to the general legal consequences attendant to the breach of an international obligation attributable to a State.[90] Relatedly, State responsibility for an internationally wrongful act arising from breach of an obligation *erga omnes*, including respect for the right to self-determination, is not criminal in nature.[91] State responsibility for an internationally wrongful act is 'flat', without distinction or gradation relative to the normative status of the obligation at issue or the gravity of its breach.[92] Under international law, 'there is a single general regime of State responsibility'.[93] Consequently, a responsible State is subject only to 'international responsibility' and the general legal consequences arising therefrom.

1. Cessation

The obligation of cessation of wrongful conduct is a primary consequence of State responsibility for an internationally wrongful act.[94] Obligations of cessation of wrongful conduct were identified by the ICJ in *Namibia* (1971), *The Wall* (2004), *Chagos Archipelago* (2019), and *Palestine* (2024). In *Namibia* (1971), ICJ found that, by maintaining its presence in Namibia, South Africa incurred international responsibility for breach of an international obligation of a continuing character and identified an obligation to bring that breach to an end.[95] In *The Wall* (2004), the ICJ found that Israel was 'bound

[87] See e.g. *Factory at Chorzów (Merits)*, PCIJ Series A No 17, Judgment No 13 (13 Sept 1928) (hereinafter *Factory at Chorzów (Merits)* (1928)) 47. See Chapter 9.d.i.2.

[88] See e.g. *Gabčíkovo-Nagymaros Project (Hungary v Slovakia)*, Judgment, ICJ Rep 1997, 7 para 114; *Palestine* (2024) para 272. See also ILC ARSIWA art 29.

[89] See Christian J. Tams, 'Do Serious Breaches Give Rise to Any Specific Obligations of the Responsible State?' (2002) 13(5) *EJIL* 1161, 1179–80.

[90] ILC ARSIWA art 41, Commentary para 13.

[91] See Thomas Weatherall, *Duality of Responsibility in International Law: The Individual, the State, and International Crimes* (Brill Nijhoff 2022) 87–90. Cf Cassese (n 14) 177–80.

[92] ILC ARSIWA art 12, Commentary para 5.

[93] Ibid. See also art 1.

[94] Ibid art 30 and Commentary para 4.

[95] *Namibia* (1971) paras 118, 133 (The ICJ did not specify precisely the obligation that had been breached). See Chapter 4.b.

to comply with its obligation to respect the right of the Palestinian people to self-determination' and that Israel 'also has an obligation to put an end to the violation of its international obligations' associated with its construction of the wall at issue.[96] In *Chagos Archipelago* (2019), the ICJ found the United Kingdom subject to an obligation to cease its breach of the obligation to respect the right to self-determination in connection with its administration of Mauritius, a former NSGT, by bringing an end to its administration of the Chagos Archipelago 'as rapidly as possible, thereby enabling Mauritius to complete the decolonization of its territory in a manner consistent with the right of peoples to self-determination'.[97] Finally, in *Palestine* (2024), regarding policies and practices of Israel found to be unlawful, including breach of the obligation to respect the right to self-determination, the ICJ found that 'Israel has an obligation to put an end to those unlawful acts', and that 'Israel has an obligation to bring an end to its presence in the [OPT] as rapidly as possible'.[98]

2. Reparation

The obligation to make reparation for an internationally wrongful act is the other primary consequence of State responsibility.[99] Reparation functions to, 'as far as possible, wipe out all the consequences of the illegal act and reestablish the situation which would, in all probability, have existed if that act had not been committed'.[100] The obligation of reparation is not contingent on material injury resulting from an internationally wrongful act.[101] The

[96] *Wall* (2004) paras 149–50. See also ibid para 163. See Chapter 4.e.

[97] *Chagos* (2019) paras 177–78, 183. See also *R (Hoareau and Bancoult) v Secretary of State for Foreign and Commonwealth Affairs* [2020] EWCA Civ 1010 [132] ('[B]oth the ICJ and the General Assembly were careful to fashion a remedy which was prospective and which entailed the UK in completing an ongoing (albeit long interrupted) complex "*process*"'). See Chapter 4.g.

[98] *Palestine* (2024) paras 267–68 ('As the Court affirmed in its *Wall* Advisory Opinion, the obligation of a State responsible for an internationally wrongful act to put an end to that act is well established in general international law, and the Court has on a number of occasions confirmed the existence of that obligation' (citing *Chagos* (2019) para 178 and *Wall* (2004) para 150)). See Chapter 4.h.

[99] *Factory at Chorzów (Jurisdiction)*, PCIJ Series A No 9, Judgment No 8 (26 July 1927) 21. See Statute of the International Court of Justice art 36(2)(d), XV UNCIO 355 (26 June 1945, entered into force 24 Oct 1945); Statute of the Permanent Court of International Justice art 36, 6 LNTS 389 (16 Dec 1920, entered into force 20 Aug 1921). See also ILC ARSIWA art 31(1).

[100] *Factory at Chorzów (Merits)* (1928) 47.

[101] *Rainbow Warrior* (1990) ss 109–10 (referring to damage 'of a moral, political and legal nature'). See ILC ARSIWA art 31(2).

available forms of reparation under international law are restitution, compensation, and satisfaction.[102] The obligation of reparation, and its particular forms, are not punitive in nature.[103] In its advisory opinions addressing the right to self-determination, the ICJ explicitly identified an obligation of reparation in *The Wall* (2004) and *Palestine* (2024).

In *The Wall* (2004), the ICJ found that Israel was under an obligation to make reparation for damages associated with breaches of various international obligations, which included respect for the right to self-determination.[104] In *Palestine* (2024), the ICJ found that Israel is 'under an obligation to provide full reparation for the damage caused by its internationally wrongful acts to all natural or legal persons concerned'.[105] The ICJ identified the three forms of reparation under international law and prescribed measures of restitution,[106] or compensation in the alternative should restitution 'prove to be materially impossible'.[107] Finally, the court recalled that these secondary obligations in the field of State responsibility do not relieve Israel from its performance of the primary obligations it was found to have breached, including the obligation to respect the right to self-determination.[108]

In neither of its advisory opinions related to decolonization, in which it had identified obligations of cessation—*Namibia* (1971) and *Chagos Archipelago* (2019)—did the ICJ similarly identify an obligation of reparation. The absence of discrete obligations of reparation in those cases might be related to the character of the specific obligations breached or the nature of the breaches themselves. Unlike *The Wall* (2004) and *Palestine* (2024), both *Namibia* (1971) and *Chagos Archipelago* (2019) concerned decolonization in relation to the administration of a former Trust Territory and NSGT, respectively. Because the function of reparation is to, 'as far as possible, wipe out all the consequences of the illegal act and reestablish the situation which would,

[102] *Palestine* (2024) para 269. See ILC ARSIWA art 34.
[103] Regarding compensation, see ILC ARSIWA art 36, Commentary para 4; James Crawford, *State Responsibility: The General Part* (CUP 2013) 526. Regarding satisfaction, see ILC ARSIWA art 37(3) and art 37, Commentary para 8.
[104] *Wall* (2004) paras 152–53, 163.
[105] *Palestine* (2024) para 269 (citing *Wall* (2004) para 152).
[106] Ibid paras 269–70.
[107] Ibid para 271.
[108] Ibid para 272.

in all probability, have existed if that act had not been committed',[109] those cases may not have presented a significant practical distinction between cessation and reparation in the view of the ICJ. Put differently, because the obligation of cessation requires a State to return to compliance with a continuing obligation, performance of such continuing obligations in those cases may have been viewed to satisfy the function of reparation.[110]

ii. Obligations of Third-States

Breaches of obligations *erga omnes* may give rise to consequences not only for the responsible State, but also for third-States. The ICJ has articulated three 'general consequences' for third-States arising from breaches of obligations *erga omnes* under the right to self-determination: obligations of non-recognition and non-maintenance of such breaches, and cooperation to bring such breaches to an end.[111] These secondary obligations of third-States, first identified by the ICJ in *Namibia* (1971), have since been restated in relation to breaches of obligations *erga omnes*, particularly the obligation to respect the right to self-determination under CIL.[112] While the ICJ has identified these third-State consequences specifically in reference to self-determination, the ILC has associated these third-State consequences more generally with breaches of obligations arising under peremptory norms (i.e. obligations *erga omnes*).[113] The ILC has referred to these third-State consequences as arising from 'serious breaches' of 'obligations under peremptory norms' at Article 41 of the Articles on State Responsibility.[114]

[109] *Factory at Chorzów (Merits)* (1928) 47; *Palestine* (2024) para 269 (quoting *Factory at Chorzów (Merits)* (1928) 47).
[110] ILC ARSIWA art 35, Commentary para 6.
[111] *Namibia* (1971) paras 119–26; *Wall* (2004) para 159; *Palestine* (2024) paras 273–79. See also *Chagos* (2019) para 180 (identifying only the obligation of cooperation).
[112] *Wall* (2004) para 159. See also *Palestine* (2024) paras 273–79; *Chagos* (2019) para 180.
[113] ILC ARSIWA arts 40–41.
[114] The ILC, at Article 40, contemplates such consequences in terms of the magnitude of a 'breach of peremptory norms' and conceives of the seriousness of a breach in terms of the organization or intensity of 'the violation . . . of the peremptory norms in question'. See ILC ARSIWA art 40, Commentary paras 7–8. By contrast, the ICJ contemplates such consequences in relation to the character of the obligation breached, without any reference to peremptory norms or a criterion of 'seriousness'. Cf *Palestine* (2024) paras 273–79; *Chagos* (2019) para 180; *Wall* (2004) para 159; *Namibia* (1971) para 126. See also *Palestine* (2024) para 280.

Unlike the obligations of cessation and reparation for a responsible State, which are regarded as part of the law of State responsibility, various sources of secondary obligations of third States have been contemplated in the context of self-determination. In *Namibia* (1971), the ICJ relied on UNSC Resolution 276 (1970) as the source of third-State obligations, though the specific obligations articulated by the court were not stipulated by the Security Council.[115] In *Chagos Archipelago* (2019) and *Palestine* (2024), the ICJ identified obligations of third-States in relation to the duty to promote the realization of the principle of self-determination articulated by the FRD.[116] In each of these cases, the ICJ identified third-State obligations in relation to the *erga omnes* character of the obligation to respect the right to self-determination; in *Chagos Archipelago* (2019), the court specifically relied on the common legal interest of States in the performance of the obligation breached, i.e. its *erga omnes* character.[117] Third-State obligations may therefore be understood as an aspect of performance of the *erga omnes* obligation to respect the right to self-determination in relation to breaches of the right.[118]

1. Non-Recognition and Non-Maintenance

Where a State is responsible for breach of an obligation *erga omnes*, one possible consequence for third-States is an obligation not to recognize the lawfulness of a situation resulting from, or maintained by, the breach of that underlying obligation. The ICJ has articulated this obligation in relation to breach of obligations related to the right to self-determination in *Namibia* (1971), *The Wall* (2004), and *Palestine* (2024).[119] In these cases, the ICJ

[115] *Namibia* (1971) paras 119–26. See S/Res/276 (30 Jan 1970) paras 2, 5.

[116] FRD Principle V, para 2 ('Every State has the duty to promote, through joint and separate action, realization of the principle of equal rights and self-determination of peoples, in accordance with the provisions of the Charter, and to render assistance to the United Nations in carrying out the responsibilities entrusted to it by the Charter regarding the implementation of the principle'). See *Chagos* (2019) para 180; *Palestine* (2024) para 275. See also *Wall* (2004) paras 155–56, 159.

[117] *Chagos* (2019) para 180; *Palestine* (2024) paras 274–75. See also *Wall* (2004) para 159 (referring to 'the character and the importance of the rights and obligations involved').

[118] It may also be the case that third-State obligations, like the obligations of cessation and reparation for a responsible State, are supplied by the law of State responsibility in relation to breaches of obligations *erga omnes* generally. See ILC ARSIWA art 41.

[119] *Namibia* (1971) para 119; *Wall* (2004) para 159; *Palestine* (2024) paras 278–79.

articulated a parallel obligation that States not aid or assist in the maintenance of such a situation.[120]

In *Chagos Archipelago* (2019), the ICJ did not refer to obligations of non-recognition and non-maintenance for third-States. Notably, in this regard, the relation between the United Kingdom and Mauritius relative to the Chagos Archipelago was characterized by the ICJ as one of incomplete decolonization rather than as a situation of occupation. Because the administration of the Chagos Archipelago by the United Kingdom derived from its authority as the administering power of a NSGT, its exercise of sovereignty over the Chagos Archipelago was distinguishable from the presence of South Africa in Namibia (*Namibia* (1971)) and the presence of Israel in the OPT (*The Wall* (2004) and *Palestine* (2024)), both of which were regarded by the ICJ as situations of occupation.[121] The obligations implicated in relation to Mauritius and the Chagos Archipelago were those of the United Kingdom as an administering power.[122] Chapter XI of the UN Charter does not, however, render relationships of subordination between administering powers and NSGTs unlawful, but instead, imposes positive obligations on administering powers based in 'progressive development' to wind down such relationships.[123] In this way, the internationally wrongful act identified by the ICJ was effectively treated as incomplete performance by the United Kingdom of its obligations as the administering power of Mauritius, a former NSGT.[124]

In *Palestine* (2024), the ICJ identified legal consequences beyond third-States for international organisations arising from the *erga omnes* character of the obligations breached, including the obligation to respect the right to self-determination.[125] In particular, the court considered that the duty of non-recognition applies to international organisations, including the United Nations, in view of the *erga omnes* character of the obligations breached.[126]

[120] Ibid. Cf ILC ARSIWA art 41(2). The ILC, at Article 41(2) of the Articles on State Responsibility, extended such third-State obligations to 'serious breaches' of obligations under peremptory norms. The obligations of non-recognition and non-maintenance identified by the ICJ in advisory opinions concerning self-determination were not, however, based on a criterion of seriousness of the breach of obligations related to the right to self-determination or any assertion of the peremptory status of the right. See Weatherall (n 91) 246–47.

[121] See Chapter 7.b.ii.1.

[122] *Chagos* (2019) Sep Op Gaja para 4.

[123] *Chagos* (2019) para 147. See Chapter 9.c.ii.

[124] *Chagos* (2019) paras 178, 183. See also *R (Hoareau and Bancoult) v Secretary of State for Foreign and Commonwealth Affairs* [2020] EWCA Civ 1010 [132].

[125] *Palestine* (2024) paras 280–81.

[126] Ibid para 280.

In this way, the court expanded the scope of legal consequences arising from the breach of the obligation *erga omnes* to respect the right to self-determination, beyond third-States, to include a duty of non-recognition for international organisations.

2. Cooperation

While the foregoing third-State obligations of non-recognition and non-maintenance are negative in character, another consequence that has been articulated for third-States in relation to breaches of obligations related to the right to self-determination is a positive obligation of cooperation to bring an end to such breaches.[127] In *Namibia* (1971), the ICJ called on States to refrain from lending support or assistance to the maintenance of the situation in Namibia, and advised on various measures to be undertaken by States directed at bringing an end to the unlawful situation resulting from South Africa's presence in Namibia.[128] The ICJ identified an obligation of cooperation to bring an end to breaches of the obligation to respect the right to self-determination in *The Wall* (2004), *Chagos Archipelago* (2019), and *Palestine* (2024). In this regard, in *The Wall* (2004), the ICJ referred to the duty to promote the realization of the right to self-determination in the FRD and called on States 'to see to it that any impediment' resulting from construction of the wall to the exercise of the right to self-determination by the Palestinian people 'is brought to an end'.[129] In *Chagos Archipelago* (2019), the ICJ articulated an obligation of cooperation for third-States and referred to the provision of the FRD regarding promotion of the right to self-determination.[130]

[127] The ILC, at Article 41(1) of the Articles on State Responsibility, extended this consequence to serious breaches of obligations under peremptory norms. The ILC acknowledged that Article 41(1) may reflect 'progressive development'. As with the obligations of non-recognition and non-maintenance discussed above, the obligation of cooperation identified by the ICJ in advisory opinions concerning self-determination was not based on a criterion of seriousness or assertion of the peremptory status of the right. See ILC ARSIWA art 41(1) and art 41, Commentary paras 2–3.

[128] *Namibia* (1971) paras 119–26.

[129] *Wall* (2004) paras 156, 159. Cf James Crawford, 'Opinion: Third Party Obligations with respect to Israeli Settlements in the Occupied Palestinian Territories' para 72 (24 Jan 2012) (referring to this language as a corollary of the obligation of non-recognition rather than as a positive obligation of cooperation).

[130] *Chagos* (2019) para 180 ('The Court considers that, while it is for the General Assembly to pronounce on the modalities required to ensure the completion of the decolonization of Mauritius, all Member States must co-operate with the United Nations to put those modalities into effect'). See FRD Principle V, para 2.

In *Palestine* (2024), the ICJ framed the obligation of cooperation by incorporating elements of its previous articulations of the obligation in *The Wall* (2004) and *Chagos Archipelago* (2019).[131] The ICJ has conditioned the performance by third-States of the obligation of cooperation by respect for the UN Charter and international law.[132]

131 *Palestine* (2024) paras 275, 279.
132 *Wall* (2004) para 159; *Palestine* (2024) para 279. See also *Chagos* (2019) para 180.

PART III
PRACTICE

Part III surveys and analyses the practice of the right to self-determination in international law. This practice is addressed by chapters on three key areas: the United Nations, international dispute settlement, and other mechanisms of implementation and enforcement.

10
The United Nations

a. Overview

The United Nations has played a central institutional role in advancing the right to self-determination. The UN Charter confers upon the United Nations authorities and functions specific to the advancement of decolonization. The Special Committee on Decolonization, discussed in detail below, contextualized the prioritization by the United Nations of bringing an end to colonialism in the following terms:

> The desire of the Members of the United Nations to bring about the final end of colonialism as speedily as possible by peaceful means was well known. It was generally recognized that the emancipation of all peoples still living in dependent status would not only remove one of the major obstacles to the maintenance of peace but would greatly contribute to the realization of the principles of equality enshrined in the Charter.[1]

That the UN Charter includes three chapters addressing aspects of decolonization is indicative of the institutional focus of the United Nations on bringing about an end to colonialism to advance the realization of self-determination for all peoples. As discussed in Part I, Chapter XI (Articles 73 and 74) of the Charter sets forth obligations for administering powers vis-à-vis Non-Self-Governing Territories (NSGTs).[2] Chapter XII (Articles 75–85) of the Charter sets out the parameters of the International Trusteeship System, including objectives for administering authorities of territories to which the Trusteeship System applied.[3] And Chapter XIII (Articles 86–91)

[1] A/5446/Rev.1 (1963) (hereinafter *1963 Special Committee Report*) ch I para 9.
[2] See Chapter 2.b.ii.
[3] See Chapter 2.b.iii.

The Right to Self-Determination in International Law. Thomas Weatherall, Oxford University Press.
 DOI: 10.1093/9780197798119.003.0011

established and provides for the functions of the UN Trusteeship Council, which monitored the administration of Trust Territories.[4]

In exercising its authorities related to decolonization, the record of the United Nations is extensive. The United Nations has been integral to supervising the administration of territories subject to Chapters XI and XII of the UN Charter, and to promoting the realization of self-government of those territories through independence or other changes in political status. A survey of UN practice in this regard is contained in Appendix 1 (Former Trust Territories and Non-Self-Governing Territories), which identifies key actions undertaken by the United Nations pertinent to changes in political status of each of the more than one hundred territories formerly subject to Chapters XI and XII of the Charter.

Such changes in political status have generally resulted from the participation of the peoples concerned in an 'act of free choice' through which their wishes were freely expressed. It has been observed that this exercise of self-determination is one area of international practice in which democratic principles have been widely respected,[5] consistent with the obligations of administering States under the UN Charter directed towards promoting representative government in NSGTs and Trust Territories.[6] The administration of such self-determination processes has often been accompanied by some form of involvement by the United Nations.[7] While such processes have frequently taken the form of a referendum, the modalities by which the peoples concerned have expressed their wishes have varied.[8] This variation was described by one survey of UN practice in the following terms:

> There were of course differences in the ways in which these territories exercised their right to self-determination by securing independence and sovereignty, as well as international recognition. . . . The legal character and the status of the territories which subsequently became sovereign States also differed. As a result, United Nations action and the procedure

[4] Ibid. See also Chapter 10.b.i.1.

[5] Thomas M. Franck, 'The Stealing of the Sahara' (1976) 70(4) *AJIL* 694, 698–99.

[6] See Chapter 9.c.

[7] 'Fifteen Years of the United Nations Declaration on the Granting of Independence to Colonial Countries and Peoples' (1975) 2 *Decolonization* No 6 (hereinafter *Fifteen Years*) 19.

[8] *Western Sahara*, Advisory Opinion, ICJ Rep 1975, 12 (hereinafter *Western Sahara* (1975)) paras 59, 71; *Legal Consequences of the Separation of the Chagos Archipelago from Mauritius in 1965*, Advisory Opinion, ICJ Rep 2019, 95 (hereinafter *Chagos* (2019)) paras 157–58,

> followed have also differed, varying according to the circumstances. . . . It is sufficient to emphasize the vital importance, whether direct or indirect, of United Nations action in these processes and the international significance of the entry of the new States into the United Nations, which in practice has become tantamount to recognition of the free and sovereign nature of those States by the international community.[9]

To be sure, there have been exceptions to this general practice, in which the United Nations has been excluded from the administration of a self-determination process,[10] or where a change in political status (i.e. independence) was achieved through force rather than a political process.[11] However, as illustrated by the survey in Appendix 1, the overwhelming trend in the achievement of self-government has been a political process to ascertain the freely expressed wishes of the people concerned, and recognition of the resultant political independence of their territory and its emergence into sovereignty through admission to the United Nations.

The work of the United Nations to advance decolonization is ongoing. There remain cases in which such a self-determination process has not yet been completed, as reflected by the seventeen NSGTs identified in Appendix 2 (Non-Self-Governing Territories).

This chapter provides an overview of the institutional mechanisms of the United Nations and their practical roles relative to the performance by States of relevant obligations related to the right to self-determination. The first section of this chapter surveys the functions of the UNGA and its relevant subsidiary bodies—the Trusteeship Council and the Special Committee on Decolonization (the 'C-24')—as well as the Special Political and Decolonization Committee (the Fourth Committee). This section also addresses the UN registry of Non-Self-Governing Territories and

[9] *The Right to Self-Determination: Implementation of United Nations Resolutions* (Study prepared by Héctor Gros Espiell, Special Rapporteur of the Sub-Commission on Prevention of Discrimination and Protection of Minorities), E/CN.4/Sub.2/405/Rev.1 (1980) (hereinafter *Espiell Report* (1980)) para 254.

[10] See e.g. *Fifteen Years* 20 (discussing refusal by France to accept a United Nations presence before and during a referendum in French Somaliland).

[11] Miguel Cardina, 'Introduction' in Miguel Cardina (ed), *The Portuguese Colonial War and the African Liberation Struggles: Memory, Politics and Uses of the Past* (Routledge 2024) (discussing the achievement of political independence by Portuguese-administered territories through conflict).

considers the processes by which territories have historically been added to, and removed from, the registry.[12] The second section of this chapter considers institutional functions of the UNSC of specific relevance to self-determination.

b. United Nations General Assembly

In *Chagos Archipelago* (2019), the ICJ observed that

> [t]he General Assembly has played a crucial role in the work of the United Nations on decolonization . . . . It has overseen the implementation of the obligations of Member States in this regard, such as they are laid down in Chapter XI of the Charter and as they arise from the practice which has developed within the Organization.[13]

The activities of the UNGA in this area are comprehensive. The UNGA has facilitated the exercise of the right to self-determination by peoples of NSGTs through monitoring the means by which the will of such peoples is expressed, and assisting in the implementation of processes, mainly referendums, to this end.[14] The UNGA has engaged in self-determination processes through formulating questions submitted for popular consultation and supervising referendums.[15] In practice, the UNGA has enjoyed 'a measure of discretion' in regard to self-determination processes.[16]

i. Identification of Non-Self-Governing Territories

The UN Charter is silent on the competence to determine that a territory is subject to Chapter XI. From the outset, the authority to designate a territory as a NSGT subject to Chapter XI was regarded as the purview of the domestic

[12] This 'registry' is reflected today in the territories remaining on the agenda of the Special Committee on Decolonization.

[13] *Chagos* (2019) para 163.

[14] Ibid para 167.

[15] For a survey of UN practice on decolonization, see *Espiell Report* (1980) ch III.

[16] *Western Sahara* (1975) paras 59, 71; *Chagos* (2019) paras 157–58.

jurisdiction of an administering power.[17] This approach follows from the limited competence of the UNGA, which is not empowered to impose obligations upon UN Member States. Accordingly, it was incumbent upon UN Member States to determine which territories were NSGTs under Chapter XI of the Charter. In its first session, the UNGA requested that the annual report of the UN Secretary-General include such information submitted by UN Member States pursuant to Article 73(e) of the Charter to the Secretary-General.[18] The Secretary-General addressed a letter of 29 June 1946 to all UN Member States requesting information about NSGTs under their jurisdiction.[19] Administering powers voluntarily submitted information on NSGTs, resulting in the initial registry of seventy-two NSGTs on the basis of information submitted to the Secretary-General by Member States, and indications of the intent of Member States to submit information regarding other territories, pursuant to Article 73(e) of the Charter.[20] In 1949, the UNGA recognized its authority 'to express its opinion on the principles which have guided or which may in [the] future guide' Member States in enumerating territories subject to Article 73(e) of the Charter.[21] The UNGA contemplated the appointment of a special committee with the mandate to examine factors to guide its determination as to 'whether any territory is or is not a territory whose people have not yet attained a full measure of self-government'.[22] Following admission of Spain and Portugal to the United Nations in 1955, and their non-performance of obligations under Article 73(e) in relation to territories under their administration, the UNGA established a special committee to study the principles which should guide UN Member States in the designation of territories subject to Chapter XI of the Charter.[23] Those

17 Hans Kelsen, *The Law of the United Nations* (London Institute of World Affairs 1950) 555–57. Cf James Crawford, *The Creation of States in International Law* (2nd edn, OUP 2006) 607–08 (attributing this view to administering powers). For an analysis of early practice, see 3 *Repertory of Practice of United Nations Organs*, Supplement No 3 (1959–1966) (hereinafter *Repertory*) paras 47–215.

18 A/Res/9 (I) (9 Feb 1946) (Non-Self-Governing Peoples).

19 *Yearbook of the United Nations, 1946–47* (1947) 208. See *Report of the Secretary-General: Problems of Transmission and Organization*, A/74 (21 Oct 1946).

20 A/Res/66 (I) (14 Dec 1946) (note that this figure depends on the treatment of the High Commission Territories of the Western Pacific (Gilbert and Ellice Islands Colony, British Solomon Islands Protectorate, and Pitcairn Islands)).

21 A/Res/334 (IV) (2 Dec 1949) para 1.

22 Ibid para 2.

23 A/Res/1467 (XIV) (12 Dec 1959).

principles are reflected in UNGA Resolution 1541.[24] And, following the contemporaneous adoption of UNGA Resolution 1514, the UNGA established the Special Committee on Decolonization to monitor implementation of UNGA Resolution 1514 by States and to make recommendations pursuant thereto.[25]

In practice, the UNGA has asserted a role alongside administering powers in the identification of territories subject to Chapter XI of the UN Charter.[26] As noted above, the initial 1946 registry of NSGTs included seventy-two territories on the basis of information voluntarily submitted to the UN Secretary-General by UN Member States pursuant to Article 73(e) of the Charter.[27] No territories were added to this list prior to 1960.[28] Before the adoption of UNGA Resolutions 1514 and 1541 in 1960, NSGTs were removed from the registry either unilaterally,[29] or by vote of the UNGA to recognize a new status by virtue of constitutional changes notified by an administering power.[30] In view of the principles articulated in UNGA Resolution 1541, the UNGA designated Portuguese territories in Resolution 1542 (1960),[31] and Southern Rhodesia in Resolution 1747

[24] See Chapter 3.c.

[25] A/Res/1654 (XVI) (27 Nov 1961).

[26] Crawford (n 17) 608.

[27] A/Res/66 (I) (14 Dec 1946).

[28] *Fifteen Years* 6.

[29] For example, the practice of France, regarding New Caledonia and French Polynesia, was to cease transmitting information under Article 73(e) of the UN Charter following the initial listing of the two territories in 1946. See A/Res/41/41 [A] (2 Dec 1986) preambular paras 1–2; A/Res/67/265 (17 May 2013) preambular para 8. These territories were then removed from the registry of NSGTs maintained by the UNGA. However, as discussed below, each territory was subsequently 'reinscribed' by the UNGA.

[30] *Cessation of the Transmission of Information: Communication from the Government of the United States of America concerning Puerto Rico*, A/AC.35/L.121 (3 Apr 1953) and A/Res/748 (VIII) (27 Nov 1953) (endorsing cessation of transmission of information under Article 73(e)); *Cessation of the Transmission of Information: Communication from the Government of Denmark Concerning Greenland*, A/AC.35/L.155 and Corr. 1 (7 Dec 1953), and A/Res/849 (IX) (22 Nov 1954) (endorsing cessation of transmission of information under Article 73(e)); *Cessation of the Transmission of Information under Article 73 e of the Charter: Communication from the Government of the Netherlands Regarding Surinam and the Netherlands Antilles*, A/AC.35/L.206 (7 Apr 1955), and A/Res/945 (X) (15 Dec 1955) (endorsing cessation of transmission of information under Article 73(e)).

[31] A/Res/1542 (XV) (15 Dec 1960). Resolution 1542 does not enumerate Spanish-administered territories, but instead 'Recall[ed] with satisfaction the statement of the representative of Spain at the 1048th meeting of the Fourth Committee that his Government agrees to transmit information to the Secretary-General in accordance with the provisions of Chapter XI of the Charter'. See A/C.4/SR.1048 (11 Nov 1960) para 1 (UNGA Fourth Committee 1048th Meeting) (Mr Aznar (Spain)). These territories were Fernando Póo and Río Muni (Equatorial

(1962),[32] as NSGTs subject to Chapter XI of the Charter. In 1963, the Special Committee on Decolonization approved what it characterized as 'a preliminary list of territories' consisting of sixty-four territories to which Chapter XI applied.[33] At the beginning of 1967, the registry of NSGTs consisted of thirty-seven territories for which administering powers had transmitted information pursuant to Article 73(e) and a further eight (the Portuguese territories and Southern Rhodesia) declared by the UNGA to be non-self-governing within the meaning of Chapter XI.[34] At the time of writing, there are seventeen territories regarded as NSGTs for purposes of Chapter XI of the Charter, as reflected by the agenda of the Special Committee on Decolonization.[35] This figure includes territories 'reinscribed' by the UNGA to the registry of NSGTs over the objections of their administering power, as reflected in resolutions concerning New Caledonia in 1986,[36] and French Polynesia in 2013.[37] The ICJ has observed that the UNGA 'reserves to itself the right to determine the territories which have to be regarded as non-self-governing for the purposes of the application of Chapter XI of the Charter'.[38]

ii. Cessation of Obligations under Chapters XI and XII of the United Nations Charter

The UN Charter does not provide for the cessation of obligations under Chapter XI or Chapter XII. The Charter therefore does not prescribe United Nations action prior to the cessation of such obligations, and the termination of such obligations is not conditioned by United Nations action under the Charter.[39]

Guinea), Ifni, and Spanish Sahara (Western Sahara). See *Repertory* para 189. See also *Report of the Secretary-General: Africa and Adjacent Territories*, A/5078/Add.3 (26 Mar 1962) (based on information transmitted by Spain pursuant to Article 73(e)).

---

32 A/Res/1747 (XVI) (28 June 1962).
33 *1963 Special Committee Report* ch I paras 27–28, 46, and Annex I.
34 *Repertory* para 215 (excluding São João Batista de Ajudá and Goa).
35 See Appendix 2.
36 A/Res/41/41 [A] (2 Dec 1986).
37 A/Res/67/265 (17 May 2013).
38 *East Timor (Portugal v Australia)*, Judgment, ICJ Rep 1995, 90 para 31.
39 Crawford (n 17) 621–22.

Regarding obligations under Chapter XI of the UN Charter, in relation to NSGTs, UNGA Resolution 1541 contemplates that the reporting obligation for an administering power under Article 73(e) terminates '[a]s soon as a territory and its peoples attain a measure of self-government'.[40] However, the UNGA maintains that it retains the competence to determine whether a NSGT has attained a 'full measure of self-government', and thus whether a State remains subject to obligations under Article 73 of the Charter.[41] The UNGA has also reserved to itself the authority to revisit the status of a territory that freely associates with a sovereign State.[42] Attainment of a 'full measure of self-government' is generally recognized by the UNGA through the adoption of a territory-specific resolution, indicating that such territory is no longer regarded as a NSGT by the UNGA for purposes of Chapter XI.[43] In this way, recognition by the UNGA of a people's attainment of self-government has in practice come to represent a key benchmark from the perspective of process.[44] Where a people has attained self-government through independence, this process has culminated in admission to the United Nations by operation of an UNGA resolution.[45]

A comparable practice is seen regarding Trust Territories subject to Chapter XII of the UN Charter. Following the attainment of self-government by each Trust Territory, the UNGA terminated the respective underlying Trusteeship agreements by adopting UNGA resolutions.[46] The ICJ has regarded an UNGA resolution terminating a Trusteeship agreement to have

[40] A/Res/1541 (XV) (15 Dec 1960) Annex, Principle II. See Crawford (n 17) 622.

[41] See e.g. A/Res/945 (X) (15 Dec 1955) preambular para 5.

[42] See e.g. A/Res/742 (VIII) Annex, Third Part, s A, para 2 (27 Nov 1953) ('Freedom of choice').

[43] Accordingly, the UNGA has consistently reaffirmed that, 'in the absence of a decision by the General Assembly itself that a Non-Self-Governing Territory has attained a full measure of self-government in terms of Chapter XI of the Charter of the United Nations, the administering Power concerned should continue to transmit information under Article 73 *e* of the Charter with respect to that Territory'. See e.g. A/Res/77/129 (15 Dec 2022) para 1; A/Res/69/97 (5 Dec 2014) para 1; A/Res/57/131 (11 Dec 2002) para 1; A/Res/51/139 (13 Dec 1996) para 2; A/Res/40/51 (2 Dec 1985) para 2 (non-exhaustive). See Chapter 10.b.iv.2.

[44] Crawford (n 17) 622–23. In exceptional cases, questions arise as to implementation of the right to self-determination notwithstanding the imprimatur of the UNGA. For one example, see Thomas D. Musgrave, 'An analysis of the 1969 Act of Free Choice in West Papua' in Christine Chinkin and Freya Baetens (eds), *Sovereignty, Statehood and State Responsibility: Essays in Honour of James Crawford* (CUP 2015) 209–28.

[45] Crawford (n 17) 622. See Appendix 1.

[46] See Chapter 10.b.iv.1. The termination of League of Nations Mandates upon achievement of self-government was comparatively less orderly: see Chapter 1.c.i.

'definitive legal effect' as to the attainment of self-government through the exercise of the right to self-determination by the people concerned.[47]

iii. Other Activities of the United Nations General Assembly

The activities of the UNGA relevant to self-determination extend beyond its practice specific to NSGTs. The UNGA adopts resolutions on a range of issues in connection with self-determination, which have played an important role in promoting the right to self-determination more broadly. Notably, while there are more United Nations resolutions referring to self-determination than can be effectively documented,[48] several UNGA resolutions in particular have been identified by the ICJ as contributing to the crystallization of the CIL of self-determination.[49] In recent years, recurring resolutions have been adopted by the UNGA on general issues pertaining to self-determination as well as territory-specific resolutions, often on an annual basis. This practice is discussed in greater detail below in reference to the UNGA Fourth Committee.[50]

One way in which the UNGA has shaped the development of the right to self-determination in international law is through the ICJ advisory procedure. The UNGA has requested advisory opinions relevant to its functions relating to decolonization,[51] as well as others implicating self-determination in situations beyond the context of decolonization.[52] Advisory opinions by the ICJ addressing self-determination rendered in response to these requests inform the content of the right to self-determination in international law.[53]

[47] *Case Concerning the Northern Cameroons (Cameroon v United Kingdom)*, Preliminary Objections, Judgment, ICJ Rep 1963, 15, 32.

[48] *Reference re Secession of Quebec* [1998] 2 SCR 217 para 117.

[49] *Chagos* (2019) paras 150–56. See Chapter 3.

[50] See Chapter 10.b.iv.3.

[51] *Chagos* (2019) paras 86–90; *Western Sahara* (1975) para 39.

[52] *Legal Consequences arising from the Policies and Practices of Israel in the Occupied Palestinian Territory, including East Jerusalem*, Advisory Opinion, ICJ Rep 2024, paras 36–37; *Accordance with International Law of the Unilateral Declaration of Independence in Respect of Kosovo*, Advisory Opinion, ICJ Rep 2010, 403 paras 55–56; *Legal Consequences of the Construction of a Wall in the Occupied Palestinian Territory*, Advisory Opinion, ICJ Rep 2004, 136 paras 48–50.

[53] See Chapter 11.d.

Although advisory opinions are not binding on any State or requesting organ, they are generally recognized to provide authoritative statements of international law.[54] Moreover, where a request for an advisory opinion implicates an ongoing dispute, the advice rendered by the ICJ may affect the complexion of that underlying dispute.[55] In this way, requests by the UNGA for advisory opinions may have a significant practical impact on disputes concerning the performance of obligations related to self-determination, as well as in developing the international law of self-determination through the caselaw of the ICJ. Chapter 11 analyses advisory proceedings of the ICJ in the context of self-determination.

iv. Subsidiary Bodies of the United Nations General Assembly

The UNGA contains subsidiary bodies—the Trusteeship Council and the Special Committee on Decolonization—to monitor, respectively, the administration of Trust Territories by administering authorities and the performance by administering powers of their obligations vis-à-vis NSGTs over which they exercise authority. The Fourth Committee of the UNGA, one of the Main Committees of the General Assembly, also plays a practical role in the exercise of UNGA decolonization authorities. Each of these bodies is considered below.

1. Trusteeship Council

Chapter XIII of the UN Charter provides for the establishment and operation of the Trusteeship Council, a subsidiary body of the UNGA with competence to monitor the administration of Trust Territories by administering authorities.[56] Article 85 of the Charter contemplates the operation of the Trusteeship Council under the authority of the UNGA in order to assist the UNGA in carrying out functions related to Trusteeship agreements, namely, those related to approval and alteration or amendment of such

[54] See Chapter 11.d.ii.
[55] See Chapter 11.d.i.
[56] For discussion of the International Trusteeship System, see Chapter 2.b.iii; Chapter 9.c.i.

agreements.[57] In 1946, Resolution 64 (I) was adopted by the UNGA to establish the Trusteeship Council, consistent with the provisions of Article 86 of the Charter concerning the composition of the Council.[58] Eleven Trust Territories were subject to the Trusteeship System.[59] As discussed in Chapter 9, administering authorities of each Trust Territory were subject to obligations under Trusteeship agreements.[60] Following attainment of self-government by each Trust Territory, its respective Trusteeship agreement was terminated by the UNGA.[61] All former Trust Territories have attained self-government and no UN Member State is subject to the performance of obligations under a Chapter XII Trusteeship agreement. Consequently, on 25 May 1994, the Trusteeship Council adopted a resolution suspending its operation.[62]

2. Special Committee on Decolonization

The Special Committee on the Situation with regard to the Implementation of the Declaration on the Granting of Independence to Colonial Countries and Peoples (also known as the 'Special Committee on Decolonization' or 'C-24') was established in 1961 as a subsidiary body of the UNGA by Resolution 1654 (XVI).[63] The Special Committee was created following the adoption of UNGA Resolution 1514.[64] The mandate of the Special Committee is 'to examine the application' of UNGA Resolution 1514 and 'to make suggestions and recommendations on the progress and extent of [its] implementation' to the UNGA.[65] Membership of the Special Committee was expanded from seventeen to twenty-four UN Member States in 1962, which accounts for the moniker 'C-24'.[66] In 1963, the Committee on Information from Non-Self-Governing Territories was dissolved by the UNGA and the Special Committee assumed responsibility for reviewing information transmitted by

[57] Charter of the United Nations art 85, XV UNCIO 335 (26 June 1945, entered into force 24 Oct 1945) (hereinafter UN Charter).
[58] A/Res/64 (I) (14 Dec 1946). See UN Charter art 86.
[59] Note that the UNSC has authority under the UN Charter with respect to 'strategic' Trust Territories: UN Charter arts 82–83. See Chapter 10.c.
[60] See supra Chapter 2 n 34 (citing Trusteeship agreements). See Chapter 9.c.i.
[61] See supra Chapter 2 n 35 (citing relevant resolutions).
[62] T/Res/2200 (LXI) (25 May 1994).
[63] A/Res/1654 (XVI) (27 Nov 1961).
[64] See Chapter 3.b.
[65] A/Res/1654 (XVI) (27 Nov 1961) para 4.
[66] A/Res/1810 (XVII) (17 Dec 1962) para 7.

administering powers under Article 73(e) of the UN Charter.[67] At the same session, in 1963, the UNGA renewed the mandate of the Special Committee and has continued to renew its mandate at subsequent sessions.[68]

Responsibility for maintaining the registry of NSGTs (i.e. territories subject to Chapter XI of the UN Charter) has been assumed by the Special Committee. As discussed above, before the adoption of UNGA Resolutions 1514 and 1541 in 1960, which articulated standards and principles addressed to UN Member States regarding the exercise of self-determination by peoples of NSGTs, and prior to the establishment of the Special Committee, NSGTs were removed from the registry either unilaterally or by vote of the UNGA.[69] In 1962, however, the UNGA invited the Special Committee to submit a report containing suggestions and recommendations on Trust Territories and NSGTs or all other territories which have not yet attained independence.[70] In response, the Special Committee approved in 1963 what it characterized as 'a preliminary list of territories' consisting of sixty-four territories in relation to which Chapter XI applied.[71] The Special Committee has continued to consider the situation of territories to which Chapter XI applies, and in exceptional cases has considered territories no longer reported under Article 73(e).[72]

The contemporary practice of the Special Committee centres on its annual review of the registry of NSGTs. Typically, the Special Committee annually adopts resolutions and a declaration addressing each remaining NSGT, as well as other more general topical and thematic resolutions, which it then recommends to the UNGA Fourth Committee, discussed further below. During its 2022 session, for example, the Special Committee adopted twenty-one draft resolutions and one decision, which it then recommended in its annual report to the UNGA Fourth Committee.[73] The Special Committee

[67] A/Res/1970 (XVIII) (16 Dec 1963). For discussion of Article 73(e), see Chapter 2.b.ii; Chapter 9.c.ii.

[68] For further discussion of the establishment and history of the Special Committee, see A/AC.109/2022/L.1 (10 Dec 2021) paras 2–14.

[69] See supra n 33.

[70] A/Res/1810 (XVII) (17 Dec 1962) para 8(c).

[71] *1963 Special Committee Report* ch I paras 27–28, 46, and Annex I.

[72] Comoros (see e.g. A/Res/3161 (XXVIII) (14 Dec 1973)), French Somaliland (Djibouti) (see e.g. A/Res/2228 (XXI) (20 Dec 1966)), and the West Indies Associated States (until disaggregation) (see e.g. A/Res/2867 (XXVI) (20 Dec 1971)) are examples of such consideration. Puerto Rico was also considered after its removal from the registry of NSGTs: see e.g. A/AC.109/2000/24 (12 July 2000). See Crawford (n 17) 610, 626–28.

[73] A/77/23 (2022) ch XIII.

also organizes regional seminars on decolonization matters and is empowered to dispatch visiting missions to NSGTs at the invitation of administering powers.[74]

3. Fourth Committee of the United Nations General Assembly

The Special Political and Decolonization Committee (also known as the 'Fourth Committee') is one of the Main Committees of the UNGA.[75] The Fourth Committee considers a range of items allocated to it by the UNGA.[76] The contemporary practice of the UNGA has seen the allocation of five agenda items related to decolonization to the Fourth Committee for consideration at each annual session: (1) information from NSGTs transmitted under Article 73(e) of the UN Charter, (2) economic and other activities which affect the interests of the peoples of NSGTs, (3) implementation of Resolution 1514 by specialized agencies and international institutions associated with the United Nations, (4) offers by UN Member States of study and training facilities for inhabitants of NSGTs, and (5) implementation of UNGA Resolution 1514.[77] The Fourth Committee submits reports on each agenda item to the UNGA plenary, which reports contain the draft resolutions for consideration at the plenary.[78] These draft resolutions generally consist of those recommended to it by the Special Committee. For illustration, as noted above, in 2022, the Special Committee adopted twenty-one draft resolutions and one decision, addressing each NSGT as well as other self-determination and decolonization-related topics, which it recommended to the Fourth Committee in its annual report.[79] The Fourth Committee then adopted these twenty-one resolutions on decolonization agenda items during the seventy-seventh session of the UNGA.[80] The

[74] For an illustration of the scope of work of the Special Committee, see A/AC.109/2022/SR.8 (17 Aug 2022).

[75] Rules of Procedure of the General Assembly, A/520/Rev.20 (2022) Rule 98.

[76] See e.g. A/77/251 (16 Sept 2022) (Agenda of the seventy-seventh regular session of the General Assembly).

[77] See e.g. A/C.4/77/1 (16 Sept 2022) (Agenda items 51–55). For background of each agenda item, including summaries of prior treatment by the UNGA, see e.g. A/77/100 (15 June 2022).

[78] For representative reports see e.g. A/77/404 (25 Oct 2022) (Agenda item 51); A/77/405 (25 Oct 2022) (Agenda item 52); A/77/406 (25 Oct 2022) (Agenda item 53); A/77/407 (25 Oct 2022) (Agenda item 54); A/77/408 (28 Oct 2022) (Agenda item 55).

[79] A/77/23 (2022) ch XIII.

[80] A/C.4/77/INF/3/Rev.1 (3 Jan 2023).

UNGA subsequently adopted these twenty-one resolutions on decolonization agenda items in December 2022.[81]

c. United Nations Security Council

Although the UNGA has primary institutional responsibility for decolonization matters within the United Nations system, the UN Charter assigns responsibility to the UNSC with respect to Trust Territories designated as 'strategic' in character.[82] Article 83(1) of the Charter provides that '[a]ll functions of the United Nations relating to strategic areas, including the approval of the terms of the trusteeship agreements and of their alteration or amendment shall be exercised by the Security Council'. The Trust Territory of the Pacific Islands was designated as a strategic area under Article 82 of the Charter, the only territory so designated.[83] The Trusteeship Agreement for the Trust Territory of the Pacific Islands was terminated by the UNSC in 1994, upon the entry of Palau into free association with the United States.[84] As discussed above, there are no territories currently subject to the Trusteeship System.

The UNSC has also exercised its general authorities under the UN Charter in self-determination matters. The UNSC has adopted resolutions on disputes implicating self-determination and, in so doing, recognized the right to self-determination of the peoples of Namibia, East Timor, and Western Sahara.[85] Resolutions by the UNSC may have binding effect on UN Member States under Article 25 of the Charter.[86] Moreover, the UNSC has exercised

[81] Ibid.

[82] UN Charter arts 82–83.

[83] *1963 Special Committee Report* 289 n b.

[84] The Federated States of Micronesia, the Marshall Islands, and Palau are States that emerged from the Trust Territory of the Pacific Islands. The Northern Mariana Islands became a commonwealth territory of the United States. The Trusteeship agreement was terminated by the UNSC upon Palau entering into free association with the United States. See S/Res/956 (10 Nov 1994). See also S/Res/683 (22 Dec 1990) (termination of Trusteeship agreement in relation to the Federated States of Micronesia, the Marshall Islands, and the Northern Mariana Islands).

[85] See e.g. S/Res/301 (20 Oct 1971) preambular para 7 (Namibia); S/Res/384 (22 Dec 1975) para 3 (East Timor); S/Res/389 (22 Apr 1976) preambular paras 5–6, para 1 (East Timor); S/Res/1598 (28 Apr 2005) preambular para 2 (Western Sahara). See also S/Res/432 (27 July 1978) (Walvis Bay).

[86] UN Charter art 25. See *Legal Consequences for States of the Continued Presence of South Africa in Namibia (South West Africa) notwithstanding Security Council Resolution 276 (1970)*,

its authority under Chapter VII of the Charter to establish missions to help achieve self-government by peoples in contentious situations. Action by the UNSC in relation to East Timor[87] and Namibia (discussed in detail below) are examples in this regard. As discussed above, where a political process to ascertain the freely expressed wishes of the people concerned results in independence, perhaps the most definitive indicia of the achievement of self-government is admission to the United Nations. Prior to admission to the United Nations by UNGA resolution, the UNSC considers the application to admit a new State and makes a recommendation to the UNGA.[88] In these ways, the UNSC has the capacity to shape the legal complexion of self-determination matters through its general authorities under the Charter.

One notable illustration of the activity of the UNSC in self-determination matters relates to the decolonization of Namibia.[89] The United Nations was seized with the manner of South Africa's administration of Namibia under the League of Nations Mandate for South West Africa. The UNSC adopted a series of resolutions concerning the situation in Namibia, notably Resolution 276 (1970), which declared the continued presence of South Africa in Namibia, following termination of the Mandate by the UNGA, to be illegal and called upon UN Member States to take action accordingly.[90] UNSC Resolution 276 (1970) was assessed to be binding on UN Member States pursuant to Article 25 of the UN Charter.[91] The UNSC subsequently requested an advisory opinion from the ICJ to ascertain 'the legal consequences for States of the continued presence of South Africa in Namibia, notwithstanding

Advisory Opinion, ICJ Rep 1971, 16 (hereinafter *Namibia* (1971)) paras 111–16 (discussing S/Res/276 (30 Jan 1970)).

[87] See *Question of East Timor: Report of the Secretary-General*, A/53/951 / S/1999/513 (5 May 1999) (Attaching agreements concerning modalities for the exercise of self-determination by the people of East Timor); S/Res/1264 (15 Sept 1999) (Taking note of the outcome of the UN-facilitated referendum through which the people of East Timor achieved self-government through independence); S/Res/1272 (25 Oct 1999) (Establishing the United Nations Transitional Administration in East Timor (UNTAET)). The UNGA subsequently recognized the independence of East Timor (A/Res/56/282 (8 May 2002)) and admitted East Timor to the United Nations (A/Res/57/3 (27 Sept 2002)).

[88] UN Charter art 4(2).

[89] See John Dugard, 'The Revocation of the Mandate for South West Africa' (1968) 62(1) *AJIL* 78; John F. Murphy, 'Whither Now Namibia' (1972) 6(1) *Cornell International Law Journal* 1, 4–11; Crawford (n 17) 591–95.

[90] S/Res/276 (30 Jan 1970).

[91] *Namibia* (1971) paras 111–16. See UN Charter art 25.

Security Council resolution 276 (1970)'.[92] Because the UNSC had already determined South Africa's presence in Namibia to be unlawful, the ICJ was asked only to identify the legal consequences flowing from that unlawful situation. The advice provided by the ICJ in response to the UNSC request for an advisory opinion, in particular the consequences for third-States arising from the unlawful conduct at issue, was itself informed by UNSC Resolution 276 (1970).[93] In Resolution 301 (1971), adopted in response to the advisory opinion, the UNSC 'recogniz[ed] the legitimacy of the movement of the people of Namibia against the illegal occupation of their Territory by the South African authorities and their right to self-determination and independence'.[94]

Later, under Resolution 435 (1978), the UNSC established the United Nations Transition Assistance Group 'to ensure the early independence of Namibia through free elections under the supervision and control of the United Nations',[95] a peacekeeping mission viewed to have been a success.[96] The UNSC ultimately recommended that Namibia be admitted to membership in the United Nations in Resolution 652 (1990),[97] following which Namibia was admitted by the UNGA.[98] The actions of the UNSC regarding the situation in Namibia are illustrative of the capacity of the UNSC to impact international law and influence matters concerning decolonization with implications for the right to self-determination more broadly.[99]

92 S/Res/284 (29 July 1970).

93 *Namibia* (1971) paras 119–24. While the basis for the binding character of UNSC Resolution 276 (1970) upon UN Member States is Article 25 of the UN Charter, the ICJ identified the legal consequences arising from the illegal situation as opposable *erga omnes* and thereby reaching beyond the UN Charter and its Member States: ibid para 126.

94 S/Res/301 (20 Oct 1971) preambular para 7. See also para 6.

95 S/Res/435 (29 Sept 1978).

96 Frederic L. Kirgis Jr, 'The Security Council's First Fifty Years' (1995) 89(3) *AJIL* 506, 538.

97 S/Res/652 (17 Apr 1990).

98 A/Res/S-18/1 (23 Apr 1990).

99 See Chapter 4.b.

11
International Dispute Settlement

a. Overview

The peaceful settlement of disputes is a cornerstone of the contemporary rules-based international order. The UN Charter, at Article 1(1), provides that one purpose of the United Nations is to 'bring about by peaceful means . . . adjustment or settlement of international disputes or situations which may lead to a breach of the peace'.[1] International organs established to this end include the ICJ, the principal judicial organ of the United Nations.[2] Situations concerning the performance of obligations related to self-determination have repeatedly been placed before the ICJ.[3] While Chapter 4 detailed the substantive content of ICJ caselaw regarding self-determination, this chapter considers procedural and structural aspects of international dispute settlement relevant in practice to the right to self-determination.

This chapter begins by identifying the entitlement of States, with a common legal interest in the performance of obligations *erga omnes*, to invoke the international responsibility of a breaching State. Next, this chapter addresses the general principle that the consent of disputing parties to adjudication is a prerequisite to the exercise of jurisdiction over States under international law. After discussing standing and jurisdiction in relation to self-determination, this chapter evaluates the way in which the ICJ advisory procedure has been utilized as an alternative to the contentious, dispute-settlement paradigm to address disputes implicating self-determination, including to adjudge State responsibility for breaches of obligations arising from the right. This chapter then discusses instances of collateral adjudication of self-determination issues in fora other than the ICJ, and how ICJ

[1] Charter of the United Nations art 1(1), XV UNCIO 335 (26 June 1945, entered into force 24 Oct 1945) (hereinafter UN Charter).

[2] Statute of the International Court of Justice art 1, XV UNCIO 355 (26 June 1945, entered into force 24 Oct 1945) (hereinafter ICJ Statute); UN Charter art 92.

[3] See Chapter 4.

The Right to Self-Determination in International Law. Thomas Weatherall, Oxford University Press.
 DOI: 10.1093/9780197798119.003.0012

caselaw has impacted such proceedings. Finally, this chapter considers historic precedents for the establishment of ad hoc bodies to address international disputes with self-determination implications.

b. Entitlement to Invoke International Responsibility

The common legal interest of States in the performance of an obligation *erga omnes* confers upon those States the entitlement to invoke the international responsibility of a State in breach of such an obligation.[4] The entitlement of a non-injured State to invoke international responsibility for breach of an obligation *erga omnes* on the basis of a common legal interest in its performance is reflected in the caselaw of the ICJ concerning obligations *erga omnes partes*.[5] This rule is reflected at Article 48 of the ILC Articles on State Responsibility.[6] This consequence of the general legal interest of States in the performance of obligations *erga omnes* is understood to apply to both obligations *erga omnes partes* arising under certain multilateral international agreements, which obligations are owed to States parties to such agreements, as well as obligations *erga omnes* under CIL, as obligations owed to

[4] See Chapter 5.d.

[5] *Application of the Convention on the Prevention and Punishment of the Crime of Genocide in the Gaza Strip (South Africa v Israel)*, Provisional Measures, Order of 26 January 2024, ICJ Rep 2024 (hereinafter *Genocide Convention (South Africa v Israel)* (2024)) para 34; *Application of the Convention against Torture and Other Cruel, Inhuman or Degrading Treatment or Punishment (Canada and Netherlands v Syrian Arab Republic)*, Provisional Measures, Order of 16 November 2023, ICJ Rep 2023, 587 (hereinafter *Torture Convention* (2023)) para 57; *Application of the Convention on the Prevention and Punishment of the Crime of Genocide (The Gambia v Myanmar)*, Preliminary Objections, Judgment, ICJ Rep 2022, 477 (hereinafter *Genocide Convention (The Gambia v Myanmar)* (2022)) paras 106–14; *Application of the Convention on the Prevention and Punishment of the Crime of Genocide (The Gambia v Myanmar)*, Provisional Measures, Order of 23 January 2020, ICJ Rep 2020, 3 (hereinafter *Genocide Convention (The Gambia v Myanmar)* (2020)) para 41; *Questions relating to the Obligation to Prosecute or Extradite (Belgium v Senegal)*, Judgment, ICJ Rep 2012, 422 (hereinafter *Prosecute or Extradite* (2012)) paras 68–70. See also *Application of the International Convention on the Elimination of All Forms of Racial Discrimination (Armenia v. Azerbaijan)*, Provisional Measures, Order of 7 December 2021, ICJ Rep 2021, 382 para 57.

[6] ILC Draft Articles on Responsibility of States for Internationally Wrongful Acts art 48(1), UN Doc A/56/10, Report of the International Law Commission on the Work of its Fifty-Third Session, [2001] II(2) *YbILC* 26 et seq, UN Doc A/CN.4/SER.A/2001/Add.1 (Part 2) (hereinafter ILC ARSIWA).

the international community as a whole.[7] The entitlement to invoke international responsibility on the basis of a common legal interest represents an expansion of the general rule governing invocation of responsibility by an injured or specially affected State.[8]

The absence of a requirement of injury or special interest by a State invoking responsibility for breach of an obligation *erga omnes* is of practical relevance to the beneficiaries of such an obligation. The ICJ noted, in *Prosecute or Extradite* (2012), that '[i]f a special interest were required for that purpose, in many cases no State would be in the position to make such a claim'.[9] Indeed, with respect to obligations *erga omnes* related to the right to self-determination, it may often be the case that no State can be said to have been injured by the breach of such an obligation; there may similarly be no State with a special interest in such a breach. Even so, it does not follow that there is no beneficiary of the obligation breached in such cases. The ICJ took note of this practical reality in *Namibia* (1971), where it recalled that 'all States should bear in mind that the injured entity is a people which must look to the international community for assistance in its progress towards the goals for which the sacred trust was instituted' under the Mandate System, i.e. 'the self-determination and independence of the peoples concerned'.[10] The ILC, in its commentary to Article 48 of the Articles on State Responsibility, noted in this regard a distinction 'between the capacity of the applicant State to raise the matter and the interests of the beneficiaries of the obligation'.[11] This distinction was illustrated by unsuccessful proceedings instituted by Ethiopia and Liberia on behalf of the people of Namibia in *South West Africa Cases* (1966) prior to *Barcelona Traction* (1970),[12] and more recently in

[7] Ibid art 48, Commentary para 6. See Chapter 5.d.i.

[8] Cf ILC ARSIWA art 42.

[9] *Prosecute or Extradite* (2012) para 69. See also *Genocide Convention (The Gambia v Myanmar)* (2022) para 108.

[10] *Legal Consequences for States of the Continued Presence of South Africa in Namibia (South West Africa) notwithstanding Security Council Resolution 276 (1970)*, Advisory Opinion, ICJ Rep 1971, 16 (hereinafter *Namibia* (1971)) paras 53, 127.

[11] ILC ARSIWA art 48, Commentary para 12.

[12] In *South West Africa Cases*, the 'injured entity' was the people of South West Africa on whose behalf Ethiopia and Liberia had instituted proceedings. See *South West Africa Cases (Ethiopia v South Africa; Liberia v South Africa)*, Preliminary Objections, Judgment, ICJ Rep 1962, 319; *South West Africa Cases (Ethiopia v South Africa; Liberia v South Africa)*, Second Phase, Judgment, ICJ Rep 1966, 6. As discussed in Chapter 5, the introduction of the *erga omnes* doctrine by the ICJ in *Barcelona Traction* (1970) may be viewed as a recalibration by the court following its rejection of claims by Ethiopia and Liberia in *South West Africa Cases* (1966).

different contexts, in proceedings successfully instituted under the Genocide Convention and the Torture Convention.[13] The beneficiaries of obligations *erga omnes* may therefore be peoples rather than States, as with obligations related to the right to self-determination, and the 'shared values' reflected by such obligations, in the view of the ICJ, give rise to a common legal interest of States in their performance in favour of their beneficiaries.[14]

As the beneficiary of an obligation *erga omnes* may differ from the State invoking responsibility for its breach, the remedies that such State might claim may differ in certain respects from those that might be claimed by an injured or specially affected State. This is reflected at Article 48(2) of the ILC Articles on State Responsibility, which contemplates the remedies that might be claimed by a State other than an injured State, in the interest of the injured State or of the beneficiaries of the obligation breached.[15] Practice illustrates that States invoking responsibility for breach of obligations *erga omnes* on the basis of their common legal interest have sought remedies that are not directed towards the benefit of the invoking State. Instead, in such cases, States invoking responsibility have sought remedies on behalf of the beneficiaries of obligations *erga omnes* or in furtherance of performance of such obligations themselves.[16]

c. Jurisdiction over States under International Law

The *erga omnes* character of an obligation does not impact the requirement that jurisdiction over a State under international law requires consent. The judgment of the ICJ in *Monetary Gold* (1954) reflects 'a well-established principle of international law' that the competence of a court to exercise

[13] *Genocide Convention (South Africa v Israel)* (2024) para 34; *Torture Convention* (2023) para 57; *Genocide Convention (The Gambia v Myanmar)* (2022) para 108. See similarly *Prosecute or Extradite* (2012) para 69.

[14] See *Genocide Convention (The Gambia v Myanmar)* (2020) para 56.

[15] ILC ARSIWA art 48(2). These remedies are cessation, assurances and guarantees of non-repetition, and performance of the obligation of reparation in the interest of the injured State or beneficiaries of the obligation breached.

[16] *Genocide Convention (South Africa v Israel)* (2024) para 2; *Torture Convention* (2023) para 2; *Genocide Convention (The Gambia v Myanmar)* (2020) para 2; *Prosecute or Extradite* (2012) paras 13–14, 71.

jurisdiction over a State depends upon the consent of that State to such jurisdiction.[17] In the absence of a State's consent to jurisdiction, a court may not exercise jurisdiction over that State. This principle is undisturbed by the *erga omnes* character of the obligation at issue in a dispute. In *East Timor* (1995), the only contentious case directly addressing the right to self-determination brought before the ICJ to date,[18] the court distinguished between consent to jurisdiction and the character of the obligation at issue.[19] The ICJ explained that the *erga omnes* character of obligations arising from the right to self-determination was insufficient to overcome the requirement of consent to the court's jurisdiction by the parties to a dispute.[20] Breach of an obligation *erga omnes* is therefore not sufficient to engage the jurisdiction of the ICJ, a point that the court restated in *Armed Activities* (2006).[21] In *Armed Activities* (2006), the ICJ extended this conclusion to peremptory norms, such that the *jus cogens* status of a rule subject to a dispute is also insufficient to overcome the requirement of consent to the court's jurisdiction by parties to such dispute.[22]

d. Advisory Proceedings before the International Court of Justice

The practice of the ICJ regarding advisory proceedings concerning self-determination has differed markedly from its contentious record. As noted above, the ICJ found that it lacked jurisdiction in *East Timor* (1995), the

[17] *Case of the Monetary Gold removed from Rome in 1943 (Italy v France, United Kingdom, and United States of America)*, Preliminary Question, Judgment, ICJ Rep 1954, 19 (hereinafter *Monetary Gold* (1954)) 32. See also *East Timor (Portugal v Australia)*, Judgment, ICJ Rep 1995, 90 (hereinafter *East Timor* (1995)) para 26; *Armed Activities on the Territory of the Congo (New Application: 2002) (Democratic Republic of the Congo v Rwanda)*, Jurisdiction and Admissibility, Judgment, ICJ Rep 2006, 6 (hereinafter *Armed Activities* (2006)) para 125.

[18] Cf *Case Concerning the Northern Cameroons (Cameroon v United Kingdom)*, Preliminary Objections, Judgment, ICJ Rep 1963, 15; *Certain Phosphate Lands in Nauru (Nauru v Australia)*, Preliminary Objections, Judgment, ICJ Rep 1992, 240 (summarized supra Chapter 4 n 7).

[19] See Chapter 4.d.

[20] *East Timor* (1995) para 29. For discussion of the indispensable third party principle in this case, see Christine M. Chinkin, 'Symposium: The East Timor Case before the International Court of Justice, East Timor Moves into the World Court' (1993) 4(2) *EJIL* 206, 218–22. See also Christian J. Tams, *Enforcing Obligations Erga Omnes in International Law* (CUP 2005) 183–85.

[21] *Armed Activities* (2006) paras 64, 125.

[22] Ibid.

single contentious case expressly addressing the right to self-determination that has been brought before it. By contrast, the ICJ has to date expressly addressed self-determination in six advisory opinions: *Namibia* (1971), *Western Sahara* (1975), *The Wall* (2004), *Kosovo* (2010), *Chagos Archipelago* (2019), and *Palestine* (2024).[23] The paucity of contentious cases squarely addressing self-determination as compared to advisory opinions may at least in part be informed by the procedural rules discussed in the previous sections. Other contributing factors might include that subjects of the right to self-determination—peoples—may not in every instance be positioned to engage mechanisms of international dispute settlement. Notably, in this regard, advisory proceedings before the ICJ concerning self-determination have generally involved a beneficiary of the right that is not the population of a State.[24] Recourse by the political organs of the United Nations to the advisory procedure of the ICJ in matters concerning self-determination may also be a product of the particular institutional role of the United Nations in monitoring implementation of associated obligations, especially in the context of decolonization.[25]

i. Nexus between Advisory Opinions and Dispute Resolution

Chapter XIV of the UN Charter confers upon the UNGA and UNSC the authority to request from the ICJ 'an advisory opinion on any legal question'.[26] This competence is distinct from that of the ICJ to adjudicate disputes in contentious proceedings between States.[27] Chapter IV of the ICJ Statute addresses the competence of the ICJ to render advisory opinions. In particular, Article 65 provides the authority to render an advisory opinion on 'any legal question' at the request of whatever bodies are so authorized under

[23] See Chapter 4.

[24] See e.g. ICJ Statute art 34(1) ('Only states may be parties in cases before the Court'). *Chagos* (2019) is the exception: the beneficiary of the right to self-determination in that opinion was the people of Mauritius. See *Legal Consequences of the Separation of the Chagos Archipelago from Mauritius in 1965*, Advisory Opinion, ICJ Rep 2019, 95 (hereinafter *Chagos* (2019)) para 170.

[25] See Chapter 10.

[26] UN Charter art 96(1). See also art 96(2) (setting out the capacity of other UN organs and specialized agencies to seek advisory opinions from the ICJ).

[27] ICJ Statute ch II. See also UN Charter art 93.

the UN Charter.[28] Article 65 is formulated in discretionary terms: the ICJ '*may* give an advisory opinion'.[29] The jurisprudence of the ICJ indicates that only 'compelling reasons' may lead the ICJ to decline to render an advisory opinion in response to a request otherwise falling within its competence.[30]

While the ICJ has not, to date, exercised its discretion to decline to render an advisory opinion, the predecessor to the ICJ, the Permanent Court of International Justice (PCIJ), once declined to render an advisory opinion, in *Eastern Carelia* (1923).[31] In *Eastern Carelia* (1923), the PCIJ declined a request by the League of Nations concerning certain obligations of Russia on the basis of the lack of Russia's consent, which consent was required as a threshold matter because Russia was not a member of the League of Nations.[32] *Eastern Carelia* (1923) is often understood to stand for the proposition that an advisory proceeding may not be utilized to adjudicate a dispute between States without their consent.[33] However, the ICJ revisited this holding in *Interpretation of Peace Treaties with Bulgaria, Hungary and Romania* (1951) and explained why, in its view, advisory proceedings do not call for the consent required to adjudicate disputes in contentious proceedings.[34] The ICJ distinguished between the consent of States parties to a dispute required to submit that dispute for adjudication and a request for an advisory opinion related to 'a legal question actually pending between States', i.e. the substance of a dispute.[35] Even where advice is requested in relation to

[28] ICJ Statute art 65.

[29] Ibid (emphasis added).

[30] *Legal Consequences arising from the Policies and Practices of Israel in the Occupied Palestinian Territory, including East Jerusalem*, Advisory Opinion, ICJ Rep 2024 (hereinafter *Palestine* (2024)) para 31; *Accordance with International Law of the Unilateral Declaration of Independence in Respect of Kosovo*, Advisory Opinion, ICJ Rep 2010, 403 para 30; *Legal Consequences of the Construction of a Wall in the Occupied Palestinian Territory*, Advisory Opinion, ICJ Rep 2004, 136 (hereinafter *Wall* (2004)) para 44; *Judgments of the Administrative Tribunal of the ILO upon Complaints Made against the UNESCO*, Advisory Opinion, ICJ Rep 1956, 77, 86.

[31] *Status of Eastern Carelia*, PCIJ Series B No 5, Advisory Opinion (1923).

[32] Ibid 27–29.

[33] Richard Falk, 'The *Kosovo* Advisory Opinion: Conflict Resolution and Precedent' (2011) 105(1) *AJIL* 50, 53.

[34] *Interpretation of Peace Treaties*, First Phase, Advisory Opinion, ICJ Rep 1950, 65, 71. See also *Western Sahara*, Advisory Opinion, ICJ Rep 1975, 12 (hereinafter *Western Sahara* (1975)) para 31; *Wall* (2004) paras 46–48.

[35] See Rules of Court (1978) art 102 (14 Apr 1978, entered into force 1 July 1978) (as amended) (discussing the procedures applicable when 'an advisory opinion is requested upon a legal question actually pending between two or more States'). Conversely, the ICJ has observed that '[t]he fact that the question put to the Court *does not* relate to a specific dispute should consequently not lead the Court to decline to give the opinion requested'. *Legality of the Threat or*

'a legal question actually pending between States', the ICJ explained, consent of the disputing parties is not required because an advisory opinion takes the form of non-binding advice to a requesting organ of the United Nations, rather than a binding judgment issued to the parties to the dispute. Where an advisory proceeding implicates a bilateral dispute, the ICJ has emphasized that the dispute has arisen in the work of the organ requesting advice.[36]

In most advisory proceedings concerning self-determination, objections were raised on the basis of the lack of consent to adjudicate a dispute as a reason for the ICJ to exercise its discretion to decline to render an advisory opinion.[37] Notwithstanding the distinction between the principles of jurisdiction applicable in its contentious and advisory proceedings, there remains a tension in the effective adjudication by the ICJ of a bilateral dispute through its advisory procedure.[38] The general principle of consent, articulated in *Monetary Gold* (1954), refers not only to jurisdiction as a general matter, but to the competence to 'decide [] a dispute', meaning '[t]o adjudicate upon the international responsibility' of the State concerned.[39] Perhaps in recognition of this tension, where an advisory proceeding related to self-determination has implicated an underlying dispute, the ICJ has attempted to distinguish its advisory proceeding from the associated dispute in various ways, including on the basis of relevant functions of the United Nations and 'the broader frame of reference' within which a request was situated.[40] In

Use of Nuclear Weapons, Advisory Opinion, ICJ Rep 1996, 266 (hereinafter *Nuclear Weapons* (1996)) para 15.

---

[36] Rosalyn Higgins, *Problems and Process: International Law and How We Use It* (Clarendon Press 1995) 200–01. See *Western Sahara* (1975) para 34; *Wall* (2004) para 50; *Chagos* (2019) paras 86, 88; *Palestine* (2024) para 35.

[37] *Namibia* (1971) para 30 (South Africa objecting); *Western Sahara* (1975) para 28 (Spain objecting); *Wall* (2004) para 46 (Israel objecting); *Legal Consequences of the Separation of the Chagos Archipelago from Mauritius in 1965* (Request by the United Nations General Assembly for an Advisory Opinion), Written Statement of the United Kingdom of Great Britain and Northern Ireland (15 Feb 2018) 101–16 (United Kingdom objecting); *Legal Consequences arising from the Policies and Practices of Israel in the Occupied Palestinian Territory, including East Jerusalem*, Statement of the State of Israel pursuant to the Court's Order of 3 February 2023 relating to the advisory proceedings initiated by UN General Assembly resolution 77/247 (24 July 2023) (Israel objecting).

[38] See John R. Crook, 'The 2004 Judicial Activity of the International Court of Justice' (2005) 99(2) *AJIL* 450, 452–53.

[39] *Monetary Gold* (1954) 32. See *East Timor* (1995) para 26; *Armed Activities* (2006) para 125. See also Chapter 11.c.

[40] *See Namibia* (1971) paras 32–33; *Western Sahara*, Order of 22 May 1975, ICJ Rep 1975, 6, 7–8 (One judge observed that the case 'assumed a quasi-contentious form . . . and was, from the

none of these cases did the ICJ invoke the *erga omnes* character of the legal obligations implicated to justify rendering an advisory opinion. Across its defences of advisory proceedings implicating ongoing disputes, the evolution of the approach of the ICJ indicates an increasing willingness to at least acknowledge the connection of its advisory procedure to a dispute. Shifting justifications suggest that the ICJ has itself grappled with the propriety of exercising its advisory function in this way.

ii. Legal Consequences and Effects of Advisory Opinions

Despite the extent to which the ICJ has attempted to distinguish its contentious and advisory proceedings in relation to an underlying dispute, advisory opinions addressing self-determination have borne hallmarks of judgments in contentious proceedings. In four advisory opinions concerning obligations related to the right to self-determination—*Namibia* (1971),[41] *The Wall* (2004),[42] *Chagos Archipelago* (2019),[43] and *Palestine* (2024)[44]—the ICJ rendered findings on the international responsibility of responsible States for internationally wrongful acts. The ICJ further identified legal consequences for such responsible States, namely obligations of cessation of wrongful conduct in each of these cases, as well as an obligation of reparation in *The Wall* (2004) and *Palestine* (2024).[45] Where the ICJ renders findings on State responsibility and associated obligations of a responsible State in the context of an ongoing dispute—i.e. 'adjudicate[s] upon the international responsibility' of a responsible State[46]—it becomes difficult to effectively differentiate between the advisory procedure and contentious proceedings related to the underlying dispute.[47]

outset, of a hybrid character': *Western Sahara* (1975) Sep Op de Castro 142); *Wall* (2004) paras 49–50; *Chagos* (2019) paras 86–90; *Palestine* (2024) paras 34–35.

---

41 *Namibia* (1971) para 118.
42 *Wall* (2004) paras 147–53.
43 *Chagos* (2019) para 177.
44 *Palestine* (2024) paras 267–72.
45 *Wall* (2004) paras 152–53, 163; *Palestine* (2024) paras 269–71.
46 *Monetary Gold* (1954) 32.
47 See *Chagos* (2019), Declaration of Judge Tomka para 8; ibid, Dissenting Opinion of Judge Donoghue para 1.

Formally, '[t]he purpose of the advisory function is . . . to offer legal advice to the organs and institutions requesting the opinion'.[48] However, although advisory opinions are not binding on any State or the requesting organ in the way that a judgment in a contentious proceeding is binding as to the parties to a dispute,[49] they are generally recognized to provide authoritative statements of international law.[50] The authoritative character of an advisory opinion was described by the International Tribunal for the Law of the Sea (ITLOS) Special Chamber in *Maritime Delimitation (Mauritius / Maldives)* (2021), in view of the legal conclusions rendered by the ICJ in *Chagos Archipelago* (2019), as having 'legal effect'.[51] This authoritative character of an ICJ advisory opinion is illustrated by the invocation of advisory opinions addressing self-determination by other international courts and tribunals. For instance, the Grand Chamber of the CJEU, in *Council of the European Union v Front Polisario* (2016),[52] and *Organisation juive européenne, Vignoble Psagot Ltd v Ministre de l'Économie et des Finances* (2019),[53] adopted and applied legal conclusions related to self-determination rendered by the ICJ in *Western Sahara* (1975) and *The Wall* (2004), respectively.[54] Pre-Trial Chamber I of the ICC, in identifying and applying the right to self-determination as an 'internationally recognized human right[]' within the meaning of Article 21(3) of the ICC Statute, relied on legal conclusions of the ICJ in *Namibia* (1971), *Western Sahara* (1975), *The Wall* (2004), and *Kosovo* (2010).[55] And,

48 *Nuclear Weapons* (1996) para 15.

49 ICJ Statute art 59.

50 See e.g. *Dispute Concerning Delimitation of the Maritime Boundary Between Mauritius and Maldives in the Indian Ocean (Mauritius / Maldives)*, ITLOS, Case No 28, Preliminary Objections, Judgment (28 Jan 2021) (hereinafter *Maritime Delimitation (Mauritius / Maldives)* (2021)); Case T-279/19 *Front populaire pour la libération de la Saguia-el-Hamra et du Rio de Oro (Front Polisario) v Council of the European Union*, General Court, Judgment (29 Sept 2021) (hereinafter *Polisario III* (2021)) para 386. See Falk (n 33) 52–54; W. Michael Reisman, 'The Constitutional Crisis in the United Nations' (1993) 87(1) *AJIL* 83, 92.

51 *Maritime Delimitation (Mauritius / Maldives)* (2021) paras 203, 205.

52 Case C-104/16 *Council of the European Union vs Front populaire pour la libération de la saguia-el-hamra et du rio de oro (Front Polisario)*, General Court, Judgment (21 Dec 2016) (hereinafter *Polisario II* (2016)) paras 88–91, 104–06. *See also Polisario III* (2021) para 386.

53 Case C-363/18 *Organisation juive européenne, Vignoble Psagot Ltd v Ministre de l'Économie et des Finances*, Grand Chamber, Judgment (12 Nov 2019) paras 35, 48, 56.

54 See Chapter 11.e.ii.

55 *Decision on the 'Prosecution request pursuant to article 19(3) for a ruling on the Court's territorial jurisdiction in Palestine'*, PTC I, ICC-01/18-143 (5 Feb 2021) (hereinafter *Situation in Palestine* (2021)) paras 119–23 (note that the PTC also referred to *East Timor* (1995)). See also Rome Statute of the International Criminal Court art 21(3), 2187 UNTS 90 (17 July 1998, entered into force 1 July 2002) (hereinafter Rome Statute). See Chapter 11.e.iii.

in *Maritime Delimitation (Mauritius / Maldives)* (2021), the ITLOS Special Chamber addressed preliminary objections to its jurisdiction on the basis that *Chagos Archipelago* (2019) had resolved the sovereignty dispute over the Chagos Archipelago,[56] a bilateral dispute which the ITLOS Tribunal had previously found it lacked jurisdiction to adjudicate.[57] These examples illustrate the authoritative nature of ICJ advisory opinions, on matters of self-determination, and demonstrate how such opinions may affect the complexion of an underlying dispute notwithstanding their non-binding character.

This practice of the ICJ in the context of self-determination signals how the court may influence international disputes through the advice it renders to requesting United Nations bodies.[58] The political impact of an advisory opinion applying the law of State responsibility to an ongoing dispute may be significant, as illustrated by negotiations between the United Kingdom and Mauritius undertaken following the advisory opinion rendered in *Chagos Archipelago* (2019), and announcement of an agreement to transfer sovereignty over the Chagos Archipelago consistent with that advisory opinion.[59] The jurisprudence of the ICJ suggests that, if what is past is prologue, self-determination issues may continue to be adjudicated primarily through its advisory procedure rather than in contentious proceedings.

e. Collateral Consideration of Disputes

Implicit in the invocation of ICJ advisory opinions by other international courts and tribunals is that disputes related to self-determination may be addressed collaterally by fora other than the ICJ. Such cases may implicate what has been referred to as 'incidental jurisdiction', or the exercise of jurisdiction by an international court or tribunal over a legal question which,

[56] *Maritime Delimitation (Mauritius / Maldives)* (2021) paras 247–51. See Chapter 11.e.i.

[57] *Award in the Arbitration regarding the Chagos Marine Protected Area between Mauritius and the United Kingdom of Great Britain and Northern Ireland*, XXXI RIAA 359 (18 Mar 2015) (hereinafter *Chagos Award* (2015)) paras 221, 547.

[58] See e.g. *Speech by H.E. Judge Shi Jiuyong, President of the International Court of Justice, to the Sixth Committee of the General Assembly of the United Nations: The advisory function of the International Court of Justice* (5 Nov 2004) 4.

[59] Press Release, *UK and Mauritius joint statement, 3 October 2024*, at https://www.gov.uk/government/news/joint-statement-between-uk-and-mauritius-3-october-2024.

while ordinarily beyond its competence, may fall within its jurisdiction because of its connection to resolving the dispute before it.[60] In some cases, legal proceedings on an ancillary issue may be undertaken with designs to achieve legal support for an underlying dispute concerning a people and its entitlement to self-determination in relation to contested territorial sovereignty. In other cases, litigation may incidentally address aspects of self-determination ancillary to the principal matter in question and, as a result, a court may opine on the self-determination implications of an underlying dispute.

i. International Tribunal for the Law of the Sea

A series of proceedings initiated by Mauritius under the UN Convention on the Law of the Sea (UNCLOS) offers an example at once of the limits of incidental jurisdiction in relation to self-determination and the way in which an ICJ advisory opinion may impact a bilateral dispute. In March 2015, a Tribunal constituted pursuant to UNCLOS Annex VII rendered its award in the arbitration regarding the Chagos Marine Protected Area.[61] Certain claims brought by Mauritius against the United Kingdom under UNCLOS concerned the establishment of a Marine Protected Area (MPA) surrounding the Chagos Archipelago, while other claims regarding the *de jure* costal State in relation to the Chagos Archipelago were 'properly characterized as relating to sovereignty over the Chagos Archipelago'.[62] The Tribunal acknowledged its jurisdiction under UNCLOS Article 288(1) 'to mak[e] such findings of fact or ancillary determinations of law as are necessary to resolve the dispute presented to it', but considered that such jurisdiction did not appertain where the 'real issue in the case' and the 'object of the claim' do no relate to interpretation or application of UNCLOS; 'an incidental connection between the dispute and some matter regulated by the Convention is insufficient to bring the dispute, as a whole', within the Tribunal's competence.[63] Because the 'dispute

[60] See e.g. *Chagos Award* (2015) para 220. See Peter Tzeng, 'The Implicated Issue Problem: Indispensable Issues and Incidental Jurisdiction' (2018) 50(2) *New York University Journal of International Law and Politics* 447, 454 n 31.
[61] *Chagos Award* (2015).
[62] Ibid para 212. See also para 230.
[63] Ibid para 220 (internal quotation and citation omitted).

regarding sovereignty' between Mauritius and the United Kingdom did not relate to interpretation or application of UNCLOS, the Tribunal found that it lacked jurisdiction to address claims based in that dispute.[64]

In June 2019, following the *Chagos Archipelago* (2019) advisory opinion rendered by the ICJ, Mauritius again instituted arbitral proceedings pursuant to UNCLOS Annex VII, this time against the Maldives, concerning delimitation of the maritime boundary with respect to the Chagos Archipelago.[65] The ITLOS Special Chamber to which the matter was referred regarded *Chagos Archipelago* (2019) as 'authoritative' and with 'legal effect' and, 'in light of the advisory opinion', rejected the 'matter-of-fact existence of a sovereignty dispute over the Chagos Archipelago'.[66] The Special Chamber proceeded to issue a judgment in April 2023 as to the delimitation of the maritime boundary between Mauritius and the Maldives relative to the Chagos Archipelago.[67] Claims by Mauritius under UNCLOS may be viewed in the context of its sustained effort to achieve legal support for its underlying sovereignty claims over the Chagos Archipelago through adjudication of UNCLOS claims.[68]

ii. Court of Justice of the European Union

A line of cases brought against the United Kingdom and institutions of the European Union provides a second illustration of the collateral invocation of an ICJ advisory opinion and its impact on the treatment of a sovereignty dispute. Claims in this line of cases were brought against the United Kingdom by Western Sahara Campaign UK, an advocacy group promoting

[64] Ibid paras 221, 230. The Tribunal found that it had jurisdiction to consider the compatibility of the MPA with certain provisions of the UNCLOS. The Tribunal found that the manner in which the United Kingdom established the MPA surrounding the Chagos Archipelago breached its obligations under UNCLOS. Ibid paras 544, 547.

[65] *Maritime Delimitation (Mauritius / Maldives)* (2021) para 1. See Thomas Burri & Jamie Trinidad, 'Introductory Note' (2021) 60(6) ILM 969.

[66] *Maritime Delimitation (Mauritius / Maldives)* (2021) paras 203, 205, 245.

[67] *Dispute Concerning Delimitation of the Maritime Boundary Between Mauritius and Maldives in the Indian Ocean (Mauritius / Maldives)*, ITLOS Case No 28, Judgment (28 Apr 2023).

[68] See Stephen Allen, 'Self-Determination, the *Chagos Advisory Opinion* and the Chagossians' (2020) 69(1) *ICLQ* 203, 205.

the self-determination of the people of Western Sahara,[69] and against institutions of the European Union by the Popular Front for the Liberation of Saguia el-Hamra and Rio de Oro (*Front Polisario*).[70] The claims in these cases challenged the applicability to Western Sahara of a tariff agreement concluded between the European Communities and Member States with Morocco,[71] and a fisheries agreement concluded between the European Community and Morocco.[72] By operation of the principle of self-determination (which provides that a NSGT maintains a separate and distinct territorial status from its administering power (including a 'de facto' administering power)), the territorial scope of treaties (VCLT Article 29), and the relative effect of treaties (VCLT Article 34, which requires the consent of a third party for it to be bound, the people of Western Sahara constituting such a third party), the Grand Chamber of the CJEU interpreted the tariff agreement as not applying to the territory of Western Sahara.[73] The same reasoning was applied by the Grand Chamber to the fisheries agreement.[74] In so finding, the

[69] Case C-266/16 *Western Sahara Campaign UK v Commissioners for Her Majesty's Revenue and Customs, Secretary of State for Environment, Food and Rural Affairs*, Grand Chamber, Judgment (27 Feb 2018) (hereinafter *Western Sahara Campaign I* (2018)) para 30.

[70] Joined Cases T-344/19 and T-356/19 *Popular Front for the Liberation of Saguia el-Hamra and Rio de Oro (Front Polisario) v Council of the European Union*, General Court, Judgment (29 Sept 2021) (hereinafter *Polisario IV* (2021)) para 6.

[71] Ibid paras 21–24. See Euro-Mediterranean Agreement establishing an association between the European Communities and their Member States, of the one part, and the Kingdom of Morocco, of the other part, (2000) *Official Journal of the European Communities* L 70/2 (18 Mar 2000). Following the withdrawal of the United Kingdom from the European Union, a new association agreement between the UK and Morocco was concluded, and its implementing regulations were unsuccessfully challenged, including on the basis that the underlying agreement was void for conflicting with a peremptory norm. See *Western Sahara Campaign UK v Secretary of State for International Trade et al* [2022] EWHC 3108 (Admin) [45], [159].

[72] *Polisario IV* (2021) paras 25–30. See Fisheries Partnership Agreement between the European Community and the Kingdom of Morocco, (2006) *Official Journal of the European Communities* L 141/4 (29 May 2006). For general background, see Eva Kassoti, 'Between *Sollen* and *Sein*: The CJEU's reliance on international law in the interpretation of economic agreements covering occupied territories' (2020) 33(2) *Leiden Journal of International Law* 371, 374–76.

[73] *Polisario II* (2016) paras 87–97, 123, 131–34. For summary and critical commentary, see Jed Odermatt, 'Council of the European Union v. Front Populaire pour la Libération de la Saguia-El-Hamra et Du Rio de Oro (Front Polisario)' (2017) 111(3) *AJIL* 731, 735–38; Kassoti (n 72) 377–83.

This overturned an earlier decision of the General Court, which had annulled the agreement: See Case T-512/12 *Front populaire pour la libération de la saguia-el-hamra et du rio de oro (Front Polisario) v Council of the European Union*, General Court, Judgment (10 Dec 2015). For summary and critical commentary, see Eva Kassoti, 'The *Front Polisario v. Council* Case: The General Court, *Völkerrechtsfreundlichkeit* and the External Aspect of European Integration (First Part)' (2017) 2(1) *European Papers* 339.

[74] *Western Sahara Campaign I* (2018) paras 61–64, 80–83. See Kassoti (n 73) 383–88.

Grand Chamber adopted and applied legal conclusions regarding the right of the people of Western Sahara to self-determination rendered by the ICJ in *Western Sahara* (1975).[75]

Each agreement was subsequently amended to expressly apply to Western Sahara, 'without prejudice to the position of Western Sahara', following consultation between EU institutions and 'the people concerned'. The General Court of the CJEU annulled both agreements on the basis that consultation of 'the people concerned' was insufficient to establish consent by the people of Western Sahara to be bound by the agreements.[76] The General Court looked to *Western Sahara* (1975), as previously applied by the Grand Chamber, for the applicable international law regarding the right of the people of Western Sahara to self-determination.[77] The foregoing CJEU cases may be contextualized as strategic litigation designed to achieve legal support for the *Front Polisario* in its opposition to Morocco's claim to sovereignty over Western Sahara.[78]

iii. International Criminal Court

Referral of the 'Situation in Palestine' to the ICC provides another example of the incidental consideration of the right to self-determination in the context of a dispute that would ordinarily fall beyond the competence of the court in question. In January 2015, Palestine lodged a declaration under the Rome Statute accepting the exercise of jurisdiction by the ICC over acts 'committed in the occupied Palestinian territory, including

[75] *Polisario II* (2016) paras 88, 91, 104–05. See also *Western Sahara Campaign I* (2018) paras 61–64.

[76] *Polisario III* (2021) paras 366, 391; *Polisario IV* (2021) paras 348, 364. The Grand Chamber dismissed appeals of these decisions. See Joined Cases C-778/21 P and C-798/21 P *European Commission and Council of the European Union v Front populaire pour la libération de la Saguia el-Hamra et du Rio de oro (Front Polisario)*, Grand Chamber, Judgment (4 Oct 2024); Joined Cases C-779/21 P and C-799/21 P *European Commission and Council of the European Union v Front populaire pour la libération de la Saguia el-Hamra et du Rio de oro (Front Polisario)*, Grand Chamber, Judgment (4 Oct 2024).

[77] *Polisario III* (2021) para 91; *Polisario IV* (2021) para 143.

[78] Cedric Ryngaert & Rutger Fransen, 'EU extraterritorial obligations with respect to trade with occupied territories: Reflections after the case of *Front Polisario* before EU courts' (2018) 2(1) *Europe and the World: A law review* 1, 19; see also Odermatt (n 73) 737.

East Jerusalem, since June 13, 2014'.[79] In order to determine the territorial scope of Palestine's acceptance of jurisdiction of the ICC over alleged crimes committed in the Occupied Palestinian Territory (OPT), in January 2020, the ICC Prosecutor requested a ruling pursuant to Article 19(3) of the Rome Statute on the court's territorial jurisdiction in Palestine.[80] A divided Pre-Trial Chamber (PTC) rendered a decision on territorial jurisdiction in February 2021.[81] After determining that Palestine, a party to the Rome Statute, is a 'State' for purposes of Article 12(2)(a),[82] the PTC determined that the territorial jurisdiction of the court in the Situation in Palestine extends to the territories occupied by Israel since 1967 (Gaza and the West Bank, including East Jerusalem).[83]

Because the territorial parameters of the Prosecutor's investigation 'implicate the right to self-determination',[84] it was necessary in the view of the PTC to consider its findings in light of Article 21(3) of the Rome Statute, which provides that '[t]he application and interpretation of law pursuant to this article must be consistent with internationally recognized human rights'.[85] The PTC accordingly considered its finding on territorial jurisdiction in light of the right of the Palestinian people to self-determination.

> [I]n the view of the Chamber, the right to self-determination amounts to an 'internationally recognized human [right]' within the meaning of article 21(3) of the Statute. The Chamber notes that the United Nations General Assembly and the International Court of Justice have affirmed that this right finds application in relation to the Occupied Palestinian Territory. . . . Accordingly, it is the view of the Chamber that the above

[79] For background on Palestine's accession to the Rome Statute, see *Situation in Palestine* (2021) paras 1–2, 100–13. See also Office of the Prosecutor, ICC, *Situation in Palestine* (3 Apr 2012) (regarding disposition of an earlier January 2009 declaration by Palestine).

[80] *Prosecution request pursuant to article 19(3) for a ruling on the Court's territorial jurisdiction in Palestine*, ICC-01/18-12 (22 Jan 2020). See Rome Statute art 19(3) ('The Prosecutor may seek a ruling from the Court regarding a question of jurisdiction or admissibility').

[81] *Situation in Palestine* (2021). For commentary, see Anne Bayefsky, 'Introductory Note' (2021) 60(6) ILM 1038.

[82] Rome Statute art 12 (Preconditions to the exercise of jurisdiction).

[83] *Situation in Palestine* (2021) para 118.

[84] Ibid para 123.

[85] Rome Statute art 21(3) (Applicable law). See Mahnoush H. Arsanjani, 'The Rome Statute of the International Criminal Court' (1999) 93(1) *AJIL* 22, 29; William A. Schabas, *The International Criminal Court: A Commentary on the Rome Statute* (2nd edn, OUP 2017) 530–34.

> conclusion [regarding the scope of territorial jurisdiction] . . . is consistent with the right to self-determination.[86]

Although its reasoning was cursory, the PTC considered its determination of the scope of the court's territorial jurisdiction in relation to the OPT to be consistent with the right of the Palestinian people to self-determination in reference to legal conclusions of the ICJ in *The Wall* (2004) and UNGA resolutions to the same effect.[87] In short, acceptance of the consent of Palestine to the exercise of territorial jurisdiction by the court over the OPT comports with recognition of the right of the Palestinian people to self-determination in relation to that territory.[88]

f. Ad Hoc Dispute Resolution

There are precedents for the establishment of ad hoc bodies to address international disputes with self-determination implications. Recourse to such bodies provides an important contribution to practice from the standpoint of process as much as the substantive guidance rendered by such bodies.

i. League of Nations and the Aaland Islands

One example of ad hoc dispute resolution regards the dispute between Sweden and Finland over the Aaland Islands. In 1920, the League of Nations convened two separate bodies to advise respectively on the jurisdiction and merits phases of the dispute. The treatment of the Aaland Islands dispute by the League of Nations provides an early point of reference regarding ad hoc dispute resolution relevant to self-determination. The case is discussed in detail in Chapter 1.[89] Its resolution and Sweden's conduct were contemporaneously 'hailed as admirable examples of ideal international procedure'.[90]

[86] *Situation in Palestine* (2021) paras 122–23.

[87] Ibid para 121. For criticism, see ibid, Judge Péter Kovács' Partly Dissenting Opinion, ICC-01/18-143-Anx1 (5 Feb 2021) para 90.

[88] For background on Palestine, see supra Chapter 4 n 77.

[89] See Chapter 1.c.ii.

[90] Norman J. Padelford & K. Gösta A. Andersson, 'The Aaland Islands Question' (1939) 33(3) *AJIL* 465, 476.

ii. Arbitration Commission on Yugoslavia

A second example of ad hoc dispute resolution is the Arbitration Commission on Yugoslavia, commonly referred to as the 'Badinter Commission' in reference to its President. The Arbitration Commission was created by the European Community (EC) and its members in connection with the International Conference for Peace in Yugoslavia on 27 August 1991.[91] The EC established the Arbitration Commission 'in the framework of the peace conference' on Yugoslavia as a body to which 'relevant authorities could submit their differences'.[92] The Arbitration Commission was created by a declaration rather than a binding agreement between States, rendering its opinions of a non-binding, advisory character.[93] The Arbitration Commission was regarded, in its view, to be a consultative organ of the Peace Conference in reference to which it was created.[94] Its opinions were considered a 'subsidiary means for the determination of rules of law' within the meaning of Article 38(1)(d) of the ICJ Statute.[95]

The Arbitration Commission ultimately rendered fifteen opinions on a range of issues including State succession and self-determination.[96] These included two opinions relevant to self-determination, in response to questions raised by Serbia—Opinion No 2 and Opinion No 3—each dated 11 January 1992.[97]

In Opinion No 2, the Arbitration Commission responded to a question concerning the scope of the right to self-determination: 'Does the Serbian population in Croatia and Bosnia-Hercegovina, as one of the constituent peoples of Yugoslavia, have the right to self-determination?'[98] In responding, the

[91] 'Joint Statement' (28 Aug 1991), (1991) 24(7/8) *Bulletin of the European Communities* 115 (1.4.25) (hereinafter Joint Statement). See Matthew C. R. Craven, 'The European Community Arbitration Commission on Yugoslavia' (1995) 66(1) *British Yearbook of International Law* 333.

[92] Joint Statement 116.

[93] *Reactions of the members of the Arbitration Commission of the International Conference on the Former Yugoslavia to the statement made by the FRY Government on its competence*, paras 5–6, reproduced in (1993) 32(6) ILM 1579, 1583 (hereinafter *Reactions on Competence*). See Craven (n 91) 337–42, 350–51.

[94] *Interlocutory Decision (Opinions No. 8, 9 and 10)*, para 7, reproduced in (1992) 31(6) ILM 1518, 1521.

[95] *Reactions on Competence* para 6. See Craven (n 91) 351.

[96] For a survey of the opinions rendered by the Arbitration Commission, see Craven (n 91) 353–409.

[97] See Alain Pellet, 'The Opinions of the Badinter Arbitration Committee: A Second Breath for the Self-Determination of Peoples' (1992) 3(1) *EJIL* 178; Craven (n 91) 380–95.

[98] Opinion No 2.

Arbitration Commission stated that, while international law does not currently 'spell out all the implications' of the right to self-determination, 'the right to self-determination must not involve changes to existing frontiers at the time of independence (*uti possidetis juris*) except where the States concerned agree otherwise'.[99] Against this backdrop, the Arbitration Commission then identified the entitlement of minority groups within a State to the 'right to the recognition of their identity under international law', and referred to obligations of States to ensure respect for the rights of minorities.[100] The Arbitration Commission made reference to the way in which common Article 1 of the two human rights covenants 'establishes that the principle of the right to self-determination serves to safeguard human rights',[101] which oriented Opinion No 2 within the frame of the domestic aspect of the right to self-determination.[102]

In Opinion No 3, the Arbitration Commission responded to a question concerning frontiers: 'Can the internal boundaries between Croatia and Serbia and between Bosnia-Hercegovina and Serbia be regarded as frontiers in terms of public international law?'[103] The Arbitration Commission contextualized its response in light of its Opinion No 1, which found Yugoslavia to be 'in the process of breaking up', then identified a series of principles to guide the frontiers of successor States arising therefrom.[104] First, the Arbitration Commission referred generally to principles of respect for external frontiers and their inalterability except by agreement 'freely arrived at'.[105] Next, the Arbitration Commission applied the principle of *uti possidetis* with reference to *Frontier Dispute (Burkina Faso v Mali)* (1986), where the ICJ found *uti possidetis* to constitute 'a general principle, which is logically connected with the phenomenon of the obtaining of independence, wherever it occurs'.[106] Finally, the Arbitration Commission referred to the principle that forcible alteration of existing frontiers or boundaries is without legal effect.[107]

[99] Ibid s 1. See Chapter 7.e.

[100] Opinion No 2 s 2.

[101] Ibid s 3.

[102] See Chapter 8.

[103] Opinion No 3 s 2.

[104] Ibid ss 1–2.

[105] Ibid s 2.

[106] Ibid; *Frontier Dispute (Burkina Faso v Mali)* (1986) para 20. For a critique of this application, see Peter Radan, 'Post-Secession International Borders: A Critical Analysis of the Opinions of the Badinter Arbitration Commission' (2000) 24(1) *Melbourne University Law Review* 50. See Chapter 7.e. See similarly Opinion No 2 s 1.

[107] Opinion No 3 s 2.

12
Implementation and Enforcement

a. Overview

The foregoing chapters in this part, which addressed the United Nations system and international dispute settlement, primarily implicate the international aspect of self-determination. In the normal course, however, the right to self-determination is exercised domestically, and it is in this sense of its domestic aspect that the right to self-determination gives rise to obligations owed by States towards the peoples within their territories.[1] This chapter considers mechanisms invoked primarily by the population of a State, or a portion thereof, in relation to its own government, which most often implicates the domestic aspect of self-determination. The first section of this chapter analyses the practice of treaty bodies of an international character in relation to the right to self-determination. The next section considers the practice of treaty bodies of a regional character, including regional courts, regarding self-determination. Finally, this chapter considers ways in which domestic authorities implement and apply the right to self-determination through national constitutions and courts.

b. Treaty Bodies of an International Character

The principal source of the right to self-determination in treaty law is common Article 1 of the two human rights covenants.[2] The practice of international treaty bodies established to monitor implementation by States of their obligations under the human rights covenants—the Human Rights Committee (HRC) and the Committee on Economic, Social and Cultural Rights (CESCR)—thereby provides a point of reference regarding claims

[1] See Chapter 8.
[2] See Chapter 2.c.

The Right to Self-Determination in International Law. Thomas Weatherall, Oxford University Press.
 DOI: 10.1093/9780197798119.003.0013

by individuals and groups against States parties regarding their obligations under common Article 1.[3]

i. Human Rights Committee

The HRC is an independent body of experts established under Article 28 of the ICCPR to monitor implementation of the ICCPR by States parties. Under Article 40(1) of the ICCPR, States parties are obligated to 'undertake to submit reports on the measures they have adopted which give effect to the rights recognized' in the ICCPR.[4] In relation to this reporting requirement, the HRC, in General Comment No 12, provided substantive guidance regarding each of the three paragraphs of ICCPR Article 1 (the right to self-determination).[5] Through its reporting requirement, the ICCPR provides for a general mechanism by which to monitor the implementation of Article 1 by States parties, and thereby promotes a degree of accountability with respect to performance of such obligations. In practice, however, reporting by States parties regarding Article 1 has been viewed to be inadequate.[6]

The Optional Protocol to the ICCPR establishes an individual complaint mechanism in relation to the ICCPR.[7] Under Article 1 of the Optional Protocol, States parties recognize the competence of the HRC 'to receive and consider communications from individuals subject to [a State Party] jurisdiction who claim to be victims of a violation by that State Party of any of the rights set forth in the Covenant'.[8] Article 2 sets out an exhaustion requirement for 'individuals who claim that any of their rights enumerated in the

[3] The Committee on the Elimination of Racial Discrimination adopted a General Recommendation on the right to self-determination: see General Recommendation XXI (48), adopted at the 1147th meeting, 8 March 1996, in *Report of the Committee on the Elimination of Racial Discrimination*, Annex VIII.B 125, A/51/18.

[4] International Covenant on Civil and Political Rights art 40(1), 999 UNTS 171 (16 Dec 1966, entered into force 23 Mar 1976).

[5] HRC, *CCPR General Comment No. 12: The Right to Self-Determination of Peoples (Art 1)* (1984) (hereinafter HRC GC 12) paras 4–6.

[6] Ibid para 3. See also Paul M. Taylor, *A Commentary on the International Covenant on Civil and Political Rights: The UN Human Rights Committee's Monitoring of ICCPR Rights* (CUP 2020) 55–56 (discussing shortcomings of reporting by States parties regarding Article 1).

[7] Optional Protocol to the International Covenant on Civil and Political Rights, 999 UNTS 171 (16 Dec 1966, entered into force 23 Mar 1976) (hereinafter ICCPR Optional Protocol).

[8] Ibid art 1.

Covenant have been violated'.[9] According to 'its constant jurisprudence' on the question,[10] the HRC has determined that claims under ICCPR Article 1 are not cognizable under the individual complaint mechanism.[11] The inadmissibility of claims under ICCPR Article 1 results from the competence of the HRC to receive and consider communications from individuals, but not peoples, under the Optional Protocol. Put differently, '[t]he Optional Protocol provides a procedure under which individuals can claim that their individual rights have been violated. These rights are set out in part III of the Covenant, articles 6 to 27, inclusive'.[12] In effect, the HRC has determined that a claim invoking ICCPR Article 1 is inadmissible under the Optional Protocol because such a claim concerns a collective right of peoples that cannot be invoked by an individual.[13]

ICCPR Article 1 may nevertheless be relevant to the interpretation and application of other rights within the competence of the HRC under the Optional Protocol. It may be recalled that the domestic aspect of the right to self-determination, and in particular the entitlement to representative government as a component of the right to self-determination, has been understood in terms of the collective exercise of particular human rights and fundamental freedoms.[14] In *J.G.A. Diergaardt et al v Namibia* (2000), members of the Rehoboth alleged that 'their right to self-determination inside the republic of Namibia (so-called internal self-determination) ha[d] been

[9] Ibid art 2.

[10] *R.L. v Canada*, Communication No 358/1989, CCPR/C/43/D/358/1989 (1991) para 6.2.

[11] See e.g. *Poma Poma v Peru*, Communication No 1457/2006, CCPR/C/95/D/1457/2006 (2009) para 6.3; *Lubicon Lake Band v Canada*, Communication No 167/1984, CCPR/C/38/D/167/1984 (1990) para 13.3; *E.P. et al v Colombia*, Communication No 318/1988, CCPR/C/39/D/318/1988 (1990) para 8.2; *Grand Chief Donald Marshall et al v Canada*, Communication No 205/1986, CCPR/C/39/D/205/1986 (1990) para 14.2; *A.B. et al v Italy*, Communication No 413/1990, CCPR/C/40/D/413/1990 (1990) para 3.2; *Ivan Kitok v Sweden*, Communication No 197/1985, CCPR/C/33/D/197/1985 (1988) para 6.3. See also *A. D. v Canada*, Communication No 78/1980 (1980) para 8.2, in *Report of the Human Rights Committee*, Annex XVI, 200, A/39/40 (20 Sept 1984).

[12] *J.G.A. Diergaardt et al v Namibia*, Communication No 760/1997, CCPR/C/69/D/760/1997 (2000) (hereinafter *J.G.A. Diergaardt v Namibia* (2000)) para 10.3; *Mahuika et al v New Zealand*, Communication No 547/1993, CCPR/C/70/D/547/1993 (2000) (hereinafter *Mahuika v New Zealand* (2000)) para 9.2.

[13] Antonio Cassese, *Self-Determination of Peoples: A Legal Reappraisal* (CUP 1995) 62–65; Manfred Nowak, *UN Covenant on Civil and Political Rights: CCPR Commentary* (2nd edn, N.P. Engel 2005) paras 15–17; James Summers, 'The Right of Peoples to Self-Determination in Article 1 of the Human Rights Covenants as a Claimable Right' (2019) 31(2) *New England Journal of Public Policy* 1, 1.

[14] See Chapter 8.b.

violated' because they were unable to pursue their economic, social, and cultural development and freely dispose of their community's natural wealth and resources.[15] While the HRC recalled the inadmissibility of claims under ICCPR Article 1, it acknowledged that 'the provisions of article 1 may be relevant in the interpretation of other rights protected by the Covenant, in particular articles 25, 26 and 27'.[16] The HRC made a similar statement regarding ICCPR Article 1 in *Mahuika et al v New Zealand* (2000), a communication by members of the Indigenous Māori concerning restriction of access and control over fishing resources by New Zealand.[17] In neither case, however, was Article 1 applied to interpret other rights under the ICCPR.

The HRC only later applied ICCPR Article 1 to evaluate the exercise of individual rights in relation to the right to self-determination in *Gillot et al v France* (2002).[18] The communication, authored by twenty-one French citizens resident in New Caledonia, concerned restrictions on participation in referendums conducted by France as part of the process of self-determination for New Caledonia, a NSGT administered by France.[19] The authors claimed, inter alia, that criteria used to determine the electorate for the referendums were discriminatory and that associated length of residence requirements were excessive; they alleged that such restrictions violated their rights under Articles 2, 25, and 26 of the ICCPR.[20] Given that the violations alleged occurred in the context of self-determination referendums, the HRC looked to ICCPR Article 1 to assess whether the individual rights asserted had been violated in that context.[21] The HRC found no violation of the ICCPR by France with respect to the referendums conducted in New Caledonia.[22] This particular example of the interpretation of individual rights in reference to ICCPR Article

[15] *J.G.A. Diergaardt v Namibia* (2000) para 3.2. See Annelies Verstichel, 'Recent Developments in the UN Human Rights Committee's Approach to Minorities, with a Focus on Effective Participation' (2005) 12(1) *International Journal on Minority and Group Rights* 25, 34–36.

[16] *J.G.A. Diergaardt v Namibia* (2000) para 10.3.

[17] *Mahuika v New Zealand* (2000) para 9.2 ('[T]he provisions of article 1 may be relevant in the interpretation of other rights protected by the Covenant, in particular article 27'). See Verstichel (n 15) 37–40.

[18] *Gillot et al v France*, Communication No 932/2000, CCPR/C/75/D/932/2000 (2002) (hereinafter *Gillot v France* (2002)). See Taylor (n 6) 53–54; Verstichel (n 15) 36–37.

[19] *Gillot v France* (2002) paras 1–2.11.

[20] Ibid paras 3.1–3.11.

[21] Ibid para 13.4.

[22] Ibid para 15.

1 is noteworthy for its justification of a relatively more restrictive application of such individual rights in relation to the right to self-determination.

This same interpretive approach is reflected in *Sanila-Aikio v Finland* (2019) and *Käkkäläjärvi et al v Finland* (2019), in which the HRC applied ICCPR Article 1 to interpret Article 25 and Article 27 in relation to the self-determination of Indigenous Peoples. These cases are discussed in detail in Chapter 8.[23]

ii. Committee on Economic, Social and Cultural Rights

The CESCR is an independent body of experts established to monitor implementation of the ICESCR by States parties. The CESCR was established under ECOSOC Resolution 1985/17 to perform the functions of the ECOSOC under Part IV of the ICESCR, particularly Articles 21 and 22.[24] Under Article 16(1) of the ICESCR, States parties are obligated to submit 'reports on the measures which they have adopted and the progress made in achieving the observance of the rights recognized' in the ICESCR.[25] The CESCR has not issued a General Comment addressing the right to self-determination under ICESCR Article 1 that corresponds to HRC General Comment No 12 on ICCPR Article 1, though CESCR General Comment No 26 on land and economic, social and cultural rights provides guidance on ICESCR Article 1 in reference to the right to self-determination of Indigenous Peoples.[26] The ICESCR reporting requirement, like the parallel reporting requirement of the ICCPR, promotes a degree of accountability with respect to performance of obligations of States parties under ICESCR Article 1.

The Optional Protocol to the ICESCR establishes an individual complaint mechanism in relation to the ICESCR.[27] Under Article 2 of the Optional Protocol, States parties recognize the competence of the CESCR to receive

[23] See Chapter 8.e.

[24] E/Res/1985/17 (28 May 1985).

[25] International Covenant on Economic, Social and Cultural Rights art 16(1), 993 UNTS 3 (16 Dec 1966, entered into force 3 Jan 1976).

[26] Committee on Economic, Social and Cultural Rights, *General Comment No. 26 (2022) on land and economic, social and cultural rights*, E/C.12/GC/26 (2023) paras 11, 16. See Chapter 8.e.

[27] Optional Protocol to the International Covenant on Economic, Social and Cultural Rights, 2922 UNTS 29 (10 Dec 2008, entered into force 5 May 2013) (hereinafter ICESCR Optional Protocol).

and consider communications 'submitted by or on behalf of individuals or groups of individuals, under the jurisdiction of a State Party, claiming to be victims of a violation of any of the economic, social and cultural rights set forth in the Covenant by that State Party'.[28] Although there are several communications pending before the CESCR that invoke ICESCR Article 1,[29] the CESCR has not yet opined on its competence to consider a claim based on an alleged violation of the right to self-determination under ICESCR Article 1.[30] Unlike Article 1 of the ICCPR Optional Protocol, which limits the competence of the HRC to communications 'from individuals . . . who claim to be victims of a violation' of a right under the ICCPR, Article 2 of the ICESCR Optional Protocol permits communications 'submitted by *or on behalf of* individuals *or groups of individuals* . . . claiming to be victims of a violation of any [] economic, social and cultural rights' under the ICESCR.[31] It is unclear whether these differences support a divergent approach in relation to the ICESCR in favour of the competence of the CESCR to consider claims based on the right to self-determination under ICESCR Article 1.[32]

c. Treaty Bodies of a Regional Character

At the regional level, treatment of claims under the ACHPR by the African Commission on Human and Peoples' Rights and the ACtHPR offers insight into the right to self-determination under the ACHPR. And, although no Inter-American instrument establishes a right to self-determination as such,[33] the IACHR and IACtHR have addressed self-determination and identified protections for Indigenous Peoples under the ACHR. Practice of these regional treaty bodies relevant to the right to self-determination is

[28] Ibid art 2.

[29] Table of pending cases before the Committee on Economic, Social and Cultural Rights, considered under the Optional Protocol to the International Covenant on Economic, Social and Cultural Rights, https://www.ohchr.org/en/treaty-bodies/cescr/table-pending-cases (last accessed 28 Oct 2024) (Communications Nos 251/2022 and 289/2022).

[30] Summers (n 13) 1.

[31] ICCPR Optional Protocol art 1; ICESCR Optional Protocol art 2 (emphasis added).

[32] For a favourable view in this regard, see Summers (n 13) 1–6.

[33] However, the non-binding ADRIP refers to the right of Indigenous Peoples to self-determination. See Chapter 8.e.iii.1. Preambular language in the Additional Protocol to the American Convention on Human Rights in the area of Economic, Social and Cultural Rights (Protocol of San Salvador) also refers to self-determination. See Chapter 2.d.iii.

considered below. Claims related to self-determination before the CJEU are discussed in Chapter 11.[34]

i. African Commission on Human and Peoples' Rights

The ACHPR provides for both an inter-State complaint mechanism,[35] and an individual complaint mechanism that confers competence to the African Commission on Human and Peoples' Rights to receive and consider communications 'relating to human and peoples' rights'.[36] The ACHPR imposes obligations upon States parties in relation to rights of peoples at Articles 19–24, including the right to self-determination (Article 20) and the right to freely dispose of wealth and natural resources (Article 21).[37] The African Commission has adopted recommendations in response to communications alleging violations of Articles 20 and 21.[38] These recommendations have primarily addressed the domestic aspect of the right to self-determination and, at times, expressly linked Article 20 to the right to participate in government under ACHPR Article 13. The African Commission has addressed the right to self-determination in relation to occupation,[39] secession,[40] a military coup,[41] natural resource exploitation,[42] and Indigenous Peoples.[43]

[34] See Chapter 11.e.ii.

[35] African [Banjul] Charter on Human and Peoples' Rights arts 47–54, OAU Doc CAB/LEG/67/3/Rev.5, 1520 UNTS 217 (27 June 1981, entered into force 21 Oct 1986) (hereinafter ACHPR).

[36] Ibid arts 55–59.

[37] See Chapter 2.d.i.

[38] For discussion including statements by the African Commission relevant to self-determination under the ACHPR outside the context of the individual complaint mechanism, see Rachel Murray, *The African Charter on Human and Peoples' Rights: A Commentary* (OUP 2019) 497–507. On free disposal of natural wealth and resources, see ibid 508–20.

[39] *Democratic Republic of Congo v Burundi, Rwanda and Uganda*, ACommHPR, Communication No 227/99 (2003). See Chapter 7.b.ii.1.A.

[40] *Katangese Peoples' Congress v Zaire*, ACommHPR, Communication No 75/92 (1995); *Mgwanga Gunme et al v Cameroon*, ACommHPR, Communication No 266/2003 (2009). See Chapter 7.c.

[41] *Jawara v The Gambia* ACommHPR, Communications Nos 147/95 & 149/96 (2000). See Chapter 8.c.i.

[42] *Front for the Liberation of the State of Cabinda v Angola*, ACommHPR, Communication No 328/06 (2013). See also *The Social and Economic Rights Action Center for Economic and Social Rights v Nigeria*, ACommHPR, Communication No 155/96 (2001). See Chapter 8.d.

[43] *Centre for Minority Rights Development (Kenya) & Minority Rights Group International on behalf of Endorois Welfare Council v Kenya*, ACommHPR, Communication No 276/2003 (2010). See Chapter 8.e.iii.2.

ii. African Court on Human and Peoples' Rights

The ACtHPR has competence to consider cases instituted by individuals and non-governmental organizations, contingent upon a separate declaration by States parties under Article 34 of the Protocol.[44] The ACtHPR has considered cases alleging violations of the right of peoples to self-determination under ACHPR Article 20, and in so doing has authoritatively interpretated the right to self-determination under the ACHPR. In *Mornah v Benin* (2022), the ACtHPR provided a comprehensive treatment of the right to self-determination under the ACHPR. The ACtHPR opined on the normative status of the right to self-determination,[45] the extraterritorial character of positive duties under ACHPR Article 20(3),[46] and the relationship between occupation and decolonization in the case of Western Sahara.[47] In the performance of obligations of assistance under Article 20(3), the ACtHPR identified a margin of appreciation, recognizing the discretion of the respondent States to select the affirmative measures they find appropriate to promote realization of the right to self-determination.[48] In *ACHPR v Kenya* (2017), the ACtHPR defined contours of groups that may be regarded as 'peoples' for purposes of collective rights in the ACHPR.[49]

iii. Inter-American Commission on Human Rights

The ACHR provides for an individual complaint mechanism pursuant to which any person or group of persons, as well as certain nongovernmental entities, may submit petitions regarding alleged violations of the ACHR

[44] Protocol to the African Charter on Human and Peoples' Rights on the Establishment of an African Court on Human and Peoples' Rights art 34(6) (10 June 1998, entered into force 25 Jan 2004). See also art 5.

[45] *Bernard Anbataayela Mornah v Benin et al*, ACtHPR, No 028/2018, Judgment, para 301 (22 Sept 2022) (hereinafter *Mornah v Benin* (2022)). See Chapter 7.d.ii.

[46] *Mornah v Benin* (2022) para 299. See Chapter 9.b.i.2.

[47] *Mornah v Benin* (2022) para 301. See Chapter 7.b.ii.1.B.

[48] *Mornah v Benin* (2022) para 314. The ACtHPR accordingly did not find that the respondent States had failed to perform their obligations under ACHPR Article 20 by not opposing Morocco's admission into the AU, or that they had violated, individually or collectively, the right to self-determination under ACHPR Article 20. Ibid paras 314–22.

[49] *ACHPR v Kenya*, Application No 006/2012, Judgment (2017) paras 195–201. See Chapter 6.e.i; Chapter 7.c.i; Chapter 8.e.iii.2. Cf *Endorois v Kenya* (2010).

by a State party.[50] No Inter-American instrument codifies the right to self-determination. An early treatment by the IACHR of the question of the self-determination of Indigenous Peoples is found in *Report on the Situation of Human Rights of a Segment of the Nicaraguan Population of Miskito Origin* (1983), in which the IACHR recognized the principle of self-determination in international law, but did not consider the right to self-determination to be applicable to minority groups within a State, including Indigenous groups.[51]

iv. Inter-American Court of Human Rights

The IACtHR is an 'autonomous judicial institution' within the OAS system with a mandate to interpret and apply the ACHR.[52] The modalities of the IACtHR are set out in Chapter VIII of the ACHR. The right to self-determination has featured in the application of provisions of the ACHR by the IACtHR in relation to Indigenous Peoples and tribal communities. These cases are discussed in Chapter 8.[53]

d. Domestic Authorities

This section considers examples of ways in which domestic authorities implement and apply the right to self-determination. The first part of this section considers references to self-determination in the national constitutions of States. The second part discusses claims before national courts based on the right to self-determination in international law.

[50] American Convention on Human Rights: 'Pact of San José, Costa Rica' arts 44–51, 1144 UNTS 143 (22 Nov 1969, entered into force 18 July 1978) (hereinafter ACHR).

[51] *Report on the Situation of Human Rights of a Segment of the Nicaraguan Population of Miskito Origin*, IACHR, OAS Doc OEA/Ser.L/V.II.62, doc 10 rev 3 (29 Nov 1983) part II.B.

[52] ACHR art 62(3). See Statute of the Inter-American Court of Human Rights art 1, OAS AG/Res 448 (IX-0/79) (31 Oct 1979).

[53] *Huilcamán Paillama et al v Chile* (Merits, Reparations and Costs), 2024 IACtHR (Ser C) No 527 (18 June 2024); *Rama and Kriol Peoples, the Black Creole Indigenous Community of Bluefields et al v Nicaragua* (Merits, Reparations and Costs), 2024 IACtHR (Ser C) No 552 (1 Apr 2024); *Kaliña and Lokono Peoples v Suriname*, Judgment (Merits, Reparations and Costs), 2015 IACtHR (Ser C) No 309 (25 Nov 2015); *Saramaka People v Suriname*, Judgment (Preliminary Objections, Merits, Reparations, and Costs), 2007 IACtHR (Ser C) No 172 (28 Nov 2007). See Chapter 8.e.iii.1.

i. National Constitutions

Some States expressly incorporate and implement aspects of the right to self-determination in their national constitutions.[54] Such references are noteworthy insofar as they indicate ways in which individual States choose to give effect to aspects of self-determination. The relatively small number of national constitutions addressing self-determination suggests, however, that express constitutional provisions are not the primary modality by which States implement their obligations under the right to self-determination. Even so, both the international and domestic aspects of the right to self-determination find expression in national constitutions.

The international aspect of the right to self-determination features most prominently in those national constitutions that refer to self-determination. A range of national constitutions refer to self-determination in various ways in their introductory sections as the basis for the State,[55] thereby invoking the entitlement of their peoples to freely determine their political status.[56] National constitutions also contemplate the conduct of foreign relations to be informed by self-determination,[57] consistent with extraterritorial obligations of States to respect the right to self-determination.[58] In some cases, this application of self-determination to foreign relations expressly supports resistance to forms of oppression.[59] The constitution of France, of relevance

[54] The survey of national constitutions discussed herein was facilitated by the dataset indexed by the Comparative Constitutions Project. See Zachary Elkins, Tom Ginsburg & James Melton, *Constitute: The World's Constitutions to Read, Search, and Compare* (at *constituteproject.org*) (last accessed 23 May 2024). National constitutions are identified by year of adoption.

[55] Belarus (1994) preamble; Croatia (1990) s I; Estonia (1992) preamble; Ethiopia (1995) preamble; Germany (1949) preamble; Hungary (2011) preamble; Latvia (1922) preamble; Nicaragua (1986/87) art 1; Russian Federation (1993) preamble; Slovakia (1992) preamble; Slovenia (1991) preamble; Timor-Leste (2002) preamble; Ukraine (1996) preamble; Venezuela (1999) preamble. See also Bangladesh Proclamation of Independence (1971) preambular para 6; Charter of Fundamental Rights and Basic Freedoms (Czech Republic) (1993) preamble. See similarly The Amended Basic Law (Palestine) (2003) preamble.

[56] See Chapter 7.b.

[57] Algeria (1989) art 32; Angola (2010) art 12(1); Brazil (1988) art 4(III); Cabo Verde (1992) art 11(2); Colombia (1991) art 9; Cuba (2019) art 16; Ecuador (2008) art 416(1); Guinea-Bissau (1984) art 18(2); Honduras (1982) art 15; Mexico (1917) art 89(X); Paraguay (1992) art 143(2); Philippines (1987) art II(7); Portugal (1976) art 7(3); Qatar (2004) art 7; Suriname (1987) art 7(1); Timor-Leste (2002) art 8(1); Venezuela (1999) art 152. See also Bangladesh (1972) art 25.

[58] See Chapter 9.b.i.2.

[59] Algeria (1989) art 32; Cabo Verde (1992) art 11(2); Cuba (2019) art 16(j); Guinea-Bissau (1984) art 18(2); Portugal (1976) art 7(3); Venezuela (1999) art 152. See Chapter 7.b.ii.2.

to its obligations as an administering power, refers to the principle of self-determination in relation to NSGTs under its administration.[60]

The domestic aspect of self-determination is also referenced in national constitutions in relation to elements of representative government and political participation.[61] The relatively limited number of constitutions expressly referring to this aspect of self-determination may reflect the way the domestic aspect of self-determination is, in practice, given effect instead through the collective exercise of human rights and fundamental freedoms.[62] A number of national constitutions of Central and South American States contain provisions addressing the self-determination of Indigenous Peoples.[63] As discussed in Chapter 8, other States give effect to the right to self-determination of Indigenous Peoples through legislation and regulations.[64] The constitution of Moldova recognizes the self-governing status of the autonomous territory of Găgăuzia in terms of self-determination.[65] Finally, the constitution of Ethiopia contains a provision on the right to self-determination that sets out parameters according to which sub-State groups may pursue secession under domestic law.[66]

There are a number of other references to self-determination in national constitutions that do not clearly relate to the principle or right as it is defined in international law.[67]

ii. National Courts

While claims based in the right to self-determination in international law do not appear to be frequently presented to national courts, there are instances

[60] France (1958) preamble. See Chapter 9.c.ii.

[61] Belarus (1994) art 9; Bolivia (2009) arts 2, 30(II); Ecuador (2008) art 96 (see also arts 351, 391); Honduras (1982) art 5; Lao People's Democratic Republic (1991) art 7; Nicaragua (1986/87) art 5; Russian Federation (1993) art 5(3); Slovenia (1991) art 3; Venezuela (1999) art 1.

[62] See Chapter 8.

[63] Bolivia (2009) arts 2, 30(II); Ecuador (2008) art 57; Mexico (1917) art 2. See also South Africa (1996) art 235 (Permitting 'recognition of the notion of the right to self-determination' to sub-State groups under domestic law).

[64] See Chapter 8.e.iv.

[65] Moldova (1994) art 111(1). The region is not regarded as a territorial unit whose people is entitled to the right to self-determination under international law, and this provision is formulated as an expression of the domestic aspect of self-determination. Cf Chapter 6.c.

[66] Ethiopia (1995) arts 39, 62(3). Cf Chapter 7.c.i.

[67] See Cuba (2019) art 88 (self-determination of the elderly); Georgia (1995) art 18 ('informational self-determination'). Two constitutions refer to duties of individuals under the right to self-determination: see Nicaragua (1986/87) art 1; Venezuela (1999) art 130.

in which national courts have addressed the right to self-determination. The most well-known cases have concerned secession claims by sub-State groups. In a number of other domestic cases, the outward-facing obligations of States related to self-determination have been invoked by litigants as a basis to challenge governmental action. Finally, it bears noting that although the right to self-determination is exercised in the normal course by a people through its collective enjoyment and exercise of human rights, the right to self-determination may not be a controlling consideration in assertions of human rights, even in cases overtly implicating the right to self-determination. Examples of litigation before national courts in each of these areas implicating the right to self-determination are considered in turn.

1. Secession Claims

The right to self-determination in international law does not contain a general entitlement to secession.[68] This aspect of the right to self-determination has been litigated repeatedly before domestic courts.[69] These cases are discussed in Chapter 7.

2. Challenges to Government Action

In several notable instances, the right to self-determination in international law has been raised by litigants in domestic courts to challenge the lawfulness of government action. Two lines of litigation in the United Kingdom sought to challenge the conformity of government action with the right to self-determination in relation to the international aspect of the right.

One line of cases, discussed in Chapter 11, challenged the applicability to Western Sahara of tariff and fisheries agreements concluded between European organs and Morocco.[70] Following withdrawal of the United Kingdom from the European Union, a new association agreement between

[68] See Chapter 7.c.i.

[69] See *Reference by the Lord Advocate of devolution issues under paragraph 34 of Schedule 6 to the Scotland Act 1998* [2022] UKSC 31; *Hikkadu Koralage Don Chandrasoma v Mawai S. Senathirajah et al*, SC SPL 03/2014 (2017); *Reference re Secession of Quebec* [1998] 2 SCR 217; Decree No 10-P of the Constitutional Court of the Russian Federation, 31 July 1995, in (1995) 31(5) *Statutes & Decisions: The Laws of the USSR and its Successor States* 48; Decree of the Constitutional Court of the RSFSR, 13 March 1992, in (1994) 30(3) *Statutes & Decisions: The Laws of the USSR and its Successor States* 32. See also *Accordance with International Law of the Unilateral Declaration of Independence in Respect of Kosovo*, Advisory Opinion, ICJ Rep 2010, 403 paras 55–56. See Chapter 7.c.

[70] See Chapter 11.e.ii.

the UK and Morocco was concluded; its implementing regulations were unsuccessfully challenged on the basis of their alleged non-conformity with the right to self-determination.[71]

A second line of cases in the United Kingdom was brought by litigants seeking resettlement of the Chagossian diaspora on the Chagos Archipelago.[72] The first in this line of cases successfully challenged Immigration Ordinance 1971, which removed the right of Chagossians to inhabit the Chagos Archipelago.[73] The next case challenged subsequent Orders in Council introduced in 2004, which again restricted the right of abode for Chagossians; the challenge succeeded before the Divisional Court and Court of Appeal but ultimately failed before the House of Lords.[74] A third case challenged, unsuccessfully, the establishment in 2010 of a Marine Protected Area (MPA) for the British Indian Ocean Territory based in part on the claim that the MPA was intended to impede resettlement by the Chagossians.[75] Following the *Chagos Archipelago* (2019) advisory opinion, a fourth case challenged a subsequent decision by the UK Government not to support resettlement of the Chagos Archipelago.[76] After dismissal by the Divisional Court, on appeal, this case focused on applicability of the European Convention for the Protection of Human Rights and Fundamental Freedoms to the Chagos Archipelago and the consequences of the *Chagos Archipelago* (2019) advisory opinion.[77] The Court of Appeal rejected the applicability of the European Convention to the Chagos Archipelago and held that 'the right to self-determination and the right of resettlement are, by their natures, related concepts but they are not legally synonymous'.[78] Accordingly, the Court of Appeal concluded that any resettlement of the Chagos Archipelago was a decision for Mauritius

[71] *Western Sahara Campaign UK v Secretary of State for International Trade et al* [2022] EWHC 3108 (Admin) [45], [159].

[72] *R (Hoareau and Bancoult) v Secretary of State for Foreign and Commonwealth Affairs* [2020] EWCA Civ 1010 (hereinafter *Bancoult* (2020)) (the most recent case in this line of cases, summarizing prior litigation at paras [18]–[43]).

[73] *R (Bancoult) v Secretary of State for the Foreign and Commonwealth Office (No 1)* [2000] EWHC 413 (Admin).

[74] *R (Bancoult) v Secretary of State for Foreign and Commonwealth Affairs (No 2)* [2008] UKHL 61.

[75] *R (Bancoult) v Secretary of State for Foreign and Commonwealth Affairs (No 3)* [2018] UKSC 3.

[76] *Bancoult* (2020).

[77] See Chapter 4.g.

[78] *Bancoult* (2020) [130], [139], [141].

governed by the laws of Mauritius rather than international law.[79] This line of cases in the United Kingdom represented but one front in a wide-ranging campaign challenging UK sovereignty over the Chagos Archipelago.[80]

The right to self-determination in international law may play a role in promoting the right of Indigenous Peoples to self-determination before domestic courts. One illustration is *Reference re An Act respecting First Nations, Inuit and Métis children, youth and families* (2024),[81] which concerned a challenge to the constitutionality of Canadian legislation implementing commitments under the UNDRIP in Canadian law.[82] In its judgment, the Supreme Court of Canada took note of the incorporation in Canadian law of the UNDRIP, aspects of its implementation, and its recognition of the exercise by Indigenous Peoples of their right to self-determination through autonomy or self-government.[83] The Supreme Court of Canada found the legislation at issue constitutional, which it described as creating a jurisdiction that 'invites Indigenous communities to work with the Crown to weave together Indigenous, national and international laws in order to protect the well-being of Indigenous children, youth and families'.[84] While the case may be unique to the Canadian legal landscape, it nonetheless demonstrates one way in which the right to self-determination may inform challenges to government action in domestic courts.[85]

3. Human Rights Claims

Although the right to self-determination is exercised by a people in the normal course through the domestic aspect of the right, it does not appear that the right under international law is a significant factor in adjudicating associated human rights claims before domestic courts. This appears to be so even in cases where the exercise of human rights squarely implicates the right to self-determination, such as the administration of political status

[79] Ibid [130].

[80] See Application no 35622/04 *Chagos Islanders v United Kingdom* [2013] 56 EHRR SE 15 (The application, concerning the removal of the Chagossians and prohibition of their return, was found inadmissible on 11 Dec 2012). See also Chapter 4.g; Chapter 11.e.i.

[81] *Reference re An Act respecting First Nations, Inuit and Métis children, youth and families* [2024] SCC 5 (2024) (hereinafter *First Nations Act* (2024)).

[82] *Act respecting First Nations, Inuit and Métis children, youth and families*, SC 2019, c 24.

[83] *First Nations Act* (2024) paras 3–4, 45, 52.

[84] Ibid paras 134, 136.

[85] See Chapter 8.e.iv.

referendums. *Davis v Guam* (2019), which concerned participation in a self-determination referendum in Guam, a NSGT, is illustrative in this regard.[86] A law enacted by Guam in 2000 contemplated a 'political status plebiscite' to ascertain the will of the 'Native Inhabitants of Guam' regarding the territory's political relationship with the United States.[87] The stated intent of the law was 'to permit the native inhabitants of Guam, as defined by the U.S. Congress' 1950 Organic Act of Guam to exercise the inalienable right to self-determination of their political relationship with the United States of America'.[88] The law provided for a registry to be used 'for the future exercise of self-determination by the Indigenous Chamorro people of Guam'.[89] The law was challenged by a non-Chamorro resident of Guam who was denied registration under the law.[90] The District Court found that the law used 'ancestry as a proxy for race' in violation of the US Constitution, a finding upheld on appeal by the Ninth Circuit Court of Appeals.[91] The Ninth Circuit took care to note that the impermissibility of race-based voting restrictions under the US Constitution, rather than any evaluation of self-determination, was the basis for its judgment.[92] The operation of domestic human rights protections thereby had the effect of promoting enjoyment of the right to self-determination of the people of Guam by safeguarding the collective exercise of human rights and fundamental freedoms by the entire population of the territory.[93] Although the case had implications for both the international and domestic aspects of the right to self-determination, the challenge to the plebiscite law in question was not adjudicated on the basis of the right to self-determination.[94]

[86] *Davis v Guam*, 932 F.3d 822 (9th Circuit 2019) (hereinafter *Davis v Guam* (2019)). For discussion, see Comment, 'Davis v. Guam' (2019) 133(2) *Harvard Law Review* 683.
[87] *Davis v Guam* (2019) 824.
[88] Ibid 828.
[89] Ibid 839.
[90] Ibid 828.
[91] Ibid 829, 843. See US Constitution, Amendment XV s 1 (prohibiting race-based voting restrictions).
[92] *Davis v Guam* (2019) 843.
[93] This result, consistent with the international aspect of self-determination, does not foreclose claims to autonomy by the indigenous Chamorro, consistent with the domestic aspect of self-determination. See Comment (n 86) 690.
[94] The HRC found non-discriminatory restrictions on participation in a political status referendum permissible in view of the right to self-determination. See *Gillot v France* (2002) (discussed supra, text accompanying nn 18–22).

Conclusion

Self-Determination's Future

The right to self-determination in international law is, at base, a right to freedom. Self-determination entails an entitlement of peoples to self-government and the pursuit of their development, whose realization is contingent upon respect by other States as well as respect for human rights and fundamental freedoms by their own State. The right serves as a bridge between conceptualizations of State sovereignty and popular sovereignty and, in effect, projects popular sovereignty onto the relations of States. It is an 'inalienable right'.[1] In this way, the right to self-determination constitutes 'an ordering principle for international society'.[2]

Restating these observations serves as a reminder of the continuing relevance of the right to self-determination. The international community has largely emerged from a profoundly formative period in the application of the right to self-determination. This period saw the acceleration of decolonization, a proliferation of new States, and the crystallization of obligations *erga omnes* arising from the right to self-determination under CIL. To be sure, decolonization remains incomplete. The few, formally outstanding cases of non-self-governing territories remain unresolved and may, for quite different reasons, remain so for some time. Such cases range from relationships in which satisfaction with the status quo has itself resembled an expression of self-determination, to situations in which an occupying power has displaced an administering power, stymying the ability of the people concerned to exercise its right to self-determination. The right to self-determination

[1] *Legal Consequences arising from the Policies and Practices of Israel in the Occupied Palestinian Territory, including East Jerusalem*, Advisory Opinion, ICJ Rep 2024, para 257. Cf *Declaration of Independence* (4 July 1776) (Referring to 'unalienable rights').

[2] Erez Manela, *The Wilsonian Moment: Self-Determination and the International Origins of Anticolonial Nationalism* (OUP 2007) 11 (quoting James Mayall, *Nationalism and International Society* (CUP 1990) 44–45).

The Right to Self-Determination in International Law. Thomas Weatherall, Oxford University Press.
 DOI: 10.1093/9780197798119.003.0014

will increasingly operate primarily to reinforce the political independence of existing States. In time, this conservative application may as a practical matter be all that remains of the international aspect of the right to self-determination as it is currently formulated in international law: a 'right to independence' of the peoples of sovereign States.[3]

As the conservative features of the right to self-determination dominate the international aspect of the right,[4] the more progressive features of the domestic aspect of the right to self-determination can be expected to garner relatively greater attention. This may entail increased scrutiny over the degree to which States are 'possessed of a government representing the whole people belonging to the territory without distinction as to race, creed or colour'.[5] One indication of such a trajectory is significant attention now directed towards the autonomy and self-government of Indigenous Peoples. Treaty bodies of both an international and regional character have addressed aspects of the right to self-determination as it applies to Indigenous Peoples, a relatively recent development. There is coherence in the way that self-determination, as the rule that deconstructed colonialism on the international plane, is now increasingly concerned on the domestic plane with the autonomy and self-government of Indigenous Peoples, whose marginalization is a direct consequence of colonialism.[6] The self-determination of Indigenous Peoples provides one indication of the way in which the domestic aspect of the right to self-determination will continue to influence the relationship between States and their peoples.

History attests to the transformative impact of self-determination in international relations. Over the course of the twentieth century, roughly half of the members of the international community would owe their independence to the right of peoples to self-determination in international law. The 'right to independence' manifested by the international aspect of self-determination is complemented by a 'right to democracy' within its domestic aspect.[7]

[3] *Accordance with International Law of the Unilateral Declaration of Independence in Respect of Kosovo*, Advisory Opinion, ICJ Rep 2010, 403 para 79. For a critical view of such a limited application of the right to self-determination, see Marc Weller, *Escaping the Self-Determination Trap* (Martinus Nijhoff 2008).

[4] James Crawford, *The Creation of States in International Law* (2nd edn, OUP 2006) 126.

[5] A/Res/2625 (24 Oct 1970) Annex, Principle V para 7.

[6] S. James Anaya, *Indigenous Peoples in International Law* (2nd edn, OUP 2004) 3–4.

[7] See Harold Hongju Koh, 'A United States Human Rights Policy for the 21st Century' (2002) 46(2) *Saint Louis University Law Journal* 293, 325.

It remains to be seen whether the right to self-determination will, in the twenty-first century, have a second act in its entitlement to democracy: Will the profound impact of the right to self-determination in advancing equality amongst peoples be matched by its effect on the relationship between peoples and their governments? Time will tell. The domestic aspect of the right to self-determination lacks the targeted remedial obligations and institutional mechanisms that helped bring an end to colonialism, meaning that self-determination as a force for democratization will look quite unlike its advancement of decolonization. Instead, realization of the democratic entitlement in international law depends upon States 'taking seriously' the obligations owed to their peoples under the right to self-determination.[8] Unrealized democratic aspirations of peoples offer further transformative potential for the right to self-determination in international law.

[8] James Crawford, 'Democracy and International Law' (1993) 64(1) *British Yearbook of International Law* 113, 123.

APPENDIX 1

Former Trust Territories and Non-Self-Governing Territories*

Administering State	Territory	Status	Year	UN Resolutions and Agreements	Explanation of Change in Status	Notes
Australia	Cocos (Keeling) Islands*	Change in status	1984	A/Res/39/30 (5 Dec 1984)	A/Res/39/30 recognized integration with Australia	*Initially administered by the United Kingdom as part of Singapore. Transmission of information on the Cocos (Keeling) Islands only began after its transfer to Australia in 1955. See Issue on Cocos (Keeling) Islands, *Decolonization*, No 11, at 6 (1978).
	Papua	Independence as Papua New Guinea*	1975	A/Res/66 (I) (14 Dec 1946), A/Res/2865 (XXVI) (20 Dec 1971), A/Res/3284 (XXIX) (13 Dec 1974); A/Res/3368 (XXX) (10 Oct 1975)		*Under A/Res/2865, Territory of Papua and Trust Territory of New Guinea become Papua New Guinea
	Trust Territory of Nauru	Independence as Nauru	1968	Trusteeship agreement for the Territory of Nauru, 10 UNTS 3 (entered into force 1 Nov 1947); A/Res/140 (II) (1 Nov 1947), A/Res/2347 (XXII) (19 Dec 1967), A/Res/54/2 (1 Oct 1999)		

	Trust Territory of New Guinea	Independence as Papua New Guinea*	1975	Trusteeship agreement for the Territory of New Guinea, 8 UNTS 181 (entered into force 13 Dec 1946); A/Res/63 (I) (13 Dec 1946), A/Res/2865 (XXVI) (20 Dec 1971), A/Res/3284 (XXIX) (13 Dec 1974), A/Res/3368 (XXX) (10 Oct 1975)	*Under A/Res/2865, Territory of Papua and Trust Territory of New Guinea become Papua New Guinea
Belgium	Belgian Congo	Independence as Congo-Leopoldville, later Zaire, now the Democratic Republic of the Congo	1960	A/Res/66 (I) (14 Dec 1946), A/Res/1480 (XV) (20 Sept 1960)	
	Trust Territory of Ruanda-Urundi*	Independence as Burundi	1962	Trusteeship agreement for the Territory of Ruanda-Urundi, 8 UNTS 105 (entered into force 13 Dec 1946); A/Res/63 (I) (13 Dec 1946), A/Res/1746 (XVI) (27 June 1962), A/Res/1579 (XV) (20 Dec 1960), A/Res/1749 (XVII) (18 Sept 1962)	*The UNGA had initially supported the 'emergence of a single state', see e.g. A/Res/1743 (XVI) (23 Feb 1962), until A/Res/1746 (XVI) (27 June 1962), which favoured emergence 'of two independent and sovereign States'.

Administering State	Territory		Status	Year	UN Resolutions and Agreements	Explanation of Change in Status	Notes
			Independence as Rwanda	1962	Trusteeship agreement for the Territory of Ruanda-Urundi, 8 UNTS 105 (entered into force 13 Dec 1946); A/Res/63 (I) (13 Dec 1946), A/Res/1746 (XVI) (27 June 1962), A/Res/1579 (XV) (20 Dec 1960), A/Res/1748 (XVII) (18 Sept 1962)		*The UNGA had initially supported the 'emergence of a single state', see e.g. A/Res/1743 (XVI) (23 Feb 1962), until A/Res/1746 (XVI) (27 June 1962), which favoured emergence 'of two independent and sovereign States'.
Denmark	Greenland		Change in status	1954	A/Res/66 (I) (14 Dec 1946), A/Res/849 (IX) (22 Nov 1954)	A/Res/849 recognized integration with Denmark	
France	French Equatorial Africa	French Equatorial Africa	Independence as Chad	1960	A/Res/66 (I) (14 Dec 1946), A/Res/1485 (XV) (20 Sept 1960)		
			Independence as Gabon	1960	A/Res/66 (I) (14 Dec 1946), A/Res/1487 (XV) (20 Sept 1960)		
		Middle Congo	Independence as Congo (Brazzaville), now the Republic of the Congo	1960	A/Res/66 (I) (14 Dec 1946), A/Res/1486 (XV) (20 Sept 1960)		

	Ubangi Shari	Independence as the Central African Republic	1960	A/Res/66 (I) (14 Dec 1946), A/Res/1488 (XV) (20 Sept 1960)		
French Establishments in India		Change in status	1948	A/Res/66 (I) (14 Dec 1946)	Integration by India without UN recognition following transfer by France*	*Agreement by Exchange of Notes Regarding the Cession of the French Loges in India to the Government of India (annex enclosed), 12 August–30 September 1947, French Diplomatic Archives, Agreement No 19470025; Agreement by Exchange of Notes Regarding the Date of Cession of the French Loges to the Government of India, 3 October–4 October 1947, French Diplomatic Archives, Agreement No 19470031.[1] See also Treaty of Cession of the Territory of the Free Town of Chandernagore (with Protocol), 203 UNTS 155 (2 Feb 1951, entered into force 9 June 1952); Indo-French Treaty ceding the French Establishments of Pondicherry, Karikal, Mahe and Yanam to India, with Protocol and Exchange of Notes—New Delhi (28 May 1956), (1965) 162 *British and Foreign State Papers* 848.

Administering State	Territory	Status	Year	UN Resolutions and Agreements	Explanation of Change in Status	Notes
	French Establishments in Oceania	Change in status	1947	A/Res/66 (I) (14 Dec 1946), A/Res/67/265 (17 May 2013)	Integrated by France without UN recognition ('reinscribed' as NSGT French Polynesia*)	*A/Res/67/265 'reinscribed' territory into the registry of NSGTs after cessation of reporting under Article 73(e) as French Polynesia
	French Guiana	Change in status	1947	A/Res/66 (I) (14 Dec 1946)	Integrated by France without UN recognition	
	French Somaliland	Independence as Djibouti	1977	A/Res/66 (I) (14 Dec 1946), A/Res/32/1 (20 Sept 1977)		
	French West Africa French West Africa	Independence as Dahomey, now Benin	1960	A/Res/66 (I) (14 Dec 1946), A/Res/1481 (XV) (20 Sept 1960)		
		Independence as Ivory Coast, now Côte d'Ivoire	1960	A/Res/66 (I) (14 Dec 1946), A/Res/1484 (XV) (20 Sept 1960)		
		Independence as Mauritania	1960	A/Res/66 (I) (14 Dec 1946), A/Res/1631 (XVI) (27 Oct 1961)		
		Independence as Senegal	1960	A/Res/66 (I) (14 Dec 1946), A/Res/1490 (XV) (28 Sept 1960)		

		Independence as Upper Volta, now Burkina Faso	1960	A/Res/66 (I) (14 Dec 1946), A/Res/1483 (XV) (20 Sept 1960)	
	French Guinea	Independence as Guinea	1958	A/Res/66 (I) (14 Dec 1946), A/Res/1325 (XIII) (12 Dec 1958)	
	French Sudan	Independence as Mali	1960	A/Res/66 (I) (14 Dec 1946), A/Res/1491 (XV) (28 Sept 1960)	
	Niger	Independence as Niger	1960	A/Res/66 (I) (14 Dec 1946), A/Res/1482 (XV) (20 Sept 1960)	
Guadeloupe and Dependencies		Change in status	1947	A/Res/66 (I) (14 Dec 1946)	Integrated by France without UN recognition
Indo-China		Independence as Cambodia	1948	A/Res/66 (I) (14 Dec 1946), A/Res/995 (X) (14 Dec 1955)	
		Independence as Laos, now the Lao People's Democratic Republic	1949	A/Res/66 (I) (14 Dec 1946), A/Res/995 (X) (14 Dec 1955)	
		Independence as Viet Nam	1948	A/Res/32/2 (20 Sept 1977)	

Administering State	Territory	Status	Year	UN Resolutions and Agreements	Explanation of Change in Status	Notes
	Madagascar and Dependencies	Independence as Madagascar	1960	A/Res/66 (I) (14 Dec 1946), A/Res/1478 (XV) (20 Sept 1960)		
		Independence as the Comoros**	1975	A/Res/66 (I) (14 Dec 1946),* A/Res/3385 (XXX) (12 Nov 1975)		*In 1972, the Special Committee on Decolonization recommended to the UNGA that the Comoro Archipelago be included on the list of territories subject to Chapter XI of the UN Charter: see A/8723/Rev.1, para 183. The UNGA approved the report of the Special Committee. See A/Res/2908 (XXVII) (2 Nov 1972) para 3. See also A/Res/3161 (14 Dec 1973) (reaffirming 'the inalienable right of the people of the Comoro Archipelago to self-determination and independence in accordance with General Assembly resolution 1514 (XV)'). **Mayotte plebiscites rejected by the UNGA: In A/Res/31/4 (21 Oct 1976), the General Assembly considered null and void the referendums of 8 February and

					11 April 1976 and condemned the presence of France in Mayotte as a violation of the national unity, territorial integrity and sovereignty of the independent Republic of the Comoros.
Martinique	Change in status	1947	A/Res/66 (I) (14 Dec 1946)	Integrated by France without UN recognition	
Morocco	Independence as Morocco	1956	A/Res/66 (I) (14 Dec 1946), A/Res/911 (X) (3 Dec 1955), A/Res/1111 (XI) (12 Nov 1956)		
New Hebrides (Under Anglo-French Condominium)	Independence as Vanuatu	1980	A/Res/66 (I) (14 Dec 1946), A/Res 36/1 (15 Sept 1981)		
Reunion	Change in status	1947	A/Res/66 (I) (14 Dec 1946)	Integrated by France without UN recognition	
St. Pierre and Miquelon	Change in status	1947	A/Res/66 (I) (14 Dec 1946)	Integrated by France without UN recognition	

Administering State	Territory	Status	Year	UN Resolutions and Agreements	Explanation of Change in Status	Notes
	Trust Territory of Cameroons under French administration	Independence as Cameroon	1960	Trusteeship agreement for the Territory of the Cameroons under French administration, 8 UNTS 135 (entered into force 13 Dec 1946); A/Res/63 (I) (13 Dec 1946), A/Res/1349 (XIII) (13 Mar 1959), A/Res/1608 (XV) (21 Apr 1961), A/Res/1476 (XV) (20 Sept 1960)		
	Trust Territory of Togoland under French administration	Independence as Togo	1960	Trusteeship agreement for the Territory of Togoland under French administration, 8 UNTS 165 (entered into force 13 Dec 1946); A/Res/63 (I) (13 Dec 1946), A/Res/1416 (XIV) (5 Dec 1959), A/Res/1477 (XV) (20 Sept 1960)		
	Tunisia	Independence as Tunisia	1956	A/Res/66 (I) (14 Dec 1946), A/Res/813 (IX) (17 Dec 1954), A/Res/1112 (XI) (12 Nov 1956)		

Italy	Trust Territory of Somaliland under Italian administration*	Independence as Somalia (uniting with British Somaliland)	1960	Trusteeship agreement for the Territory of Somaliland under Italian Administration, 118 UNTS 255 (entered into force 8 Jan 1952); A/Res/289 (IV) (21 Nov 1949); A/Res/442 (V) (2 Dec 1950) A/Res/1418 (XIV) (5 Dec 1959), A/Res/1479 (XV) (20 Sept 1960)		* Placed under trusteeship for fixed, ten-year period in 1950.
Netherlands	Netherlands Antilles (formerly Curaçao)	Change in status	1955	A/Res/66 (I) (14 Dec 1946), A/Res/945 (X) (15 Dec 1955)	A/Res/945 recognized approval of new constitutional order through freely-elected representative bodies	
	Netherlands Indies*	Independence as Indonesia	1949	A/Res/66 (I) (14 Dec 1946), A/Res/301 (IV) (7 Dec 1949), A/Res/448 (V) (12 Dec 1950), A/Res/491 (V) (28 Sept 1950); A/Res/1752 (XVII) (21 Sept 1962); A/Res/2504 (XXIV) (19 Nov 1969)		* West Irian (West New Guinea) was ceded to Indonesia by agreement in 1962. See Agreement Between the Republic of Indonesia and the Kingdom of the Netherlands concerning West New Guinea (West Irian) 437 UNTS 274 (15 Aug 1962, entered into force 21 Sept 1962). The status of West Irian was the subject of a UN-supervised referendum. See Report of the Secretary-General Concerning the Act of Self-Determination in West Irian, A/7723 (6 Nov 1969).

Administering State	Territory	Status	Year	UN Resolutions and Agreements	Explanation of Change in Status	Notes
	West Papua	Change in status (joined with Indonesia as Irian Jaya)	1963	A/Res/448 (V) (12 Dec 1950), A/Res/2504 (XXIV) (19 Nov 1969)	Administered separately from Indonesia following Indonesia's independence. A/Res/2504 recognized 'act of free choice' in joining Indonesia.*	* See also General Assembly decision of 6 Nov 1963 (modalities of UN involvement)
	Suriname	Change in status (later independent as Suriname in 1975)	1955	A/Res/66 (I) (14 Dec 1946), A/Res/945 (X) (15 Dec 1955), A/Res/3413 (XXX) (4 Dec 1975)	A/Res/945 recognized approval of new constitutional order through freely-elected representative bodies	
New Zealand	Cook Islands	Change in status	1965	A/Res/66 (I) (14 Dec 1946), A/Res/2064 (XX) (16 Dec 1965)	A/Res/2064 recognized attainment of internal self-government vis-à-vis New Zealand	

	Niue	Change in status	1974	A/Res/3155 (XXVIII) (14 Dec 1973), A/Res/3285 (XXIX) (13 Dec 1974)	A/Res/3285 recognized independence in free association with New Zealand
	Trust Territory of Samoa	Independence as Western Samoa, now Samoa	1962	Trusteeship agreement for the Territory of Western Samoa (with Annex), 8 UNTS 71 (entered into force 13 Dec 1946); A/Res/63 (I) (13 Dec 1946), A/Res/1626 (XVI) (18 Oct 1961), A/Res/31/104 (15 Dec 1976)	
Portugal	Angola, including the enclave of Cabinda	Independence as Angola	1975	A/Res/1542 (XV) (15 Dec 1960), Alvar Agreement (15 Jan 1975) in A/10040 (22 Jan 1975), A/Res/31/44 (1 Dec 1976)	
	Cape Verde Archipelago	Independence as Cape Verde, now Cabo Verde	1975	A/Res/1542 (XV) (15 Dec 1960), Lisbon Agreement (18 Dec 1974) in A/10054 (11 Mar 1975), A/Res/3363 (XXX) (16 Sept 1975)	

Administering State	Territory	Status	Year	UN Resolutions and Agreements	Explanation of Change in Status	Notes
	Goa and Dependencies	Change in status	1962	A/Res/1542 (XV) (15 Dec 1960)	Integration by India without UN recognition	
	Macau and Dependencies	Change in status	1972	A/Res/1542 (XV) (15 Dec 1960)	Integration by China*	* See A/AC.109/396 (Letter Dated 8 March 1972 from the Permanent Representative of China to the United Nations Addressed to the Chairman of the Special Committee) (opposing treatment of Macau and Hong Kong as NSGTs)). A working group of the Special Committee on Decolonization recommended, in consideration of the letter, that the Special Committee recommend to the UNGA that Hong Kong and Macau and dependencies be excluded from the list of territories subject to Chapter XI of the UN Charter. See A/AC.109/L.795 (1972) at 1–2 (Sixty-Sixth Report of the Working Group). The Special Committee approved that recommendation, see A/AC.109/PV.873 (1972) at 19–20

					(Record of the 873rd Meeting of the Special Committee), and included that recommendation in its 1972 report: see A/8723/ Rev.1, para 183. The UNGA approved the report of the Special Committee. See A/ Res/2908 (XXVII) (2 Nov 1972) para 3.
Mozambique	Independence as Mozambique	1975	A/Res/1542 (XV) (15 Dec 1960), Lusaka Agreement (7 Sept 1974) in A/9769 (24 Sept 1974) and (1974) 13(6) ILM 1467, A/Res/ 3365 (XXX) (16 Sept 1975)		
Portuguese Guinea	Independence as Guinea-Bissau	1974	A/Res/1542 (XV) (15 Dec 1960), A/Res/3061 (XXVIII) (2 Nov 1973), A/ Res 3205 (XXIX) (17 Sept 1974)		
São João Batista de Ajudá	Change in status	1962	A/Res/1542 (XV) (15 Dec 1960)	Integration by Dahomey (now Benin) without UN recognition*	* See *Yearbook of the United Nations, 1961*, at 420.

Administering State	Territory	Status	Year	UN Resolutions and Agreements	Explanation of Change in Status	Notes
	São Tome and Principe	Independence as São Tome and Principe	1975	A/Res/1542 (XV) (15 Dec 1960), Algiers Agreement (16 Nov 1974) in (1975) 14(1) ILM 39, A/Res/3364 (XXX) (16 Sept 1975)		
	Timor/East Timor*	Independence as Timor-Leste	2002	A/Res/1542 (XV) (15 Dec 1960), A/Res/56/282 (1 May 2002), A/Res/57/3 (27 Sept 2002)		* Initially administered by Portugal. Under Indonesian control between 1975 and 1999. Attained independence in May 2002. Joined the United Nations in September 2002 as Timor-Leste. See S/Res/1264 (15 Sept 1999) (establishing the United Nations Mission in East Timor (UNAMET) and taking note of the outcome of the UN-facilitated referendum through which the people of East Timor achieved self-governance through independence); Question of East Timor, Report of the Secretary General, A/53/951, S/1999/513 (5 May 1999) (attaching agreements concerning modalities for the exercise of self-determination by the people of East Timor).

					See also S/Res/1272 (25 Oct 1999) (establishing the United Nations Transitional Administration in East Timor (UNTAET)). The UNGA subsequently recognized the independence of East Timor, A/Res/56/282 (1 May 2002), and admitted East Timor to the United Nations, A/Res/57/3 (27 Sept 2002).
South Africa	South West Africa	Termination of the Mandate of South Africa by the General Assembly*	1966	A/Res/2145 (XXI) (27 Oct 1966)	*United Nations Council for South West Africa established to administer the Territory: A/Res/2248 (S-V) (19 May 1967)
		Independence as Namibia	1990	S/Res/435 (29 Sept 1978), A/Res/S-18/1 (23 Apr 1990)	
Spain	Fernando Póo and Río Muni	Independence as Equatorial Guinea	1968	A/Res/1542 (XV) (15 Dec 1960), A/Res/2067 (XX) (16 Dec 1965), A/Res/2355 (XXII) (19 Dec 1967), A/Res/2384 (XXIII) (12 Nov 1968)	

Administering State	Territory	Status	Year	UN Resolutions and Agreements	Explanation of Change in Status	Notes
	Ifni	Change in status	1969	A/Res/1542 (XV) (15 Dec 1960), A/Res/2072 (XX) (16 Dec 1965), A/Res/2229 (XXI) (20 Dec 1966), A/Res/2354 (XXII) (19 Dec 1967), A/Res/2428 (XXIII) (18 Dec 1968)	Integration by Morocco*	*See *Western Sahara*, Advisory Opinion, ICJ Rep 1975, 12, para 63 ('Decolonized' by transfer to Morocco)
United Kingdom	Aden	Independence as South Yemen, later Yemen (uniting with Yemen Arab Republic)	1967	A/Res/66 (I) (14 Dec 1946), A/Res/2183 (XXI) (12 Dec 1966), A/Res/2310 (XXII) (14 Dec 1967)		
	Antigua (Leeward Islands)	Independence as Antigua and Barbuda	1981	A/Res/66 (I) (14 Dec 1946), A/Res/36/26 (11 Nov 1981)		
	Bahamas	Independence as the Bahamas	1973	A/Res/66 (I) (14 Dec 1946), A/Res/3051 (XXVIII) (18 Sept 1973)		
	Barbados	Independence as Barbados	1966	A/Res/66 (I) (14 Dec 1946), A/Res/2069 (XX) (16 Dec 1965), A/Res/2175 (XXI) (9 Dec 1966)		

Basutoland	Independence as Lesotho	1966	A/Res/66 (I) (14 Dec 1946), A/Res/2063 (XX) (16 Dec 1965), A/Res/2134 (XXI) (29 Sept 1966), A/Res/2137 (XXI) (17 Oct 1966)
Bechuanaland	Independence as Botswana	1966	A/Res/66 (I) (14 Dec 1946), A/Res/2063 (XX) (16 Dec 1965), A/Res/2134 (XXI) (29 Sept 1966), A/Res/2136 (XXI) (17 Oct 1966)
British Guiana	Independence as Guyana	1966	A/Res/66 (I) (14 Dec 1946), A/Res/2071 (XX) (16 Dec 1965), A/Res/2133 (XXI) (20 Sept 1966)
British Honduras	Independence as Belize	1981	A/Res/66 (I) (14 Dec 1946), A/Res/3432 (XXX) (8 Dec 1975), A/Res/36/3 (25 Sept 1981)
British Somaliland	Independence as Somalia (joining the Trust Territory of Somaliland under Italian administration)	1960	A/Res/66 (I) (14 Dec 1946), A/Res/1418 (XIV) (5 Dec 1959), A/Res/1479 (XV) (20 Sept 1960)

Administering State	Territory	Status	Year	UN Resolutions and Agreements	Explanation of Change in Status	Notes
	Brunei	Independence, now Brunei Darussalam	1984	A/Res/66 (I) (14 Dec 1946), A/Res/39/1 (21 Sept 1984)		
	Cyprus	Independence as Cyprus	1960	A/Res/66 (I) (14 Dec 1946), A/Res/1287 (XIII) (5 Dec 1958), A/Res/1489 (XV) (20 Sept 1960)		
	Dominica (Windward Islands)	Independence as Dominica	1978	A/Res/66 (I) (14 Dec 1946), A/Res/33/107 (18 Dec 1978)		
	Fiji	Independence as Fiji	1970	A/Res/66 (I) (14 Dec 1946), A/Res/1951 (XVIII) (11 Dec 1963), A/Res/2068 (XX) (16 Dec 1965), A/Res/2350 (XXII) (19 Dec 1967), A/Res/2622 (XXV) (13 Oct 1970)		
	Gambia	Independence as The Gambia	1965	A/Res/66 (I) (14 Dec 1946), A/Res/2008 (XX) (21 Sept 1965)		
	Gilbert and Ellice Islands	Independence as Kiribati	1979	A/Res/66 (I) (14 Dec 1946), A/Res/54/1 (1 Oct 1999)		
		Independence as Tuvalu	1978	A/Res/66 (I) (14 Dec 1946), A/Res/55/1 (6 Oct 2000)		
	Gold Coast	Independence as Ghana	1957	A/Res/66 (I) (14 Dec 1946), A/Res/1118 (XI) (8 Mar 1957)		
	Grenada (Windward Islands)	Independence as Grenada	1974	A/Res/66 (I) (14 Dec 1946), A/Res/3204 (XXIX) (17 Sept 1974)		

Hong Kong	Change in status	1972	A/Res/66 (I) (14 Dec 1946)	Integration by China*	* See A/AC.109/396 (Letter Dated 8 March 1972 from the Permanent Representative of China to the United Nations Addressed to the Chairman of the Special Committee) (opposing treatment of Macau and Hong Kong as NSGTs)). A working group of the Special Committee on Decolonization recommended, in consideration of the letter, that the Special Committee recommend to the UNGA that Hong Kong and Macau and dependencies be excluded from the list of territories subject to Chapter XI of the UN Charter. See A/AC.109/L.795 (1972) at 1–2 (Sixty-Sixth Report of the Working Group). The Special Committee approved that recommendation, see A/AC.109/PV.873 (1972) at 19–20 (Record of the 873rd Meeting of the Special Committee), and included that recommendation in its 1972 report: see A/8723/Rev.1, para 183. The UNGA approved the report of the Special Committee. See A/Res/2908 (XXVII) (2 Nov. 1972) para 3.

Administering State	Territory	Status	Year	UN Resolutions and Agreements	Explanation of Change in Status	Notes
	Jamaica	Independence as Jamaica	1962	A/Res/66 (I) (14 Dec 1946), A/Res/1750 (XVII) (18 Sept 1962)		
	Kenya	Independence as Kenya	1963	A/Res/66 (I) (14 Dec 1946), A/Res/1812 (XVII) (17 Dec 1962), A/Res/1976 (XVIII) (16 Dec 1963)		
	Malayan Union	Independence as the Federation of Malaya, now Malaysia*	1957	A/Res/66 (I) (14 Dec 1946), A/Res/1134 (XII) (17 Sept 1957)		* In 1963, the Federation of Malaya became Malaysia, following admission to the new federation of Singapore, Sabah (North Borneo) and Sarawak. Singapore became independent in 1965. See *Yearbook of the United Nations, 1963*, at 41-44.
	Malta	Independence as Malta	1964	A/Res/66 (I) (14 Dec 1946), A/Res/1950 (XVIII) (11 Dec 1963), Decision of 1 December 1964*		* The General Assembly adopted a decision to admit Malta during its nineteenth session at the 1286th meeting held on 1 December 1964.
	Mauritius	Independence as Mauritius	1968	A/Res/66 (I) (14 Dec 1946), A/Res/2371 (XXII) (24 Apr 1968)		

Nigeria	Independence as Nigeria	1960	A/Res/66 (I) (14 Dec 1946), A/Res/1492 (XV) (7 Oct 1960)		
North Borneo	Change in status	1963	A/Res/66 (I) (14 Dec 1946)	In 1963, the Federation of Malaya became Malaysia, following admission to the new federation of Singapore, Sabah (North Borneo) and Sarawak. Singapore became independent in 1965.*	* See *Yearbook of the United Nations, 1963*, at 41–44.
Northern Rhodesia	Independence as Zambia	1964	A/Res/66 (I) (14 Dec 1946), A/Res/1952 (XVIII) (11 Dec 1963), Decision of 1 December 1964*		* The General Assembly adopted a decision to admit Zambia during its nineteenth session at the 1286th meeting held on 1 December 1964.
Nyasaland	Independence as Malawi	1964	A/Res/66 (I) (14 Dec 1946), A/Res/1953 (XVIII) (11 Dec 1963), Decision of 1 December 1964*		* The General Assembly adopted a decision to admit Malawi during its nineteenth session at the 1286th meeting held on 1 December 1964.

Administering State	Territory	Status	Year	UN Resolutions and Agreements	Explanation of Change in Status	Notes
	Sarawak	Change in status	1963	A/Res/66 (I) (14 Dec 1946)	In 1963, the Federation of Malaya became Malaysia, following admission to the new federation of Singapore, Sabah (North Borneo) and Sarawak. Singapore became independent in 1965.*	* See *Yearbook of the United Nations, 1963*, at 41–44.
	Seychelles	Independence as Seychelles	1976	A/Res/66 (I) (14 Dec 1946), A/Res/3287 (XXIX) (13 Dec 1974), A/Res/31/1 (21 Sept 1976)		
	Sierra Leone	Independence as Sierra Leone	1961	A/Res/66 (I) (14 Dec 1946), A/Res/1623 (XVI) (27 Sept 1961)		
	Singapore	Independence as Singapore*	1965	A/Res/66 (I) (14 Dec 1946), A/Res/2010 (XX) (21 Sept 1965)		* In 1963, the Federation of Malaya became Malaysia, following admission to the new federation of Singapore, Sabah (North Borneo) and Sarawak. Singapore became independent in 1965. See *Yearbook of the United Nations, 1963*, at 41-44.

Solomon Islands	Independence as Solomon Islands	1978	A/Res/66 (I) (14 Dec 1946), A/Res/33/1 (19 Sept 1978)
Southern Rhodesia	Independence as Zimbabwe	1980	A/Res/1747(XVI) (28 June 1962), A/Res/34/192 (18 Dec 1979), A/Res/S-11/1 (25 Aug 1980)
St. Kitts-Nevis-Anguilla (Leeward Islands)	Independence as Saint Kitts and Nevis (separated from Anguilla)	1983	A/Res/66 (I) (14 Dec 1946), A/Res/38/1 (23 Sept 1983)
St. Lucia (Windward Islands)	Independence as Saint Lucia	1979	A/Res/66 (I) (14 Dec 1946), A/Res/34/1 (18 Sept 1979)
St. Vincent (Windward Islands)	Independence as Saint Vincent and the Grenadines	1979	A/Res/66 (I) (14 Dec 1946), A/Res/35/1 (16 Sept 1980)
Swaziland	Independence as Swaziland, now Eswatini	1968	A/Res/66 (I) (14 Dec 1946), A/Res/2063 (XX) (16 Dec 1965), A/Res/2134 (XXI) (29 Sept 1966), A/Res/2376 (XXIII) (24 Sept 1968)

Administering State	Territory	Status	Year	UN Resolutions and Agreements	Explanation of Change in Status	Notes
	Trinidad and Tobago	Independence as Trinidad and Tobago	1962	A/Res/66 (I) (14 Dec 1946), A/Res/1751 (XVII) (18 Sept 1962)		
	Trust Territory of Cameroons under British administration	Change in status as Northern Cameroons (joined with Nigeria)	1961	Trusteeship agreement for the Territory of the Cameroons under British administration, 8 UNTS 119 (entered into force 13 Dec 1946); A/Res/63 (I) (13 Dec 1946), A/Res/1350 (XIII) (13 May 1959), A/Res/1608 (XV) (21 Apr 1961)	Following plebiscites for Northern Cameroons and Southern Cameroons conducted under the auspices of the United Nations, Southern Cameroons joined the Republic of Cameroon and Northern Cameroons joined the Federation of Nigeria. UNGA Resolution 1608 (XV) endorsed the plebiscites and terminated the Trusteeship agreement.	
		Change in status as Southern Cameroons (joined with Cameroon)	1961			

Trust Territory of Tanganyika	Independence as Tanganyika (now the United Republic of Tanzania)*	1961	Trusteeship agreement for the Territory of Tanganyika, 8 UNTS 91 (entered into force 13 Dec 1946); A/Res/63 (I) (13 Dec 1946), A/Res/1609 (XV) (21 Apr 1961), A/Res/1642 (XVI) (6 Nov 1961), A/Res/1667 (XVI) (14 Dec 1961)		*Following ratification of the Articles of Union between Tanganyika and Zanzibar on 26 April 1964, the United Republic of Tanganyika and Zanzibar became one Member of the United Nations. Its name changed on 1 November 1964 to the United Republic of Tanzania.
Trust Territory of Togoland under British administration	Change in status	1957	Trusteeship agreement for the Territory of Togoland under British administration, 8 UNTS 151 (entered into force 13 Dec 1946); A/Res/63 (I) (13 Dec 1946), A/Res/1044 (XI) (13 Dec 1956), A/Res/1118 (XI) (8 Mar 1957)	United with the Gold Coast, a Non-Self-Governing Territory, to form Ghana	
Uganda	Independence as Uganda	1962	A/Res/66 (I) (14 Dec 1946), A/Res/1758 (XVII) (25 Oct 1962)		
Zanzibar	Independence as Zanzibar, now the United Republic of Tanzania*	1963	A/Res/66 (I) (14 Dec 1946), A/Res/1811 (XVII) (17 Dec 1962), A/Res/1975 (XVIII) (16 Dec 1963)		*Following ratification of the Articles of Union between Tanganyika and Zanzibar on 26 April 1964, the United Republic of Tanganyika and Zanzibar became one Member of the United Nations. Its name changed on 1 November 1964 to the United Republic of Tanzania.

Administering State	Territory	Status	Year	UN Resolutions and Agreements	Explanation of Change in Status	Notes
United States	Alaska	Change in status	1959	A/Res/66 (I) (14 Dec 1946), A/Res/1469 (XIV) (12 Dec 1959)	Constituent state of the United States	
	Hawaii	Change in status	1959	A/Res/66 (I) (14 Dec 1946), A/Res/1469 (XIV) (12 Dec 1959)	Constituent state of the United States	
	Panama Canal Zone	Change in status	1947	A/Res/66 (I) (14 Dec 1946)	Integration by Panama*	*See UNGA Fourth Committee, Summary Record of Meetings 1 November–12 December 1946, A/C.4/SR.13–27 (Part I) 113–14 (Protest by Panama that Panama Canal Zone had been considered subject to UN Charter Article 73(e) in error).
	Puerto Rico	Change in status	1952	A/Res/66 (I) (14 Dec 1946), A/Res/748 (VIII) (27 Nov 1953)	Commonwealth of the United States	
	Trust Territory of the Pacific Islands	Change in status as the Federated States of Micronesia	1990	Trusteeship agreement for the former Japanese Mandated Islands, Approved by the Security Council on 2 April 1947, 8 UNTS 189 (entered into force 18 July 1947); S/Res/683 (22 Dec 1990)	Fully self-governing in free association with the United States	

Change in status as the Marshall Islands	1990	Trusteeship agreement for the former Japanese Mandated Islands, Approved by the Security Council on 2 April 1947, 8 UNTS 189 (entered into force 18 July 1947); S/Res/683 (22 Dec 1990)	Fully self-governing in free association with the United States
Change in status as the Northern Mariana Islands	1990	Trusteeship agreement for the former Japanese Mandated Islands, Approved by the Security Council on 2 April 1947, 8 UNTS 189 (entered into force 18 July 1947); S/Res/683 (22 Dec 1990)	Commonwealth of the United States
Change in status as Palau	1994	Trusteeship agreement for the former Japanese Mandated Islands, Approved by the Security Council on 2 April 1947, 8 UNTS 189 (entered into force 18 July 1947); S/Res/956 (10 Nov 1994)	Fully self-governing in free association with the United States

*Note: The territories included on this list, as well as information on administering power/authority, status, and relevant year, are derived from a table maintained by the United Nations, available at https://www.un.org/dppa/decolonization/en/history/former-trust-and-nsgts (last visited 27 Dec 2023).
The five 'A' Mandates under the League of Nations Mandate System did not come under the purview of the Trusteeship System and are therefore not reflected on this list. Although the 'C' Mandate of South West Africa did not come under the purview of the Trusteeship System, it is included on this list given the activity of the United Nations regarding the administration of the Territory. See Chapter 1.c.i (Mandate System).

[1] Cited in Jamie Trinidad, *Self-Determination in Disputed Colonial Territories* (CUP 2018) 181.

APPENDIX 2

Non-Self-Governing Territories*

Administering Power	Territory	UN Resolutions	Notes	
France	French Polynesia*	A/Res/66 (I) (14 Dec 1946), A/Res/67/265 (17 May 2013)	*A/Res/67/265 'reinscribed' territory into the registry of NSGTs after cessation of reporting under Article 73(e)	
	New Caledonia*	A/Res/66 (I) (14 Dec 1946), A/Res/41/41-A (2 Dec 1986)	*A/Res/41/41-A 'reinscribed' territory into the registry of NSGTs after cessation of reporting under Article 73(e)	
New Zealand	Tokelau	A/Res/66 (I) (14 Dec 1946)		
Spain*	Western Sahara	A/Res/1542 (XV) (15 Dec 1960)**	* In 1976, Spain informed the UN Secretary-General that it had, inter alia, withdrawn as administering power of Western Sahara and considered itself exempt from associated obligations under the UN Charter. See *Letter dated 26 February 1967 from the Permanent Representative of Spain to the United Nations addressed to the Secretary-General*, A/31/56, S/11997 (26 Feb 1976) 3.	** Resolution 1542 does not enumerate Spanish-administered territories, but instead '[r]ecall[ed] with satisfaction the statement of the representative of Spain at the 10th meeting of the Fourth Committee that his Government agrees to transmit information to the Secretary-General in accordance with the provisions of Chapter XI of the Charter'. See A/C.4/SR.1048 (11 Nov 1960) para 1 (UNGA Fourth Committee 1048th Meeting) (Mr Aznar (Spain)). These territories included Western Sahara. See *3 Repertory of Practice of United Nations Organs, Supplement No 3 (1959–1966)* para 189.

United Kingdom	Anguilla	A/Res/66 (I) (14 Dec 1946)
	Bermuda	A/Res/66 (I) (14 Dec 1946)
	British Virgin Islands	A/Res/66 (I) (14 Dec 1946)
	Cayman Islands	A/Res/66 (I) (14 Dec 1946)
	Falkland Islands / Malvinas	A/Res/66 (I) (14 Dec 1946)
	Gibraltar	A/Res/66 (I) (14 Dec 1946)
	Montserrat	A/Res/66 (I) (14 Dec 1946)
	Pitcairn	A/Res/66 (I) (14 Dec 1946)
	Saint Helena	A/Res/66 (I) (14 Dec 1946)
	Turks and Caicos Islands	A/Res/66 (I) (14 Dec 1946)
United States	American Samoa	A/Res/66 (I) (14 Dec 1946)
	Guam	A/Res/66 (I) (14 Dec 1946)
	United States Virgin Islands	A/Res/66 (I) (14 Dec 1946)

*Note: Information on administering power and territory reflects the list of territories remaining on the agenda of the Special Committee on Decolonization. See https://www.un.org/dppa/decolonization/en/nsgt.

Index

For the benefit of digital users, indexed terms that span two pages (e.g., 52–53) may, on occasion, appear on only one of those pages.

C